Microsoft Excel 2013

Step by Step

Curtis D. Frye

ISBN: 978-0-7356-8101-9

Third Printing: April 2014

Printed and bound in the United States of America.

Microsoft Press books are available through booksellers and distributors worldwide. If you need support related to this book, email Microsoft Press Book Support at mspinput@microsoft.com. Please tell us what you think of this book at *http://www.microsoft.com/learning/booksurvey*.

Microsoft and the trademarks listed at *http://www.microsoft.com/about/legal/en/us/IntellectualProperty/ Trademarks/EN-US.aspx* are trademarks of the Microsoft group of companies. All other marks are property of their respective owners.

The example companies, organizations, products, domain names, email addresses, logos, people, places, and events depicted herein are fictitious. No association with any real company, organization, product, domain name, email address, logo, person, place, or event is intended or should be inferred.

This book expresses the author's views and opinions. The information contained in this book is provided without any express, statutory, or implied warranties. Neither the authors, O'Reilly Media, Inc., Microsoft Corporation, nor its resellers, or distributors will be held liable for any damages caused or alleged to be caused either directly or indirectly by this book.

Acquisitions and Developmental Editor: Kenyon Brown

Production Editor: Melanie Yarbrough

Editorial Production: Online Training Solutions, Inc. (OTSI)

Technical Reviewer: Andy Pope

Indexer: Judith McConville

Cover Design: Girvin

Cover Composition: Zyg Group, LLC

Illustrator: Online Training Solutions, Inc. (OTSI)

For Virginia.

Contents

12 Working with macros and forms 361

13 Working with other Office programs 393

14 Collaborating with colleagues 411

Introduction

Part of the Microsoft Office 2013 suite of programs, Microsoft Excel 2013 is a full-featured spreadsheet program that helps you quickly and efficiently develop dynamic, professional workbooks to summarize and present your data. *Microsoft Excel 2013 Step by Step* offers a comprehensive look at the features of Excel that most people will use most frequently.

Who this book is for

Microsoft Excel 2013 Step by Step and other books in the *Step by Step* series are designed for beginning-level to intermediate-level computer users. Examples shown in the book generally pertain to small and medium businesses but teach skills that can be used in organizations of any size. Whether you are already comfortable working in Excel and want to learn about new features in Excel 2013 or are new to Excel, this book provides invaluable hands-on experience so that you can create, modify, and share workbooks with ease.

How this book is organized

This book is divided into 14 chapters. Chapters 1–4 address basic skills such as identifying the different Excel programs, customizing the program window, setting up workbooks, managing data within workbooks, creating formulas to summarize your data, and formatting your workbooks. Chapters 5–10 show you how to analyze your data in more depth through sorting and filtering, creating alternative data sets for scenario analysis, summarizing data by using charts, and creating PivotTables and PivotCharts. Chapters 11–14 cover printing, working with macros and forms, working with other Microsoft Office programs, and collaborating with colleagues.

The first part of Chapter 1 contains introductory information that will primarily be of interest to readers who are new to Excel or are upgrading from Excel 2010 or an earlier version. If you have worked with a more recent version of Excel, you might want to skip that material.

This book has been designed to lead you step by step through all the tasks you're most likely to want to perform with Excel 2013. If you start at the beginning and work your way through all the exercises, you will gain enough proficiency to be able to create and work with most types of Excel workbooks. However, each topic is self-contained, so you can jump in anywhere to acquire exactly the skills you need.

Download the practice files

Before you can complete the exercises in this book, you need to download the book's practice files to your computer. These practice files can be downloaded from the following page:

http://go.microsoft.com/FWLink/?Linkid=275457

> **IMPORTANT** The Excel 2013 program is not available from this website. You should purchase and install that program before using this book.

The following table lists the practice files for this book.

Chapter	File
Chapter 1: Getting started with Excel 2013	DataLabels.xlsx
	ExceptionSummary.xlsx
	ExceptionTracking.xlsx
	MisroutedPackages.xlsx
	PackageCounts.xlsx
	RouteVolume.xlsx
Chapter 2: Working with data and Excel tables	2013Q1ShipmentsByCategory.xlsx
	AverageDeliveries.xlsx
	DriverSortTimes.xlsx
	MailingNames.xlsx
	Series.xlsx
	ServiceLevels.xlsx
Chapter 3: Performing calculations on data	ConveyerBid.xlsx
	FuelSurcharges.xlsx
	ITExpenses.xlsx
	PackagingCosts.xlsx
	SavingsIncentive.xlsx
	VehicleMiles.xlsx

Chapter	File
Chapter 4: Changing workbook appearance	CallCenter.xlsx
	Dashboard.xlsx
	ExecutiveSearch.xlsx
	HourlyExceptions.xlsx
	HourlyTracking.xlsx
	VehicleMileSummary.xlsx
Chapter 5: Focusing on specific data by using filters	Credit.xlsx
	ForFollowUp.xlsx
	PackageExceptions.xlsx
	Slicers.xlsx
Chapter 6: Reordering and summarizing data	GroupByQuarter.xlsx
	ShipmentLog.xlsx
	ShippingCustom.xlsx
	ShippingSummary.xlsx
Chapter 7: Combining data from multiple sources	Consolidate.xlsx
	DailyCallSummary.xlsx
	FebruaryCalls.xlsx
	FleetOperatingCosts.xlsx
	JanuaryCalls.xlsx
	OperatingExpenseDashboard.xlsx
Chapter 8: Analyzing data and alternative data sets	2DayScenario.xlsx
	AdBuy.xlsx
	DriverSortTimes.xlsx
	MultipleScenarios.xlsx
	PackageAnalysis.xlsx
	RateProjections.xlsx
	TargetValues.xlsx
Chapter 9: Creating charts and graphics	FutureVolumes_start.xlsx
	MonthAndCategory_start.xlsx
	OrgChart_start.xlsx
	RevenueAnalysis_start.xlsx
	RevenueSummary_start.xlsx
	Shapes_start.xlsx
	VolumeByCenter_start.xlsx
	YearlyPackageVolume_start.xlsx

Chapter	File
Chapter 10: Using PivotTables and PivotCharts	Creating.txt
	Creating.xlsx
	Editing.xlsx
	Focusing.xlsx
	Formatting.xlsx
	RevenueAnalysis.xlsx
Chapter 11: Printing worksheets and charts	ConsolidatedMessenger.png
	CorporateRevenue.xlsx
	HourlyPickups.xlsx
	PickupsByHour.xlsx
	RevenueByCustomer.xlsx
	SummaryByCustomer.xlsx
Chapter 12: Working with macros and forms	PackageWeight.xlsm
	PerformanceDashboard.xlsm
	RunOnOpen.xlsm
	VolumeHighlights.xlsm
	YearlySalesSummary.xlsm
Chapter 13: Working with other Office programs	2013YearlyRevenueSummary.pptx
	Hyperlink.xlsx
	LevelDescriptions.xlsx
	RevenueByServiceLevel.xlsx
	RevenueChart.xlsx
	RevenueSummary.pptx
	SummaryPresentation.xlsx
Chapter 14: Collaborating with colleagues	CategoryXML.xlsx
	CostProjections.xlsx
	ExceptionTracking.xml
	ProjectionChangeTracking.xlsx
	ProjectionsDistro.xlsx
	ProjectionsForComment.xlsx
	ProjectionsSigned.xlsx
	SecureInfo.xlsx
	ShipmentSummary.xlsx
	SkyDriveFile.xlsx

Your companion ebook

With the ebook edition of this book, you can do the following:

- Search the full text
- Print
- Copy and paste

To download your ebook, please see the instruction page at the back of the book.

Getting support and giving feedback

The following sections provide information about getting help with Excel 2013 or the contents of this book and contacting us to provide feedback or report errors.

Errata

We've made every effort to ensure the accuracy of this book and its companion content. Any errors that have been reported since this book was published are listed on our Microsoft Press site:

http://go.microsoft.com/FWLink/?Linkid=275456

If you find an error that is not already listed, you can report it to us through the same page.

If you need additional support, email Microsoft Press Book Support at *mspinput@microsoft.com*.

Please note that product support for Microsoft software is not offered through the addresses above.

We want to hear from you

At Microsoft Press, your satisfaction is our top priority, and your feedback our most valuable asset. Please tell us what you think of this book at:

http://www.microsoft.com/learning/booksurvey

The survey is short, and we read every one of your comments and ideas. Thanks in advance for your input!

Stay in touch

Let's keep the conversation going! We're on Twitter at: *http://twitter.com/MicrosoftPress*.

Chapter at a glance

Customize

Customize the Excel 2013 program window,
page 13

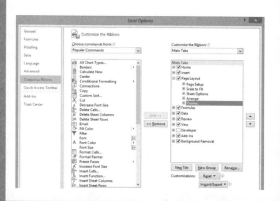

Create

Create workbooks,
page 25

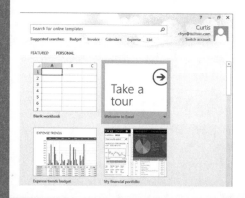

Modify

Modify workbooks,
page 30

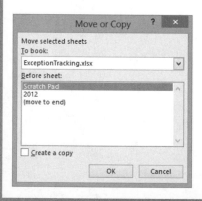

Merge

Merge and unmerge cells,
page 39

Getting started with Excel 2013

1

IN THIS CHAPTER, YOU WILL LEARN HOW TO

- Identify the different Excel 2013 programs.

- Identify new features of Excel 2013.

- Customize the Excel 2013 program window.

- Create workbooks.

- Modify workbooks.

- Modify worksheets.

- Merge and unmerge cells.

When you create a Microsoft Excel 2013 workbook, the program presents a blank workbook that contains one worksheet. You can add or delete worksheets, hide worksheets within the workbook without deleting them, and change the order of your worksheets within the workbook. You can also copy a worksheet to another workbook or move the worksheet without leaving a copy of the worksheet in the first workbook. If you and your colleagues work with a large number of documents, you can define property values to make your workbooks easier to find when you and your colleagues attempt to locate them by searching in File Explorer or by using Windows 8 Search.

TIP In Windows 8, File Explorer has replaced Windows Explorer. Throughout this book, this browsing utility is referred to by its Windows 8 name. If your computer is running Windows 7, use Windows Explorer instead.

You can also make Excel easier to use by customizing the Excel program window to fit your work style. If you have several workbooks open at the same time, you can move between the workbook windows quickly. However, if you switch between workbooks frequently, you might find it easier to resize the workbooks so they don't take up the entire Excel window. If you do this, you can switch to the workbook that you want to modify by clicking the title bar of the workbook you want.

The Microsoft Office User Experience team has enhanced your ability to customize the Excel user interface. If you find that you use a command frequently, you can add it to the Quick Access Toolbar so it's never more than one click away. If you use a set of commands frequently, you can create a custom ribbon tab so they appear in one place. You can also hide, display, or change the order of the tabs on the ribbon.

In this chapter, you'll get an overview of the different Excel programs that are available and discover features that are available in Excel 2013. You'll also create and modify workbooks and worksheets, make workbooks easier to find, and customize the Excel 2013 program window.

PRACTICE FILES To complete the exercises in this chapter, you need the practice files contained in the Chapter01 practice file folder. For more information, see "Download the practice files" in this book's Introduction.

Identifying the different Excel 2013 programs

The Microsoft Office 2013 suite includes programs that give you the ability to create and manage every type of file you need to work effectively at home, business, or school. The programs include Microsoft Word 2013, Excel 2013, Outlook 2013, PowerPoint 2013, Access 2013, InfoPath 2013, Lync 2013, OneNote 2013, and Publisher 2013. You can purchase the programs as part of a package that includes multiple programs or purchase most of the programs individually.

With the Office 2013 programs, you can find the tools you need quickly and, because they were designed as an integrated package, you'll find that most of the skills you learn in one program transfer readily to the others. That flexibility extends well beyond your personal computer. In addition to the traditional desktop Excel program, you can also use Excel 2013 on devices with ARM chips and over the web. The following describes the different Excel 2013 programs that are available to you:

- **Microsoft Excel 2013 desktop edition** This program is installed directly on your computer. It includes all of the capabilities built into Excel 2013. You can purchase the desktop edition as part of an Office program suite, as a separate program, or as part of the Office 365 subscription package that lets you install the desktop versions of Office programs over the Internet.

- **Microsoft Excel 2013 RT** Microsoft developed an edition of Windows 8 for devices powered by an ARM processor. Devices running this edition of Windows 8, called Windows RT, come with an edition of Office 2013 named Microsoft Office 2013 RT. The Office 2013 RT program suite includes Excel, OneNote, PowerPoint, and Word.

  Excel 2013 RT takes advantage of ARM devices' touch screen capabilities by including Touch Mode. When you enable Touch Mode, the Excel 2013 RT interface changes slightly to make it easier to work with the program by tapping the screen with your finger or a stylus and by providing an on-screen keyboard through which you can enter data. You can also work with Excel 2013 RT by using a physical keyboard, a mouse, and your device's track pad.

- **Microsoft Excel 2013 Web App** Information workers require their data to be available to them at all times, not just when they're using their personal computers. To provide mobile workers with access to their data, Microsoft developed Office Web Apps, which include online versions of Excel, Word, PowerPoint, and OneNote. Office Web Apps are available as part of an Office 365 subscription or for free as part of the Microsoft SkyDrive cloud service.

  You can use Excel Web App to edit files stored in your SkyDrive account or on a Microsoft SharePoint site. Excel Web App displays your Excel 2010 and Excel 2013 files as they appear in the desktop program and includes all of the functions you use to summarize your data. You can also view and manipulate (but not create) PivotTables, add charts, and format your data to communicate its meaning clearly.

  Excel Web App also includes the capabilities to share your workbooks online, to embed them as part of another webpage, and to create web-accessible surveys that save user responses directly to an Excel workbook in your SkyDrive account.

  After you open a file by using Excel Web App, you can choose to continue editing the file in your browser (such as Windows Internet Explorer 10) or open the file in the desktop program. When you open the file in your desktop program, any changes you save are written to the version of the file on your SkyDrive account. This practice means that you will always have access to the most recent version of your file, regardless of where and how you access it.

- **Microsoft Excel Mobile** If you have a Windows Phone 8 device, you can use Excel Mobile to view and manipulate your workbooks. You can create formulas, change the formatting of worksheet cells, sort and filter your data, and summarize your data by using charts. You can also connect your phone to your SkyDrive account, so all of those files will be available even if you don't have a notebook or other computer to work with at the moment.

Identifying new features of Excel 2013

Excel 2013 includes all of the most useful capabilities included in previous versions of the program. If you've used an earlier version of Excel, you probably want to know about the new features introduced in Excel 2013. The following sections summarize the most important changes from Excel 2010, Excel 2007, and Excel 2003.

If you are upgrading from Excel 2010

For users of Excel 2010, you'll find that Excel 2013 extends the program's existing capabilities and adds some very useful new ones. The features introduced in Excel 2013 include:

- **Windows 8 functionality** Excel 2013, like all Office 2013 programs, takes full advantage of the capabilities of the Windows 8 operating system. When it is running on a computer running Windows 8, Excel embodies the new presentation elements and enables you to use a touch interface to interact with your data.

- **A window for each workbook** Every workbook now has its own program window.

- **New functions** More than 50 new functions are available, which you can use to summarize your data, handle errors in your formulas, and bring in data from online resources.

- **Flash Fill** If your data is in list form, you can combine, extract, or format the data in a cell. When you continue the operation, Excel detects your pattern and offers to extend it for every row in the list.

- **Quick Analysis Lens** Clicking the Quick Analysis action button, which appears next to a selected cell range, displays different ways to visually represent your data. Clicking an icon creates the analysis instantly.

- **Recommended PivotTable** PivotTables create interactive and flexible data summaries. You can have Excel recommend a series of PivotTables to create from your data, click the one you want, and keep working.

- **Recommended Charts** As with Recommended PivotTables, Excel recommends the most suitable charts based on patterns in your data. You can display the suggested charts, click the one you want, and modify it so it's perfect.

- **Chart formatting control** You can fine-tune your charts quickly and easily. Change the title, layout, or other elements of your charts from a new and interactive interface.

- **Chart animations** When you change the underlying data in a chart, Excel updates your chart and highlights the change by using an animation.

- **Cloud capability** You can now share workbooks stored online or post part of a workbook to your social network by posting a link to the file.

- **Online presentation capability** You can share your workbook and collaborate in real time with others as part of a Microsoft Lync conversation or meeting. You can also allow others to take control of your workbook during the conversation or meeting.

If you are upgrading from Excel 2007

In addition to the features added in Excel 2013, the Excel programming team introduced the following features in Excel 2010:

- **Manage Excel files and settings in the Backstage view** When the User Experience and Excel teams focused on the Excel 2007 user interface, they discovered that several workbook management tasks that contained content-related tasks were sprinkled among the ribbon tabs. The Excel team moved all of the workbook management tasks to the Backstage view, which users can access by clicking the File tab.

- **Preview data by using Paste Preview** With this feature, you can preview how your data will appear in the worksheet before you commit to the paste.

- **Customize the Excel 2010 user interface** The ability to make simple modifications to the Quick Access Toolbar has been broadened to include many more options for changing the ribbon interface. You can hide or display built-in ribbon tabs, change the order of built-in ribbon tabs, add custom groups to a ribbon tab, and create custom ribbon tabs, which can also contain custom groups.

- **Summarize data by using more accurate functions** In earlier versions of Excel, the program contained statistical, scientific, engineering, and financial functions that would return inaccurate results in some relatively rare circumstances. The Excel programming team identified the functions that returned inaccurate results and collaborated with academic and industry analysts to improve the functions' accuracy.

- **Summarize data by using sparklines** In his book *Beautiful Evidence* (Graphics Press), Edward Tufte describes sparklines as "intense, simple, wordlike graphics." Sparklines take the form of small charts that summarize data in a single cell. These small but powerful additions to Excel 2010 and Excel 2013 enhance the program's reporting and summary capabilities.

- **Filter PivotTable data by using slicers** Slicers visually indicate which values appear in a PivotTable and which are hidden. They are particularly useful when you are presenting data to an audience that contains visual thinkers who might not be skilled at working with numerical values.

- **Filter PivotTable data by using search filters** Excel 2007 introduced several new ways to filter PivotTables. These filtering capabilities have been extended with the introduction of search filters. With a search filter, you begin entering a sequence of characters that occur in the term (or terms) by which you want to filter. As you enter these characters, the filter list of the PivotTable field displays only those terms that reflect the values entered into the search filter box.

- **Visualize data by using improved conditional formats** The Excel programming team greatly extended the capabilities of the data bar and icon set conditional formats introduced in Excel 2007. The team also enabled you to create conditional formats that refer to cells on worksheets other than the one on which you're defining the format.

- **Create and display math equations** With the updated equation designer, you can create any equation you require. The editor has several common equations built in, such as the quadratic formula and the Pythagorean theorem, but it also contains numerous templates that you can use to create custom equations quickly.

- **Edit pictures within Excel 2010** One very helpful capability is the ability to remove the background elements of an image. Removing an image's background enables you to create a composite image in which the foreground elements are placed in front of another background. For example, you can focus on a flower's bloom and remove most of the leaves and stem from the photo. After you isolate the foreground image, you can place the bloom in front of another background.

If you are upgrading from Excel 2003

In addition to the changes in Excel 2010 and Excel 2013, users upgrading from Excel 2003 will notice several more significant changes:

- **The ribbon** Unlike in previous versions of Excel, in which you hunted through a complex toolbar and menu system to find the commands you wanted, you can use the ribbon user interface to find everything you need at the top of the program window.

- **Larger data collection capability** The larger worksheet includes more than 1 million rows and 16,000 columns.

- **New file format** The Excel file format (.xlsx) uses XML and file compression techniques to reduce the size of a typical file by 50 percent.

- **Expanded cell and worksheet formatting** Vast improvements have been made to the color management and formatting options found in previous versions of the program. You can have as many different colors in a workbook as you like, for example, and you can assign a design theme to a workbook.

- **Excel tables** These enable you to enter and summarize your data efficiently. If you want to enter data in a new table row, all you have to do is enter the data in the row below the table. When you press Tab or Enter after entering the last cell's values, Excel expands the table to include your new data. You can also have Excel display a Totals row, which summarizes your table's data by using a function that you specify.

- **Improved charting** With the charting engine, you can create more attractive charts.

- **Formula AutoComplete** When you enter formulas into an Excel worksheet cell, the program displays a list of options from which you can choose for each formula element, greatly accelerating formula entry.

- **Additional formulas** With the added formulas, such as AVERAGEIFS, users can summarize data conditionally.

- **Conditional formatting** With conditional formats, users can create data bars and color scales, assign icon sets to values, assign multiple conditional formats to a cell, and assign more than three conditional formatting rules to a cell.

Working with the ribbon

As with all Office 2013 programs, the Excel ribbon is dynamic, meaning that as its width changes, its buttons adapt to the available space. As a result, a button might be large or small, it might or might not have a label, or it might even be an entry in a list.

For example, when sufficient horizontal space is available, the buttons on the Home tab are spread out, and the available commands in each group are visible.

If you decrease the horizontal space available to the ribbon, small button labels disappear and entire groups of buttons might hide under one button that represents the entire group. Clicking the group button displays a list of the commands available in that group.

When the ribbon becomes too narrow to display all the groups, a scroll arrow appears at its right end. Clicking the scroll arrow displays the hidden groups.

The width of the ribbon depends on three factors:

- **Program window width** Maximizing the program window provides the most space for the ribbon. To maximize the window, click the **Maximize** button, drag the borders of a nonmaximized window, or drag the window to the top of the screen.

- **Screen resolution** Screen resolution is the size of your screen display expressed as pixels wide × pixels high. Your screen resolution options are dependent on the display adapter installed in your computer, and on your monitor. Common screen resolutions range from 800 × 600 to 2560 × 1600. The greater the number of pixels wide (the first number), the greater the number of buttons that can be shown on the ribbon.

  To change your screen resolution:

  1 Display the **Screen Resolution** control panel item in one of the following ways:

     - Right-click the Windows desktop, and then click **Screen Resolution**.

     - Enter screen resolution in Windows 8 Search, and then click **Adjust screen resolution** in the **Settings** results.

     - Open the **Display** control panel item, and then click **Adjust resolution**.

  2 On the **Screen Resolution** page, click the **Resolution** arrow, click or drag to select the screen resolution you want, and then click **Apply** or **OK**.

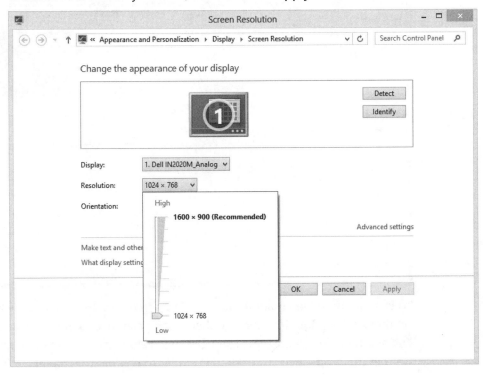

- **The magnification of your screen display** If you change the screen magnification setting in Windows, text and user interface elements are larger and therefore more legible, but fewer elements fit on the screen. You can set the magnification from 100 to 500 percent.

You can change the screen magnification from the Display page of the Appearance And Personalization control panel item. You can display the Display page directly from Control Panel or by using one of the following methods:

- Right-click the Windows desktop, click **Personalize**, and then in the lower-left corner of the **Personalization** window, click **Display**.

- Enter display in Windows 8 Search, and then click **Display** in the **Settings** results.

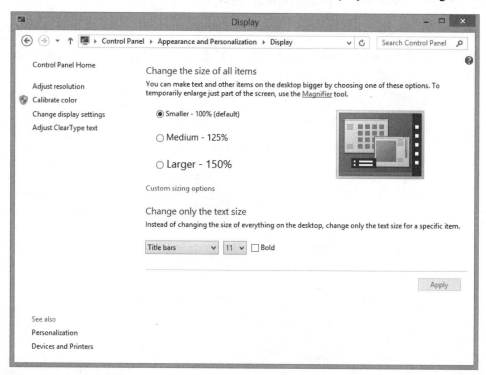

To change the screen magnification to 125 percent or 150 percent, click that option on the Display page. To select another magnification, click the Custom Sizing Options link and then, in the Custom Sizing Options dialog box, click the magnification you want in the drop-down list or drag the ruler to change the magnification even more.

After you click OK in the Custom Sizing Options dialog box, the custom magnification is shown on the Display page along with any warnings about possible problems with selecting that magnification. Click Apply on the Display page to apply the selected magnification.

Customizing the Excel 2013 program window

How you use Excel 2013 depends on your personal working style and the type of data collections you manage. The Excel product team interviews customers, observes how differing organizations use the program, and sets up the user interface so that many users won't need to change it to work effectively. If you do want to change the program window, including the user interface, you can. You can change how Excel displays your worksheets; zoom in on worksheet data; add frequently used commands to the Quick Access Toolbar; hide, display, and reorder ribbon tabs; and create custom tabs to make groups of commands readily accessible.

Zooming in on a worksheet

One way to make Excel easier to work with is to change the program's zoom level. Just as you can "zoom in" with a camera to increase the size of an object in the camera's viewer, you can use the zoom setting to change the size of objects within the Excel program window. For example, if Peter Villadsen, the Consolidated Messenger European Distribution Center Manager, displayed a worksheet that summarized his distribution center's package volume by month, he could click the View tab and then, in the Zoom group, click the Zoom button to open the Zoom dialog box. The Zoom dialog box contains controls that he can use to select a preset magnification level or to enter a custom magnification level. He could also use the Zoom control in the lower-right corner of the Excel window.

Clicking the Zoom In control increases the size of items in the program window by 10 percent, whereas clicking the Zoom Out control decreases the size of items in the program window by 10 percent. If you want more fine-grained control of your zoom level, you can use the slider control to select a specific zoom level or click the magnification level indicator, which indicates the zoom percentage, and use the Zoom dialog box to set a custom magnification level.

The Zoom group on the View tab contains the Zoom To Selection button, which fills the program window with the contents of any selected cells, up to the program's maximum zoom level of 400 percent.

TIP The minimum zoom level in Excel is 10 percent.

Arranging multiple workbook windows

As you work with Excel, you will probably need to have more than one workbook open at a time. For example, you could open a workbook that contains customer contact information and copy it into another workbook to be used as the source data for a mass mailing you create in Word. When you have multiple workbooks open simultaneously, you can switch between them by clicking the View tab and then, in the Window group, clicking the Switch Windows button and clicking the name of the workbook you want to view.

You can arrange your workbooks on the desktop so that most of the active workbook is shown but the others are easily accessible. To do so, click the View tab and then, in the Window group, click the Arrange All button. Then, in the Arrange Windows dialog box, click Cascade.

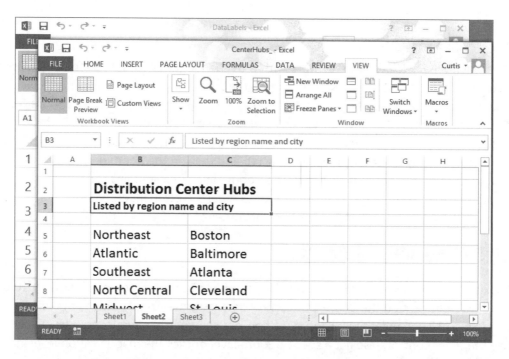

Many Excel workbooks contain formulas on one worksheet that derive their value from data on another worksheet, which means you need to change between two worksheets every time you want to test how modifying your data changes the formula's result. However, an easier way to approach this is to display two copies of the same workbook simultaneously, displaying the worksheet that contains the data in the original window and displaying the worksheet with the formula in the new window. When you change the data in either copy of the workbook, Excel updates the other copy. To display two copies of the same workbook, open the workbook and then, on the View tab, in the Window group, click New Window to opens a second copy of the workbook. To display the workbooks side by side, on the View tab, click Arrange All. Then, in the Arrange Windows dialog box, click Vertical and then click OK.

If the original workbook's name is MisroutedPackages, Excel displays the name MisroutedPackages:1 on the original workbook's title bar and MisroutedPackages:2 on the second workbook's title bar.

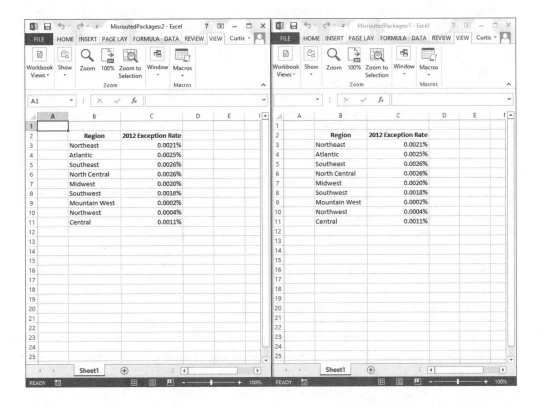

TROUBLESHOOTING If the controls in the Window group on the View tab don't affect your workbooks as you expect, you might have a program, such as SkyDrive for PC, open in the background that prevents those capabilities from functioning.

Adapting exercise steps

The screen shots shown in this book were captured at a screen resolution of 1024 × 768, at 100-percent magnification. If your settings are different, the ribbon on your screen might not look the same as the one shown in this book. As a result, exercise instructions that involve the ribbon might require a little adaptation. This book's instructions use this format:

- On the **Insert** tab, in the **Illustrations** group, click the **Chart** button.

If the command is in a list, the instructions use this format:

- On the **Home** tab, in the **Editing** group, click the **Find** arrow and then, in the **Find** list, click **Go To**.

If your display settings cause a button to appear differently on your screen than it does in this book, you can easily adapt the steps to locate the command. First click the specified tab, and then locate the specified group. If a group has been collapsed into a group list or under a group button, click the list or button to display the group's commands. If you can't immediately identify the button you want, point to likely candidates to display their names in ScreenTips.

This book provides instructions based on traditional keyboard and mouse input methods. If you're using Excel on a touch-enabled device, you might be giving commands by tapping with your finger or with a stylus. If so, substitute a tapping action any time the instructions ask you to click a user interface element. Also note that when the instructions ask you to enter information in Excel, you can do so by typing on a keyboard, tapping in the entry field under discussion to display and use the on-screen keyboard, or even speaking aloud, depending on your computer setup and your personal preferences.

In this exercise, you'll change a worksheet's zoom level, zoom to maximize the display of a selected cell range, switch between workbooks, and arrange all open workbooks on your screen.

 SET UP **You need the PackageCounts and MisroutedPackages workbooks located in the Chapter01 practice file folder to complete this exercise. Open both workbooks, and then follow the steps.**

1   In the **MisroutedPackages** workbook, in the lower-right corner of the Excel window, click the **Zoom In** control five times to change the worksheet's zoom level to **150%**.

2   Select cells **B2:C11**.

3   On the **View** tab, in the **Zoom** group, click the **Zoom to Selection** button to display the selected cells so that they fill the program window.

	A	B	C
2		**Region**	**2012 Exception Rate**
3		Northeast	0.0021%
4		Atlantic	0.0025%
5		Southeast	0.0026%
6		North Central	0.0026%
7		Midwest	0.0020%
8		Southwest	0.0018%
9		Mountain West	0.0002%
10		Northwest	0.0004%
11		Central	0.0011%

Sheet1   ⊕

4   On the **View** tab, in the **Zoom** group, click the **Zoom** button to open the **Zoom** dialog box.

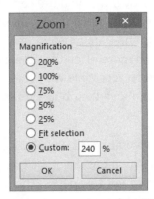

5   Click **100%**, and then click **OK** to return the worksheet to its default zoom level.

6   On the **View** tab, in the **Window** group, click the **Switch Windows** button, and then click **PackageCounts** to display the **PackageCounts** workbook.

7   On the **View** tab, in the **Window** group, click the **Arrange All** button to open the **Arrange Windows** dialog box.

8   Click **Cascade**, and then click **OK** to cascade the open workbook windows.

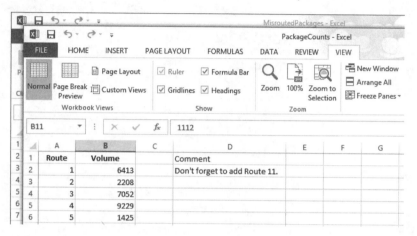

 CLEAN UP Close the PackageCounts and MisroutedPackages workbooks, saving your changes if you want to.

Adding buttons to the Quick Access Toolbar

As you continue to work with Excel 2013, you might discover that you use certain commands much more frequently than others. If your workbooks draw data from external sources, for example, you might find yourself displaying the Data tab and then, in the Connections group, clicking the Refresh All button much more often than the program's designers might have expected. You can make any button accessible with one click by adding the button to the Quick Access Toolbar, located just above the ribbon in the upper-left corner of the Excel program window.

To add a button to the Quick Access Toolbar, click the File tab to display the Backstage view, and then click Options in the left pane. In the Excel Options dialog box, display the Customize The Quick Access Toolbar page. This page contains two panes. The pane on the left lists all of the controls that are available within a specified category, and the pane on the right lists the controls currently displayed on the Quick Access Toolbar. To add a command to the Quick Access Toolbar, in the Choose Commands From list, click the category that contains the control you want to add. Excel displays the available commands in the pane below the Choose Commands From field. Click the control you want, and then click the Add button.

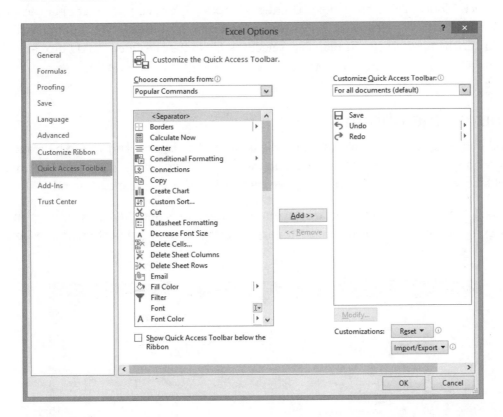

You can change a button's position on the Quick Access Toolbar by clicking its name in the right pane and then clicking either the Move Up or Move Down button at the right edge of the dialog box. To remove a button from the Quick Access Toolbar, click the button's name in the right pane, and then click the Remove button. When you're done making your changes, click the OK button. If you prefer not to save your changes, click the Cancel button. If you saved your changes but want to return the Quick Access Toolbar to its original state, click the Reset button and then click either Reset Only Quick Access Toolbar, which removes any changes you made to the Quick Access Toolbar, or Reset All Customizations, which returns the entire ribbon interface to its original state.

You can also choose whether your Quick Access Toolbar changes affect all your workbooks or just the active workbook. To control how Excel applies your change, in the Customize Quick Access Toolbar list, click either For All Documents to apply the change to all of your workbooks or For Workbook to apply the change to the active workbook only.

If you'd like to export your Quick Access Toolbar customizations to a file that can be used to apply those changes to another Excel 2013 installation, click the Import/Export button and then click Export All Customizations. Use the controls in the dialog box that opens to save your file. When you're ready to apply saved customizations to Excel, click the Import/Export button, click Import Customization File, select the file in the File Open dialog box, and click Open.

Customizing the ribbon

Excel enhances your ability to customize the entire ribbon by enabling you to hide and display ribbon tabs, reorder tabs displayed on the ribbon, customize existing tabs (including tool tabs, which appear when specific items are selected), and create custom tabs.

To begin customizing the ribbon, display the Backstage view and then click Options. In the Excel Options dialog box, click Customize Ribbon to display the Customize The Ribbon page.

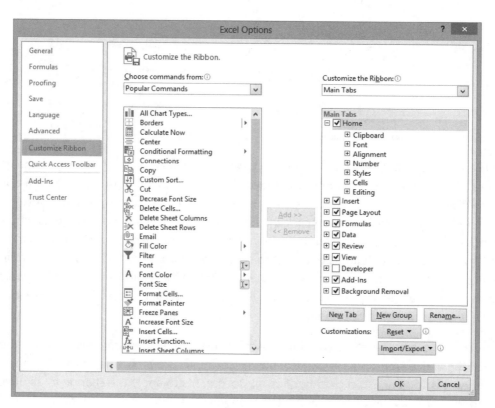

To select which tabs appear in the tabs pane on the right side of the screen, click the Customize The Ribbon field's arrow and then click either Main Tabs, which displays the tabs that can appear on the standard ribbon; Tool Tabs, which displays the tabs that appear when you click an item such as a drawing object or PivotTable; or All Tabs.

TIP The procedures taught in this section apply to both the main tabs and the tool tabs.

Each tab's name has a check box next to it. If a tab's check box is selected, then that tab appears on the ribbon. You can hide a tab by clearing the check box and bring the tab back by selecting the check box. You can also change the order in which the tabs are displayed on the ribbon. To do so, click the name of the tab you want to move and then click the Move Up or Move Down arrow to reposition the selected tab.

Just as you can change the order of the tabs on the ribbon, you can change the order in which groups of commands appear on a tab. For example, the Page Layout tab contains five groups: Themes, Page Setup, Scale To Fit, Sheet Options, and Arrange. If you use the Themes group less frequently than the other groups, you could move the group to the right end of the tab by clicking the group's name and then clicking the Move Down button until the group appears in the position you want.

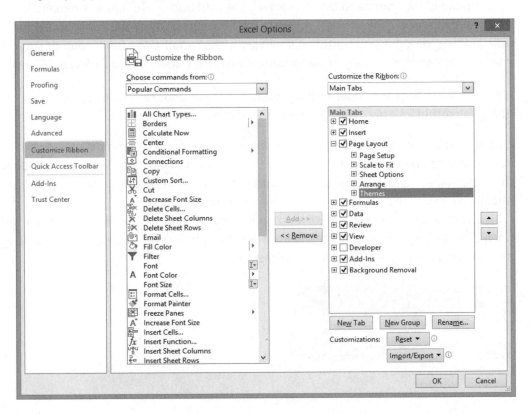

To remove a group from a built-in tab, click the name of the group in the right pane and click the Remove button. If you remove a group from a built-in tab and later decide you want to put it back on the tab, display the tab in the right pane. Then, click the Choose Commands From field's arrow and click Main Tabs. With the tab displayed, in the left pane, click the expand control (which looks like a plus sign) next to the name of the tab that contains the group you want to add back. You can now click the name of the group in the left pane and click the Add button to put the group back on the selected tab.

The built-in tabs are designed efficiently, so adding new command groups might crowd the other items on the tab and make those controls harder to find. Rather than adding controls to an existing tab, you can create a custom tab and then add groups and commands to it. To create a custom tab, click the New Tab button on the Customize The Ribbon page of the Excel Options dialog box. When you do, a new tab named New Tab (Custom), which contains a group named New Group (Custom), appears in the tab list.

You can add an existing group to your new tab by clicking the Choose Commands From field's arrow, selecting a collection of commands, clicking the group you want to add, and then clicking the Add button. You can also add individual commands to your tab by clicking a command in the command list and clicking the Add button. To add a command to your tab's custom group, click the new group in the right tab list, click the command in the left list, and then click the Add button. If you want to add another custom group to your new tab, click the new tab, or any of the groups within that tab, and then click New Group.

TIP You can change the order of the groups and commands on your custom ribbon tabs by using the techniques described earlier in this section.

The New Tab (Custom) name doesn't tell you anything about the commands on your new tab, so you can rename it to reflect its contents. To rename any tab on the ribbon, display the Customize The Ribbon page of the Excel Options dialog box, click the tab you want to modify, and then click the Rename button. Enter the tab's new name in the Rename dialog box, and click OK. To rename any group on the ribbon, click the name of the group, and then click Rename. When you do, the Rename dialog box appears. Enter a new name for the group in the Display Name box and click OK.

If you'd like to export your ribbon customizations to a file that can be used to apply those changes to another Excel 2013 installation, click the Import/Export button and then click Export All Customizations. Use the controls in the dialog box that opens to save your file. When you're ready to apply saved customizations to Excel, click the Import/Export button, click Import Customization File, select the file in the File Open dialog box, and click Open.

When you're done customizing the ribbon, click the OK button to save your changes or click Cancel to keep the user interface as it was before you started this round of changes. You can also change a tab, or the entire ribbon, back to the state it was in when you installed Excel. To restore a single tab, click the tab you want to restore, click the Reset button, and then click Reset Only Selected Ribbon Tab. To restore the entire ribbon, including the Quick Access Toolbar, click the Reset button and then click Reset All Customizations.

Maximizing usable space in the program window

You can increase the amount of space available inside the program window by hiding the ribbon, the formula bar, or the row and column labels.

To hide the ribbon, double-click the active tab label. The tab labels remain visible at the top of the program window, but the tab content is hidden. To temporarily redisplay the ribbon, click the tab label you want. Then click any button on the tab, or click away from the tab, to rehide it. To permanently redisplay the ribbon, double-click any tab label.

KEYBOARD SHORTCUT Press Ctrl+F1 to hide and unhide the ribbon. For a complete list of keyboard shortcuts, see "Keyboard shortcuts" at the end of this book.

To hide the formula bar, clear the Formula Bar check box in the Show/Hide group on the View tab. To hide the row and column labels, clear the Headings check box in the Show/Hide group on the View tab.

In this exercise, you'll add a button to the Quick Access Toolbar and customize the ribbon.

 SET UP You need the PackageCounts workbook located in the Chapter01 practice file folder to complete this exercise. Open the workbook, and then follow the steps.

1 Click the **File** tab to display the **Backstage** view, and then click **Options** to open the **Excel Options** dialog box.

2 Click **Quick Access Toolbar** to display the **Customize The Quick Access Toolbar** page.

3   Click the **Choose commands from** arrow, and then in the list, click **Review Tab** to display the commands in the **Review Tab** category in the command list.

4   Click the **Spelling** command, and then click **Add** to add the **Spelling** command to the **Quick Access Toolbar**.

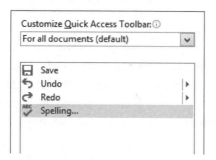

5   Click **Customize Ribbon** to display the **Customize The Ribbon** page of the **Excel Options** dialog box.

6   If necessary, click the **Customize the Ribbon** box's arrow and click **Main Tabs**. In the right tab list, click the **Review** tab and then click the **Move Up** button three times to move the **Review** tab between the **Insert** and **Page Layout** tabs.

7   Click the **New Tab** button to create a tab named **New Tab (Custom)**, which appears below the most recently active tab in the **Main Tabs** list.

8   Click the **New Tab (Custom)** tab name, click the **Rename** button, enter My Commands in the **Display Name** box, and click **OK** to change the new tab's name to **My Commands**.

9   Click the **New Group (Custom)** group's name and then click the **Rename** button. In the **Rename** dialog box, click the icon that looks like a paint palette (second row, fourth from the right). Then, in the **Display name** box, enter Formatting, and click **OK** to change the new group's name to **Formatting**.

10   In the right tab list, click the **My Commands** tab name. Then, on the left side of the dialog box, click the **Choose Commands From** box's arrow and click **Main Tabs** to display that group of tabs in the left tab list.

11 In the left tab list, click the **Home** tab's expand control, click the **Styles** group's name, and then click the **Add** button to add the **Styles** group to the **My Commands** tab.

12 In the left tab list, below the **Home** tab, click the **Number** group's expand control to display the commands in the **Number** group.

13 In the right tab list, click the **Formatting** group you created earlier. Then, in the left tab list, click the **Number Format** item and click the **Add** button to add the **Number Format** item to the **Formatting** custom group.

14 Click **OK** to save your ribbon customizations, and then click the **My Commands** tab on the ribbon to display the contents of the new tab.

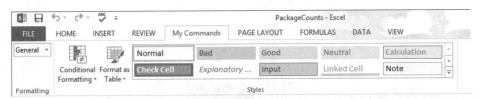

IMPORTANT The remaining exercises in this book assume that you are using Excel 2013 as it was installed on your computer. After you complete this exercise, you should reset the ribbon to its original configuration so that the instructions in the remaining exercises in the book are consistent with your copy of Excel.

✖ CLEAN UP Close all open workbooks, saving your changes if you want to.

Creating workbooks

Every time you want to gather and store data that isn't closely related to any of your other existing data, you should create a new workbook. The default workbook in Excel has one worksheet, although you can add more worksheets or delete existing worksheets if you want. Creating a workbook is a straightforward process—you just display the Backstage view, click New, and click the tile that represents the type of workbook you want.

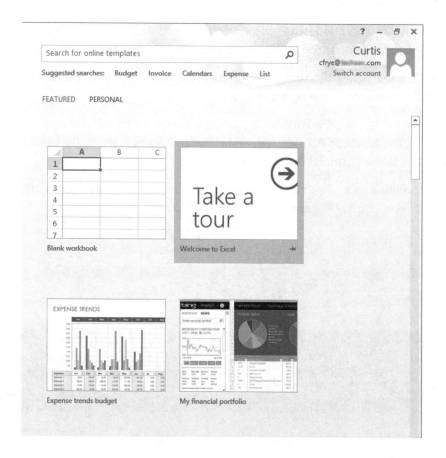

KEYBOARD SHORTCUT Press Ctrl+N to create a blank workbook.

When you start Excel, the program displays the Start experience. With the Start experience, you can select which type of workbook to create. You can create a blank workbook by clicking the Blank Workbook tile or click one of the built-in templates available in Excel. You can then begin to enter data into the worksheet's cells. You could also open an existing workbook and work with its contents. In this book's exercises, you'll work with workbooks created for Consolidated Messenger, a fictional global shipping company. After you make changes to a workbook, you can save it to preserve your work.

KEYBOARD SHORTCUT Press Ctrl+S to save a workbook.

TIP Readers frequently ask, "How often should I save my files?" It is good practice to save your changes every half hour or even every five minutes, but the best time to save a file is whenever you make a change that you would hate to have to make again.

When you save a file, you overwrite the previous copy of the file. If you have made changes that you want to save, but you also want to keep a copy of the file as it was when you saved it previously, you can use the Save As command to specify a name for the new file. To open the Save As dialog box, in the Backstage view, click Save As.

KEYBOARD SHORTCUT Press F12 to open the Save As dialog box.

You can also use the controls in the Save As dialog box to specify a different format for the new file and a different location in which to save the new version of the file. For example, Lori Penor, the chief operating officer of Consolidated Messenger, might want to save an Excel file that tracks consulting expenses as an Excel 2003 file if she needs to share the file with a consulting firm that uses Excel 2003.

After you create a file, you can add information to make the file easier to find when you search by using File Explorer or Windows 8 Search to search for it. Each category of information, or property, stores specific information about your file. In Windows, you can search for files based on the file's author or title, or by keywords associated with the file. A file that tracks the postal code destinations of all packages sent from a vendor might have the keywords *postal*, *destination*, and *origin* associated with it.

To set values for your workbook's built-in properties, you can display the Backstage view, click Info, click Properties, and then click Show Document Panel to display the Document Properties panel below the ribbon. The standard version of the Document Properties panel has fields for the file's author, title, subject, keywords, category, and status, and any comments about the file.

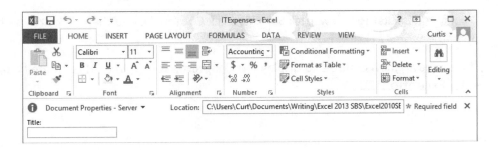

You can also create custom properties by clicking the arrow located to the right of the Document Properties label, and clicking Advanced Properties to open the Properties dialog box. On the Custom page of the Properties dialog box, you can click one of the existing custom categories or create your own by entering a new property name in the Name field, clicking the Type arrow and selecting a data type (for example, Text, Date, Number, or Yes/No), selecting or entering a value in the Value field, and then clicking Add. If you want to delete an existing custom property, point to the Properties list, click the property you want to get rid of, and click Delete. After you finish making your changes, click the OK button. To hide the Document Properties panel, click the Close button in the upper-right corner of the panel.

When you're done modifying a workbook, you should save your changes and then, to close the file, display the Backstage view and then click Close. You can also click the Close button in the upper-right corner of the workbook window.

KEYBOARD SHORTCUT Press Ctrl+W to close a workbook.

In this exercise, you'll close an open workbook, create a new workbook, save the workbook with a new name, assign values to the workbook's standard properties, and create a custom property.

 SET UP You need the ExceptionSummary workbook located in the Chapter01 practice file folder to complete this exercise. Open the workbook, and then follow the steps.

1   Click the **File** tab to display the **Backstage** view, and then click **Close** to close the ExceptionSummary workbook.

2   Display the **Backstage** view, and then click **New** to display the **New** page.

3   Click **Blank workbook**, and then click **Create** to open a new, blank workbook.

4   Display the **Backstage** view, click **Save As**, click **Computer**, and then click **Browse** to open the **Save As** dialog box.

5   Use the navigation controls to display the **Chapter01** folder. In the **File name** field, enter **Exceptions2013**.

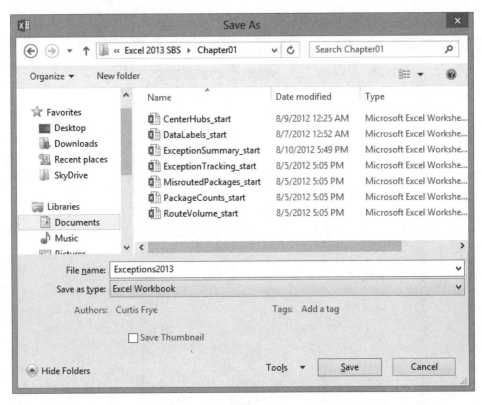

6   Click the **Save** button to save your work and close the **Save As** dialog box.

7   Display the **Backstage** view, click **Info**, click **Properties**, and then click **Show Document Panel** to display the **Document Properties** panel.

8   In the **Keywords** field, enter exceptions, regional, percentage.

9   In the **Category** field, enter performance.

10 Click the arrow at the right end of the **Document Properties** button, and then click **Advanced Properties** to open the **Exceptions2013 Properties** dialog box.

11 Click the **Custom** tab to display the **Custom** page.

12   In the **Name** field, enter Performance.

13   In the **Value** field, enter Exceptions.

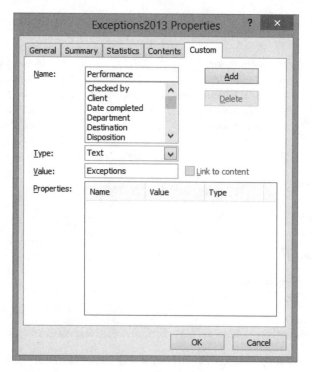

14   Click the **Add** button, and then click **OK** to save the properties and close the **Exceptions2013 Properties** dialog box.

❌ CLEAN UP Close the Exceptions2013 workbook, saving your changes if you want to.

Modifying workbooks

Most of the time, you create a workbook to record information about a particular activity, such as the number of packages that a regional distribution center handles or the average time a driver takes to complete all deliveries on a route. Each worksheet within that workbook should represent a subdivision of that activity. To display a particular worksheet, click the worksheet's tab on the tab bar (just below the grid of cells).

In the case of Consolidated Messenger, the workbook used to track daily package volumes could have a separate worksheet for each regional distribution center. As mentioned earlier, new Excel workbooks contain one worksheet; because Consolidated Messenger uses nine regional distribution centers, you would need to create eight new worksheets. To create a new worksheet, click the New Sheet button (which looks like a plus sign in a circle) at the right edge of the tab bar.

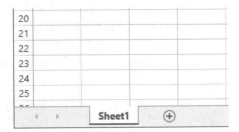

When you create a worksheet, Excel assigns it a generic name such as *Sheet2*, *Sheet3*, or *Sheet4*. After you decide what type of data you want to store on a worksheet, you should change the default worksheet name to something more descriptive. For example, you could change the name of Sheet1 in the regional distribution center tracking workbook to *Northeast*. When you want to change a worksheet's name, double-click the worksheet's tab on the tab bar to highlight the worksheet name, enter the new name, and press Enter.

Another way to work with more than one worksheet is to copy a worksheet from another workbook to the current workbook. One circumstance in which you might consider copying worksheets to the current workbook is if you have a list of your current employees in another workbook. You can copy worksheets from another workbook by right-clicking the tab of the sheet you want to copy and, on the shortcut menu, clicking Move Or Copy to open the Move Or Copy dialog box.

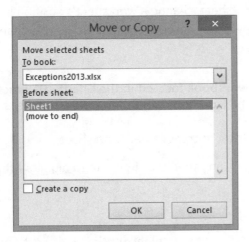

TIP When you select the Create A Copy check box, Excel leaves the copied worksheet in its original workbook, whereas clearing the check box causes Excel to delete the worksheet from its original workbook.

After the worksheet is in the target workbook, you can change the worksheets' order to make the data easier to locate within the workbook. To change a worksheet's location in the workbook, you drag its sheet tab to the location you want on the tab bar. If you want to remove a worksheet from the tab bar without deleting the worksheet, you can do so by right-clicking the worksheet's tab on the tab bar and clicking Hide on the shortcut menu. When you want Excel to redisplay the worksheet, right-click any visible sheet tab and then click Unhide. In the Unhide dialog box, click the name of the sheet you want to display, and click OK.

To differentiate a worksheet from others, or to visually indicate groups or categories of worksheets in a multiple-worksheet workbook, you can change the color of a worksheet tab. To do so, right-click the tab, point to Tab Color, and then click the color you want.

TIP If you copy a worksheet to another workbook, and the destination workbook has the same Office Theme applied as the active workbook, the worksheet retains its tab color. If the destination workbook has another theme applied, the worksheet's tab color changes to reflect that theme. For more information about Office themes, see Chapter 4, "Changing workbook appearance."

If you determine that you no longer need a particular worksheet, such as one you created to store some figures temporarily, you can delete the worksheet quickly. To do so, right-click its sheet tab, and then click Delete.

In this exercise, you'll insert and rename a worksheet, change a worksheet's position in a workbook, hide and unhide a worksheet, copy a worksheet to another workbook, change a worksheet's tab color, and delete a worksheet.

 SET UP **You need the ExceptionTracking workbook located in the Chapter01 practice file folder to complete this exercise. Open the workbook, and then follow the steps.**

1   On the tab bar, click the **New Sheet** button to create a new worksheet.

2   Right-click the new worksheet's sheet tab, and then click **Rename** to highlight the new worksheet's name.

3   Enter **2013**, and then press **Enter**.

4   On the tab bar, double-click the **Sheet1** sheet tab to highlight the worksheet's name.

5   Enter **2012**, and then press **Enter**.

6   Right-click the **2013** sheet tab, point to **Tab Color**, and then, in the **Standard Colors** palette, click the green swatch to change the **2013** sheet tab to green.

7   On the tab bar, drag the **2012** sheet tab to the right of the **Scratch Pad** sheet tab.

8   Right-click the **2013** sheet tab, and then click **Hide** to remove the **2013** sheet tab from the tab bar.

9   Right-click the **2012** sheet tab, and then click **Move or Copy** to open the **Move or Copy** dialog box.

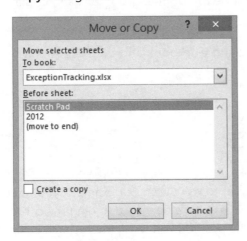

10   Click the **To book** arrow, and then in the list, click **(new book)**.

11   Select the **Create a copy** check box.

12   Click **OK** to create a new workbook and copy the selected worksheet into it.

13   On the **Quick Access Toolbar**, click **Save** to open the **Save As** dialog box.

14   In the **File name** field, enter **2012 Archive**, and then press **Enter** to save the workbook.

15   On the **View** tab, click the **Switch Windows** button, and then click **ExceptionTracking** to display the **ExceptionTracking** workbook.

16   On the tab bar, right-click the **Scratch Pad** sheet tab, and then click **Delete**. In the dialog box that opens, click **Delete** to confirm the operation.

17   Right-click the **2012** sheet tab, and then click **Unhide** to open the **Unhide** dialog box.

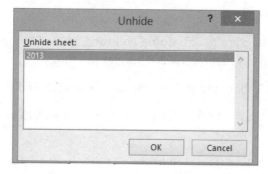

18 Click **2013**, and then click **OK** to close the **Unhide** dialog box and display the **2013** worksheet in the workbook.

✖ CLEAN UP Close the ExceptionTracking workbook and the 2012 Archive workbook, saving your changes if you want to.

Modifying worksheets

After you put up the signposts that make your data easy to find, you can take other steps to make the data in your workbooks easier to work with. For example, you can change the width of a column or the height of a row in a worksheet by dragging the column's right border or the row's bottom border to the position you want. Increasing a column's width or a row's height increases the space between cell contents, making your data easier to read and work with.

TIP You can apply the same change to more than one row or column by selecting the rows or columns you want to change and then dragging the border of one of the selected rows or columns to the location you want. When you release the mouse button, all the selected rows or columns change to the new height or width.

Inserting rows, columns, and cells

Modifying column width and row height can make a workbook's contents easier to work with, but you can also insert a row or column between cells that contain data to make your data easier to read. Adding space between the edge of a worksheet and cells that contain data, or perhaps between a label and the data to which it refers, makes the workbook's contents less crowded. You insert rows by clicking a cell and clicking the Home tab on the ribbon. Then, in the Cells group, in the Insert list, click Insert Sheet Rows. Excel inserts a row above the row that contains the active cell. You insert a column in much the same way, by choosing Insert Sheet Columns from the Insert list. When you do this, Excel inserts a column to the left of the active cell.

When you insert a row, column, or cell in a worksheet that has had formatting applied, the Insert Options button appears. When you click the Insert Options button, Excel displays a list of choices you can make about how the inserted row or column should be formatted, as described in the following table.

Option	Action
Format Same As Above	Applies the formatting of the row above the inserted row to the new row
Format Same As Below	Applies the formatting of the row below the inserted row to the new row
Format Same As Left	Applies the formatting of the column to the left of the inserted column to the new column
Format Same As Right	Applies the formatting of the column to the right of the inserted column to the new column
Clear Formatting	Applies the default format to the new row or column

If you want to delete a row or column, right-click the row or column head and then, on the shortcut menu that appears, click Delete. You can temporarily hide rows or columns by selecting those rows or columns and then, on the Home tab, in the Cells group, clicking the Format button, pointing to Hide & Unhide, and then clicking either Hide Rows or Hide Columns. The rows or columns you selected disappear, but they aren't gone for good as they would be if you'd used Delete. Instead, they have just been removed from the display until you call them back. To return the hidden rows to the display, select the row or column headers on either side of the hidden rows or columns. Then, on the Home tab, in the Cells group, click the Format button, point to Hide & Unhide, and then click either Unhide Rows or Unhide Columns.

Just as you can insert rows or columns, you can insert individual cells into a worksheet. To insert a cell, click the cell that is currently in the position where you want the new cell to appear. On the Home tab, in the Cells group, in the Insert list, click Insert Cells to open the Insert dialog box. In the Insert dialog box, you can choose whether to shift the cells surrounding the inserted cell down (if your data is arranged as a column) or to the right (if your data is arranged as a row). When you click OK, the new cell appears, and the contents of affected cells shift down or to the right, as appropriate. Similarly, if you want to delete a block of cells, select the cells, and on the Home tab, in the Cells group, in the Delete list, click Delete Cells to open the Delete dialog box—complete with options that you can use to choose how to shift the position of the cells around the deleted cells.

TIP The Insert dialog box also includes options you can click to insert a new row or column; the Delete dialog box has similar options for deleting an entire row or column.

If you want to move the data in a group of cells to another location in your worksheet, select the cells you want to move and point to the selection's border. When the pointer changes to a four-pointed arrow, you can drag the selected cells to the desired location on the worksheet. If the destination cells contain data, Excel displays a dialog box asking whether you want to overwrite the destination cells' contents. If you want to replace the existing values, click OK. If you don't want to overwrite the existing values, click Cancel and insert the required number of cells to accommodate the data you want to move.

In this exercise, you'll insert a column and row into a worksheet, specify insert options, hide a column, insert a cell into a worksheet, delete a cell from a worksheet, and move a group of cells within the worksheet.

SET UP You need the RouteVolume workbook located in the Chapter01 practice file folder to complete this exercise. Open the workbook, and then follow the steps.

1   On the **May 12** worksheet, select cell **A1**.

2   On the **Home** tab, in the **Cells** group, click the **Insert** arrow, and then in the list, click **Insert Sheet Columns** to create a new column **A**.

3   In the **Insert** list, click **Insert Sheet Rows** to create a new row **1**.

4   Click the **Insert Options** button that appears below the lower-right corner of the selected cell, and then click **Clear Formatting** to remove the formatting from the new row **1**.

5   Right-click the column header of column **E**, and then click **Hide** to remove column **E** from the display.

◢	A	B	C	D	F
1					
2		Route	Volume		
3		1	6413		
4		2	2208		
5		3	7052		
6		4	9229		
7		5	1425		
8		6	4329		
9		7	8410		
10		8	8785		
11		9	5812		
12		10	1112		
13					

6   On the tab bar, click the **May 13** sheet tab to display the worksheet of the same name.

7   Click cell **B6**.

8   On the **Home** tab, in the **Cells** group, click the **Delete** arrow, and then in the list, click **Delete Cells** to open the **Delete** dialog box.

9   If necessary, click **Shift cells up**, and then click **OK**. Excel deletes cell **B6**, moving the cells below it up to fill in the gap.

10   Click cell **C6**.

11   In the **Cells** group, in the **Insert** list, click **Insert Cells** to open the **Insert** dialog box.

12   If necessary, click **Shift cells down**, and then click **OK** to close the **Insert** dialog box, create a new cell **C6**, and move cells **C6:C11** down to accommodate the inserted cell.

13   In cell **C6**, enter **4499**, and then press **Enter**.

14   Select cells **E13:F13**.

15   Point to the border of the selected cells. When the pointer changes to a four-pointed arrow, drag the selected cells to cells **B13:C13**. The dragged cells replace cells **B13:C13**.

	A	B	C	D
1				
2		Route	Volume	
3		1	6413	
4		2	2208	
5		3	7052	
6		4	4499	
7		5	9229	
8		6	1425	
9		7	4329	
10		8	8410	
11		9	8785	
12		10	5812	
13		11	5509	
14				
15				

❌ CLEAN UP Close the RouteVolume workbook, saving your changes if you want to.

Merging and unmerging cells

Most Excel worksheets contain data about a specific subject, such as packages shipped, revenue, or operating costs. One of the best ways to communicate the contents of a worksheet is to use a label. For example, you might create a list of Consolidated Messenger's delivery regions with the city where the region's distribution hub is located.

◢	A	B	C
1			
2		**Distribution Center Hubs**	
3		**Listed by region name and city**	
4			
5		Northeast	Boston
6		Atlantic	Baltimore
7		Southeast	Atlanta
8		North Central	Cleveland
9		Midwest	St. Louis
10		Southwest	Albuquerque
11		Mountain West	Denver
12		Northwest	Portland
13		Central	Omaha
14			

The text *Distribution Center Hubs* appears to span two cells, B2 and C2, but is in fact contained within cell B2. If you select cell B2, Excel highlights the cell's border, which obscures the text. If you want to combine cells B2 and C2 into a single cell, you can do so by merging the cells into a single cell.

To merge two or more cells, you select the cells, click the Home tab, click Merge & Center, and then click Merge Cells. Now when you click cell B2, the selection border extends along the entire merged cell without blocking the text.

	A	B	C
1			
2		**Distribution Center Hubs**	
3		Listed by region name and city	
4			
5		Northeast	Boston
6		Atlantic	Baltimore
7		Southeast	Atlanta
8		North Central	Cleveland
9		Midwest	St. Louis
10		Southwest	Albuquerque
11		Mountain West	Denver
12		Northwest	Portland
13		Central	Omaha
14			

IMPORTANT When you merge two or more cells, Excel retains just the text in the range's top left cell. All other text is deleted.

When you click the Merge & Center button, a list of options appears. In addition to merging cells, you can click Merge & Center to combine the selected cells into a single cell and center the text within the merged cell. You should strongly consider using the Merge & Center option for label text, such as above a list of data where the title spans more than one column.

You can also merge the cells in multiple rows at the same time. For example, suppose your list has a main heading and a subheading. You can merge the cells in the two rows that contain headings by clicking the Home tab, clicking Merge & Center, and then clicking Merge Across.

	A	B	C
1			
2		**Distribution Center Hubs**	
3		Listed by region name and city	
4			
5		Northeast	Boston
6		Atlantic	Baltimore
7		Southeast	Atlanta
8		North Central	Cleveland
9		Midwest	St. Louis
10		Southwest	Albuquerque
11		Mountain West	Denver
12		Northwest	Portland
13		Central	Omaha
14			

IMPORTANT When you select the header cells, click the Home tab, click Merge & Center, and then click either Merge & Center or Merge Cells, Excel deletes any text that's not in the top-left cell of the selected range.

If you want to split merged cells into their individual cells, click the Home tab, click Merge & Center, and then click Unmerge Cells.

In this exercise, you will merge cells, unmerge cells, merge and center cells, and use Merge Across to combine cells in several rows into one merged cell per row.

1   Select cells **B2:D2**.

2   Click the **Home** tab, click the **Merge & Center** arrow, and then click **Merge Cells** to merge the cells into a single cell.

3   Select cells **B3:F3**.

4   Click the **Home** tab, click the **Merge & Center** arrow, and then click **Merge & Center** to merge the cells into a single cell and center its contents.

5   Select cells **B5:E8**.

6   Click the **Home** tab, click the **Merge & Center** arrow, and then click **Merge Across** to merge the cells in each row into a single cell. The operation creates four merged cells.

◢	A	B	C	D	E	F
1						
2		**Delivery Category**				
3		**Brief descriptions of each category**				
4						
5		Overnight: next day delivery by 3PM				
6		2Day: second-day delivery by 6PM				
7		3Day: third-day delivery by 6PM				
8		Ground: delivery in 3-5 days by 6PM				
9						

7   Select cell **B2**.

8   Click the **Home** tab, click the **Merge & Center** arrow, and then click **Unmerge Cells** to split the merged cell into its original cells.

9   Select cells **B2:D2**.

10   Click the **Home** tab, click the **Merge & Center** arrow, and then click **Merge & Center** to merge the cells into a single cell and center its contents.

✖ **CLEAN UP** Close the DataLabels workbook, saving your changes if you want to.

Key points

- Save your work whenever you do something you'd hate to have to do again.

- Assigning values to a workbook's properties makes it easier to find your workbook by searching in File Explorer or by using Windows 8 Search.

- Be sure to give your worksheets descriptive names.

- If you want to use a worksheet's data in another workbook, you can send a copy of the worksheet to that other workbook without deleting the original worksheet.

- You can delete a worksheet you no longer need, but you can also hide a worksheet in a workbook. When you need the data on the worksheet, you can unhide it.

- You can save yourself a lot of cutting and pasting by inserting and deleting worksheet cells, columns, and rows.

- By merging cells, you can add data labels that span multiple columns.

- Customize your Excel 2013 program window by changing how it displays your workbooks, zooming in on data, adding frequently used buttons to the Quick Access Toolbar, and rearranging or customizing the ribbon to meet your needs.

Chapter at a glance

Manage

Manage data by using Flash Fill,
page 50

Rearrange

Move data within a workbook,
page 54

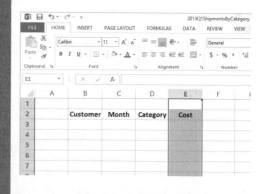

Find

Find and replace data,
page 58

Define

Define Excel tables,
page 67

	A	B	C	D
1				
2		Customer	Month	Program Savings
3		Contoso	January	$ 182,423
4		Contoso	February	$ 173,486
5		Contoso	March	$ 88,027
6		Fabrikam	January	$ 139,434
7		Fabrikam	February	$ 29,461
8		Fabrikam	March	$ 91,295
9		Lucerne Publishing	January	$ 136,922
10		Lucerne Publishing	February	$ 161,370
11		Lucerne Publishing	March	$ 160,250
12		Wide World Importers	January	$ 109,903
13		Wide World Importers	February	$ 102,243
14		Wide World Importers	March	$ 105,077
15		Total		$ 1,479,891

Working with data and Excel tables

2

IN THIS CHAPTER, YOU WILL LEARN HOW TO

- Enter and revise data.

- Manage data by using Flash Fill.

- Move data within a workbook.

- Find and replace data.

- Correct and expand upon worksheet data.

- Define Excel tables.

With Microsoft Excel 2013, you can visualize and present information effectively by using charts, graphics, and formatting, but the data is the most important part of any workbook. By learning to enter data efficiently, you will make fewer data entry errors and give yourself more time to analyze your data so you can make decisions about your organization's performance and direction.

Excel provides a wide variety of tools you can use to enter and manage worksheet data effectively. For example, you can organize your data into Excel tables, which enables you to store and analyze your data quickly and efficiently. Also, you can enter a data series quickly, repeat one or more values, and control how Excel formats cells, columns, and rows moved from one part of a worksheet to another with a minimum of effort. With Excel, you can check the spelling of worksheet text, look up alternative words by using the Thesaurus, and translate words to foreign languages.

In this chapter, you'll enter and revise Excel data, manage data by using Flash Fill, move data within a workbook, find and replace existing data, use proofing and reference tools to enhance your data, and organize your data by defining Excel tables.

PRACTICE FILES To complete the exercises in this chapter, you need the practice files contained in the Chapter02 practice file folder. For more information, see "Download the practice files" in this book's Introduction.

Entering and revising data

After you create a workbook, you can begin entering data. The simplest way to enter data is to click a cell and enter a value. This method works very well when you're entering a few pieces of data, but it is less than ideal when you're entering long sequences or series of values. For example, Craig Dewar, the VP of Marketing for Consolidated Messenger, might want to create a worksheet that lists the monthly program savings that large customers can realize if they sign exclusive delivery contracts with Consolidated Messenger. To record those numbers, he would need to create a worksheet tracking each customer's monthly program savings.

	A	B	C	D	E
1					
2		**Customer**	**Month**	**Program Savings**	
3		Contoso	January	$ 182,423	
4		Contoso	February	$ 173,486	
5		Contoso	March	$ 88,027	
6		Fabrikam	January	$ 139,434	
7		Fabrikam	February	$ 29,461	
8		Fabrikam	March	$ 91,295	
9		Lucerne Publishing	January	$ 136,922	
10		Lucerne Publishing	February	$ 161,370	
11		Lucerne Publishing	March	$ 160,250	
12		Wide World Importers	January	$ 109,903	
13		Wide World Importers	February	$ 102,243	
14		Wide World Importers	March	$ 105,077	
15					

Repeatedly entering the sequence January, February, March, and so on can be handled by copying and pasting the first occurrence of the sequence, but there's an easier way to do it: use AutoFill. With AutoFill, you enter the first element in a recognized series, click the fill handle at the lower-right corner of the cell, and drag the fill handle until the series extends far enough to accommodate your data. By using a similar tool, FillSeries, you can enter two values in a series and use the fill handle to extend the series in your worksheet. For example, if you want to create a series starting at 2 and increasing by 2, you can enter 2 in the first cell and 4 in the second cell, select both cells, and then use the fill handle to extend the series to the end value you want.

You do have some control over how Excel extends the values in a series when you drag the fill handle. For example, if you drag the fill handle up (or to the left), Excel extends the series to include previous values. If you enter January in a cell and then drag that cell's fill handle up (or to the left), Excel places December in the first cell, November in the second cell, and so on.

Another way to control how Excel extends a data series is by pressing the Ctrl key while you drag the fill handle. For example, if you press the Ctrl key while you drag the fill handle, Excel repeats the value January in each cell you add to the series.

TIP Be sure to experiment with how the fill handle extends your series and how pressing the Ctrl key changes that behavior. Using the fill handle can save you a lot of time entering data.

Other data entry techniques you'll use in this section are AutoComplete, which detects when a value you're entering is similar to previously entered values; Pick From Drop-Down List, from which you can choose a value from among the existing values in the active cell's worksheet column; and Ctrl+Enter, which you can use to enter a value in multiple cells simultaneously.

TROUBLESHOOTING If an AutoComplete suggestion doesn't appear as you begin entering a cell value, the option might be turned off. To turn on AutoComplete, click the File tab, and then click Options. In the Excel Options dialog box, display the Advanced page. In the Editing Options area of the page, select the Enable AutoComplete For Cell Values check box, and then click OK.

The following table summarizes these data entry techniques.

Method	Action
AutoFill	Enter the first value in a recognized series and use the fill handle to extend the series.
FillSeries	Enter the first two values in a series and use the fill handle to extend the series.
AutoComplete	Enter the first few letters in a cell, and if a similar value exists in the same column, Excel suggests the existing value.
Pick From Drop-Down List	Right-click a cell, and then click Pick From Drop-Down List. A list of existing values in the cell's column is displayed. Click the value you want to enter into the cell.
Ctrl+Enter	Select a range of cells, each of which you want to contain the same data, enter the data in the active cell, and press Ctrl+Enter.

Another handy feature in Excel is the AutoFill Options button that appears next to data you add to a worksheet by using the fill handle.

Clicking the AutoFill Options button displays a list of actions Excel can take regarding the cells affected by your fill operation. The options in the list are summarized in the following table.

Option	Action
Copy Cells	This copies the contents of the selected cells to the cells indicated by the fill operation.
Fill Series	This action fills the cells indicated by the fill operation with the next items in the series.
Fill Formatting Only	This copies the format of the selected cell to the cells indicated by the fill operation, but does not place any values in the target cells.
Fill Without Formatting	This action fills the cells indicated by the fill operation with the next items in the series, but ignores any formatting applied to the source cells.
Fill Days (or Fill Weekdays, Fill Months, and so on)	The appearance of this option changes according to the series you extend. For example, if you extend the values Wed, Thu, and Fri, Excel presents two options, Fill Days and Fill Weekdays, and you can select which one you intended. If you do not use a recognized sequence, this option does not appear.
Flash Fill	This action fills the cells by using the Flash Fill capability, which fills the values by identifying a pattern in the worksheet's data.

In this exercise, you'll enter data by using multiple methods and control how Excel formats an extended data series.

SET UP You need the Series workbook located in the Chapter02 practice file folder to complete this exercise. Start Excel, and open the workbook. Then follow the steps.

1 On the **Monthly** worksheet, select cell **B3**, and then drag the fill handle down through **B7** to repeat the value **Fabrikam** in cells **B4:B7**.

2 Select cell **C3**, and while pressing the **Ctrl** key, drag the fill handle down through **C7** to repeat the value **January** in cells **C4:C7**.

3 Select cell **B8**, and then enter the letter **F**, which causes Excel to display the characters **abrikam** highlighted in gray.

	A	B	C	D	E	F
1						
2		Customer	Month	Category	Amount	
3		Fabrikam	January	Ground	$ 14,501.98	
4		Fabrikam	January	3Day	$ 3,501.75	
5		Fabrikam	January	2Day	$ 5,599.10	
6		Fabrikam	January	Overnight	$ 35,907.82	
7		Fabrikam	January	Priority Overnight	$ 17,333.25	
8		Fabrikam				
9						

4 Press **Tab** to accept the value **Fabrikam** for the cell.

5 In cell **C8**, enter **February**.

6 Right-click cell **D8**, and then click **Pick From Drop-down List** to display a list of values in column **D**.

	A	B	C	D	E	F
1						
2		Customer	Month	Category	Amount	
3		Fabrikam	January	Ground	$ 14,501.98	
4		Fabrikam	January	3Day	$ 3,501.75	
5		Fabrikam	January	2Day	$ 5,599.10	
6		Fabrikam	January	Overnight	$ 35,907.82	
7		Fabrikam	January	Priority Overnight	$ 17,333.25	
8		Fabrikam	February			
9				2Day		
10				3Day		
11				Ground		
12				Overnight		
				Priority Overnight		

7   From the list, click **2Day**, which then appears in cell **D8**.

8   In cell **E8**, enter **11802.14**, and then press **Tab** or **Enter** to enter the value into the cell.

9   Select cell **B2**, and then drag the fill handle through cells **C2:E2** to fill the cells with the value **Customer**.

10   Click the **AutoFill Options** button, and then click **Fill Formatting Only** to restore the original values in cells **C2:E2** and apply the formatting of cell **B2** to those cells.

✖ CLEAN UP Close the Series workbook, saving your changes if you want to.

Managing data by using Flash Fill

When you manage data in Excel, you will often find that you want to combine values from several cells into a single value. For example, Consolidated Messenger might have a list of individuals to contact about arranging bulk shipping contracts for their companies.

	A	B	C	D
1	**LastName**	**FirstName**	**Initial**	**FullName**
2	Ray	Mike		
3	Basalik	Evan	B	
4	Roth	Daniel	C	
5	Kahn	Wendy		

The contacts' names appear in three columns: LastName, FirstName, and Initial. Note that not every contact has a middle initial. If you want to combine each row's LastName, FirstName, and Initial value into a single name, you click in the blank cell to the right of the first row's Initial column and enter the combination as you want it to appear. When you're done, press Enter to move down a row and enter the second row's value. After you start typing, Flash Fill, which is new in Excel 2013, displays suggestions based on how it predicts you want to fill in the rest of the values.

	A	B	C	D
1	**LastName**	**FirstName**	**Initial**	**FullName**
2	Ray	Mike		Mike Ray
3	Basalik	Evan	B	Evan Basalik
4	Roth	Daniel	C	Daniel Roth
5	Kahn	Wendy		Wendy Kahn
6				

Note that the Flash Fill suggestions did not include Initial values for rows that have a value in that cell. You can correct that omission by clicking in the FullName cell next to a row that does contain an Initial value and then entering the name as you would like it to appear. When you do, Flash Fill recognizes the new pattern for this subset of the data and offers to fill in the values.

	A	B	C	D
1	**LastName**	**FirstName**	**Initial**	**FullName**
2	Ray	Mike		Mike Ray
3	Basalik	Evan	B	Evan B Basalik
4	Roth	Daniel	C	Daniel C Roth
5	Kahn	Wendy		Wendy Kahn
6				

IMPORTANT For Flash Fill to function, you must enter the desired value in a cell next to the data you based your list on and make two consecutive edits. "Two consecutive edits" means that you must enter the desired value in one cell and then immediately start entering a value in a cell in the range you want Flash Fill to populate.

With Flash Fill, you can also pull data segments out of a larger, compound value. For example, suppose you received a customer database where the city, state, and postal code of each mailing address was combined in a single cell.

◢	A	B	C
1	**CityStateZip**	**State**	
2	Vienna, VA 22180		
3	Portland, OR 97220		
4	Mt. Crawford, VA 22841		
5	Syracuse, NY 13214		
6			

This data follows a consistent pattern, with the city followed by a comma before the two-letter state abbreviation. Because Flash Fill can detect this pattern, you can perform two consecutive edits to have the program suggest values for the remaining cells to the right of the existing data.

◢	A	B	C
1	**CityStateZip**	**State**	
2	Vienna, VA 22180	VA	
3	Portland, OR 97220	OR	
4	Mt. Crawford, VA 22841	VA	
5	Syracuse, NY 13214	NY	
6			

TIP If for some reason Flash Fill doesn't offer to complete the values in a data range, click a cell in the range you want Flash Fill to populate and then, on the Data tab of the ribbon, click Flash Fill.

In this exercise, you'll combine and correct data by using Flash Fill.

➡ SET UP You need the MailingNames workbook located in the Chapter02 practice file folder to complete this exercise. Open the workbook, and then follow the steps.

1   On the **Names** worksheet, enter **Mark Hassall** in cell **D2** and press **Enter**.

2   In cell **D3**, start entering the first name **Justin**. As you do, the Flash Fill logic suggests a series of values to fill in cells **D3:D5**.

3   Press **Enter** to accept the suggestions, even though some of them don't include the individual's middle initial.

4   Edit the value in cell **D3** so it reads Justin K. Harrison, and press **Enter** to have Flash Fill update the name in cell **D3** and the name in **D4**.

	A	B	C	D
1	**LastName**	**FirstName**	**Initial**	**FullName**
2	Hassall	Mark		Mark Hassall
3	Harrison	Justin	K	Justin K. Harrison
4	Pionsky	Idan	L	Idan L. Pionsky
5	Preston	Chris		Chris Preston

5   On the tab bar, click the **Addresses** sheet tab to display the **Addresses** worksheet.

6   Select cells **E2:F5** and then, on the **Home** tab, click the **Number Format** arrow. Then click **Text**.

7   In cell **F2**, enter 03214, and then press **Enter**.

8   In cell **F3**, start entering 07921 to have Flash Fill suggest values for the corrected series.

9   Press **Enter** to accept the suggested values.

10 Edit the value in cell **F4** so it reads 98012.

✖ CLEAN UP Close the MailingNames workbook, saving your changes if you want to.

Moving data within a workbook

You can move to a specific cell in lots of ways, but the most direct method is to click the desired cell. The cell you click will be outlined in black, and its contents, if any, will appear in the formula bar. When a cell is outlined, it is the active cell, meaning that you can modify its contents. You use a similar method to select multiple cells (referred to as a *cell range*)—just click the first cell in the range, and drag the mouse pointer over the remaining cells you want to select. After you select the cell or cells you want to work with, you can cut, copy, delete, or change the format of the contents of the cell or cells. For instance, Gregory Weber, the Northwest Distribution Center Manager for Consolidated Messenger, might want to copy the cells that contain a set of column labels to a new page that summarizes similar data.

> **IMPORTANT** If you select a group of cells, the first cell you click is designated as the active cell.

You're not limited to selecting cells individually or as part of a range. For example, you might need to move a column of price data one column to the right to make room for a column of headings that indicate to which service category (ground, three-day express, two-day express, overnight, or priority overnight) a set of numbers belongs. To move an entire column (or entire columns) of data at a time, you click the column's header, located at the top of the worksheet. Clicking a column header highlights every cell in that column and enables you to copy or cut the column and paste it elsewhere in the workbook. Similarly, clicking a row's header highlights every cell in that row, enabling you to copy or cut the row and paste it elsewhere in the workbook.

When you copy a cell, cell range, row, or column, Excel copies the cells' contents and formatting. In versions prior to Excel 2010, you would paste the cut or copied items and then click the Paste Options button to select which aspects of the cut or copied cells to paste into the target cells. The problem with using the Paste Options button was that there was no way to tell what your pasted data would look like until you completed the paste operation. If you didn't like the way the pasted data looked, you had to click the Paste Options button again and try another option.

With the Paste Live Preview capability in Excel, you can view what your pasted data will look like before committing to the paste operation. To preview your data by using Paste Live Preview, cut or copy worksheet data and then, on the Home tab of the ribbon, in the Clipboard group, click the Paste button's arrow to display a menu containing the Paste gallery, and point to one of the icons. When you do, Excel displays a preview of how your data will appear if you click that paste option.

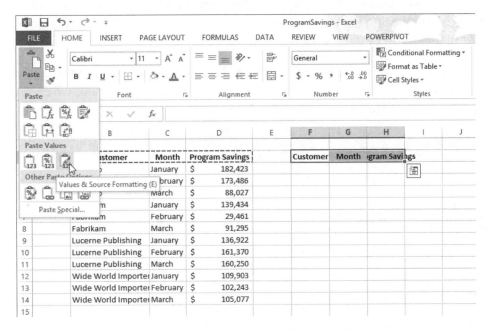

If you position the pointer over one icon in the Paste gallery and then move it over another icon without clicking, Excel will update the preview to reflect the new option. Depending on the cells' contents, two or more of the paste options might lead to the same result.

TROUBLESHOOTING If pointing to an icon in the Paste gallery doesn't result in a live preview, that option might be turned off. To turn Paste Live Preview on, click the File tab, and then click Options to open the Excel Options dialog box. Click General, select the Enable Live Preview check box, and click OK.

After you click an icon to complete the paste operation, Excel displays the Paste Options button next to the pasted cells. Clicking the Paste Options button displays the Paste Options gallery as well, but pointing to one of those icons doesn't generate a preview. If you want to display Paste Live Preview again, you will need to press Ctrl+Z to undo the paste operation and, if necessary, cut or copy the data again to use the icons in the Home tab's Clipboard group.

TROUBLESHOOTING If the Paste Options button doesn't appear, you can turn the feature on by clicking the File tab and then clicking Options to open the Excel Options dialog box. In the Excel Options dialog box, display the Advanced page and then, in the Cut, Copy, And Paste area, select the Show Paste Options Buttons When Content Is Pasted check box. Click OK to close the dialog box and save your setting.

After cutting or copying data to the Microsoft Office Clipboard, you can access additional paste options from the Paste gallery and from the Paste Special dialog box, which you display by clicking Paste Special at the bottom of the Paste menu.

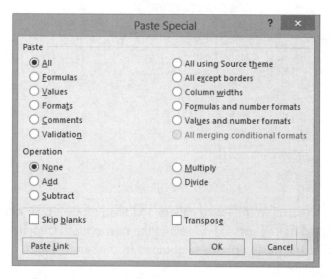

In the Paste Special dialog box, you can specify the aspect of the Clipboard contents you want to paste, restricting the pasted data to values, formats, comments, or one of several other options. You can perform mathematical operations involving the cut or copied data and the existing data in the cells you paste the content into. You can transpose data—change rows to columns and columns to rows—when you paste it, by clicking the Transpose thumbnail in the Paste gallery or by selecting the Transpose check box in the Paste Special dialog box.

In this exercise, you'll copy a set of data headers to another worksheet, move a column of data within a worksheet, and use Paste Live Preview to control the appearance of copied data.

SET UP **You need the 2013Q1ShipmentsByCategory workbook located in the Chapter02 practice file folder to complete this exercise. Open the workbook, and then follow the steps.**

1   On the **Count** worksheet, select cells **B2:D2**.

2   On the **Home** tab, in the **Clipboard** group, click the **Copy** button to copy the contents of cells **B2:D2** to the Clipboard.

    KEYBOARD SHORTCUT Press Ctrl+C to copy worksheet contents to the Clipboard. For a complete list of keyboard shortcuts, see "Keyboard shortcuts" at the end of this book.

3   On the tab bar, click the **Sales** tab to display that worksheet.

4   Select cell **B2**.

5   On the **Home** tab, in the **Clipboard** group, click the **Paste** button's arrow, point to the first icon in the **Paste** group, and then click the **Keep Source Formatting** icon (the final icon in the first row of the **Paste** gallery). Notice that Excel displays how the data would look if you pasted the copied values without formatting, and then pastes the header values into cells **B2:D2**, retaining the original cells' formatting.

6   Right-click the column header of column **I**, and then click **Cut**, which causes Excel to outline column **I** with a marquee.

7   Right-click the header of column **E**, and then, in the **Paste Options** area, click **Paste** to paste the contents of column **I** into column **E**.

    KEYBOARD SHORTCUT Press Ctrl+V to paste worksheet contents exactly as they appear in the original cell.

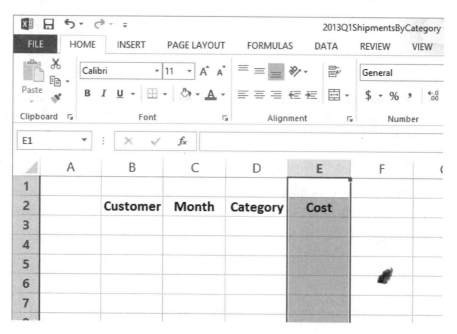

CLEAN UP Close the 2013Q1ShipmentsByCategory workbook, saving your changes if you want to.

Finding and replacing data

Excel worksheets can hold more than one million rows of data, so in large data collections, it's unlikely that you would have the time to move through a worksheet one row at a time to locate the data you want to find. You can locate specific data in an Excel worksheet by using the Find And Replace dialog box, which has two pages (one named Find, the other named Replace) that you can use to search for cells that contain particular values. Using the controls on the Find page identifies cells that contain the data you specify; by using the controls on the Replace page, you can substitute one value for another. For example, if one of Consolidated Messenger's customers changes its company name, you can change every instance of the old name to the new name by using the Replace functionality.

When you need more control over the data that you find and replace—for instance, if you want to find cells in which the entire cell value matches the value you're searching for—you can click the Options button to expand the Find And Replace dialog box.

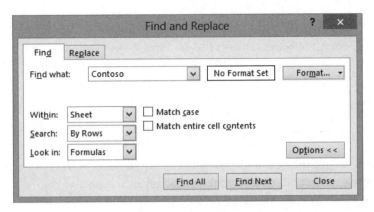

One way you can use the extra options in the Find And Replace dialog box is to use a specific format to identify data that requires review. As an example, Consolidated Messenger VP of Marketing Craig Dewar could make corporate sales plans based on a projected budget for the next year and mark his trial figures by using a specific format. After the executive board finalizes the numbers, he could use the Find Format capability in the Find And Replace dialog box to locate the old values and change them by hand.

The following table summarizes the Find And Replace dialog box controls' functions.

Control	Function
Find What field	Contains the value you want to find or replace
Find All button	Identifies every cell that contains the value in the Find What field
Find Next button	Selects the next cell that contains the value in the Find What field
Replace With field	Contains the value to overwrite the value in the Find What field
Replace All button	Replaces every instance of the value in the Find What field with the value in the Replace With field
Replace button	Replaces the highlighted occurrence of the value in the Find What field and highlights the next cell that contains that value
Options button	Expands the Find And Replace dialog box to display additional capabilities
Format button	Opens the Find Format dialog box, which you can use to specify the format of values to be found or values to be replaced
Within box	Enables you to select whether to search the active worksheet or the entire workbook
Search box	Enables you to select whether to search by rows or by columns
Look In box	Enables you to select whether to search cell formulas or values

Control	Function
Match Case check box	When selected, requires that all matches have the same capitalization as the text in the Find What field (for example, cat doesn't match Cat)
Match Entire Cell Contents check box	Requires that the cell contain exactly the same value as in the Find What field (for example, Cat doesn't match Catherine)
Close button	Closes the Find And Replace dialog box

To change a value by hand, select the cell, and then either enter a new value in the cell or, in the formula bar, select the value you want to replace and enter the new value. You can also double-click a cell and edit its contents within the cell.

In this exercise, you'll find a specific value in a worksheet, replace every occurrence of a company name in a worksheet, and find a cell that has a specific formatting.

 SET UP You need the AverageDeliveries workbook located in the Chapter02 practice file folder to complete this exercise. Open the workbook, and then follow the steps.

1   If necessary, click the **Time Summary** sheet tab to display the **Time Summary** worksheet.

2   On the **Home** tab, in the **Editing** group, click **Find & Select**, and then click **Find** to display the **Find** page of the **Find and Replace** dialog box.

KEYBOARD SHORTCUT Press Ctrl+F to display the Find page of the Find And Replace dialog box.

3   In the **Find what** field, enter **103**.

4   Click **Find Next** to have Excel select cell **B5**, which contains the value **103**.

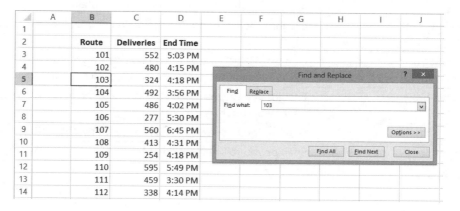

5   Delete the value in the **Find what** field, and then click the **Options** button to display additional search options.

6   Click **Format** to open the **Find Format** dialog box.

7   Click the **Font** tab to display the **Font** page of the dialog box.

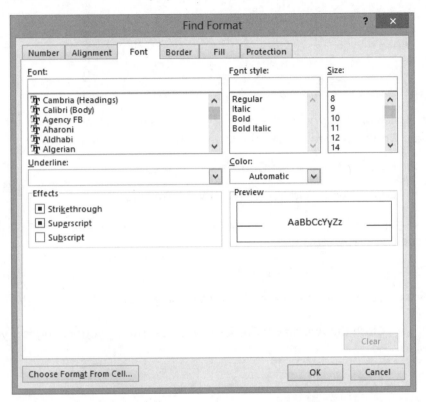

8   In the **Font style** list, click **Italic**, and then click **OK** to close the **Find Format** dialog box.

9   Click **Find Next**, which causes Excel to select cell **D25**.

10 Click **Close** to close the **Find and Replace** dialog box.

11 On the tab bar, click the **Customer Summary** sheet tab to display the **Customer Summary** worksheet.

12 On the **Home** tab, in the **Editing** group, click **Find & Select**, and then click **Replace** to open the **Find and Replace** dialog box with the **Replace** page displayed.

   KEYBOARD SHORTCUT Press Ctrl+H to display the Replace page of the Find And Replace dialog box.

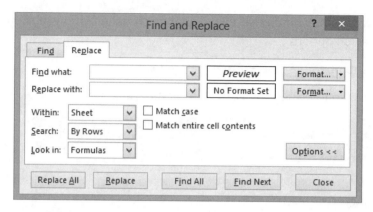

13   Click the **Format** arrow to the right of the **Find what** field, and then in the list, click **Clear Find Format** to remove the format from the **Find What** field.

14   In the **Find what** field, enter **Contoso**.

15   In the **Replace with** field, enter **Northwind Traders**.

16   Click **Replace All**, which causes Excel to display a message box indicating that Excel made three replacements.

17   Click **OK** to close the message box.

18   Click **Close** to close the **Find and Replace** dialog box.

❌ CLEAN UP Close the AverageDeliveries workbook, saving your changes if you want to.

Correcting and expanding upon worksheet data

After you enter your data, you should take the time to check and correct it. You do need to verify visually that each piece of numeric data is correct, but you can make sure that your worksheet's text is spelled correctly by using the Excel spelling checker. When the spelling checker encounters a word it doesn't recognize, it highlights the word and offers suggestions representing its best guess of the correct word. You can then edit the word directly, pick the proper word from the list of suggestions, or have the spelling checker ignore the misspelling. You can also use the spelling checker to add new words to a custom dictionary so that Excel will recognize them later, saving you time by not requiring you to identify the words as correct every time they occur in your worksheets.

TIP After you make a change in a workbook, you can usually remove the change as long as you haven't closed the workbook. To undo a change, click the Undo button on the Quick Access Toolbar. If you decide you want to keep a change, you can use the Redo command to restore it.

If you're not sure of your word choice, or if you use a word that is almost but not quite right for your intended meaning, you can check for alternative words by using the Thesaurus. Several other research tools are also available, such as the Bing search engine and the Microsoft Encarta dictionary, to which you can refer as you create your workbooks. To display those tools, on the Review tab, in the Proofing group, click Research to display the Research pane.

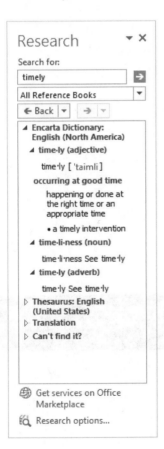

Finally, if you want to translate a word from one language to another, you can do so by selecting the cell that contains the value you want to translate, displaying the Review tab, and then, in the Language group, clicking Translate. The Research pane opens (or changes if it's already open) and displays controls you can use to select the original and destination languages.

IMPORTANT Excel translates a sentence by using word substitutions, which means that the translation routine doesn't always pick the best word for a given context. The translated sentence might not capture your exact meaning.

In this exercise, you'll check a worksheet's spelling, add two new terms to a dictionary, search for an alternative word by using the Thesaurus, and translate a word from English into French.

SET UP You need the ServiceLevels workbook located in the Chapter02 practice file folder to complete this exercise. Open the workbook, and then follow the steps.

1   On the **Review** tab, in the **Proofing** group, click **Spelling** to open the **Spelling** dialog box with the first misspelled word in the worksheet displayed in the **Not in Dictionary** field.

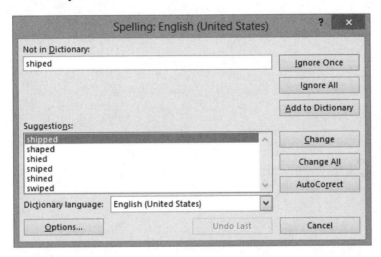

2   Verify that the word **shipped** is highlighted in the **Suggestions** pane, and then click **Change** to correct the word and display the next questioned word: **withn**.

3   Click **Change** to correct the word and display the next questioned word: **TwoDay**.

4   Click **Add to Dictionary** to add the word to the dictionary and display the next questioned word: **ThreeDay**.

5   Click **Add to Dictionary** to add the word to the dictionary.

6   If necessary, click **Close** to close the **Spelling** dialog box. When you do, the **Spelling** dialog box closes and a message box appears, indicating that the spelling check is complete for the worksheet.

7   Click **OK** to close the message box.

8   Click cell **B6** and then, on the **Review** tab, in the **Proofing** group, click **Thesaurus** to display a list of synonyms for the word **Overnight**.

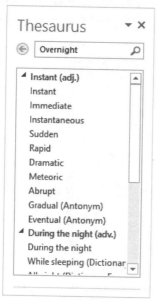

9   On the **Review** tab, in the **Language** group, click **Translate** to display the translation tools in the **Research** pane.

10 If necessary, in the **From** list, click **English (U.S.)**.

11 In the **To** list, click **French (France)**. The **Research** pane displays French words that mean *overnight*.

CLEAN UP Close the ServiceLevels workbook, saving your changes if you want to.

Defining Excel tables

With Excel, you've always been able to manage lists of data effectively, enabling you to sort your worksheet data based on the values in one or more columns, limit the data displayed by using criteria (for example, show only those routes with fewer than 100 stops), and create formulas that summarize the values in visible (that is, unfiltered) cells. In Excel 2007, the Excel product team extended your ability to manage your data by introducing Excel tables. Excel 2013 offers you the same capability.

	A	B	C	D
1				
2		**Customer** ▾	**Month** ▾	**Program Savings** ▾
3		Contoso	January	$ 182,423
4		Contoso	February	$ 173,486
5		Contoso	March	$ 88,027
6		Fabrikam	January	$ 139,434
7		Fabrikam	February	$ 29,461
8		Fabrikam	March	$ 91,295
9		Lucerne Publishing	January	$ 136,922
10		Lucerne Publishing	February	$ 161,370
11		Lucerne Publishing	March	$ 160,250
12		Wide World Importers	January	$ 109,903
13		Wide World Importers	February	$ 102,243
14		Wide World Importers	March	$ 105,077
15				

To create an Excel table, enter a series of column headers in adjacent cells, and then enter a row of data below the headers. Click any header or data cell into which you just entered, and then, on the Home tab, in the Styles group, click Format As Table. Then, from the gallery that appears, click the style you want to apply to the table. When the Format As Table dialog box opens, verify that the cells in the Where Is The Data For Your Table? field reflect your current selection and that the My Table Has Headers check box is selected, and then click OK.

Excel can also create an Excel table from an existing cell range as long as the range has no blank rows or columns within the data and there is no extraneous data in cells immediately below or next to the list. To create the Excel table, click any cell in the range and then, on the Home tab, in the Styles group, click the Format As Table button and select a table style. If your existing data has formatting applied to it, that formatting remains applied to those cells when you create the Excel table. If you want Excel to replace the existing formatting with the Excel table's formatting, right-click the table style you want to apply and then click Apply And Clear Formatting.

When you want to add data to an Excel table, click the rightmost cell in the bottom row of the Excel table and press the Tab key to create a new row. You can also select a cell in the row immediately below the last row in the table or a cell in the column immediately to the right of the table and enter a value into the cell. After you enter the value and move out of the cell, the AutoCorrect Options action button appears. If you didn't mean to include the data in the Excel table, you can click Undo Table AutoExpansion to exclude the cells from the Excel table. If you never want Excel to include adjacent data in an Excel table again, click Stop Automatically Expanding Tables.

TIP To stop Table AutoExpansion before it starts, click the File tab, and then click Options. In the Excel Options dialog box, click Proofing, and then click the AutoCorrect Options button to open the AutoCorrect dialog box. Click the AutoFormat As You Type tab, clear the Include New Rows And Columns In Table check box, and then click OK twice.

You can add rows and columns to an Excel table, or remove them from an Excel table without deleting the cells' contents, by dragging the resize handle at the Excel table's lower-right corner. If your Excel table's headers contain a recognizable series of values (such as Region1, Region2, and Region3), and you drag the resize handle to create a fourth column, Excel creates the column with the label *Region4*—the next value in the series.

Excel tables often contain data that you can summarize by calculating a sum or average, or by finding the maximum or minimum value in a column. To summarize one or more columns of data, you can add a Total row to your Excel table.

	A	B	C	D
1				
2		Customer ▾	Month ▾	Program Savings ▾
3		Contoso	January	$ 182,423
4		Contoso	February	$ 173,486
5		Contoso	March	$ 88,027
6		Fabrikam	January	$ 139,434
7		Fabrikam	February	$ 29,461
8		Fabrikam	March	$ 91,295
9		Lucerne Publishing	January	$ 136,922
10		Lucerne Publishing	February	$ 161,370
11		Lucerne Publishing	March	$ 160,250
12		Wide World Importers	January	$ 109,903
13		Wide World Importers	February	$ 102,243
14		Wide World Importers	March	$ 105,077
15		Total		$ 1,479,891 ▾
16				

When you add the Total row, Excel creates a formula that summarizes the values in the rightmost Excel table column. To change that summary operation, or to add a summary operation to any other cell in the Total row, click the cell, click the arrow that appears, and then click the summary operation you want to apply. Clicking the More Functions menu item opens the Insert Function dialog box, from which you can select any of the functions available in Excel.

Much as it does when you create a new worksheet, Excel gives your Excel tables generic names such as Table1 and Table2. You can change an Excel table's name to something easier to recognize by clicking any cell in the table, clicking the Design tool tab, and then, in the Properties group, editing the value in the Table Name box. Changing an Excel table name might not seem important, but it helps make formulas that summarize Excel table data much easier to understand. You should make a habit of renaming your Excel tables so you can recognize the data they contain.

SEE ALSO For more information about using the Insert Function dialog box and about referring to tables in formulas, see "Creating formulas to calculate values" in Chapter 3, "Performing calculations on data."

If for any reason you want to convert your Excel table back to a normal range of cells, click any cell in the Excel table and then, on the Design tool tab, in the Tools group, click Convert To Range. When Excel displays a message box asking if you're sure you want to convert the table to a range, click OK.

In this exercise, you'll create an Excel table from existing data, add data to an Excel table, add a Total row, change that row's summary operation, and rename the Excel table.

 SET UP **You need the DriverSortTimes workbook located in the Chapter02 practice file folder to complete this exercise. Open the workbook, and then follow the steps.**

1   Select cell **B2**.

2   On the **Home** tab, in the **Styles** group, click **Format as Table**, and then select a table style to open the **Format As Table** dialog box.

3   Verify that the range =$B$2:$C$17 is displayed in the **Where is the data for your table?** field and that the **My table has headers** check box is selected, and then click **OK** to create an Excel table from your data and display the **Design** tool tab.

4   In cell **B18**, enter D116, press **Tab**, enter 100 in cell **C18**, and then press **Enter** to have Excel include the data in your Excel table.

5   Select a cell in the table. Then on the **Design** tool tab, in the **Table Style Options** group, select the **Total Row** check box to add a **Total** row to the bottom of your Excel table.

6   Select cell **C19**, click the arrow that appears at the right edge of the cell, and then click **Average** to change the summary operation to **Average**.

Driver	Sorting Minutes
D101	102
D102	162
D103	165
D104	91
D105	103
D106	127
D107	112
D108	137
D109	102
D110	147
D111	163
D112	109
D113	91
D114	107
D115	93
D116	100
Total	119.4375

7   On the **Design** tool tab, in the **Properties** group, enter the value SortTimes in the **Table Name** field, and then press **Enter** to rename your Excel table.

❌ CLEAN UP Close the DriverSortTimes workbook, saving your changes if you want to.

Key points

- You can enter a series of data quickly by entering one or more values in adjacent cells, selecting the cells, and then dragging the fill handle. To change how dragging the fill handle extends a data series, hold down the Ctrl key.

- Dragging a fill handle displays the Auto Fill Options button, which you can use to specify whether to copy the selected cells' values, extend a recognized series, or apply the selected cells' formatting to the new cells.

- Managing data by using Flash Fill enables you to separate cell entries into their components, apply formatting, and fix values such as postal codes that have had their leading zeros removed.

- With Excel, you can enter data by selecting items from a list, using AutoComplete, or pressing Ctrl+Enter. You should experiment with these techniques and use the one that best fits your circumstances.

- When you copy (or cut) and paste cells, columns, or rows, you can use the Paste Live Preview capability to preview how your data will appear before you commit to the paste operation.

- After you paste cells, rows, or columns into your worksheet, Excel displays the Paste Options action button. You can use its controls to change which aspects of the cut or copied elements Excel applies to the pasted elements.

- By using the options in the Paste Special dialog box, you can paste only specific aspects of cut or copied data, perform mathematical operations, transpose data, or delete blank cells when pasting.

- You can find and replace data within a worksheet by searching for specific values or by searching for cells that have a particular format applied.

- Excel provides a variety of powerful proofing and research tools, enabling you to check your workbook's spelling, find alternative words by using the Thesaurus, and translate words between languages.

- With Excel tables, you can organize and summarize your data effectively.

2

Chapter at a glance

Name

Name groups of data,
page 76

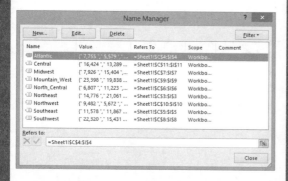

Summarize

Summarize data that meets specific
conditions, page 90

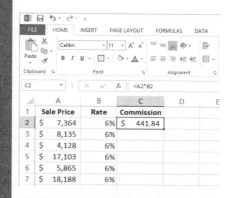

Calculate

Use array formulas,
page 96

	A	B	C
1	**Insurance Rate**	2.5%	
2			
3	**PackageID**	**Value**	**Premium**
4	PK000352	$ 591.00	=B1*B4:B6
5	PK000353	$1,713.00	
6	PK000354	$3,039.00	
7			

Correct

Find and correct errors in calculations,
page 99

	A	B	C	D
1				
2		Conveyer		
3		350' track	$ 14,012.00	
4		Catch bin	$ 895.00	
5		Motor	$ 1,245.00	
6		Chain drive	$ 1,495.00	
7		Sorting table	$ 675.00	
8		*Subtotal*		$ 18,326.00
9				

Performing calculations on data

3

IN THIS CHAPTER, YOU WILL LEARN HOW TO

- Name groups of data.

- Create formulas to calculate values.

- Summarize data that meets specific conditions.

- Work with iterative calculation options and automatic workbook calculation.

- Use array formulas.

- Find and correct errors in calculations.

Microsoft Excel 2013 workbooks give you a handy place to store and organize your data, but you can also do a lot more with your data in Excel. One important task you can perform is to calculate totals for the values in a series of related cells. You can also use Excel to discover other information about the data you select, such as the maximum or minimum value in a group of cells. By finding the maximum or minimum value in a group, you can identify your best salesperson, product categories you might need to pay more attention to, or suppliers that consistently give you the best deal. Regardless of your bookkeeping needs, Excel gives you the ability to find the information you want. And if you make an error, you can find the cause and correct it quickly.

Many times, you can't access the information you want without referencing more than one cell, and it's also often true that you'll use the data in the same group of cells for more than one calculation. Excel makes it easy to reference a number of cells at once, enabling you to define your calculations quickly.

In this chapter, you'll streamline references to groups of data on your worksheets and create and correct formulas that summarize an organization's business operations.

Naming groups of data

When you work with large amounts of data, it's often useful to identify groups of cells that contain related data. For example, you can create a worksheet in which cells C3:I3 hold the number of packages Consolidated Messenger's Northeast processing facility handled from 5:00 P.M. to 12:00 A.M. on the previous day.

	A	B	C	D	E	F	G	H	I	J
1										
2			5:00 PM	6:00 PM	7:00 PM	8:00 PM	9:00 PM	10:00 PM	11:00 PM	
3		Northeast	14,776	21,061	22,111	13,412	11,459	11,038	5,732	
4		Atlantic	7,755	5,579	13,778	13,774	5,352	17,209	15,822	
5		Southeast	11,578	11,867	5,627	5,625	7,148	24,487	20,262	
6		North Central	6,807	11,223	12,136	24,653	23,876	9,817	7,410	
7		Midwest	7,926	15,404	7,702	10,338	10,734	14,021	20,557	
8		Southwest	22,320	15,431	24,276	8,968	10,066	23,602	11,216	
9		Mountain West	23,398	19,838	21,591	24,305	21,431	8,338	6,941	
10		Northwest	9,482	5,672	14,689	18,795	9,388	8,069	19,776	
11		Central	16,424	13,289	18,546	19,762	20,770	11,202	6,403	
12										

Instead of specifying the cells individually every time you want to use the data they contain, you can define those cells as a range (also called a *named range*). For example, you can group the items from the cells described in the preceding paragraph into a range named *NortheastPreviousDay*. Whenever you want to use the contents of that range in a calculation, you can simply use the name of the range instead of specifying each cell individually.

TIP Yes, you could just name the range *Northeast*, but if you use the range's values in a formula in another worksheet, the more descriptive range name tells you and your colleagues exactly what data is used in the calculation.

To create a named range, select the cells you want to include in your range, click the Formulas tab, and then, in the Defined Names group, click Define Name to display the New Name dialog box. In the New Name dialog box, enter a name in the Name field, verify that the cells you selected appear in the Refers To field, and then click OK. You can also add a comment about the range in the Comment field and select whether you want to make the name available for formulas in the entire workbook or just on an individual worksheet.

If the cells you want to define as a named range have labels in a row or column that's part of the cell group, you can use those labels as the names of the named ranges. For example, if your data appears in worksheet cells B4:I12 and the values in column B are the row labels, you can make each row its own named range. To create a series of named ranges from a group of cells, select all of the data cells, including the labels, click the Formulas tab and then, in the Defined Names group, click Create From Selection to open the Create Names From Selection dialog box. In the Create Names From Selection dialog box, select the check box that represents the labels' position in the selected range, and then click OK.

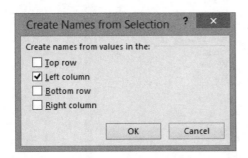

A final way to create a named range is to select the cells you want in the range, click in the Name box next to the formula box, and then enter the name for the range. You can display the ranges available in a workbook by clicking the Name arrow.

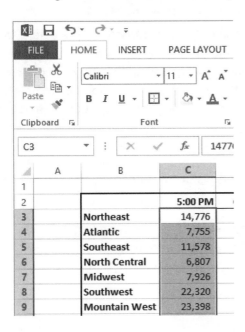

To manage the named ranges in a workbook, click the Formulas tab, and then, in the Defined Names group, click Name Manager to open the Name Manager dialog box.

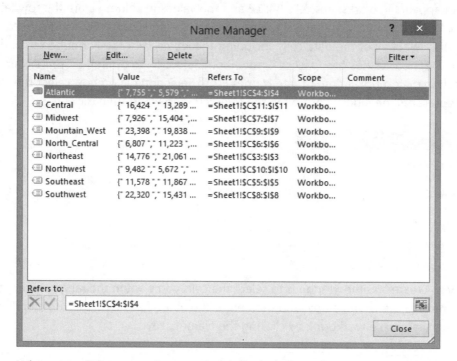

When you click a named range, Excel displays the cells it encompasses in the Refers To field. Clicking the Edit button opens the Edit Name dialog box, which is a version of the New Name dialog box, enabling you to change a named range's definition; for example, by adding a column. You can also use the controls in the Name Manager dialog box to delete a named range (the range, not the data) by clicking it, clicking the Delete button, and then clicking OK in the confirmation dialog box that opens.

TIP If your workbook contains a lot of named ranges, you can click the Filter button in the Name Manager dialog box and select a criterion to limit the names displayed in the Name Manager dialog box.

In this exercise, you'll create a named range to streamline references to a group of cells. You'll also edit a named range and use a named range in a formula.

 SET UP You need the VehicleMiles workbook located in the Chapter03 practice file folder to complete this exercise. Open the workbook, and then follow the steps.

1   Select cells **C4:G4**, intentionally leaving cell H4 out of this selection. You will edit the named range later in this exercise.

2   In the **Name** box at the left end of the formula bar, enter V101LastWeek, and then press **Enter** to create a named range named *V101LastWeek*.

3   On the **Formulas** tab, in the **Defined Names** group, click **Name Manager** to open the **Name Manager** dialog box.

4   Click the **V101LastWeek** name. The cell range to which the **V101LastWeek** name refers appears in the **Refers to** box at the bottom of the **Name Manager** dialog box.

5   Edit the cell range in the **Refers to** box to =MilesLastWeek!$C$4:$H$4 (change the **G** to an **H**), and then click the check mark button to the left of the box to finalize the update.

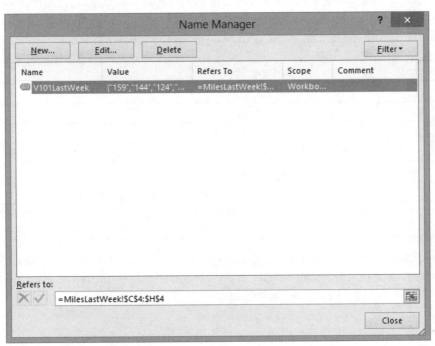

6   Click **Close** to close the **Name Manager** dialog box.

7   Select the cell range **C5:H5**.

8   On the **Formulas** tab, in the **Defined Names** group, click **Define Name** to open the **New Name** dialog box.

9   In the **Name** field, enter **V102LastWeek**.

10   Verify that the definition in the **Refers to** field is **=MilesLastWeek!$C$5:$H$5**.

11   Click **OK** to create the name and close the **New Name** dialog box.

12   In cell **A1**, enter the formula **=SUM(V102LastWeek)** and press **Enter**. When you do, the total of all miles for vehicle V102 appears in the cell.

❌ CLEAN UP **Close the VehicleMiles workbook, saving your changes if you want to.**

Operators and precedence

When you create an Excel formula, you use the built-in functions and arithmetic operators that define operations such as addition and multiplication. In Excel, mathematical operators are evaluated in the order shown in the following table.

Operator	Description
−	Negation (e.g., −1)
%	Percentage
^	Exponentiation
* and /	Multiplication and Division
+ and −	Addition and Subtraction
&	Concatenation (adding two strings together)
=, >, <, >=, <=, and <>	Equals, Greater Than, Less Than, Greater Than or Equal To, Less Than or Equal To, and Not Equal To

If two operators at the same level, such as + and −, occur in the same equation, Excel evaluates them in left-to-right order. For example, the operations in the formula = *4 + 8 * 3 − 6* would be evaluated in this order:

1   *8 * 3*, with a result of 24

2   *4 + 24*, with a result of 28

3   *28 − 6*, with a final result of 22

You can control the order in which operations are evaluated by using parentheses. Operations in parentheses are always evaluated first. For example, if the previous equation were rewritten as = *(4 + 8) * 3 – 6*, the operations would be evaluated in this order:

1   *(4 + 8)*, with a result of 12
2   *12 * 3*, with a result of 36
3   *36 – 6*, with a final result of 30

If you have multiple levels of parentheses, Excel evaluates the expressions within the innermost set of parentheses first and works its way out. As with operations on the same level, such as + and –, expressions in the same parenthetical level are evaluated in left-to-right order.

For example, the formula = *4 + (3 + 8 * (2 + 5)) – 7* would be evaluated in this order:

1   *(2 + 5)*, with a result of 7
2   *7 * 8*, with a result of 56
3   *56 + 3*, with a result of 59
4   *4 + 59*, with a result of 63
5   *63 – 7*, with a final result of 56

Creating formulas to calculate values

After you add your data to a worksheet and define ranges to simplify data references, you can create a formula, which is an expression that performs calculations on your data. For example, you can calculate the total cost of a customer's shipments, figure the average number of packages for all Wednesdays in the month of January, or find the highest and lowest daily package volumes for a week, month, or year.

To write an Excel formula, you begin the cell's contents with an equal (=) sign; when Excel identifies it, it knows that the expression following it should be interpreted as a calculation, not text. After the equal sign, enter the formula. For example, you can find the sum of the numbers in cells C2 and C3 by using the formula =*C2+C3*. After you have entered a formula into a cell, you can revise it by clicking the cell and then editing the formula in the formula box. For example, you can change the preceding formula to =C3-C2, which calculates the difference between the contents of cells C2 and C3.

TROUBLESHOOTING If Excel treats your formula as text, make sure the equal sign is the first character. If Excel still displays your formula as text, check whether the cell has the Text format applied to it. If it does, change the cell's format to a format that suits the value you want to calculate.

Entering the cell references for 15 or 20 cells in a calculation would be tedious, but Excel makes it easy to enter complex calculations. To create a new calculation, click the Formulas tab, and then in the Function Library group, click Insert Function. The Insert Function dialog box opens, with a list of functions, or predefined formulas, from which you can choose.

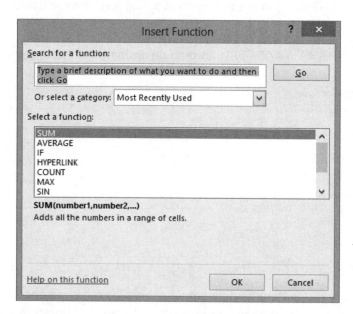

The following table describes some of the most useful functions in the list.

Function	Description
SUM	Finds the sum of the numbers in the specified cells
AVERAGE	Finds the average of the numbers in the specified cells
COUNT	Finds the number of cells in the specified range that contain numbers
MAX	Finds the largest value in the specified cells
MIN	Finds the smallest value in the specified cells

Two other functions you might use are the *NOW* and *PMT* functions. The *NOW* function displays the time Excel updated the workbook's formulas, so the value will change every time the workbook recalculates. The proper form for this function is =*NOW()*. To update the value to the current date and time, press the F9 key or display the Formulas tab and then, in the Calculation group, click the Calculate Now button.

The *PMT* function is a bit more complex. It calculates payments due on a loan, assuming a constant interest rate and constant payments. To perform its calculations, the *PMT* function requires an interest rate, the number of payments, and the starting balance. The elements to be entered into the function are called *arguments* and must be entered in a certain order. That order is written as *PMT(rate, nper, pv, fv, type)*. The following table summarizes the arguments in the *PMT* function.

Argument	Description
rate	The interest rate, to be divided by 12 for a loan with monthly payments, by 4 for quarterly payments, and so on
nper	The total number of payments for the loan
pv	The amount loaned (pv is short for present value, or principal)
fv	The amount to be left over at the end of the payment cycle (usually left blank, which indicates 0)
type	0 or 1, indicating whether payments are made at the beginning or at the end of the month (usually left blank, which indicates 0, or the end of the month)

If Consolidated Messenger wanted to borrow $2,000,000 at a 6 percent interest rate and pay the loan back over 24 months, you could use the *PMT* function to figure out the monthly payments. In this case, the function would be written =*PMT(6%/12, 24, 2000000)*, which calculates a monthly payment of $88,641.22.

TIP Because the payment calculated by the *PMT* function represents money that flows out of your bank account, the result is a negative number. If you want the result to be expressed as a positive number, multiply the formula's result by -1.

You can also use the names of any ranges you defined to supply values for a formula. For example, if the named range NortheastLastDay refers to cells C4:I4, you can calculate the average of cells C4:I4 with the formula =*AVERAGE(NortheastLastDay)*. With Excel, you can add functions, named ranges, and table references to your formulas more efficiently by using the Formula AutoComplete capability. Just as AutoComplete offers to fill in a cell's text value when Excel recognizes that the value you're entering matches a previous entry, Formula AutoComplete offers to help you fill in a function, named range, or table reference while you create a formula.

As an example, consider a worksheet that contains a two-column Excel table named *Exceptions*. The first column is labeled *Route*; the second is labeled *Count*.

	A	B
1	Route	Count
2	101	8
3	102	5
4	103	8
5	104	12
6	105	5
7	106	2
8	107	4
9	108	4
10	109	2
11	110	7
12		

You refer to a table by entering the table name, followed by the column or row name in square brackets. For example, the table reference *Exceptions[Count]* would refer to the Count column in the Exceptions table.

To create a formula that finds the total number of exceptions by using the *SUM* function, you begin by entering =SU. When you enter the letter *S*, Formula AutoComplete lists functions that begin with the letter *S*; when you enter the letter *U*, Excel narrows the list down to the functions that start with the letters *SU*.

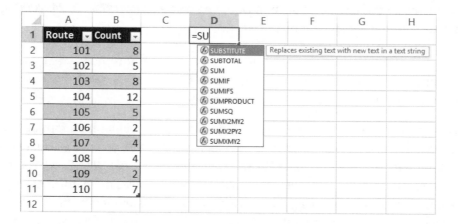

To add the *SUM* function (followed by an opening parenthesis) to the formula, click *SUM* and then press Tab. To begin adding the table reference, enter the letter *E*. Excel displays a list of available functions, tables, and named ranges that start with the letter *E*. Click Exceptions, and press Tab to add the table reference to the formula. Then, because you want to summarize the values in the table's Count column, enter a left square bracket and then, in the list of available table items, click Count. To finish creating the formula, enter a right square bracket followed by a closing parenthesis to create the formula *=SUM(Exceptions[Count])*.

If you want to include a series of contiguous cells in a formula, but you haven't defined the cells as a named range, you can click the first cell in the range and drag to the last cell. If the cells aren't contiguous, hold down the Ctrl key and select all of the cells to be included. In both cases, when you release the mouse button, the references of the cells you selected appear in the formula.

TIP Excel highlights each cell range used in a formula in one of several colors.

⬚	A	B	C	D	E	F	G	H	I	J	K
1											
2		Conveyer									
3		350' track	$14,012.00								
4		Catch bin	$ 895.00								
5		Motor	$ 1,249.00								
6		Chain drive	$ 1,495.00			=sum(C3,C6,C14,C17					
7		Sorting table	$ 675.00			SUM(number1, [number2], [number3], **[number4]**, [number5], …)					
8		Subtotal		$ 18,326.00							
9											
10		**Loading Dock**									
11		Concrete	$ 2,169.00								
12		Labor	$ 4,500.00								
13		Posts	$ 300.00								
14		Excavation	$ 2,500.00								
15		Drain	$ 1,800.00								
16		Rails	$ 495.00								
17		Stairs	$ 1,295.00								
18		Subtotal		$ 13,059.00							
19											
20		**Build Total**		$ 31,385.00							
21		**Labor Percentage**									

In addition to using the Ctrl key to add cells to a selection, you can expand a selection by using a wide range of keyboard shortcuts.

The following table summarizes many of those shortcuts.

Key sequence	Description
Shift+Right Arrow	Extend the selection one cell to the right.
Shift+Left Arrow	Extend the selection one cell to the left.
Shift+Up Arrow	Extend the selection up one cell.
Shift+Down Arrow	Extend the selection down one cell.
Ctrl+Shift+Right Arrow	Extend the selection to the last non-blank cell in the row.
Ctrl+Shift+Left Arrow	Extend the selection to the first non-blank cell in the row.
Ctrl+Shift+Up Arrow	Extend the selection to the first non-blank cell in the column.
Ctrl+Shift+Down Arrow	Extend the selection to the last non-blank cell in the column.
Ctrl+*	Select the entire active region.
Shift+Home	Extend the selection to the beginning of the row.
Ctrl+Shift+Home	Extend the selection to the beginning of the worksheet.
Ctrl+Shift+End	Extend the selection to the end of the worksheet.
Shift+Page Down	Extend the selection down one screen.
Shift+Page Up	Extend the selection up one screen.

SEE ALSO For a complete list of keyboard shortcuts, see "Keyboard shortcuts" at the end of this book.

After you create a formula, you can copy it and paste it into another cell. When you do, Excel tries to change the formula so that it works in the new cells. For instance, suppose you have a worksheet in which cell D8 contains the formula *=SUM(C2:C6)*. Clicking cell D8, copying the cell's contents, and then pasting the result into cell D16 writes *=SUM(C10:C14)* into cell D16. Excel has reinterpreted the formula so that it fits the surrounding cells! Excel knows it can reinterpret the cells used in the formula because the formula uses a relative reference, or a reference that can change if the formula is copied to another cell. Relative references are written with just the cell row and column (for example, *C14*).

Relative references are useful when you summarize rows of data and want to use the same formula for each row. As an example, suppose you have a worksheet with two columns of data, labeled *SalePrice* and *Rate*, and you want to calculate your sales representative's commission by multiplying the two values in a row. To calculate the commission for the first sale, you would enter the formula *=A2*B2* in cell C2.

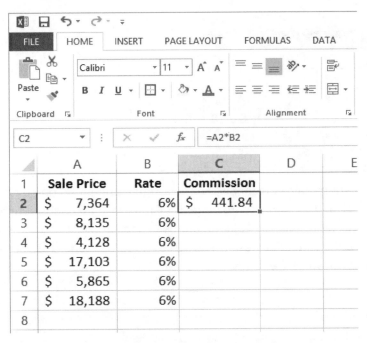

Selecting cell C2 and dragging the fill handle through cell C7 copies the formula from cell C2 into each of the other cells. Because you created the formula by using relative references, Excel updates each cell's formula to reflect its position relative to the starting cell (in this case, cell C2.) The formula in cell C7, for example, is *=A7*B7*.

	A	B	C
1	**Sale Price**	**Rate**	**Commission**
2	$ 7,364	6%	$ 441.84
3	$ 8,135	6%	$ 488.10
4	$ 4,128	6%	$ 247.68
5	$ 17,103	6%	$ 1,026.18
6	$ 5,865	6%	$ 351.90
7	$ 18,188	6%	$ 1,091.28

fx =A7*B7

You can use a similar technique when you add a formula to an Excel table column. If the sale price and rate data were in an Excel table and you created the formula *=A2*B2* in cell C2, Excel would apply the formula to every other cell in the column. Because you used relative references in the formula, the formulas would change to reflect each cell's distance from the original cell.

	A	B	C
1	Sale Price	Rate	Commission
2	$ 7,364	6%	$ 441.84
3	$ 8,135	6%	$ 488.10
4	$ 4,128	6%	$ 247.68
5	$ 17,103	6%	$ 1,026.18
6	$ 5,865	6%	$ 351.90
7	$ 18,188	6%	$ 1,091.28

If you want a cell reference to remain constant when the formula using it is copied to an-other cell, you can use an absolute reference. To write a cell reference as an absolute refer-ence, enter $ before the row letter and the column number. For example, if you want the formula in cell D16 to show the sum of values in cells C10 through C14 regardless of the cell into which it is pasted, you can write the formula as =SUM($C$10:$C$14).

TIP Another way to ensure that your cell references don't change when you copy the for-mula to another cell is to click the cell that contains the formula, copy the formula's text in the formula bar, press the Esc key to exit cut-and-copy mode, click the cell in which you want to paste the formula, and press Ctrl+V. Excel doesn't change the cell references when you copy your formula to another cell in this manner.

One quick way to change a cell reference from relative to absolute is to select the cell refer-ence in the formula box and then press F4. Pressing F4 cycles a cell reference through the four possible types of references:

- Relative columns and rows (for example, C4)

- Absolute columns and rows (for example, $C$4)

- Relative columns and absolute rows (for example, C$4)

- Absolute columns and relative rows (for example, $C4)

In this exercise, you'll create a formula manually, revise it to include additional cells, create a formula that contains an Excel table reference, create a formula with relative references, and change the formula so it contains absolute references.

 SET UP You need the ITExpenses workbook located in the Chapter03 practice file folder to complete this exercise. Open the workbook, and then follow the steps.

1   If necessary, display the **Summary** worksheet. Then, in cell **F9**, enter =C4, and press **Enter** to create the formula and display the value **$385,671.00** in cell **F9**.

2   Select cell **F9** and enter =SU to erase the existing formula and display the **Formula AutoComplete** list, which contains possible functions to use in the formula.

3   In the **Formula AutoComplete** list, click **SUM**, and then press **Tab** to change the contents of the formula bar to =SUM(.

4   Click cell **C3**, press **Ctrl+Shift+Down Arrow** to extend the selection to cell **C8**, enter) (a closing parenthesis) to make the formula bar's contents =SUM(C3:C8), and then press **Enter** to display the value **$2,562,966.00** in cell **F9**.

5   In cell **F10**, enter =SUM(C4:C5), and then press **Enter**.

6   In cell **D4**, enter =SUM($C$3:C4) and press **Enter** to add the formula to the cell.

7   Click cell **D4** and then drag the cell's fill handle until the selection covers cell **D8**. The formulas keep the cell reference **$C$3** absolute, but change the second cell reference to reflect the new cells' positions relative to the original formula.

8   On the tab bar, click the **JuneLabor** sheet tab to display the **JuneLabor** worksheet.

9   In cell **F13**, enter =SUM(J to display **JuneSummary**, the name of the table in the **JuneLabor** worksheet, in the **Formula AutoComplete** list.

10   Press **Tab** to extend the formula to read =SUM(JuneSummary.

11   Enter [, and then in the **Formula AutoComplete** list, click **Labor Expense**, and press **Tab** to extend the formula to read =SUM(JuneSummary[Labor Expense.

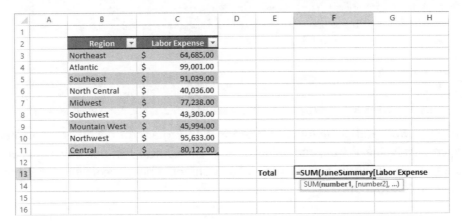

12　Enter **])** to complete the formula, and then press **Enter** to display the value **$637,051.00** in cell **F13**.

❌ CLEAN UP **Close the ITExpenses workbook, saving your changes if you want to.**

Summarizing data that meets specific conditions

Another use for formulas is to display messages when certain conditions are met. For instance, Consolidated Messenger's VP of Marketing, Craig Dewar, might have agreed to examine the rates charged to corporate customers who were billed for more than $100,000 during a calendar year. This kind of formula is called a *conditional formula*; one way to create a conditional formula in Excel is to use the *IF* function. To create a conditional formula, you click the cell to hold the formula and open the Insert Function dialog box. From within the dialog box, click *IF* in the list of available functions, and then click OK. When you do, the Function Arguments dialog box opens.

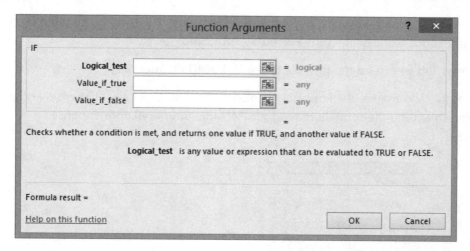

When you work with an *IF* function, the Function Arguments dialog box has three boxes: Logical_test, Value_if_true, and Value_if_false. The Logical_test box holds the condition you want to check. If the customer's year-to-date shipping bill appears in cell G8, the expression would be *G8>100000*.

Now you need to have Excel display messages that indicate whether Craig Dewar should evaluate the account for a possible rate adjustment. To have Excel print a message from an *IF* function, you enclose the message in quotes in the Value_if_true or Value_if_false box. In this case, you would enter *"High-volume shipper—evaluate for rate decrease"* (including the quotation marks) in the Value_if_true box and *"Does not qualify at this time."* in the Value_if_false box.

Excel also includes several other conditional functions you can use to summarize your data, as shown in the following table.

Function	Description
AVERAGEIF	Finds the average of values within a cell range that meet a specified criterion
AVERAGEIFS	Finds the average of values within a cell range that meet multiple criteria
COUNT	Counts the number of cells in a range that contain a numerical value
COUNTA	Counts the number of cells in a range that are not empty
COUNTBLANK	Counts the number of cells in a range that are empty
COUNTIF	Counts the number of cells in a range that meet a specified criterion
COUNTIFS	Counts the number of cells in a range that meet multiple criteria
IFERROR	Displays one value if a formula results in an error and another if it doesn't
SUMIF	Finds the sum of values in a range that meet a single criterion
SUMIFS	Finds the sum of values in a range that meet multiple criteria

You can use the *IFERROR* function to display a custom error message, instead of relying on the default Excel error messages to explain what happened. For example, you could use an *IFERROR* formula when looking up the CustomerID value from cell G8 in the Customers table by using the *VLOOKUP* function. One way to create such a formula is by using *=IFERROR(VLOOKUP(G8,Customers,2,false),"Customer not found")*. If the function finds a match for the CustomerID in cell G8, it displays the customer's name; if it doesn't find a match, it displays the text *Customer not found*.

SEE ALSO For more information about the VLOOKUP function, see "Looking up information in a worksheet" in Chapter 6, "Reordering and summarizing data."

Just as the *COUNTIF* function counts the number of cells that meet a criterion and the *SUMIF* function finds the total of values in cells that meet a criterion, the *AVERAGEIF* function finds the average of values in cells that meet a criterion. To create a formula by using the *AVERAGEIF* function, you define the range to be examined for the criterion, the criterion, and, if required, the range from which to draw the values. As an example, consider a worksheet that lists each customer's ID number, name, state, and total monthly shipping bill.

	A	B	C	D
1	CustomerID	CustomerName	State	Total
2	OD100	Contoso	WA	$118,476.00
3	OD101	Fabrikam	WA	$125,511.00
4	OD102	Northwind Traders	OR	$103,228.00
5	OD103	Adventure Works	WA	$ 86,552.00
6				

If you want to find the average order value for customers from the state of Washington (abbreviated in the worksheet as WA), you can create the formula =AVERAGEIF(C2:C5, "=WA", D2:D5).

The *SUMIFS*, *AVERAGEIFS*, and *COUNTIFS* functions extend the capabilities of the *SUMIF*, *AVERAGEIF*, and *COUNTIF* functions to allow for multiple criteria. If you want to find the sum of all orders of at least $100,000 placed by companies in Washington, you can create the formula =SUMIFS(D2:D5, C2:C5, "=WA", D2:D5, ">=100000").

The *AVERAGEIFS* and *SUMIFS* functions start with a data range that contains values that the formula summarizes; you then list the data ranges and the criteria to apply to that range. In generic terms, the syntax runs =AVERAGEIFS(data_range, criteria_range1, criteria1[,criteria_range2, criteria2...]). The part of the syntax in square brackets (which aren't used when you create the formula) is optional, so an *AVERAGEIFS* or *SUMIFS* formula that contains a single criterion will work. The *COUNTIFS* function, which doesn't perform any calculations, doesn't need a data range—you just provide the criteria ranges and criteria. For example, you could find the number of customers from Washington who were billed at least $100,000 by using the formula =COUNTIFS(C2:C5, "=WA", D2:D5, ">=100000").

In this exercise, you'll create a conditional formula that displays a message if a condition is true, find the average of worksheet values that meet one criterion, and find the sum of worksheet values that meet two criteria.

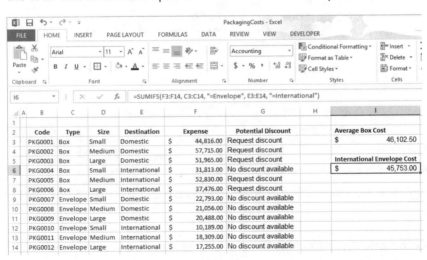

→ SET UP You need the PackagingCosts workbook located in the Chapter03 practice file folder to complete this exercise. Open the workbook, and then follow the steps.

1 In cell **G3**, enter the formula =IF(F3>=35000, "Request discount", "No discount available"), and press **Enter** to create the formula, which displays *Request discount* if the value in cell F3 is at least 35,000 and displays *No discount available* if not. The value **Request discount** appears in cell **G3**.

2 Click cell **G3**, and drag the fill handle down until it covers cell **G14**. Excel copies the formula in cell **G3** to cells **G4:G14**, adjusting the formula to reflect the cells' addresses. The results of the copied formulas appear in cells **G4:G14**.

3 In cell **I3**, enter the formula =AVERAGEIF(C3:C14, "=Box", F3:F14) and press **Enter** to display the average cost per category of boxes, **$46,102.50**, in cell **I3**.

4 In cell **I6**, enter =SUMIFS(F3:F14, C3:C14, "=Envelope", E3:E14, "=International"), and press **Enter** to display the value **$45,753.00**, which represents the total cost of all envelopes used for international shipments, in cell **I6**.

	A	B	C	D	E	F	G	H	I
1									
2		Code	Type	Size	Destination	Expense	Potential Discount		Average Box Cost
3		PKG0001	Box	Small	Domestic	$ 44,816.00	Request discount		$ 46,102.50
4		PKG0002	Box	Medium	Domestic	$ 57,715.00	Request discount		
5		PKG0003	Box	Large	Domestic	$ 51,965.00	Request discount		International Envelope Cost
6		PKG0004	Box	Small	International	$ 31,813.00	No discount available		$ 45,753.00
7		PKG0005	Box	Medium	International	$ 52,830.00	Request discount		
8		PKG0006	Box	Large	International	$ 37,476.00	Request discount		
9		PKG0007	Envelope	Small	Domestic	$ 22,793.00	No discount available		
10		PKG0008	Envelope	Medium	Domestic	$ 21,056.00	No discount available		
11		PKG0009	Envelope	Large	Domestic	$ 20,488.00	No discount available		
12		PKG0010	Envelope	Small	International	$ 10,189.00	No discount available		
13		PKG0011	Envelope	Medium	International	$ 18,309.00	No discount available		
14		PKG0012	Envelope	Large	International	$ 17,255.00	No discount available		

✖ CLEAN UP Close the PackagingCosts workbook, saving your changes if you want to.

Working with iterative calculation options and automatic workbook calculation

Excel formulas use values in other cells to calculate their results. If you create a formula that refers to the cell that contains the formula, you have created a circular reference. Under most circumstances, Excel treats circular references as a mistake for two reasons. First, the vast majority of Excel formulas don't refer to their own cell, so a circular reference is unusual enough to be identified as an error. The second, more serious consideration is that a formula with a circular reference can slow down your workbook. Because Excel repeats, or iterates, the calculation, you need to set limits on how many times the program repeats the operation.

You can control your workbook's calculation options by clicking the File tab on the ribbon, clicking Options to open the Excel Options dialog box, clicking Formulas to display that page of the Excel Options dialog box, and selecting the calculation option you want.

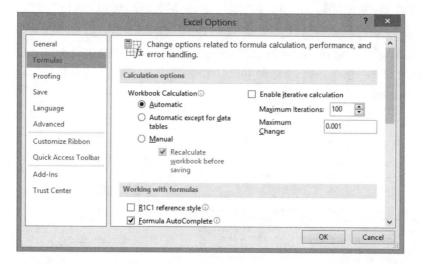

The Calculation Options section of the Formulas page in the dialog box has three available settings:

- **Automatic** The default setting, which recalculates a worksheet whenever a value affecting a formula changes

- **Automatic except for data tables** Recalculates a worksheet whenever a value changes but doesn't recalculate data tables

- **Manual** Requires you to press **F9** or click the **Formulas** tab and click the **Calculate Now** button to recalculate your worksheet

In the Calculation Options section, you can also choose to allow or disallow iterative calculations. Selecting the Enable Iterative Calculation check box lets Excel repeat calculations for cells that contain formulas with circular references. The default Maximum Iterations value of 100 and Maximum Change of 0.001 are appropriate for all but the most unusual circumstances. Click OK to accept your changes.

TIP You can also have Excel recalculate its formulas by clicking the Formulas tab on the ribbon, clicking the Calculation Options button, and selecting the behavior you want.

In this exercise, you'll create a formula that has a circular reference and then change the program's iterative calculation options to find the result.

 SET UP You need the SavingsIncentive workbook located in the Chapter03 practice file folder to complete this exercise. Open the workbook, and then follow the steps.

1 Click the **Formulas** tab, click the **Calculation Options** button, and then click **Manual**.

2 In cell **B6**, enter the formula **=B7*B9** and press **Enter** to display the initial result of the formula, which is **$1,600.00**. Note that this result is incorrect because the Gross Savings minus the Savings Incentive should equal the Net Savings value, which it does not.

3 Press **F9** to recalculate the worksheet. When you do, Excel displays a message box indicating that you have created a circular reference.

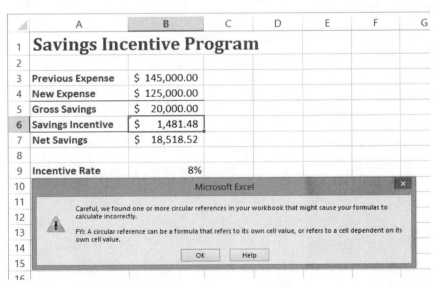

4   Click **OK** to close the message box.

5   Click the **File** tab and then click **Options** to open the **Excel Options** dialog box.

6   Click the **Formulas** category label.

7   Select the **Enable iterative calculation** check box, and then click **OK** to close the **Excel Options** dialog box.

8   Press **F9** to recalculate the worksheet. The correct values of **$1,481.48** and **$18,518.52** appear in cells **B6** and **B7**, respectively.

9   Click the **Formulas** tab, click the **Calculation Options** button, and then click **Automatic**.

✖ CLEAN UP Close the PackagingCosts workbook, saving your changes if you want to.

Using array formulas

Most Excel formulas calculate values to be displayed in a single cell. For example, you could add the formulas *=B1*B4*, *=B1*B5*, and *=B1*B6* to consecutive worksheet cells to calculate shipping insurance costs based on the value of a package's contents.

	A	B	C
1	**Insurance Rate**	2.5%	
2			
3	**PackageID**	**Value**	**Premium**
4	PK000352	$ 591.00	
5	PK000353	$1,713.00	
6	PK000354	$3,039.00	
7			

Rather than add the same formula to multiple cells one cell at a time, you can add a formula to every cell in the target range at once by creating an array formula. To create an array formula, you enter the formula's arguments and press Ctrl+Shift+Enter to identify the formula as an array formula. To calculate package insurance rates for values in the cell range B4:B6 and the rate in cell B1, you would select a range of cells with the same shape as the value range and enter the formula =B1*B4:B6. In this case, the values are in a three-cell column, so you must select a range of the same shape, such as C4:C6.

	A	B	C
1	**Insurance Rate**	2.5%	
2			
3	**PackageID**	**Value**	**Premium**
4	PK000352	$ 591.00	=B1*B4:B6
5	PK000353	$1,713.00	
6	PK000354	$3,039.00	
7			

IMPORTANT If you enter the array formula into a range of the wrong shape, Excel displays duplicate results, incomplete results, or error messages depending on how the target range differs from the value range.

When you press Ctrl+Shift+Enter, Excel creates an array formula in the selected cells. The formula appears within a pair of curly braces to indicate it is an array formula. In this case, the formula in cells C4:C6 is {=B1*B4:B6}.

IMPORTANT You can't add curly braces to a formula to make it an array formula—you must press Ctrl+Shift+Enter to create it.

In addition to creating an array formula that combines a single cell's value with an array, you can create array formulas that use two separate arrays. For example, Consolidated Messenger might establish a goal to reduce sorting time in each of four distribution centers.

	A	B	C	D
1	Center	Previous Time	Target Percentage	Target Time
2	North	145	85%	
3	South	180	90%	
4	East	195	75%	
5	West	205	70%	
6				

This worksheet stores the previous sorting times in minutes and percentage target in cells B2:B5 and C2:C5, respectively. The array formula to calculate the targets for each of the four centers is *=B2:B5*C2:C5*, which, when entered into cells D2:D5 by pressing Ctrl+Shift+Enter, would appear as *{= B2:B5*C2:C5}*.

To edit an array formula, you must select every cell that contains the array formula, click the formula bar to activate it, edit the formula on the formula bar, and then press Ctrl+Shift+Enter to re-enter the formula as an array formula.

TIP Many operations that used to require an array formula can now be calculated by using functions such as *SUMIFS* and *COUNTIFS*.

In this exercise, you'll create and edit array formulas.

➡ SET UP You need the FuelSurcharges workbook located in the Chapter03 practice file folder to complete this exercise. Open the workbook, and then follow the steps.

1   If necessary, click the **Fuel** sheet tab to display the **Fuel** worksheet.

2   Select cells **C11:F11**.

3   Enter the formula =C3*C9:F9 and then press **Ctrl+Shift+Enter** to add the formula {=C3*C9:F9} to cells **C11:F11**.

4   With cells **C11:F11** still selected, click the formula bar, edit the formula so it reads =C3*C10:F10, and then press **Ctrl+Shift+Enter** to change the array formula to {=C3*C10:F10}.

5   Click the **Volume** sheet tab to display the **Volume** worksheet.

6   Select cells **D4:D7**.

7   Enter the formula =B4:B7*C4:C7 and then press **Ctrl+Shift+Enter** to add the formula {=B4:B7*C4:C7} to cells **D4:D7**.

✖ CLEAN UP Close the FuelSurcharges workbook, saving your changes if you want to.

Finding and correcting errors in calculations

Including calculations in a worksheet gives you valuable answers to questions about your data. As is always true, however, it is possible for errors to creep into your formulas. With Excel, you can find the source of errors in your formulas by identifying the cells used in a particular calculation and describing any errors that have occurred. The process of examining a worksheet for errors is referred to as *auditing*.

Excel identifies errors in several ways. The first way is to display an error code in the cell holding the formula that is generating the error.

⊿	A	B	C	D	E	F
1						
2		Category	Expenses			
3		Hardware	$1,469,002.00			
4		Desktop Software	$ 385,671.00			
5		Server Software	$ 599,101.00			
6		Maintenance	$ 64,703.00			
7		Cable	$ 11,240.00			
8		Backup Power Supply	$ 33,249.00			
9					Total	#NAME?
10					Software Total	
11						

When a cell with an erroneous formula is the active cell, an Error button is displayed next to it. Pointing to the Error button causes it to display an arrow on the button's right edge. Clicking the arrow displays a menu with options that provide information about the error and offer to help you fix it.

The following table lists the most common error codes and what they mean.

Error code	Description
#####	The column isn't wide enough to display the value.
#VALUE!	The formula has the wrong type of argument (such as text in a cell where a numerical value is required).
#NAME?	The formula contains text that Excel doesn't recognize (such as an unknown named range).
#REF!	The formula refers to a cell that doesn't exist (which can happen whenever cells are deleted).
#DIV/0!	The formula attempts to divide by zero.
#N/A!	The formula attempts to use a value that is not available in the target range. This error often occurs when a user enters an invalid lookup value in a VLOOKUP formula.

Another technique you can use to find the source of formula errors is to ensure that the appropriate cells are providing values for the formula. For example, you might want to calculate the total number of deliveries for a service level, but you could accidentally create a formula referring to the service levels' names instead of their package quantities. You can identify the source of an error by having Excel trace a cell's *precedents*, which are the cells that have values used in the active cell's formula. To do so, click the Formulas tab, and then in the Formula Auditing group, click Trace Precedents. When you do, Excel identifies those cells by drawing a blue tracer arrow from the precedents to the active cell.

You can also audit your worksheet by identifying cells that contain formulas that use a value from a given cell. For example, you might use one region's daily package total in a formula that calculates the average number of packages delivered for all regions on a given day. Cells that use another cell's value in their calculations are known as *dependents*, meaning that they depend on the value in the other cell to derive their own value. As with tracing precedents, you can click the Formulas tab, and then in the Formula Auditing group, click Trace Dependents to have Excel draw blue arrows from the active cell to those cells that have calculations based on that value.

	A	B	C	D	E	F
1						
2		Category	Expenses			
3		Hardware	$1,469,002.00			
4		Desktop Software	$ •385,671.00			
5		Server Software	$ 599,101.00			
6		Maintenance	$ 64,703.00			
7		Cable	$ 11,240.00			
8		Backup Power Supply	$ 33,249.00			
9					Total	$ 2,562,966.00
10					Software Total	$ 984,772.00
11						

If the cells identified by the tracer arrows aren't the correct cells, you can hide the arrows and correct the formula. To hide the tracer arrows on a worksheet, display the Formulas tab, and then in the Formula Auditing group, click Remove Arrows.

If you prefer to have the elements of a formula error presented as text in a dialog box, you can use the Error Checking dialog box to view the error and the formula in the cell in which the error occurs. To open the Error Checking dialog box, display the Formulas tab, and then in the Formula Auditing group, click the Error Checking button. You can use the controls in the Error Checking dialog box to move through the formula one step at a time, to choose to ignore the error, or to move to the next or the previous error. If you click the Options button in the dialog box, you can also use the controls in the Excel Options dialog box to change how Excel determines what is an error and what isn't.

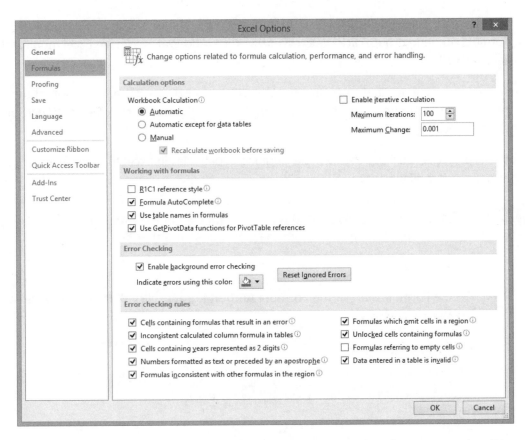

TIP You can have the Error Checking tool ignore formulas that don't use every cell in a region (such as a row or column). If you clear the Formulas Which Omit Cells In A Region check box, you can create formulas that don't add up every value in a row or column (or rectangle) without Excel marking them as an error.

For times when you just want to display the results of each step of a formula and don't need the full power of the Error Checking tool, you can use the Evaluate Formula dialog box to move through each element of the formula. To open the Evaluate Formula dialog box, you display the Formulas tab and then, in the Formula Auditing group, click the Evaluate Formula button. The Evaluate Formula dialog box is useful for examining formulas that don't produce an error but aren't generating the result you expect.

Finally, you can monitor the value in a cell regardless of where in your workbook you are by opening a Watch Window that displays the value in the cell. For example, if one of your formulas uses values from cells in other worksheets or even other workbooks, you can set a watch on the cell that contains the formula and then change the values in the other cells.

To set a watch, click the cell you want to monitor, and then on the Formulas tab, in the Formula Auditing group, click Watch Window. Click Add Watch to have Excel monitor the selected cell.

As soon as you enter the new value, the Watch Window displays the new result of the formula. When you're done watching the formula, select the watch, click Delete Watch, and close the Watch Window.

In this exercise, you'll use the formula-auditing capabilities in Excel to identify and correct errors in a formula.

 SET UP You need the ConveyerBid workbook located in the Chapter03 practice file folder to complete this exercise. Open the workbook, and then follow the steps.

1   Click cell **D21**.

2   On the **Formulas** tab, in the **Formula Auditing** group, click **Watch Window** to open the **Watch Window**.

Watch Window					
Add Watch...	Delete Watch				
Book	Sheet	Name	Cell	Value	Formula

3   Click **Add Watch**, and then in the **Add Watch** dialog box, click **Add** to add cell **D21** to the watch list.

4   Click cell **D8**, which activates the cell and displays **=SUM(C3:C7)** in the formula bar.

5   On the **Formulas** tab, in the **Formula Auditing** group, click the **Trace Precedents** button to display a blue arrow that begins at the cell range **C3:C7** and points to cell **D8**, indicating that the cells in the range **C3:C7** provide the values for the formula in cell **D8**.

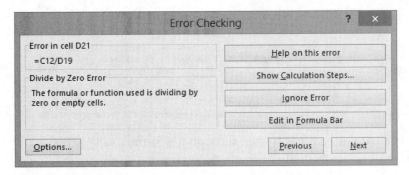

◢	A	B	C	D
1				
2		**Conveyer**		
3		350' track	$ 14,012.00	
4		Catch bin	$ 895.00	
5		Motor	$ 1,249.00	
6		Chain drive	$ 1,495.00	
7		Sorting table	$ 675.00	
8		*Subtotal*		$ 18,326.00
9				

6   On the **Formulas** tab, in the **Formula Auditing** group, click the **Remove Arrows** button to remove the tracer arrow.

7   Click cell **A1**.

8   On the **Formulas** tab, in the **Formula Auditing** group, click the **Error Checking** button to open the **Error Checking** dialog box, which displays the error found in cell D21.

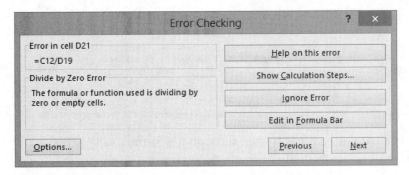

9   Click **Next** to move to the next error. Excel displays a message box indicating that there are no more errors in the worksheet.

10 Click **OK** to close both the message box and the **Error Checking** dialog box.

11 On the **Formulas** tab, in the **Formula Auditing** group, click the **Error Checking** arrow, and then in the list, click **Trace Error**. Blue arrows appear, pointing to cell **D21** from cells **C12** and **D19**. These arrows indicate that using the values (or lack of values, in this case) in the indicated cells generates the error in cell D21.

12   On the **Formulas** tab, in the **Formula Auditing** group, click **Remove Arrows** to hide the arrows.

13   In the formula box, delete the existing formula, enter =C12/D20, and then press **Enter**. The value **14%** appears in cell **D21** and the change is reflected in the Watch Window.

14   Click cell **D21**.

15   On the **Formulas** tab, in the **Formula Auditing** group, click the **Evaluate Formula** button to open the **Evaluate Formula** dialog box, which displays the formula from cell **D21**.

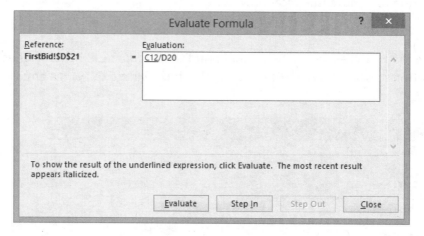

16   Click **Evaluate** three times to step through the formula's elements, and then click **Close** to close the **Evaluate Formula** dialog box.

17   In the **Watch Window**, click the watch in the list.

18   Click **Delete Watch** to erase the watch.

19   On the **Formulas** tab, in the **Formula Auditing** group, click **Watch Window** to close the **Watch Window**.

✖ CLEAN UP Close the ConveyerBid workbook, saving your changes if you want to.

Key points

- You can add a group of cells to a formula by entering the formula, and then at the spot in the formula in which you want to name the cells, selecting the cells.

- By creating named ranges, you can refer to entire blocks of cells by using a single term, saving you lots of time and effort. You can use a similar technique with Excel table data, referring to an entire Excel table or one or more table columns.

- When you write a formula, be sure you use absolute referencing ($A$1) if you want the formula to remain the same when it's copied from one cell to another, or use relative referencing (A1) if you want the formula to change to reflect its new position in the worksheet.

- Instead of entering a formula from scratch, you can use the Insert Function dialog box to help you.

- With iterative calculations, you can manage formulas that have circular references.

- You can use array formulas to summarize ranges of values by creating a single formula.

- You can monitor how the value in a cell changes by adding a watch to the Watch Window.

- To find out which formulas refer to the values in the selected cell, use Trace Dependents; if you want to find out which cells provide values for the formula in the active cell, use Trace Precedents.

- You can step through the calculations of a formula in the Evaluate Formula dialog box or go through a more rigorous error-checking procedure by using the Error Checking tool.

3

Chapter at a glance

Define

Define styles,
page 113

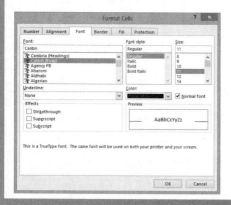

Apply

Apply workbook themes and Excel table
styles, page 119

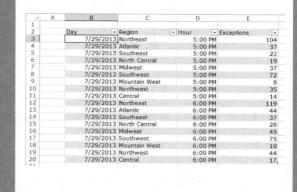

Change

Change the appearance of data based on its
value, page 131

Distribution Capacity		
Northeast		47%
Atlantic		75%
Southeast		39%
North Central		54%
Midwest		40%
Southwest		73%
Mountain West		51%
Northwest		69%
Central		41%

Add

Add images to worksheets,
page 138

	A	B	C	D
1				
2		Call Volume		
3		Northeast	13,769	
4		Atlantic	19,511	
5		Southeast	11,111	
6		North Central	24,972	
7		Midwest	11,809	
8		Southwest	20,339	
9		Mountain West	20,127	
10		Northwest	12,137	
11		Central	20,047	
12				

Changing workbook appearance

IN THIS CHAPTER, YOU WILL LEARN HOW TO

- Format cells.

- Define styles.

- Apply workbook themes and Excel table styles.

- Make numbers easier to read.

- Change the appearance of data based on its value.

- Add images to worksheets.

Entering data into a workbook efficiently saves you time, but you must also ensure that your data is easy to read. Microsoft Excel 2013 gives you a wide variety of ways to make your data easier to understand; for example, you can change the font, character size, or color used to present a cell's contents. Changing how data appears on a worksheet helps set the contents of a cell apart from the contents of surrounding cells. The simplest example of that concept is a data label. If a column on your worksheet contains a list of days, you can easily set apart a label (for example, *Day*) by presenting it in bold type that's noticeably larger than the type used to present the data to which it refers. To save time, you can define several custom formats and then apply them quickly to the desired cells.

You might also want to specially format a cell's contents to reflect the value in that cell. For example, Lori Penor, the chief operating officer of Consolidated Messenger, might want to create a worksheet that displays the percentage of improperly delivered packages from each regional distribution center. If that percentage exceeds a threshold, she could have Excel display a red traffic light icon, indicating that the center's performance is out of tolerance and requires attention.

In this chapter, you'll change the appearance of data, apply existing formats to data, make numbers easier to read, change data's appearance based on its value, and add images to worksheets.

Formatting cells

Excel spreadsheets can hold and process lots of data, but when you manage numerous spreadsheets it can be hard to remember from a worksheet's title exactly what data is kept in that worksheet. Data labels give you and your colleagues information about data in a worksheet, but it's important to format the labels so that they stand out visually. To make your data labels or any other data stand out, you can change the format of the cells that hold your data.

	A	B	C	D
1				
2		**Call Volume**		
3		Northeast	13,769	
4		Atlantic	19,511	
5		Southeast	11,111	
6		North Central	24,972	
7		Midwest	11,809	
8		Southwest	20,339	
9		Mountain West	20,127	
10		Northwest	12,137	
11		Central	20,047	
12				

Most of the tools you need to change a cell's format can be found on the Home tab. You can apply the formatting represented on a button by selecting the cells you want to apply the style to and then clicking that button. If you want to set your data labels apart by making them appear bold, click the Bold button. If you have already made a cell's contents bold, selecting the cell and clicking the Bold button will remove the formatting.

TIP Deleting a cell's contents doesn't delete the cell's formatting. To delete a selected cell's formatting, on the Home tab, in the Editing group, click the Clear button (which looks like an eraser), and then click Clear Formats. Clicking Clear All from the same list will remove the cell's contents and formatting.

Buttons in the Home tab's Font group that give you choices, such as Font Color, have an arrow at the right edge of the button. Clicking the arrow displays a list of options accessible for that button, such as the fonts available on your system or the colors you can assign to a cell.

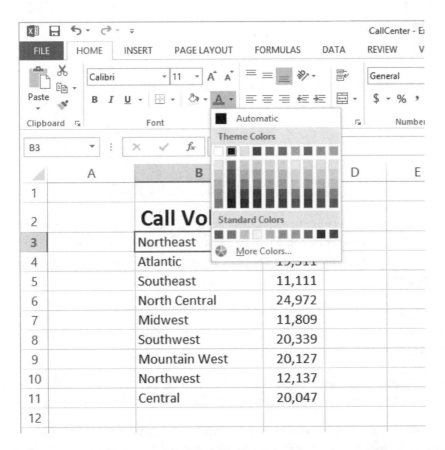

Another way you can make a cell stand apart from its neighbors is to add a border around the cell. To place a border around one or more cells, select the cells, and then choose the border type you want by selecting from the Border list in the Font group. Excel does provide more options: to display the full range of border types and styles, in the Border list, click More Borders. The Border page of the Format Cells dialog box contains the full range of tools you can use to define your cells' borders.

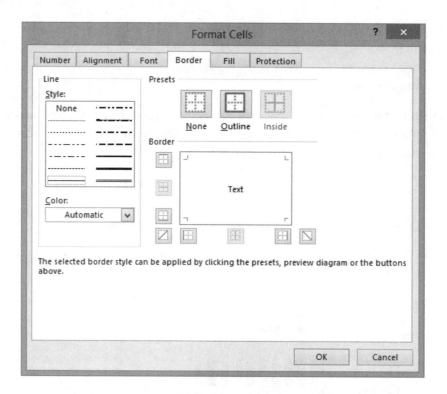

You can also make a group of cells stand apart from its neighbors by changing its shading, which is the color that fills the cells. On a worksheet that tracks total package volume for the past month, Lori Penor could change the fill color of the cells holding her data labels to make the labels stand out even more than by changing the labels' text formatting.

TIP You can display the most commonly used formatting controls by right-clicking a selected range. When you do, a Mini Toolbar containing a subset of the Home tab formatting tools appears above the shortcut menu.

If you want to change the attributes of every cell in a row or column, you can click the header of the row or column you want to modify and then select the format you want.

One task you can't perform by using the tools on the Home tab is to change the standard font for a workbook, which is used in the Name box and on the formula bar. The standard font when you install Excel is Calibri, a simple font that is easy to read on a computer screen and on the printed page. If you want to choose another font, click the File tab, and then click Options. On the General page of the Excel Options dialog box, set the values in the Use This Font and Font Size list boxes to pick your new display font.

In this exercise, you'll emphasize a worksheet's title by changing the format of cell data, and you'll add a border to a cell range and then change a cell range's fill color. After those tasks are complete, you'll change the default font for the workbook.

→ SET UP You need the VehicleMileSummary workbook located in the Chapter04 practice file folder to complete this exercise. Open the workbook, and then follow the steps.

1 Click cell **D2**.

2 On the **Home** tab, in the **Font** group, click the **Bold** button to display the cell's contents in bold type.

3 In the **Font** group, click the **Font Size** arrow, and then in the list, click **18** to increase the size of the text in cell **D2**.

⁄	A	B	C	D	E	F	G	H	I
1									
2				**Vehicle Mile Summary**					
3									
4			Day						
5		VehicleID	Monday	Tuesday	Wednesday	Thursday	Friday	Saturday	
6		V101	159	144	124	108	125	165	
7		V102	113	106	111	116	119	97	
8		V103	87	154	124	128	111	100	
9		V104	137	100	158	96	127	158	
10		V105	86	132	154	97	154	165	
11		V106	159	163	155	101	89	160	
12		V107	111	165	155	92	91	94	
13		V108	101	162	123	87	93	140	
14		V109	164	159	116	97	149	120	
15		V110	100	107	143	144	152	132	

4 Click cell **B5**, hold down the **Ctrl** key, and click cell **C4** to select the noncontiguous cells.

5 On the **Home** tab, in the **Font** group, click the **Bold** button to display the cells' contents in bold type.

6 Select the cell ranges **B6:B15** and **C5:H5**.

7   In the **Font** group, click the **Italic** button to display the cell's contents in italic type.

◢	A	B	C	D	E	F	G	H
1								
2				**Vehicle Mile Summary**				
3								
4			Day					
5		VehicleID	Monday	Tuesday	Wednesday	Thursday	Friday	Saturday
6		V101	159	144	124	108	125	165
7		V102	113	106	111	116	119	97
8		V103	87	154	124	128	111	100
9		V104	137	100	158	96	127	158
10		V105	86	132	154	97	154	165
11		V106	159	163	155	101	89	160
12		V107	111	165	155	92	91	94
13		V108	101	162	123	87	93	140
14		V109	164	159	116	97	149	120
15		V110	100	107	143	144	152	132
16								

8   Select the cell range **C6:H15**.

9   In the **Font** group, click the **Border** arrow, and then in the list, click **Outside Borders** to place a border around the outside edge of the selected cells.

10   Select the cell range **B4:H15**.

11   In the **Border** list, click **Thick Box Border** to place a thick border around the outside edge of the selected cells.

12   Select the cell ranges **B4:B15** and **C4:H5**.

13   In the **Font** group, click the **Fill Color** arrow, and then in the **Standard Colors** palette, click the yellow swatch to change the selected cells' background color to yellow.

⁄	A	B	C	D	E	F	G	H
1								
2				**Vehicle Mile Summary**				
3								
4			Day					
5		VehicleID	Monday	Tuesday	Wednesday	Thursday	Friday	Saturday
6		V101	159	144	124	108	125	165
7		V102	113	106	111	116	119	97
8		V103	87	154	124	128	111	100
9		V104	137	100	158	96	127	158
10		V105	86	132	154	97	154	165
11		V106	159	163	155	101	89	160
12		V107	111	165	155	92	91	94
13		V108	101	162	123	87	93	140
14		V109	164	159	116	97	149	120
15		V110	100	107	143	144	152	132

14   Click the **File** tab, and then click **Options** to open the **Excel Options** dialog box.

15   If necessary, click **General** to display the **General** page.

16   In the **When creating new workbooks** area, in the **Use this as the default font** list, click **Verdana**. **Verdana** appears in the **Use This Font** field.

17   Click **Cancel** to close the **Excel Options** dialog box without saving your change.

✖ CLEAN UP Close the VehicleMileSummary workbook, saving your changes if you want to.

Defining styles

As you work with Excel, you will probably develop preferred formats for data labels, titles, and other worksheet elements. Instead of adding a format's characteristics one element at a time to the target cells, you can have Excel store the format and recall it as needed. You can find the predefined formats by displaying the Home tab, and then in the Styles group, clicking Cell Styles.

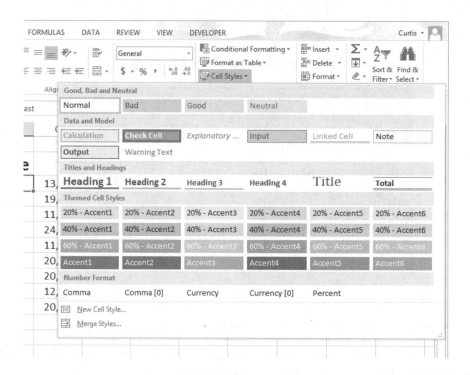

Clicking a style from the Cell Styles gallery applies the style to the selected cells, but Excel also displays a live preview of a format when you point to it. If none of the existing styles is what you want, you can create your own style by clicking New Cell Style below the gallery to display the Style dialog box. In the Style dialog box, enter the name of your new style in the Style Name field, and then click Format. The Format Cells dialog box opens.

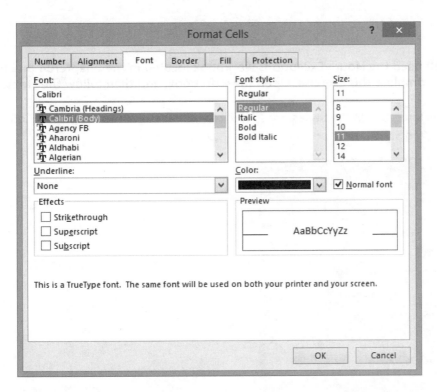

After you set the characteristics of your new style, click OK to make your style available in the Cell Styles gallery. If you ever want to delete a custom style, display the Cell Styles gallery, right-click the style, and then click Delete.

The Style dialog box is quite versatile, but it's overkill if all you want to do is apply formatting changes you made to a cell to the contents of another cell. To do so, use the Format Painter button, found in the Home tab's Clipboard group. Just click the cell that has the format you want to copy, click the Format Painter button, and select the target cells to have Excel apply the copied format to the target range.

TIP If you want to apply the same formatting to multiple cells by using the Format Painter button, double-click the Format Painter button and then click the cells to which you want to apply the formatting. When you're done applying the formatting, press the Esc key.

In this exercise, you'll create a style and apply the new style to a data label.

SET UP You need the HourlyExceptions workbook located in the Chapter04 practice file folder to complete this exercise. Open the workbook, and then follow the steps.

1   On the **Home** tab, in the **Styles** group, click **Cell Styles**, and then click **New Cell Style** to open the **Style** dialog box.

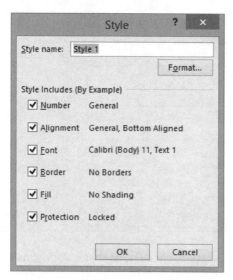

2   In the **Style name** field, enter **Crosstab Column Heading**.

3   Click the **Format** button to open the **Format Cells** dialog box.

4   Click the **Alignment** tab.

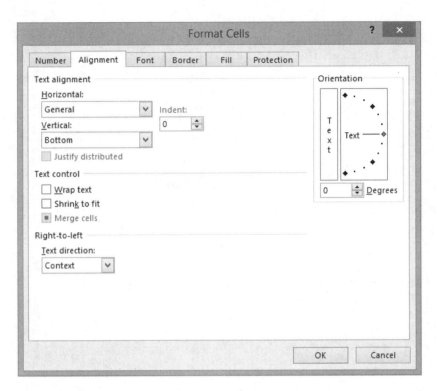

5   In the **Horizontal** list, click **Center**. **Center** appears in the **Horizontal** field.

6   Click the **Font** tab.

7   In the **Font style** list, click **Italic** to display the text in the **Preview** pane in italicized text.

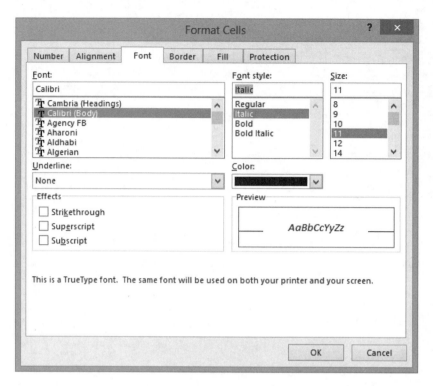

8 Click the **Number** tab to display the **Number** page of the **Format Cells** dialog box.

9 In the **Category** list, click **Time** to display the available time formats.

10 In the **Type** pane, click **1:30 PM**.

11 Click **OK** to save your changes. The **Format Cells** dialog box closes, and your new style's definition appears in the **Style** dialog box.

12 Click **OK** to close the **Style** dialog box.

13 Select cells **C4:N4**.

14 On the **Home** tab, in the **Styles** group, click **Cell Styles**. Your new style appears at the top of the gallery, in the **Custom** area.

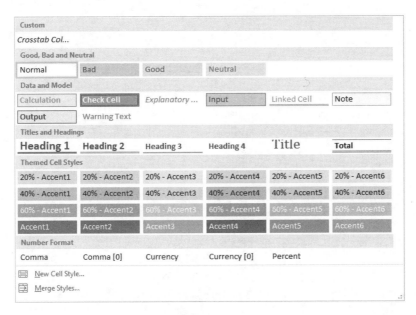

15 Click the **Crosstab Column Heading** style to apply your new style to the selected cells.

❌ CLEAN UP **Close the HourlyExceptions workbook, saving your changes if you want to.**

Applying workbook themes and Excel table styles

Microsoft Office 2013 includes powerful design tools that you can use to create attractive, professional documents quickly. The Excel product team implemented the new design capabilities by defining workbook themes and Excel table styles. A theme is a way to specify the fonts, colors, and graphic effects that appear in a workbook. Excel comes with many themes installed.

To apply an existing workbook theme, display the Page Layout tab. Then, in the Themes group, click Themes, and click the theme you want to apply to your workbook. By default, Excel applies the Office theme to your workbooks.

When you apply formatting to a workbook element, Excel displays colors that are available within the active theme. For example, selecting a worksheet cell and then clicking the Font Color button's arrow displays a menu containing two palettes of colors you can use. The theme colors appear in the Theme Colors palette, the standard colors appear in the Standard Colors palette, and the More Colors link, which displays the Colors dialog box, appears at the bottom of the menu. If you format workbook elements by using colors from the Theme Colors palette, applying a different theme changes that object's colors.

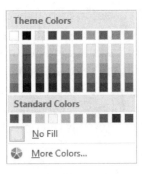

You can change a theme's colors, fonts, and graphic effects by displaying the Page Layout tab and then, in the Themes group, selecting new values from the Colors, Fonts, and Effects lists. To save your changes as a new theme, display the Page Layout tab, and in the Themes group, click Themes, and then click Save Current Theme. Use the controls in the Save Current Theme dialog box that opens to record your theme for later use. Later, when you click the Themes button, your custom theme will appear at the top of the gallery.

TIP When you save a theme, you save it as an Office Theme file. You can apply the theme to other Office 2013 documents as well.

Just as you can define and apply themes to entire workbooks, you can apply and define Excel table styles. You select an Excel table's initial style when you create it; to create a new style, display the Home tab, and in the Styles group, click Format As Table. In the Format As Table gallery, click New Table Style to open the New Table Style dialog box.

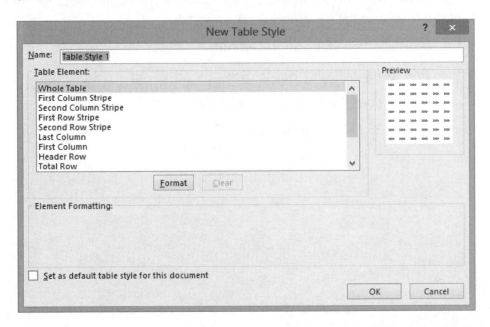

Enter a name for the new style, select the first table element you want to format, and then click Format to display the Format Cells dialog box. Define the element's formatting, and then click OK. When the New Table Style dialog box reopens, its Preview pane displays the overall table style and the Element Formatting area describes the selected element's appearance. Also, in the Table Element list, Excel displays the element's name in bold to indicate it has been changed. To make the new style the default for new Excel tables created in the current workbook, select the Set As Default Table Style For This Document check box. When you click OK, Excel saves the new table style.

TIP To remove formatting from a table element, click the name of the table element and then click the Clear button.

In this exercise, you'll create a new workbook theme, change a workbook's theme, create a new table style, and apply the new style to an Excel table.

 SET UP **You need the HourlyTracking workbook located in the Chapter04 practice file folder to complete this exercise. Open the workbook, and then follow the steps.**

1 If necessary, click any cell in the Excel table to make the table active.

2 On the **Home** tab, in the **Styles** group, click **Format as Table**, and then click the style at the upper-left corner of the **Table Styles** gallery. Doing so applies the style to the table.

3 On the **Home** tab, in the **Styles** group, click **Format as Table**, and then click **New Table Style** to open the **New Table Style** dialog box.

4 In the **Name** field, enter **Exception Default**.

5 In the **Table Element** list, click **Header Row**.

6 Click **Format** to open the **Format Cells** dialog box.

7 Click the **Fill** tab to display the **Fill** page.

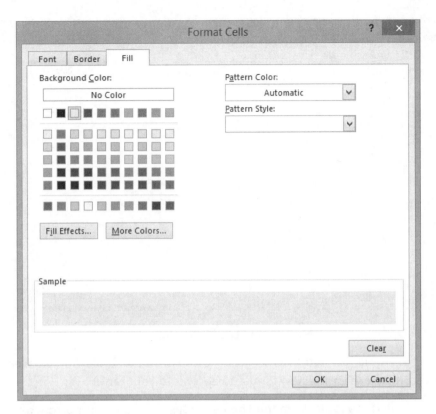

8   In the first row of color swatches, just below the **No Color** button, click the third swatch from the left to display that new background color in the **Sample** pane of the dialog box.

9   Click **OK** to close the **Format Cells** dialog box. When the **New Table Style** dialog box reopens, the **Header Row** table element appears in bold, and the **Preview** pane's header row is shaded.

10 In the **Table Element** list, click **Second Row Stripe**, and then click **Format** to open the **Format Cells** dialog box.

11 Just below the **No Color** button, click the third swatch from the left again to have the new background color appear in the **Sample** pane of the dialog box.

12 Click **OK** to close the **Format Cells** dialog box. When the **New Table Style** dialog box reopens, the **Second Row Stripe** table element appears in bold, and every second row is shaded in the **Preview** pane.

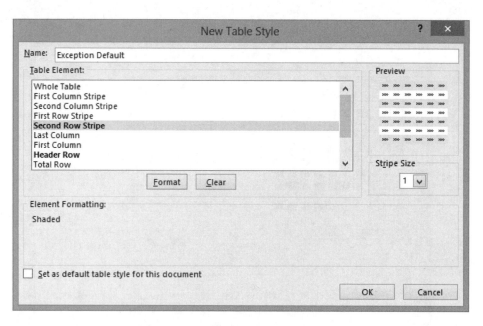

13   Click **OK** to close the **New Table Style** dialog box.

14   On the **Home** tab, in the **Styles** group, click **Format as Table**. In the gallery, in the **Custom** area, click the new format to apply it to your table.

15   On the **Page Layout** tab, in the **Themes** group, click the **Fonts** arrow, and then in the list, click **Consolas-Verdana** to change the theme's font.

16 In the **Themes** group, click the **Themes** button, and then click **Save Current Theme** to open the **Save Current Theme** dialog box.

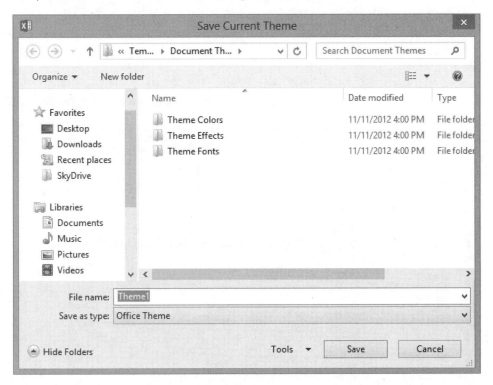

17 In the **File name** field, enter **Verdana Office**, and then click **Save** to save your theme.

18 In the **Themes** group, click the **Themes** button, and then click **Organic** to apply the new theme to your workbook.

✖ CLEAN UP **Close the HourlyTracking workbook, saving your changes if you want to.**

Making numbers easier to read

Changing the format of the cells in your worksheet can make your data much easier to read, both by setting data labels apart from the actual data and by adding borders to define the boundaries between labels and data even more clearly. Of course, using formatting options to change the font and appearance of a cell's contents doesn't help with idiosyncratic data types such as dates, phone numbers, or currency values.

As an example, consider US phone numbers. These numbers are 10 digits long and have a 3-digit area code, a 3-digit exchange, and a 4-digit line number written in the form (###) ###-####. Although it's certainly possible to enter a phone number with the expected formatting in a cell, it's much simpler to enter a sequence of 10 digits and have Excel change the data's appearance.

You can tell Excel to expect a phone number in a cell by displaying the Number page of the Format Cells dialog box and displaying the formats available for the Special category.

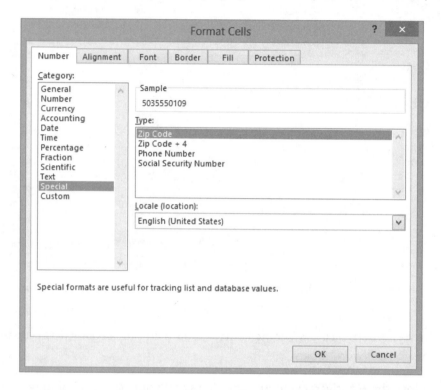

Clicking Phone Number in the Type list tells Excel to format 10-digit numbers in the standard phone number format. You can view this in operation if you compare the contents of the active cell and the contents of the formula box for a cell with the Phone Number formatting.

C3			✕	✓	fx	5035550109		

◢	A	B	C	D	E
1					
2			**Phone Number**		
3			(503) 555-0109		
4					
5					

TROUBLESHOOTING If you enter a 9-digit number in a field that expects a phone number, no error message will appear; instead, a 2-digit area code appears. For example, the number 425550012 would be displayed as (42) 555-0012. An 11-digit number would be displayed with a 4-digit area code. If the phone number doesn't look right, you probably left out a digit or included an extra one, so you should make sure your entry is correct.

Just as you can instruct Excel to expect a phone number in a cell, you can also have it expect a date or a currency amount. You can make those changes from the Format Cells dialog box by choosing either the Date category or the Currency category. Using the Date category, you can pick the format for the date (and determine whether the date's appearance changes due to the Locale setting of the operating system on the computer viewing the workbook). In a similar vein, selecting the Currency category displays controls to set the number of places after the decimal point, the currency symbol to use, and the way in which Excel should display negative numbers.

TIP With the Excel user interface, you can make the most common format changes by displaying the Home tab of the ribbon and then, in the Number group, either clicking a button representing a built-in format or selecting a format from the Number Format list.

You can also create a custom numeric format to add a word or phrase to a number in a cell. For example, you can add the phrase *per month* to a cell that has a formula that calculates average monthly sales for a year to ensure that you and your colleagues will recognize the figure as a monthly average. To create a custom number format, click the Home tab, and then click the Number dialog box launcher (found at the lower-right corner of the Number group on the ribbon) to display the Format Cells dialog box. Then, if necessary, click the Number tab.

In the Category list, click Custom to display the available custom number formats in the Type list. You can then click the base format you want and modify it in the Type box. For example, clicking the 0.00 format causes Excel to format any number in a cell with two digits to the right of the decimal point.

TIP The zeros in the format indicate that the position in the format can accept any number as a valid value.

To customize the format, click in the Type box and add any symbols or text you want to the format. For example, entering a dollar ($) sign to the left of the existing format and then entering *"per month"* (including quote marks) to the right of the existing format causes the number 1,500 to be displayed as *$1500.00 per month*.

IMPORTANT You need to enclose any text to be displayed as part of the format in quotes so that Excel recognizes the text as a string to be displayed in the cell.

In this exercise, you'll assign date, phone number, and currency formats to ranges of cells.

 SET UP **You need the ExecutiveSearch workbook located in the Chapter04 practice file folder to complete this exercise. Open the workbook, and then follow the steps.**

1   Click cell **A3**.

2   On the **Home** tab, click the **Font** dialog box launcher to open the **Format Cells** dialog box.

3   If necessary, click the **Number** tab.

4   In the **Category** list, click **Date** to display the available date formats in the **Type** list.

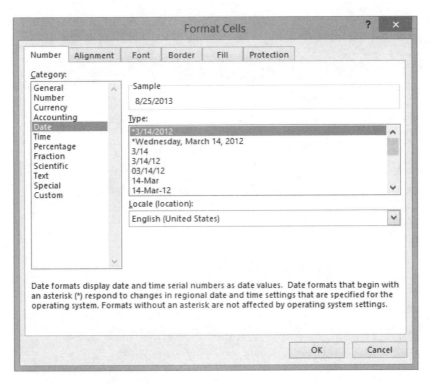

5   In the **Type** list, click **3/14/12**.

6   Click **OK** to display the contents of cell **A3** using the new format.

7   Click cell **G3**.

8   On the **Home** tab, in the **Number** group, click the **Number Format** arrow, and then click **More Number Formats**.

9   If necessary, click the **Number** tab in the **Format Cells** dialog box.

10   In the **Category** list, click **Special** to display the available special formats in the **Type** list.

11   In the **Type** list, click **Phone Number**, and then click **OK** to display the contents of the cell as **(425) 555-0102**, matching the format you selected, and to close the **Format Cells** dialog box.

12   Click cell **H3**.

13   Click the **Font** dialog box launcher.

14   If necessary, click the **Number** tab in the **Format Cells** dialog box.

15   In the **Category** list, click **Custom** to display the available custom formats in the **Type** list.

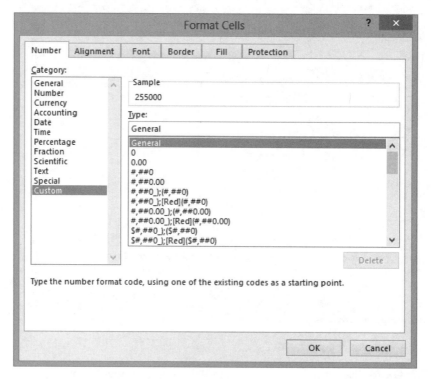

16   In the **Type** list, click the **#,##0** item to display #,##0 in the **Type** box.

17   In the **Type** box, click to the left of the existing format, and enter **$**. Then click to the right of the format, and type " before bonuses" (note the space after the opening quote).

18   Click **OK** to close the dialog box.

D	E	F	G	H	I
City	State	ZIP	Phone	CurrentSalary	
Redmond	WA	22841	(425) 555-0102	$255,000 before bonuses	

CLEAN UP Close the ExecutiveSearch workbook, saving your changes if you want to.

Changing the appearance of data based on its value

By recording package volumes, vehicle miles, and other business data in a worksheet, you can make important decisions about your operations. As explained earlier in this chapter, you can change the appearance of data labels and the worksheet itself to make interpreting your data easier.

Another way you can make your data easier to interpret is to have Excel change the appearance of your data based on its value. These formats are called *conditional formats* because the data must meet certain conditions, defined in conditional formatting rules, to have a format applied to it. For example, if chief operating officer Lori Penor wanted to highlight any Thursdays with higher-than-average weekday package volumes, she could define a conditional format that tests the value in the cell recording total sales and changes the format of the cell's contents when the condition is met.

To create a conditional format, you select the cells to which you want to apply the format, display the Home tab, and then in the Styles group, click Conditional Formatting to display a menu of possible conditional formats. In Excel, you can define conditional formats that change how the program displays data in cells that contain values above or below the average values of the related cells, that contain values near the top or bottom of the value range, or that contain values duplicated elsewhere in the selected range.

When you select which kind of condition to create, Excel opens a dialog box that contains fields and controls that you can use to define your rule. To display all of the rules for the selected cells, display the Home tab, and then in the Styles group, click Conditional Formatting. On the menu, click Manage Rules to display the Conditional Formatting Rules Manager dialog box.

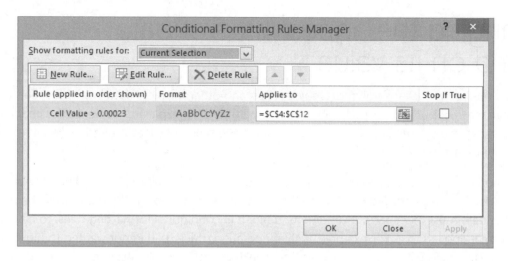

With the Conditional Formatting Rules Manager, you can control your conditional formats in the following ways:

- Create a new rule by clicking the **New Rule** button.

- Change a rule by clicking the rule and then clicking the **Edit Rule** button.

- Remove a rule by clicking the rule and then clicking the **Delete Rule** button.

- Move a rule up or down in the order by clicking the rule and then clicking the **Move Up** button or **Move Down** button.

- Control whether Excel continues evaluating conditional formats after it finds a rule to apply by selecting or clearing a rule's **Stop If True** check box.

- Save any new rules and close the **Conditional Formatting Rules Manager** by clicking **OK**.

- Save any new rules without closing the **Conditional Formatting Rules Manager** by clicking **Apply**.

- Discard any unsaved changes by clicking **Cancel**.

TIP Clicking the New Rule button in the Conditional Formatting Rules Manager opens the New Formatting Rule dialog box. The commands in the New Formatting Rule dialog box duplicate the options displayed when you click the Conditional Formatting button in the Styles group on the Home tab.

After you create a rule, you can change the format applied if the rule is true by clicking the rule and then clicking the Edit Rule button to display the Edit Formatting Rule dialog box.

In that dialog box, click the Format button to display the Format Cells dialog box. After you define your format, click OK to display the rule.

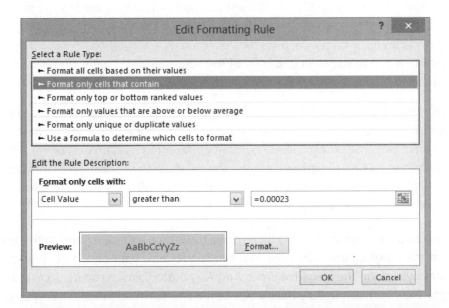

IMPORTANT Excel doesn't check to make sure that your conditions are logically consistent, so you need to be sure that you plan and enter your conditions correctly.

Using Excel, you can also create three other types of conditional formats: data bars, color scales, and icon sets. Data bars summarize the relative magnitude of values in a cell range by extending a band of color across the cell.

Distribution Capacity	
Northeast	47%
Atlantic	75%
Southeast	39%
North Central	54%
Midwest	40%
Southwest	73%
Mountain West	51%
Northwest	69%
Central	41%

You can create two types of data bars in Excel 2013: solid fill and gradient fill. When data bars were introduced in Excel 2007, they filled cells with a color band that decreased in intensity as it moved across the cell. This gradient fill pattern made it a bit difficult to determine the relative length of two data bars because the end points weren't as distinct as they would have been if the bars were a solid color. In Excel 2013, you can choose between a solid fill pattern, which makes the right edge of the bars easier to discern, and a gradient fill, which you can use if you share your workbook with colleagues who use Excel 2007.

Excel also draws data bars differently than was done in Excel 2007. Excel 2007 drew a very short data bar for the lowest value in a range and a very long data bar for the highest value. The problem was that similar values could be represented by data bars of very different lengths if there wasn't much variance among the values in the conditionally formatted range. In Excel 2013, data bars compare values based on their distance from zero, so similar values are summarized by using data bars of similar lengths.

TIP Excel 2013 data bars summarize negative values by using bars that extend to the left of a baseline that the program draws in a cell. You can control how your data bars summarize negative values by clicking the Negative Value And Axis button, which can be accessed from either the New Formatting Rule dialog box or the Edit Formatting Rule dialog box.

Color scales compare the relative magnitude of values in a cell range by applying colors from a two-color or three-color set to your cells. The intensity of a cell's color reflects the value's tendency toward the top or bottom of the values in the range.

Distribution Capacity	
Northeast	47%
Atlantic	75%
Southeast	39%
North Central	54%
Midwest	40%
Southwest	73%
Mountain West	51%
Northwest	69%
Central	41%

Icon sets are collections of three, four, or five images that Excel displays when certain rules are met.

Distribution Capacity		
Northeast	●	47%
Atlantic	●	75%
Southeast	●	39%
North Central	○	54%
Midwest	●	40%
Southwest	●	73%
Mountain West	○	51%
Northwest	●	69%
Central	●	41%

When icon sets were introduced in Excel 2007, you could apply an icon set as a whole, but you couldn't create custom icon sets or choose to have Excel 2007 display no icon if the value in a cell met a criterion. In Excel 2013, you can display any icon from any set for any criterion or display no icon.

When you click a color scale or icon set in the Conditional Formatting Rules Manager and then click the Edit Rule button, you can control when Excel applies a color or icon to your data.

IMPORTANT Be sure that you do not include cells that contain summary formulas in your conditionally formatted ranges. The values, which could be much higher or lower than your regular cell data, could throw off your comparisons.

In this exercise, you'll create a series of conditional formats to change the appearance of data in worksheet cells that display the package volume and delivery exception rates of a regional distribution center.

 SET UP **You need the Dashboard workbook located in the Chapter04 practice file folder to complete this exercise. Open the workbook, and then follow the steps.**

1   Select cells **C4:C12**.

2   On the **Home** tab, in the **Styles** group, click **Conditional Formatting**. On the menu, point to **Color Scales**, and then in the top row of the palette, click the second pattern from the left to apply the format to the selected range.

Package Exception Rate	
Northeast	0.003%
Atlantic	0.008%
Southeast	0.013%
North Central	0.004%
Midwest	0.018%
Southwest	0.001%
Mountain West	0.045%
Northwest	0.002%
Central	0.038%

3   Select cells **F4:F12**.

4   On the **Home** tab, in the **Styles** group, click **Conditional Formatting**. On the menu, point to **Data Bars**, and then, in the **Solid Fill** group, click the orange data bar format to apply the format to the selected range.

5   Select cells **I4:I12**.

6   On the **Home** tab, in the **Styles** group, click **Conditional Formatting**. On the menu, point to **Icon Sets**, and then in the left column of the list of formats, click the three traffic lights that have black borders to apply that format to the selected cells.

Distribution Capacity		
Northeast	●	47%
Atlantic	●	75%
Southeast	●	39%
North Central	○	54%
Midwest	●	40%
Southwest	●	73%
Mountain West	○	51%
Northwest	●	69%
Central	●	41%

7   With the range **I4:I12** still selected, on the **Home** tab, in the **Styles** group, click **Conditional Formatting**, and then click **Manage Rules** to open the **Conditional Formatting Rules Manager**.

8   Click the **Icon Set** rule, and then click **Edit Rule** to open the **Edit Formatting Rule** dialog box.

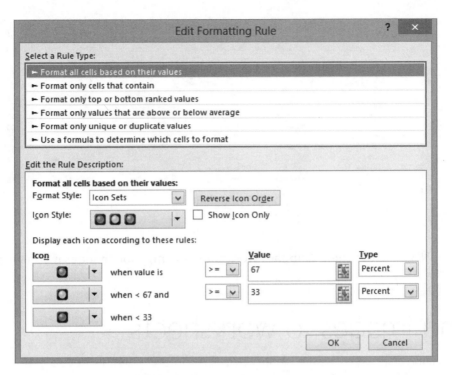

9   Click the **Reverse Icon Order** button to reconfigure the rules so the red light icon is at the top and the green light icon is at the bottom.

10   In the red light icon's row, in the **Type** list, click **Number**.

11   In the red light icon's **Value** field, enter 0.7.

12   In the yellow light icon's row, in the **Type** list, click **Number**.

13   In the yellow light icon **Value** field, enter 0.5.

14   Click **OK** twice to close the **Edit Formatting Rule** dialog box and the **Conditional Formatting Rules Manager** to apply the format to the selected cell range.

15   Click cell **C15**.

16   On the **Home** tab, in the **Styles** group, click **Conditional Formatting**. On the menu, point to **Highlight Cells Rules**, and then click **Less Than** to open the **Less Than** dialog box.

17   In the left field, enter 96%.

18   In the **With** list, click **Red text**.

19   Click **OK** to close the **Less Than** dialog box. Excel displays the text in cell **C15** in red.

▲	A	B	C	D	E	F	G	H	I	J
1										
2										
3		Package Exception Rate			Package Volume			Distribution Capacity		
4		Northeast	0.003%		Northeast	1,912,447		Northeast	◐	47%
5		Atlantic	0.008%		Atlantic	1,933,574		Atlantic	◐	75%
6		Southeast	0.013%		Southeast	1,333,292		Southeast	◐	39%
7		North Central	0.004%		North Central	1,811,459		North Central	○	54%
8		Midwest	0.018%		Midwest	1,140,803		Midwest	◐	40%
9		Southwest	0.001%		Southwest	1,911,884		Southwest	◐	73%
10		Mountain West	0.045%		Mountain West	1,787,293		Mountain West	○	51%
11		Northwest	0.002%		Northwest	1,631,350		Northwest	○	69%
12		Central	0.038%		Central	1,660,040		Central	◐	41%
13										
14										
15		Customer Satisfaction	88%							
16										

✖ CLEAN UP **Close the Dashboard workbook, saving your changes if you want to.**

Adding images to worksheets

Establishing a strong corporate identity helps customers remember your organization in addition to the products and services you offer. Setting aside the obvious need for sound management, two important physical attributes of a strong retail business are a well-conceived shop space and an eye-catching, easy-to-remember logo. After you or your graphic artist has created a logo, you should add the logo to all your documents, especially any that might be viewed by your customers. Not only does the logo mark the documents as coming from your company, it also serves as an advertisement, encouraging anyone who views your worksheets to call or visit your company.

One way to add a picture to a worksheet is to display the Insert tab, and then in the Illustrations group, click Picture. Clicking Picture displays the Insert Picture dialog box, from which you can locate the picture you want to add from your hard disk. When you insert a picture, the Format tool tab appears on the ribbon. You can use the tools on the Format tool tab to change the picture's contrast, brightness, and other attributes. With the controls in the Picture Styles group, you can place a border around the picture, change the picture's shape, or change a picture's effects (such as shadow, reflection, or three-dimensional effects). Other tools, found in the Arrange and Size groups, enable you to rotate, reposition, and resize the picture.

▲	A	B	C	D	E	F	G	H	I
1									
2		**Call Volume**							
3		Northeast	13,769						
4		Atlantic	19,511						
5		Southeast	11,111						
6		North Central	24,972						
7		Midwest	11,809						
8		Southwest	20,339						
9		Mountain West	20,127						
10		Northwest	12,137						
11		Central	20,047						
12									
13									

You can also resize a picture by clicking it and then dragging one of the handles that appears on the graphic. If you accidentally resize a graphic by dragging a handle, just click the Undo button to remove your change.

Excel 2013 includes a built-in capability that you can use to remove the background of an image you insert into a workbook. To do so, click the image and then, on the Format tool tab, in the Adjust group, click Remove Background. When you do, Excel attempts to identify the foreground and background of the image.

You can drag the handles on the inner square of the background removal tool to change how the tool analyzes the image. When you have adjusted the outline to identify the elements of the image you want to keep, click the Keep Changes button on the Background Removal tool tab to complete the operation.

If you want to generate a repeating image in the background of a worksheet to form a tiled pattern behind your worksheet's data, you can display the Page Layout tab, and then in the Page Setup group, click Background. In the Insert Pictures dialog box, click Browse to open the Sheet Background dialog box, navigate to the folder that contains the image you want to serve as the background for your worksheet, click the image, and click OK.

TIP To remove a background image from a worksheet, display the Page Layout tab, and then in the Page Setup group, click Delete Background.

To achieve a watermark-type effect that has words displayed behind the worksheet data, save the watermark information as an image, and then use the image as the sheet background; you could also insert the image in the header or footer, and then resize or scale it to position the watermark information where you want it.

In this exercise, you'll add an image to an existing worksheet, change its location on the worksheet, reduce the size of the image, and then set another image as a repeating background for the worksheet.

→ SET UP **You need the CallCenter workbook and the phone and texture images located in the Chapter04 practice file folder to complete this exercise. Open the workbook, and then follow the steps.**

1   On the **Insert** tab, in the **Illustrations** group, click **Pictures** to open the **Insert Picture** dialog box.

2   Navigate to the **Chapter04** practice file folder, and then double-click the **phone** image file to add the image to your worksheet.

3   On the **Format** tool tab, in the **Adjust** group, click **Remove Background** to have Excel attempt to separate the image's foreground from its background.

4   Drag the handles at the upper-left and lower-right corners of the outline until the entire phone, including the cord, is within the frame.

5   On the **Background Removal** tab, click **Keep Changes** to remove the highlighted image elements.

6   Move the image to the upper-left corner of the worksheet, click and hold the handle at the lower-right corner of the image, and drag it up and to the left until the image no longer obscures the **Call Volume** label.

	A	B	C	D
1				
2		**Call Volume**		
3		Northeast	13,769	
4		Atlantic	19,511	
5		Southeast	11,111	
6		North Central	24,972	
7		Midwest	11,809	
8		Southwest	20,339	
9		Mountain West	20,127	
10		Northwest	12,137	
11		Central	20,047	
12				

7   On the **Page Layout** tab, in the **Page Setup** group, click **Background** to open the **Insert Pictures** dialog box.

8   Next to **From a File**, click **Browse** to open the **Sheet Background** dialog box.

9   Navigate to the **Chapter04** practice file folder, and then double-click the **texture** image file to repeat the image as a background pattern.

▲	A	B	C	D
1				
2		**Call Volume**		
3		Northeast	13,769	
4		Atlantic	19,511	
5		Southeast	11,111	
6		North Central	24,972	
7		Midwest	11,809	
8		Southwest	20,339	
9		Mountain West	20,127	
10		Northwest	12,137	
11		Central	20,047	
12				

10 On the **Page Layout** tab, in the **Page Setup** group, click **Delete Background** to remove the background image.

❌ CLEAN UP **Close the CallCenter workbook, saving your changes if you want to.**

Key points

- If you don't like the default font in which Excel displays your data, you can change it.

- You can use cell formatting, including borders, alignment, and fill colors, to emphasize certain cells in your worksheets. This emphasis is particularly useful for making column and row labels stand out from the data.

- Excel comes with several existing styles that you can use to change the appearance of individual cells. You can also create new styles to make formatting your workbooks easier.

- If you want to apply the formatting from one cell to another cell, use the Format Painter to copy the format quickly.

- You can choose from quite a few built-in document themes and Excel table formats to apply to groups of cells. If you find one you like, use it and save yourself lots of formatting time.

- Using conditional formats, you can set rules so that Excel changes the appearance of a cell's contents based on its value.

- Adding images can make your worksheets more visually appealing and make your data easier to understand. Excel 2013 greatly enhances your ability to manage your images without leaving Excel.

4

Chapter at a glance

Restrict

Limit data that appears on your screen,
page 146

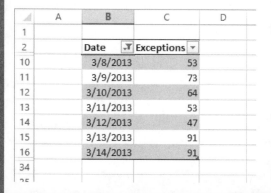

Filter

Filter Excel table data by using slicers,
page 153

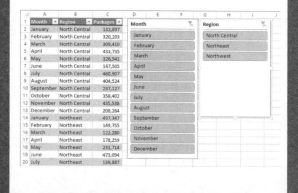

Manipulate

Manipulate worksheet data,
page 158

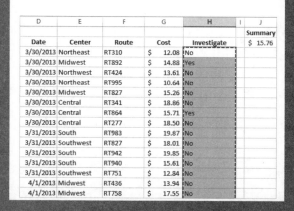

Define

Define valid sets of values for ranges of cells,
page 166

Focusing on specific data by using filters

5

IN THIS CHAPTER, YOU WILL LEARN HOW TO

- Limit data that appears on your screen.

- Filter Excel table data by using slicers.

- Manipulate worksheet data.

- Define valid sets of values for ranges of cells.

With Microsoft Excel 2013, you can manage huge data collections, but storing more than 1 million rows of data doesn't help you make business decisions unless you have the ability to focus on the most important data in a worksheet. Focusing on the most relevant data in a worksheet facilitates decision making, whether that data represents the 10 busiest days in a month or revenue streams that you might need to reevaluate. Excel offers a number of powerful and flexible tools with which you can limit the data displayed in your worksheet. When your worksheet displays the subset of data you need to make a decision, you can perform calculations on that data. You can discover what percentage of monthly revenue was earned in the 10 best days in the month, find your total revenue for particular days of the week, or locate the slowest business day of the month.

Just as you can limit the data displayed by your worksheets, you can create validation rules that limit the data entered into them as well. By setting rules for data entered into cells, you can catch many of the most common data entry errors, such as entering values that are too small or too large, or attempting to enter a word in a cell that requires a number. If you add a validation rule to worksheet cells after data has been entered into them, you can circle any invalid data so that you know what to correct.

In this chapter, you'll limit the data that appears on your screen, manipulate worksheet data, and create validation rules that limit data entry to appropriate values.

Limiting data that appears on your screen

Excel spreadsheets can hold as much data as you need them to, but you might not want to work with all the data in a worksheet at the same time. For example, you might want to review the revenue figures for your company during the first third, second third, and final third of a month. You can limit the data shown on a worksheet by creating a filter, which is a rule that selects rows to be shown in a worksheet.

To create a filter, you click a cell in the data you want to filter and then, on the Home tab, in the Editing group, click Sort & Filter and then click Filter. When you do, Excel displays a filter arrow at the right edge of the top cell in each column of the data. The arrow indicates that the Excel AutoFilter capability is active.

> **IMPORTANT** When you turn on filtering, Excel treats the cells in the active cell's column as a range. To ensure that the filtering works properly, you should always have a label at the top of the column you want to filter. If you don't, Excel treats the first value in the list as the label and doesn't include it in the list of values by which you can filter the data.

Clicking the filter arrow displays a menu of filtering options and a list of the unique values in the column. The first few commands in the list are sorting commands, followed by the Clear Filter command and then the Filter By Color command. The next command that appears in the list depends on the type of data in the column. For example, if the column contains a set of dates, the command will be Date Filters. Clicking the command displays a list of commands specific to that data type.

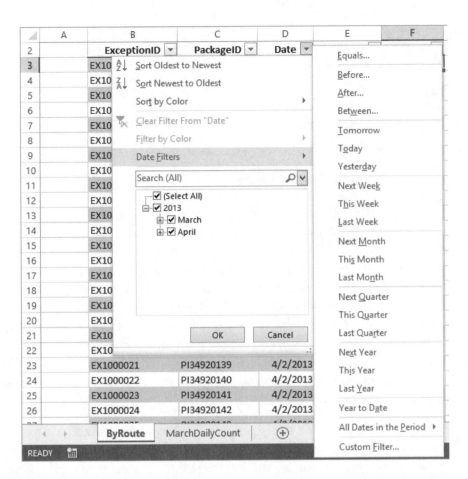

TIP When a column contains several types of data, the filter command becomes Number Filters.

When you click a filtering option, Excel displays a dialog box in which you can define the filter's criteria. As an example, you could create a filter that displays only dates after 3/31/2013.

	A	B	C	D	E	F
2		ExceptionID ▼	PackageID ▼	Date ▼	Center ▼	Route ▼
16		EX1000014	PI34920132	4/1/2013	Midwest	RT436
17		EX1000015	PI34920133	4/1/2013	Midwest	RT758
18		EX1000016	PI34920134	4/1/2013	Midwest	RT529
19		EX1000017	PI34920135	4/1/2013	Northeast	RT243
20		EX1000018	PI34920136	4/1/2013	Northeast	RT189
21		EX1000019	PI34920137	4/1/2013	Northwest	RT714
22		EX1000020	PI34920138	4/2/2013	Central	RT151
23		EX1000021	PI34920139	4/2/2013	Midwest	RT543
24		EX1000022	PI34920140	4/2/2013	Southwest	RT208
25		EX1000023	PI34920141	4/2/2013	South	RT145
26		EX1000024	PI34920142	4/2/2013	Central	RT250
27		EX1000025	PI34920143	4/2/2013	Midwest	RT852

If you want to display the highest or lowest values in a data column, you can create a Top 10 filter. Choosing the Top 10 command from the menu doesn't just limit the display to the top 10 values. Instead, it opens the Top 10 AutoFilter dialog box. From within this dialog box, you can choose whether to show values from the top or bottom of the list, define the number of items you want to display, and choose whether the number in the middle box indicates the number of items or the percentage of items to be shown when the filter is applied. By using the Top 10 AutoFilter dialog box, you can find your top 10 salespeople or identify the top 5 percent of your customers.

Excel 2013 includes a capability called the *search filter*, which you can use to type a search string that Excel uses to identify which items to display in an Excel table or a data list. To use a search filter, click a column's filter arrow and start entering a character string in the Search box. As you enter the character string, Excel limits the items displayed at the bottom of the filter panel to those that contain the character or characters you've entered. When the filter list's items represent the values you want to display, click OK.

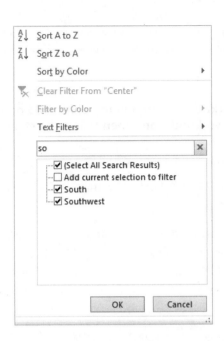

When you point to Text Filters (or Date Filters for date values or Number Filters for number values) and then click Custom Filter, you can define a rule that Excel uses to decide which rows to show after the filter is applied. For instance, you can create a rule that determines that only days with package volumes of less than 100,000 should be shown in your work-sheet. With those results in front of you, you might be able to determine whether the weather or another factor resulted in slower business on those days.

Excel indicates that a column has a filter applied by changing the appearance of the col-umn's filter arrow to include an icon that looks like a funnel. After you finish examining your data by using a filter, you can remove the filter by clicking the column's filter arrow and then clicking Clear Filter. To turn off filtering entirely and remove the filter arrows, dis-play the Home tab and then, in the Editing group, click Sort & Filter and then click Filter.

In this exercise, you'll filter worksheet data by using a series of AutoFilter commands, create a filter showing the five days with the highest delivery exception counts in a month, create a search filter, and create a custom filter.

SET UP You need the **PackageExceptions** workbook located in the Chapter05 practice file folder to complete this exercise. Open the workbook, and then follow the steps.

1   On the **ByRoute** worksheet, click any cell in the cell range **B2:F27**.

2   On the **Home** tab, in the **Editing** group, click **Sort & Filter**, and then click **Filter** to display a filter arrow in each column's header cell.

3   Click the **Date** column filter arrow and then, from the menu that appears, clear the **March** check box. When you do, Excel removes the check from the **March** check box and changes the state of the **Select All** and **2013** check boxes to indicate that some items within those categories have been filtered.

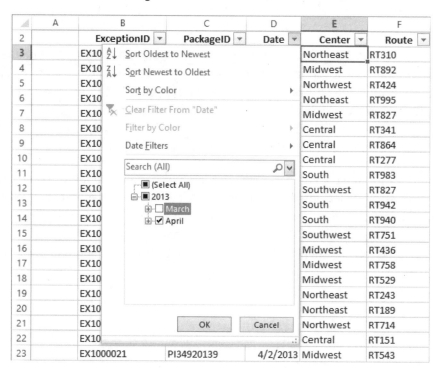

4   Click **OK** to hide all rows that contain a date from the month of March.

5   Click the **Center** column filter arrow and then, from the menu that appears, clear the **Select All** check box to clear all the check boxes in the list.

6   Select the **Midwest** check box, and then click **OK** to display only those exceptions that occurred in the Midwest distribution center during the month of April.

A	B	C	D	E	F
	ExceptionID ▼	PackageID ▼	Date ▾▼	Center ▾▼	Route ▼
	EX1000014	PI34920132	4/1/2013	Midwest	RT436
	EX1000015	PI34920133	4/1/2013	Midwest	RT758
	EX1000016	PI34920134	4/1/2013	Midwest	RT529
	EX1000021	PI34920139	4/2/2013	Midwest	RT543
	EX1000025	PI34920143	4/2/2013	Midwest	RT852

7   On the **Home** tab, in the **Editing** group, click **Sort & Filter**, and then click **Clear** to clear all active filters but leave the filter arrows in place.

8   Click the **Route** column header's filter arrow, and then enter **RT9** in the **Search** box to narrow the filter list so it displays only those routes with an identifier that includes the characters *RT9*.

9   Click **OK** to apply the filter and display exceptions that occurred on routes with identifiers that contain the string *RT9*.

10   Click the **MarchDailyCount** sheet tab to display its worksheet.

11   Click any cell in the Excel table.

12   Click the **Exceptions** column filter arrow, point to **Number Filters**, and then click **Top 10** to open the **Top 10 AutoFilter** dialog box.

13 In the middle field, enter **5** and then click **OK** to display the table rows that contain the five highest values in the **Exceptions** column.

◢	A	B	C	D
1				
2		Date ▾	Exceptions ⫧	
18		3/16/2013	144	
21		3/19/2013	128	
22		3/20/2013	144	
23		3/21/2013	138	
24		3/22/2013	137	
34				

14 Click the **Exceptions** column filter arrow, and then click **Clear Filter from "Exceptions"** to remove the filter.

15 Click the **Date** column filter arrow, point to **Date Filters**, and then click **Custom Filter** to open the **Custom AutoFilter** dialog box.

16 In the upper-left list, click **is after or equal to**.

17 In the upper-right list, click **3/8/2013**.

18 In the lower-left list, click **is before or equal to**.

19 In the lower-right list, click **3/14/2013**.

20 Click **OK**. Because you left the **And** option selected, Excel displays all table rows that contain a date from 3/8/2013 to 3/14/2013, inclusive.

◢	A	B	C	D
1				
2		Date ⫧	Exceptions ▾	
10		3/8/2013	53	
11		3/9/2013	73	
12		3/10/2013	64	
13		3/11/2013	53	
14		3/12/2013	47	
15		3/13/2013	91	
16		3/14/2013	91	
34				
35				

21   On the **Quick Access Toolbar**, click the **Undo** button to remove your filter and restore the table to its unfiltered state.

✖ CLEAN UP Close the PackageExceptions workbook, saving your changes if you want to.

Filtering Excel table data by using slicers

In versions of Excel prior to Excel 2013, the only visual indication that you have applied a filter to an Excel table column is the indicator added to a column's filter arrow. The indicator lets users know that there is an active filter applied to that column but provides no information about which values are displayed and which are hidden. Beginning with Excel 2010, you could use slicers to provide a visual indication of which items are currently displayed or hidden in a PivotTable. Excel 2013 extends that ability to filtering an Excel table.

To create a slicer, click any cell in an Excel table and then, on the Insert tab, in the Filters group, click Slicer to display the Insert Slicers dialog box.

Select the check box next to the columns for which you want to create a slicer, and click OK. When you do, Excel displays a slicer for each column you identified.

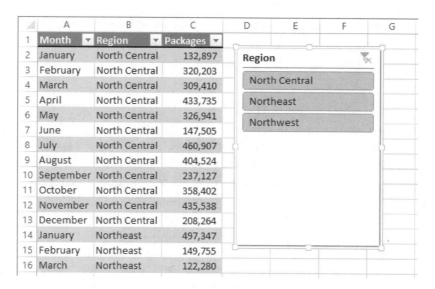

TIP If you have already applied a filter to the column for which you display a slicer, the slicer reflects the filter's result.

A slicer displays the values within the Excel table column you identified. Any value displayed in color (or gray if you select a gray-and-white color scheme) appears within the table. Values displayed in light gray or white do not appear in the table.

Clicking an item in a slicer changes that item's state—if a value is currently displayed in a table, clicking the value hides it. If it's hidden, clicking its value in the slicer displays it in the table. As with other objects in an Excel workbook, you can use the Shift and Ctrl keys to help define your selections. For example, suppose you create a slicer for the Month column while every month is displayed.

If you want to hide every month except January, February, and March, you click the January item to hide every month except January. Then hold down the Shift key and click March to have Excel display just the data for the months of January, February, and March. You can then add another month, such as July, to the filter by holding down the Ctrl key and clicking July in the slicer.

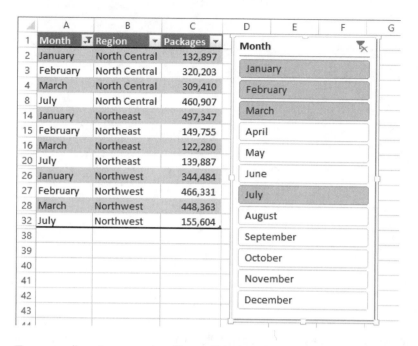

	A	B	C	D	E	F	G
1	Month	Region	Packages				
2	January	North Central	132,897				
3	February	North Central	320,203				
4	March	North Central	309,410				
8	July	North Central	460,907				
14	January	Northeast	497,347				
15	February	Northeast	149,755				
16	March	Northeast	122,280				
20	July	Northeast	139,887				
26	January	Northwest	344,484				
27	February	Northwest	466,331				
28	March	Northwest	448,363				
32	July	Northwest	155,604				
38							
39							
40							
41							
42							
43							

Month slicer: January, February, March, April, May, June, July, August, September, October, November, December

To use a slicer to remove a filter, click the Clear Filter button in the upper-right corner of the slicer. If you want to resize a slicer, you can do so by dragging the resize handle in the lower-right corner of the slicer. To delete the slicer, right-click its title bar and then click the menu command that starts with the word *Remove*. For example, the Month column's menu command would be Remove Month.

TIP You can change a slicer's formatting by clicking the slicer and then, on the Slicer Tools Options tool tab, clicking a style in the Slicer Styles gallery.

In this exercise, you'll filter the contents of an Excel table by using a slicer.

 SET UP **You need the Slicers workbook located in the Chapter05 practice file folder to complete this exercise. Open the workbook, and then follow the steps.**

1 Click any cell in the Excel table.

2 On the **Insert** tab of the ribbon, click the **Slicer** button to display the **Insert Slicers** dialog box.

3   Select the **Month** and **Region** check boxes, and then click **OK** to add slicers for the **Month** and **Region** columns.

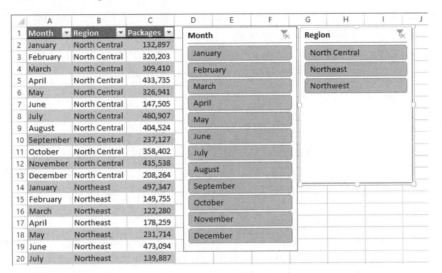

4   In the **Month** slicer, click the **January** item and then, holding down the **Shift** key, click the **April** item. Excel updates your table to display values for the months of January, February, March, and April.

5   In the **Region** slicer, click the **North Central** item and then, holding down the **Ctrl** key, click the **Northwest** item. Excel updates your table to display values for the North Central and Northwest regions.

6   Right-click the **Region** slicer and then click **Remove "Region"** to delete it. Excel deletes the slicer and removes its filter from the table.

7   In the **Month** slicer, click the **June** item to display results for the month of June.

8   In the **Month** slicer, click the **Clear Filter** button to remove the filter and display the entire table.

9   Right-click the **Month** slicer and then click **Remove "Month"** to delete it.

✖ CLEAN UP **Close the Slicers workbook, saving your changes if you want to.**

Manipulating worksheet data

Excel offers a wide range of tools you can use to summarize worksheet data. This section shows you how to select rows at random by using the *RAND* and *RANDBETWEEN* functions, how to summarize worksheet data by using the *SUBTOTAL* and *AGGREGATE* functions, and how to display a list of unique values within a data set.

Selecting list rows at random

In addition to filtering the data that is stored in your Excel worksheets, you can choose rows at random from a list. Selecting rows randomly is useful for choosing which customers will receive a special offer, deciding which days of the month to audit, or picking prize winners at an employee party.

To choose rows randomly, you can use the *RAND* function, which generates a random value between 0 and 1, and compare the value it returns with a test value included in the formula. As an example, suppose Consolidated Messenger wanted to offer approximately 30 percent of its customers a discount on their next shipment. A formula that returns a *TRUE* value 30 percent of the time would be *RAND<=0.3*; that is, whenever the random value was between 0 and 0.3, the result would be *TRUE*. You could use this formula to select each row in a list with a probability of 30 percent. A formula that displays *TRUE* when the value is equal to or less than 30 percent, and *FALSE* otherwise, would be =*IF(RAND()<=0.3,"True","False")*.

If you recalculate this formula 10 times, it's very unlikely that exactly three *TRUE* results and seven *FALSE* results would occur. Just as flipping a coin can result in the same result 10 times in a row by chance, so can the *RAND* function's results appear to be off if you only recalculate it a few times. However, if you were to recalculate the function 10,000 times, it is extremely likely that the number of *TRUE* results would be very close to 30 percent.

TIP Because the *RAND* function is a volatile function (it recalculates its results every time you update the worksheet), you should copy the cells that contain the *RAND* function in a formula and paste the formulas' values back into their original cells. To do so, select the cells that contain the *RAND* formulas and press Ctrl+C to copy the cell's contents. Then, on the Home tab, in the Clipboard group, in the Paste list, click Paste Values to replace the formula with its current result. If you don't replace the formulas with their results, you will never have a permanent record of which rows were selected.

The *RANDBETWEEN* function generates a random whole number within a defined range. For example, the formula *=RANDBETWEEN(1,100)* would generate a random integer value from 1 to 100, inclusive. The *RANDBETWEEN* function is very useful for creating sample data collections for presentations. Before the *RANDBETWEEN* function was introduced, you had to create formulas that added, subtracted, multiplied, and divided the results of the *RAND* function, which are always decimal values between 0 and 1, to create your data.

Summarizing worksheets by using hidden and filtered rows

The ability to analyze the data that's most vital to your current needs is important, but there are some limitations to how you can summarize your filtered data by using functions such as *SUM* and *AVERAGE*. One limitation is that any formulas you create that include the *SUM* and *AVERAGE* functions don't change their calculations if some of the rows used in the formula are hidden by the filter.

Excel provides two ways to summarize just the visible cells in a filtered data list. The first method is to use AutoCalculate. To use AutoCalculate, you select the cells you want to summarize. When you do, Excel displays the average of the values in the cells, the sum of the values in the cells, and the number of visible cells (the count) in the selection. You'll find the display on the status bar at the lower edge of the Excel window.

When you use AutoCalculate, you aren't limited to finding the sum, average, and count of the selected cells. To display the other functions you can use, right-click the status bar and select the function you want from the shortcut menu. If a check mark appears next to a function's name, that function's result appears on the status bar. Clicking a selected function name removes that function from the status bar.

AutoCalculate is great for finding a quick total or average for filtered cells, but it doesn't make the result available in the worksheet. Formulas such as *=SUM(C3:C26)* always consider every cell in the range, regardless of whether you hide a cell's row by right-clicking the row's header and then clicking Hide, so you need to create a formula by using either the *SUBTOTAL* function or the *AGGREGATE* function to summarize just those values that are visible in your worksheet. With the *SUBTOTAL* function, you can summarize every value in a range or summarize only those values in rows you haven't manually hidden. The *SUBTOTAL* function has this syntax: *SUBTOTAL(function_num, ref1, ref2, ...)*. The *function_num* argument holds the number of the operation you want to use to summarize your data. (The operation numbers are summarized in a table later in this section.) The *ref1*, *ref2*, and further arguments represent up to 29 ranges to include in the calculation.

As an example, assume you have a worksheet where you hid rows 20 through 26 manually. In this case, the formula *=SUBTOTAL(9, C3:C26, E3:E26, G3:G26)* would find the sum of all values in the ranges C3:C26, E3:E26, and G3:G26, regardless of whether that range contained any hidden rows. The formula *=SUBTOTAL(109, C3:C26, E3:E26, G3:G26)* would find the sum of all values in cells C3:C19, E3:E19, and G3:G19, ignoring the values in the manually hidden rows.

> **IMPORTANT** Be sure to place your *SUBTOTAL* formula in a row that is even with or above the headers in the range you're filtering. If you don't, your filter might hide the formula's result!

The following table lists the summary operations available for the *SUBTOTAL* formula. Excel displays the available summary operations as part of the Formula AutoComplete functionality, so you don't need to remember the operation numbers or look them up in the Help system.

Operation number (includes hidden values)	Operation number (ignores values in manually hidden rows)	Function	Description
1	101	AVERAGE	Returns the average of the values in the range
2	102	COUNT	Counts the cells in the range that contain a number
3	103	COUNTA	Counts the nonblank cells in the range
4	104	MAX	Returns the largest (maximum) value in the range
5	105	MIN	Returns the smallest (minimum) value in the range
6	106	PRODUCT	Returns the result of multiplying all numbers in the range

Operation number (includes hidden values)	Operation number (ignores values in manually hidden rows)	Function	Description
7	107	STDEV.S	Calculates the standard deviation of the values in the range by examining a sample of the values
8	108	STDEV.P	Calculates the standard deviation of the values in the range by using all the values
9	109	SUM	Returns the result of adding all numbers in the range together
10	110	VAR.S	Calculates the variance of the values in the range by examining a sample of the values
11	111	VAR.P	Calculates the variance of the values in the range by using all of the values

As the previous table shows, the *SUBTOTAL* function has two sets of operations. The first set (operations 1 through 11) represents operations that include hidden values in their summary, and the second set (operations 101 through 111) represents operations that summarize only values visible in the worksheet. Operations 1 through 11 summarize all cells in a range, regardless of whether the range contains any manually hidden rows. By contrast, operations 101 through 111 ignore any values in manually hidden rows. What the *SUBTOTAL* function doesn't do, however, is change its result to reflect rows hidden by using a filter.

The *AGGREGATE* function extends the capabilities of the *SUBTOTAL* function. With it, you can select from a broader range of functions and use another argument to determine which, if any, values to ignore in the calculation. *AGGREGATE* has two possible syntaxes, depending on the summary operation you select. The first syntax is *=AGGREGATE(function_num, options, ref1…)*, which is similar to the syntax of the *SUBTOTAL* function. The other possible syntax, *=AGGREGATE(function_num, options, array, [k])*, is used to create *AGGREGATE* functions that use the *LARGE, SMALL, PERCENTILE.INC, QUARTILE.INC, PERCENTILE.EXC,* and *QUARTILE.EXC* operations.

The following table summarizes the summary operations available for use in the *AGGREGATE* function.

Number	Function	Description
1	AVERAGE	Returns the average of the values in the range.
2	COUNT	Counts the cells in the range that contain a number.
3	COUNTA	Counts the nonblank cells in the range.
4	MAX	Returns the largest (maximum) value in the range.
5	MIN	Returns the smallest (minimum) value in the range.
6	PRODUCT	Returns the result of multiplying all numbers in the range.
7	STDEV.S	Calculates the standard deviation of the values in the range by examining a sample of the values.
8	STDEV.P	Calculates the standard deviation of the values in the range by using all the values.
9	SUM	Returns the result of adding all numbers in the range together.
10	VAR.S	Calculates the variance of the values in the range by examining a sample of the values.
11	VAR.P	Calculates the variance of the values in the range by using all of the values.
12	MEDIAN	Returns the value in the middle of a group of values.
13	MODE.SNGL	Returns the most frequently occurring number from a group of numbers.
14	LARGE	Returns the k-th largest value in a data set; k is specified by using the last function argument. If k is left blank, Excel returns the largest value.
15	SMALL	Returns the k-th smallest value in a data set; k is specified by using the last function argument. If k is left blank, Excel returns the smallest value.
16	PERCENTILE.INC	Returns the k-th percentile of values in a range, where k is a value from 0 to 1, inclusive.

Number	Function	Description
17	QUARTILE.INC	Returns the quartile value of a data set, based on a percentage from 0 to 1, inclusive.
18	PERCENTILE.EXC	Returns the k-th percentile of values in a range, where k is a value from 0 to 1, exclusive.
19	QUARTILE.EXC	Returns the quartile value of a data set, based on a percentage from 0 to 1, exclusive.

With the second argument, *options*, you can select which items the *AGGREGATE* function should ignore. These items can include hidden rows, errors, and *SUBTOTAL* and *AGGREGATE* functions. The following table summarizes the values available for the *options* argument and the effect they have on the function's results.

Number	Description
0	Ignore nested *SUBTOTAL* and *AGGREGATE* functions
1	Ignore hidden rows and nested *SUBTOTAL* and *AGGREGATE* functions
2	Ignore error values and nested *SUBTOTAL* and *AGGREGATE* functions
3	Ignore hidden rows, error values, and nested *SUBTOTAL* and *AGGREGATE* functions
4	Ignore nothing
5	Ignore hidden rows
6	Ignore error values
7	Ignore hidden rows and error values

Finding unique values within a data set

Summarizing numerical values can provide valuable information that helps you run your business. It can also be helpful to know how many different values appear within a column. For example, you might want to display all of the countries in which Consolidated Messenger has customers. If you want to display a list of the unique values in a column, click any cell in the data set, display the Data tab and then, in the Sort & Filter group, click Advanced to display the Advanced Filter dialog box.

In the List Range field, enter the reference of the cell range you want to examine for unique values, select the Unique Records Only check box, and then click OK to have Excel display the row that contains the first occurrence of each value in the column.

> **IMPORTANT** Excel treats the first cell in the data range as a header cell, so it doesn't consider the cell as it builds the list of unique values. Be sure to include the header cell in your data range!

In this exercise, you'll select random rows from a list of exceptions to identify package delivery misadventures to investigate, create an *AGGREGATE* formula to summarize the visible cells in a filtered worksheet, and find the unique values in one column of data.

 SET UP **You need the ForFollowUp workbook located in the Chapter05 practice file folder to complete this exercise. Open the workbook, and then follow the steps.**

1   Select cells **G3:G27**. When you do, the average of the values in the selected cells, the number of cells selected, and the total of the values in the selected cells appear in the **AutoCalculate** area of the status bar.

2   In cell **J2**, enter the formula **=AGGREGATE(1,1,G3:G27)**. The value *$15.76* appears in cell **J2**.

3   On the **Data** tab, in the **Sort & Filter** group, click **Advanced** to open the **Advanced Filter** dialog box.

4   In the **List range** field, enter **E2:E27**.

5   Select the **Unique records only** check box, and then click **OK** to display the rows that contain the first occurrence of each different value in the selected range.

> **TIP** Remember that you must include cell E2, the header cell, in the List Range field so that the filter doesn't display two occurrences of Northeast in the unique values list. To test what happens when you don't include the header cell, try changing the range in the List Range field to E3:E27, selecting the Unique Records Only check box, and clicking OK.

	B	C	D	E	F	G	H	I	J	K
2	ExceptionID	PackageID	Date	Center	Route	Cost	Investigate		$ 15.76	
3	EX1000001	PI34920119	3/30/2013	Northeast	RT310	$ 12.08				
4	EX1000002	PI34920120	3/30/2013	Midwest	RT892	$ 14.88				
5	EX1000003	PI34920121	3/30/2013	Northwest	RT424	$ 13.61				
8	EX1000006	PI34920124	3/30/2013	Central	RT341	$ 18.86				
11	EX1000009	PI34920127	3/31/2013	South	RT983	$ 19.87				
12	EX1000010	PI34920128	3/31/2013	Southwest	RT827	$ 18.01				
28										

6   On the **Data** tab, in the **Sort & Filter** group, click **Clear** to remove the filter.

7   In cell **H3**, enter the formula **=IF(RAND()<0.15,"Yes","No")**, and press **Enter**. A value of *Yes* or *No* appears in cell **H3**, depending on the *RAND* function result.

8   Select cell **H3**, and then drag the fill handle down until it covers cell **H27** to copy the formula into every cell in the range **H3:H27**.

9   With the range **H3:H27** still selected, on the **Home** tab, in the **Clipboard** group, click the **Copy** button. Excel copies the cell range's contents to the Microsoft Office Clipboard.

10   Click the **Paste** arrow, and then in the **Paste** gallery that appears, click the first icon in the **Paste Values** group to replace the cells' formulas with the formulas' current results.

D	E	F	G	H	I	J
						Summary
Date	**Center**	**Route**	**Cost**	**Investigate**		$ 15.76
3/30/2013	Northeast	RT310	$ 12.08	No		
3/30/2013	Midwest	RT892	$ 14.88	Yes		
3/30/2013	Northwest	RT424	$ 13.61	No		
3/30/2013	Northeast	RT995	$ 10.64	No		
3/30/2013	Midwest	RT827	$ 15.26	No		
3/30/2013	Central	RT341	$ 18.86	No		
3/30/2013	Central	RT864	$ 15.71	Yes		
3/30/2013	Central	RT277	$ 18.50	No		
3/31/2013	South	RT983	$ 19.87	No		
3/31/2013	Southwest	RT827	$ 18.01	No		
3/31/2013	South	RT942	$ 19.85	No		
3/31/2013	South	RT940	$ 15.61	No		
3/31/2013	Southwest	RT751	$ 12.84	No		
4/1/2013	Midwest	RT436	$ 13.94	No		
4/1/2013	Midwest	RT758	$ 17.55	No		

✖ CLEAN UP Close the ForFollowUp workbook, saving your changes if you want to.

Defining valid sets of values for ranges of cells

Part of creating efficient and easy-to-use worksheets is to do what you can to ensure the data entered into your worksheets is as accurate as possible. Although it isn't possible to catch every typographical or transcription error, you can set up a validation rule to make sure that the data entered into a cell meets certain standards.

To create a validation rule, display the Data tab on the ribbon and then, in the Data Tools group, click the Data Validation button to open the Data Validation dialog box. You can use the controls in the Data Validation dialog box to define the type of data that Excel should allow in the cell and then, depending on the data type you choose, to set the conditions data must meet to be accepted in the cell. For example, you can set the conditions so that Excel knows to look for a whole number value between 1,000 and 2,000.

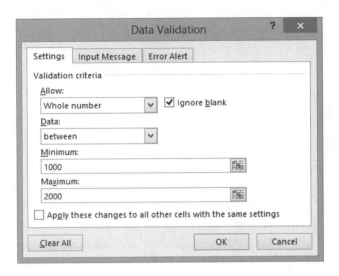

Setting accurate validation rules can help you and your colleagues avoid entering a customer's name in the cell designated to hold the phone number or setting a credit limit above a certain level. To require a user to enter a numeric value in a cell, display the Settings page of the Data Validation dialog box, and, depending on your needs, choose either Whole Number or Decimal from the Allow list.

If you want to set the same validation rule for a group of cells, you can do so by selecting the cells to which you want to apply the rule (such as a column in which you enter the credit limit of customers of Consolidated Messenger) and setting the rule by using the Data Validation dialog box. One important fact you should keep in mind is that, with Excel, you can create validation rules for cells in which you have already entered data. Excel doesn't tell you whether any of those cells contain data that violates your rule at the moment you create the rule, but you can find out by having Excel circle any worksheet cells containing data that violates the cell's validation rule. To do so, display the Data tab and then, in the Data Tools group, click the Data Validation arrow. On the menu, click the Circle Invalid Data button to circle cells with invalid data.

	A	B	C	D
1				
2		Date	Exceptions	
3		3/1/2013	73	
4		3/2/2013	89	
5		3/3/2013	47	
6		3/4/2013	109	
7		3/5/2013	115	
8		3/6/2013	109	
9		3/7/2013	118	
10		3/8/2013	53	
11		3/9/2013	73	
12		3/10/2013	64	

When you're ready to hide the circles, in the Data Validation list, click Clear Validation Circles.

Of course, it's frustrating if you want to enter data into a cell and, when a message box appears that tells you the data you tried to enter isn't acceptable, you aren't given the rules you need to follow. With Excel, you can create a message that tells the user which values are expected before the data is entered and then, if the conditions aren't met, reiterate the conditions in a custom error message.

You can turn off data validation in a cell by displaying the Settings page of the Data Validation dialog box and clicking the Clear All button in the lower-left corner of the dialog box.

In this exercise, you'll create a data validation rule that limits the credit line of Consolidated Messenger customers to $25,000, add an input message mentioning the limitation, and then create an error message if someone enters a value greater than $25,000. After you create your rule and messages, you'll test them.

 **SET UP** You need the Credit workbook located in the Chapter05 practice file folder to complete this exercise. Open the workbook, and then follow the steps.

1 Select the cell range **J4:J7**. Note that cell **J7** is currently blank; you will add a value to it later in this exercise.

2 On the **Data** tab, in the **Data Tools** group, click **Data Validation** to open the **Data Validation** dialog box, which displays the **Settings** page.

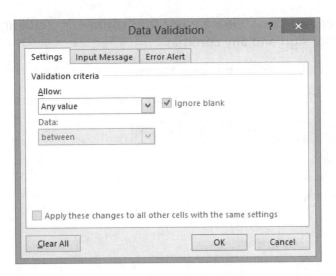

3   In the **Allow** list, click **Whole Number**. Boxes labeled **Minimum** and **Maximum** appear below the **Data** box.

4   In the **Data** list, click **less than or equal to** remove the **Minimum** box.

5   In the **Maximum** box, enter 25000.

6   Clear the **Ignore blank** check box.

7   Click the **Input Message** tab to display the **Input Message** page.

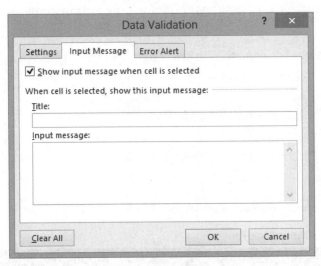

8   In the **Title** box, enter Enter Limit.

9   In the **Input Message** box, enter **Please enter the customer's credit limit, omitting the dollar sign and any commas.**

10   Click the **Error Alert** tab to display the **Error Alert** page.

11   In the **Style** list, click **Stop** to change the icon that appears on your message box.

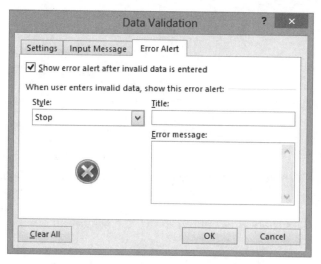

12   In the **Title** box, enter **Error**, and then click **OK**.

13   Click cell **J7**. When you do, a ScreenTip with the title *Enter Limit* and the text *Please enter the customer's credit limit, omitting the dollar sign and any commas* appears near cell **J7**.

14   Enter **25001**, and press **Enter**. A stop box with the title **Error** opens. Leaving the **Error message** box blank in step 12 causes Excel to use its default message.

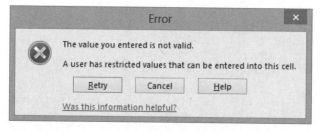

15   Click **Cancel** to close the error box.

> **IMPORTANT** By clicking Retry, you can edit the bad value, whereas clicking Cancel deletes the entry.

16   Click cell **J7** to make it the active cell and display the ScreenTip.

17   Enter **25000**, and press **Enter**.

18   On the **Data** tab, in the **Data Tools** group, click the **Data Validation** arrow and then, in the list, click **Circle Invalid Data**. A red circle appears around the value in cell **J4**.

E	F	G	H	I	J
Address	**City**	**State**	**ZIP**	**Phone**	**Limit**
11020 Microsoft Way	Redmond	WA	98073	(425) 555-1001	$ 26,000.00
1480 Microsoft Way	Redmond	WA	98073	(425) 555-1098	$ 7,500.00
891A Microsoft Way	Redmond	WA	98073	(425) 555-1287	$ 15,000.00
					$ 25,000.00

19   In the **Data Validation** list, click **Clear Validation Circles** to remove the red circle from around the value in cell **J4**.

✖ CLEAN UP Close the Credit workbook, saving your changes if you want to.

Key points

- A number of filters are defined in Excel. (You might find that the one you want is already available.)

- Filtering an Excel worksheet based on values in a single column is easy to do, but you can create a custom filter to limit your data based on the values in more than one column as well.

- With the search filter capability, you can limit the data in your worksheets based on characters the terms contain.

- Don't forget that you can get a running total (or an average, or any one of several other summary operations) for the values in a group of cells. Just select the cells and look on the status bar: the result will be there.

- Use data validation techniques to improve the accuracy of data entered into your worksheets and to identify data that doesn't meet the guidelines you set.

Chapter at a glance

Sort

Sort worksheet data,
page 174

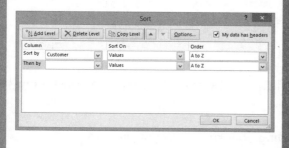

Customize

Sort data by using custom lists,
page 179

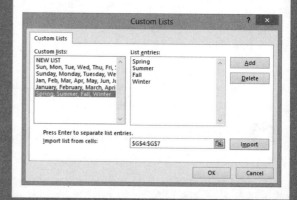

Organize

Organize data into levels,
page 183

Find

Look up information in a worksheet,
page 189

Reordering and summarizing data

6

IN THIS CHAPTER, YOU WILL LEARN HOW TO

- Sort worksheet data.

- Sort data by using custom lists.

- Organize data into levels.

- Look up information in a worksheet.

Most of the time, when you enter data in a Microsoft Excel worksheet, you will enter it in chronological order. For example, you could enter hourly shipment data in a worksheet, starting with the first hour of the day and ending with the last hour. The data would naturally be displayed in the order you entered it, but that might not always be the best arrangement to answer your questions. For instance, you might want to sort your data so that the top row in your worksheet shows the day of the month with the highest package volume, with subsequent rows displaying the remaining days in decreasing order of package volumes handled. You can also sort data based on the contents of more than one column. A good example is sorting package handling data by week, day, and then hour of the day.

After you have sorted your data into the order you want, you can find partial totals, or subtotals, for groups of cells within a given range. Yes, you can create formulas to find the sum, average, or standard deviation of data in a cell range, but you can do the same thing much more quickly by having Excel calculate the total for rows that have the same value in one of their columns. For example, if your worksheet holds sales data for a list of services, you can calculate subtotals for each product category.

When you calculate subtotals in a worksheet, Excel creates an outline that marks the cell ranges used in each subtotal. For example, if the first 10 rows of a worksheet contain overnight shipping data, and the second 10 rows contain second-day shipping data, Excel divides the rows into two units. You can use the markers on the worksheet to hide or display the rows used to calculate a subtotal; in this case, you can hide all the rows that contain overnight shipping data, hide all the rows that contain second-day shipping data, hide both, or show both.

Excel also has a capability you might expect to find only in a database program—you can enter a value in a cell and have Excel look in a named range to find a corresponding value. For instance, you can have a two-column named range with one column displaying customer identification numbers and the second column displaying the name of the company assigned each number. When you use a VLOOKUP formula that references the named range, colleagues using your workbook can enter a customer identification number in a cell and have the name of the corresponding company appear in the cell that has the formula.

In this chapter, you'll sort your data by using one or more criteria, calculate subtotals, organize your data into levels, and look up information in a worksheet.

PRACTICE FILES To complete the exercises in this chapter, you need the practice files contained in the Chapter06 practice file folder. For more information, see "Download the practice files" in this book's Introduction.

Sorting worksheet data

Although Excel makes it easy to enter your business data and to manage it after you've saved it in a worksheet, unsorted data will rarely answer every question you want to ask it. For example, you might want to discover which of your services generates the most profits or which service costs the most for you to provide. You can discover that information by sorting your data.

When you sort data in a worksheet, you rearrange the worksheet rows based on the contents of cells in a particular column or set of columns. For instance, you can sort a worksheet to find your highest-revenue services.

You can sort a group of rows in a worksheet in a number of ways, but the first step is to identify the column that will provide the values by which the rows should be sorted. In the revenue example, you could find the highest revenue totals by sorting on the cells in the Revenue column. First you would select the cells in the Revenue column and display the

Home tab. Then, in the Editing group, in the Sort & Filter list, click Sort Largest To Smallest. Clicking Sort Largest To Smallest makes Excel put the row with the highest value in the Revenue column at the top of the worksheet and continue down to the lowest value.

⁄	A	B	C	D
1				
2		Service	Revenue	
3		Overnight	$ 1,598,643	
4		3Day	$ 1,000,142	
5		Ground	$ 994,775	
6		2Day	$ 745,600	
7		Priority Overnigh	$ 502,991	
8				
9				

If you want to sort the rows in the opposite order, from the lowest revenue to the highest, select the cells in the Revenue column and then, in the Sort & Filter list, click Sort Smallest To Largest.

TIP The exact set of values that appears in the Sort & Filter list changes to reflect the data in your column. If your column contains numerical values, you'll find the options Sort Largest To Smallest, Sort Smallest To Largest, and Custom List. If your column contains text values, the options are Sort A To Z (ascending order), Sort Z To A (descending order), and Custom List. And if your column contains dates, the options are Sort Newest To Oldest, Sort Oldest To Newest, and Custom List.

By using the Sort Smallest To Largest and Sort Largest To Smallest options, you can sort rows in a worksheet quickly, but you can use these options only to sort the worksheet based on the contents of one column, even though you might want to sort by two columns. For example, you might want to order the worksheet rows by service category and then by total so that you can display the customers that use each service category most frequently. You can sort rows in a worksheet by the contents of more than one column by using the Sort dialog box, in which you can pick any number of columns to use as sort criteria and choose whether to sort the rows in ascending or descending order.

6

To open the Sort dialog box, click Custom Sort in the Sort & Filter list.

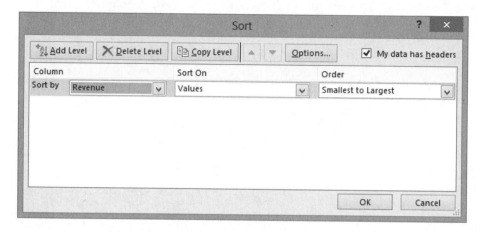

If your data has a header row, select the My Data Has Headers check box so the column headers will appear in the Sort By list. After you identify the column by which you want to sort, you can use the options in the Sort On list to select whether you want to sort by a cell's value (the default), a cell's fill color, a cell's font color, or an icon displayed in the cell.

SEE ALSO For more information about creating conditional formats that change a cell's formatting or display an icon to reflect the cell's value, see "Changing the appearance of data based on its value" in Chapter 4, "Changing workbook appearance."

Finally, from the Order list, you can select how you want Excel to sort the column values. As with the Sort & Filter button's list, the exact values that appear in the Order list change to reflect the data to be sorted.

Adding, moving, copying, and deleting sorting levels are a matter of clicking the appropriate button in the Sort dialog box. To add a second level to your sort, click the Add Level button.

TIP In Excel 2003 and earlier versions of the program, you could define a maximum of three sorting levels. Beginning with Excel 2007, you can create up to 64 sorting levels.

To delete a level, click the level in the list, and then click Delete Level. By clicking the Copy Level button, you can put all the settings from one rule into another, saving yourself some work if you need to change only one item. By clicking the Move Up and Move Down buttons, which display an upward-pointing arrow and a downward-pointing arrow, respectively, you can change a sorting level's position in the order. Finally, clicking the Options button opens the Sort Options dialog box, which you can use to make a sorting level case sensitive and to change the orientation of the sort.

In this exercise, you'll sort worksheet data, sort by multiple criteria, change the order in which sorting criteria are applied, and sort data by color.

SET UP You need the ShippingSummary workbook located in the Chapter06 practice file folder to complete this exercise. Open the workbook, and then follow the steps.

1   Click cell **C3**. On the **Home** tab, in the **Editing** group, click the **Sort & Filter** button and then, in the list, click **Sort A to Z**. Excel sorts the data by season, with the seasons listed in alphabetical order.

2   In the **Sort & Filter** list, click **Custom Sort** to open the **Sort** dialog box and display the parameters of the sort you just applied.

3   If it's not already selected, select the **My data has headers** check box.

4   In the **Column** list, click **Customer**. If necessary, in the **Sort On** list, click **Values**; then in the **Order** list, click **A to Z**.

5   Click **Add Level** to create a new sorting level.

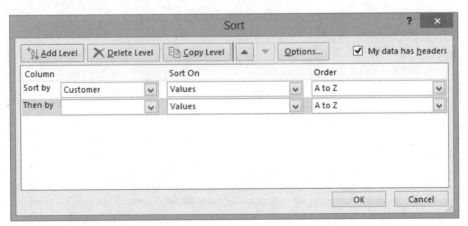

6   In the new **Column** list, click **Revenue**.

7   In the new **Order** list, click **Largest to Smallest**.

8   Click **OK** to close the **Sort** dialog box and sort the data list.

◢	A	B	C	D	E
1					
2		**Customer**	**Season**	**Revenue**	
3		Contoso	Spring	$201,438.00	
4		Contoso	Winter	$183,651.00	
5		Contoso	Fall	$118,299.00	
6		Contoso	Summer	$114,452.00	
7		Fabrikam	Fall	$255,599.00	
8		Fabrikam	Summer	$183,632.00	
9		Fabrikam	Spring	$139,170.00	
10		Fabrikam	Winter	$100,508.00	
11		Northwind Traders	Fall	$188,851.00	
12		Northwind Traders	Winter	$174,336.00	
13		Northwind Traders	Summer	$129,732.00	
14		Northwind Traders	Spring	$120,666.00	
15					

9   In the **Sort & Filter** list, click **Custom Sort** to open the **Sort** dialog box.

10   Click **Then by**, which selects the **Revenue** sorting rule.

11   Click the **Move Up** button to move the **Revenue** sorting rule above the **Customer** sorting rule.

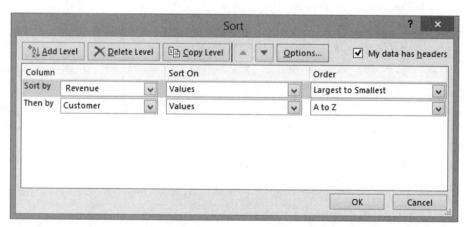

12 Click **OK** to close the **Sort** dialog box and sort the data list.

13 Click cell **C3**. Then on the **Home** tab, in the **Editing** group, click **Sort & Filter**, and click **Custom Sort** to open the **Sort** dialog box.

14 In the **Sort by** row, in the **Column** list, click **Revenue**.

15 In the **Sort on** list, click **Cell Color**.

16 In the new list control that appears in the **Sort by** row, click **On Bottom** to have Excel put the **Revenue** cells that have no cell color on the bottom.

17 Click **OK** to have Excel sort the data list.

❌ CLEAN UP **Close the ShippingSummary workbook, saving your changes if you want to.**

Sorting data by using custom lists

6

The default setting for Excel is to sort numbers according to their values and to sort words in alphabetical order, but that pattern doesn't work for some sets of values. One example in which sorting a list of values in alphabetical order would yield incorrect results is the months of the year. In an alphabetical calendar, April is the first month and September is the last! Fortunately, Excel recognizes a number of special lists, such as days of the week and months of the year. You can have Excel sort the contents of a worksheet based on values in a known list; if needed, you can create your own list of values. For example, the default lists of weekdays in Excel start with Sunday. If you keep your business records based on a Monday-through-Sunday week, you can create a new list that has Monday as the first day and Sunday as the last.

To create a new list, enter the list of values you want to use as your list into a contiguous cell range, select the cells, click the File tab, and then click Options. On the Advanced page of the Excel Options dialog box, in the General group near the bottom of the page, click the Edit Custom Lists button to open the Custom Lists dialog box.

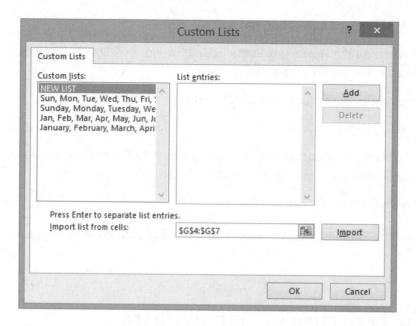

The selected cell range's reference appears in the Import List From Cells field. To record your list, click the Import button.

If you prefer, you can enter the list in the List Entries box, to the right of the Custom Lists box.

TIP Another benefit of creating a custom list is that dragging the fill handle of a list cell that contains a value causes Excel to extend the series for you. For example, if you create the list *Spring, Summer, Fall, Winter,* then enter *Summer* in a cell and drag the cell's fill handle, Excel extends the series as *Fall, Winter, Spring, Summer, Fall,* and so on.

To use a custom list as a sorting criterion, open the Sort dialog box, click the rule's Order arrow, click Custom List, and select your list from the dialog box that opens.

TIP The Data tab of the ribbon also contains a Sort & Filter group with controls you can use to sort and filter your data.

In this exercise, you'll sort data by using a custom list.

→ SET UP You need the ShippingCustom workbook located in the Chapter06 practice file folder to complete this exercise. Open the workbook, and then follow the steps.

1 Select cells **G4:G7**, click the **File** tab, and then click **Options** to open the **Excel Options** dialog box.

2 On the **Advanced** page, in the **General** group toward the bottom of the page, click **Edit Custom Lists** to open the **Custom Lists** dialog box.

3 Verify that the cell range **$G$4:$G$7** appears in the **Import list from cells** field, and then click **Import** to add the new list to the **Custom Lists** box.

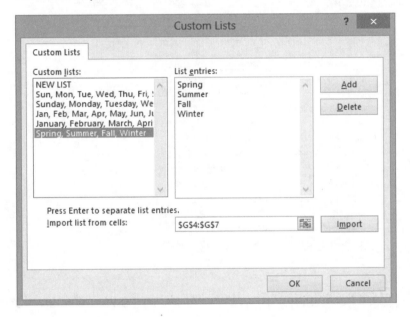

4 Click **OK** twice to close the **Custom Lists** dialog box and the **Excel Options** dialog box.

5 Click cell **C3**.

6   On the **Home** tab, in the **Editing** group, click **Sort & Filter**, and then click **Custom Sort** to open the **Sort** dialog box.

7   Click the rule in the **Sort by** row, and then click **Delete Level** to remove the sorting rule.

8   If necessary, in the new **Sort by** row, in the **Column** list, click **Season**.

9   In the same row, in the **Order** list, click **Custom List** to open the **Custom Lists** dialog box.

10   In the **Custom lists** box, click **Spring, Summer, Fall, Winter**.

11   Click **OK** twice to close the **Custom Lists** dialog box and the **Sort** dialog box so that Excel sorts the data list.

	A	B	C	D	E
1					
2		Customer	Season	Revenue	
3		Contoso	Spring	$201,438.00	
4		Fabrikam	Spring	$139,170.00	
5		Northwind Traders	Spring	$120,666.00	
6		Contoso	Summer	$114,452.00	
7		Fabrikam	Summer	$183,632.00	
8		Northwind Traders	Summer	$129,732.00	
9		Contoso	Fall	$118,299.00	
10		Fabrikam	Fall	$255,599.00	
11		Northwind Traders	Fall	$188,851.00	
12		Contoso	Winter	$183,651.00	
13		Fabrikam	Winter	$100,508.00	
14		Northwind Traders	Winter	$174,336.00	
15					

✖ CLEAN UP **Close the ShippingCustom workbook, saving your changes if you want to.**

Organizing data into levels

After you have sorted the rows in an Excel worksheet or entered the data so that it doesn't need to be sorted, you can have Excel calculate subtotals or totals for a portion of the data. In a worksheet with sales data for three different product categories, for example, you can sort the products by category, select all the cells that contain data, and then open the Subtotal dialog box. To open the Subtotal dialog box, display the Data tab and then, in the Outline group, click Subtotal.

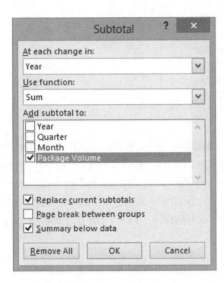

In the Subtotal dialog box, you can choose the column on which to base your subtotals (such as every change of value in the Year column), the summary calculation you want to perform, and the column or columns that have values to be summarized. After you define your subtotals, they appear in your worksheet.

1 2 3		A	B	C	D
	1	Year	Quarter	Month	Package Volume
	2	2012	1	January	5,213,292
	3	2012	1	February	2,038,516
	4	2012	1	March	2,489,601
	5	2012	2	April	9,051,231
	6	2012	2	May	5,225,156
	7	2012	2	June	3,266,644
	8	2012	3	July	2,078,794
	9	2012	3	August	1,591,434
	10	2012	3	September	8,518,985
	11	2012	4	October	1,973,050
	12	2012	4	November	7,599,195
	13	2012	4	December	9,757,876
	14	2012 Total			58,803,774
	15	2013	1	January	5,304,039
	16	2013	1	February	5,465,096
	17	2013	1	March	1,007,799

When you add subtotals to a worksheet, Excel also defines groups based on the rows used to calculate a subtotal. The groupings form an outline of your worksheet based on the criteria you used to create the subtotals. For example, all the rows representing months in the year 2012 could be in one group, rows representing months in 2013 in another, and so on. The outline area at the left of your worksheet holds controls you can use to hide or display groups of rows in your worksheet.

Three types of controls can appear in the outline area: Hide Detail buttons, Show Detail buttons, and level buttons. The Hide Detail button beside a group can be clicked to hide the rows in that group. In a worksheet that has a subtotal group consisting of rows 2 through 13, clicking the Hide Detail button next to row 14 would hide rows 2 through 13 but leave the row holding the subtotal for that group, row 14, visible.

1 2 3		A	B	C	D	E
	1	Year	Quarter	Month	Package Volume	
+	14	**2012 Total**			58,803,774	
	15	2013	1	January	5,304,039	
	16	2013	1	February	5,465,096	
	17	2013	1	March	1,007,799	
	18	2013	2	April	4,010,287	
	19	2013	2	May	4,817,070	
	20	2013	2	June	8,155,717	
	21	2013	3	July	6,552,370	
	22	2013	3	August	2,295,635	
	23	2013	3	September	7,115,883	
	24	2013	4	October	1,362,767	
	25	2013	4	November	8,935,488	
	26	2013	4	December	9,537,077	
−	27	**2013 Total**			64,559,228	
−	28	**Grand Total**			123,363,002	
	29					

When you hide a group of rows, the button displayed next to the group changes to a Show Detail button. Clicking a group's Show Detail button restores the rows in the group to the worksheet.

The level buttons are the other buttons in the outline area of a worksheet that has subtotals. Each button represents a level of organization in a worksheet; clicking a level button hides all levels of detail below that of the button you clicked. The following table describes the data contained at each level of a worksheet that has three levels of organization.

Level	Description
1	Grand total
2	Subtotals for each group
3	Individual rows in the worksheet

Clicking the Level 2 button in the worksheet would hide the rows with data on, for example, each month's revenue, but would leave the row that contains the grand total (Level 1) and all rows that contain the subtotal for each year (Level 2) visible in the worksheet.

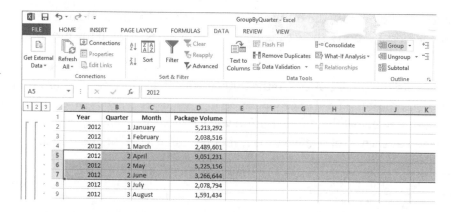

				A	B	C	D	E
			1	Year	Quarter	Month	Package Volume	
+			14	2012 Total			58,803,774	
+			27	2013 Total			64,559,228	
−			28	Grand Total			123,363,002	
			29					

If you want to, you can add levels of detail to the outline that Excel creates. For example, you might want to be able to hide revenues from April to June, which you know are traditionally strong months. To create a new outline group within an existing group, select the rows you want to group; on the Data tab, in the Outline group, point to Group, and then click Group.

You can remove a group by selecting the rows in the group and then, in the Outline group, clicking Ungroup.

TIP If you want to remove all subtotals from a worksheet, open the Subtotal dialog box, and click the Remove All button.

In this exercise, you'll add subtotals to a worksheet and then show and hide different groups of data in your worksheet by using the outline that appears.

SET UP You need the GroupByQuarter workbook located in the Chapter06 practice file folder to complete this exercise. Open the workbook, and then follow the steps.

1 Click any cell in the data list. Then, on the **Data** tab, in the **Outline** group, click **Subtotal** to open the **Subtotal** dialog box. The **Subtotal** dialog box displays the default options to add a subtotal at every change in the **Year** column, to return the sum of the values in the subtotaled rows, and to add a row with the subtotal of values in the **Package Volume** column below the final selected row.

2 Click **OK** to close the **Subtotal** dialog box. New rows appear with subtotals for package volume during each year represented in the worksheet. The new rows are numbered **14** and **27**. A row that contains the grand total of all rows also appears; that row is row **28**. A new area with outline bars and group-level indicators appears to the left of column **A**.

	Year	Quarter	Month	Package Volume	E
1	Year	Quarter	Month	Package Volume	
2	2012	1	January	5,213,292	
3	2012	1	February	2,038,516	
4	2012	1	March	2,489,601	
5	2012	2	April	9,051,231	
6	2012	2	May	5,225,156	
7	2012	2	June	3,266,644	
8	2012	3	July	2,078,794	
9	2012	3	August	1,591,434	
10	2012	3	September	8,518,985	
11	2012	4	October	1,973,050	
12	2012	4	November	7,599,195	
13	2012	4	December	9,757,876	
14	2012 Total			58,803,774	
15	2013	1	January	5,304,039	
16	2013	1	February	5,465,096	
17	2013	1	March	1,007,799	
18	2013	2	April	4,010,287	
19	2013	2	May	4,817,070	
20	2013	2	June	8,155,717	
21	2013	3	July	6,552,370	
22	2013	3	August	2,295,635	
23	2013	3	September	7,115,883	
24	2013	4	October	1,362,767	
25	2013	4	November	8,935,488	
26	2013	4	December	9,537,077	
27	2013 Total			64,559,228	
28	Grand Total			123,363,002	

Sheet1 ⊕

6

3   Click the row heading of row **5**, and drag to the row heading of row **7** to select rows **5** through **7**.

4   On the **Data** tab, in the **Outline** group, click **Group** to make rows **5** through **7** into a new group. An outline bar appears on a new level in the outline area, and a corresponding **Level 4** button appears at the top of the outline area.

5   In the outline area, click the **Hide Detail** button next to row **8** to hide rows **5** through **7**. The **Hide Detail** button you clicked changes to a **Show Detail** button.

	A	B	C	D	E
2	2012	1	January	5,213,292	
3	2012	1	February	2,038,516	
4	2012	1	March	2,489,601	
8	2012	3	July	2,078,794	
9	2012	3	August	1,591,434	
10	2012	3	September	8,518,985	
11	2012	4	October	1,973,050	
12	2012	4	November	7,599,195	
13	2012	4	December	9,757,876	
14	**2012 Total**			58,803,774	
15	2013	1	January	5,304,039	
16	2013	1	February	5,465,096	
17	2013	1	March	1,007,799	

6   In the outline area, click the **Show Detail** button next to row **8** to display rows **5** through **7**. In the outline area, click the **Level 1** button to hide all rows except row **1** with the column headings and row **28** with the grand total.

7   In the outline area, click the **Level 2** button to display the rows that have the subtotals for each year.

8   In the outline area, click the **Level 3** button to display all rows except rows **5** through **7**.

9   In the outline area, click the **Level 4** button to display rows **5** through **7**.

✖ CLEAN UP Close the GroupByQuarter workbook, saving your changes if you want to.

Looking up information in a worksheet

Whenever you create a worksheet that holds information about a list of distinct items, such as products offered for sale by a company, you should ensure that at least one column in the list contains a unique value that distinguishes that row (and the item the row represents) from every other row in the list. Assigning each row a column that contains a unique value means that you can associate data in one list with data in another list. For example, if you assign every customer a unique identification number, you can store a customer's contact information in one worksheet and all orders for that customer in another worksheet. You can then associate the customer's orders and contact information without writing the contact information in a worksheet every time the customer places an order.

In the case of shipments handled by Consolidated Messenger, the column that contains those unique values, also known as the *primary key column*, is the ShipmentID column.

	A	B	C	D	E	F
1						
2		ShipmentID	Destination			
3						
4						
5						
6		ShipmentID	CustomerID	Date	OriginationPostalCode	DestinationPostalCode
7		SI3049210	CI384471	5/20/2007 59686		77408
8		SI3049211	CI495231	5/20/2007 24348		91936
9		SI3049212	CI429120	5/20/2007 70216		83501
10		SI3049213	CI418125	5/20/2007 84196		21660
11		SI3049214	CI782990	5/20/2007 13193		92518
12		SI3049215	CI102300	5/20/2007 27910		76842
13		SI3049216	CI560742	5/20/2007 73820		21393
14		SI3049217	CI483289	5/20/2007 34245		33975

If you know a shipment's ShipmentID, it's no trouble to look through a list of 20 or 30 items to find a particular shipment. If, however, you have a list of many thousands of shipments, looking through the list to find one would take quite a bit of time. Instead, you can use the *VLOOKUP* function so that your colleagues can enter a ShipmentID in a cell and have the corresponding details appear in another cell.

The *VLOOKUP* function finds a value in the leftmost column of a named range, such as a table, and then returns the value from the specified cell to the right of the cell that has the found value. A properly formed *VLOOKUP* function has four arguments (data that is passed to the function), as shown in the following definition: =*VLOOKUP(lookup_value, table_array, col_index_num, range_lookup)*.

The following table summarizes the values Excel expects for each of these arguments.

Argument	Expected value
lookup_value	The value to be found in the first column of the named range specified by the *table_array* argument. The *lookup_value* argument can be a value, a cell reference, or a text string.
table_array	The multicolumn range or name of the range or Excel table to be searched.
col_index_num	The number of the column in the named range that has the value to be returned.
range_lookup	A *TRUE* or *FALSE* value, indicating whether the function should find an approximate match (*TRUE*) or an exact match (*FALSE*) for the *lookup_value*. If left blank, the default value for this argument is *TRUE*.

IMPORTANT When *range_lookup* is left blank or set to *TRUE*, for *VLOOKUP* to work properly the rows in the named range specified in the *table_array* argument must be sorted in ascending order based on the values in the leftmost column of the named range.

The *VLOOKUP* function works a bit differently depending on whether the *range_lookup* argument is set to *TRUE* or *FALSE*. The following list summarizes how the function works based on the value of *range_lookup*:

- If the *range_lookup* argument is left blank or set to *TRUE*, and *VLOOKUP* doesn't find an exact match for *lookup_value*, the function returns the largest value that is less than *lookup_value*.

- If the *range_lookup* argument is left blank or set to *TRUE*, and *lookup_value* is smaller than the smallest value in the named range, an *#N/A* error is returned.

- If the *range_lookup* argument is left blank or set to *TRUE*, and *lookup_value* is larger than all values in the named range, the largest value in the named range is returned.

- If the *range_lookup* argument is set to *FALSE*, and *VLOOKUP* doesn't find an exact match for *lookup_value*, the function returns an *#N/A* error.

As an example of a *VLOOKUP* function, consider an Excel table that has its headers in row 1 and the first column in column A of the worksheet. If the =*VLOOKUP (D2, Table1, 2, TRUE)* formula is used, when you enter *CI02* in cell D2 and press Enter, the *VLOOKUP* function searches the first column of the table, finds an exact match, and returns the value *Northwind Traders* to cell E2.

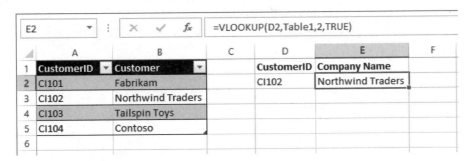

TIP The related *HLOOKUP* function matches a value in a column of the first row of a table and returns the value in the specified row number of the same column. The letter "H" in the *HLOOKUP* function name refers to the horizontal layout of the data, just as the "V" in the *VLOOKUP* function name refers to the data's vertical layout. For more information on using the *HLOOKUP* function, click the Excel Help button, enter *HLOOKUP* in the search terms box, and then click Search.

> **IMPORTANT** Be sure to format the cell in which you enter the *VLOOKUP* formula with the same format as the data you want the formula to display. For example, if you create a *VLOOKUP* formula in cell G14 that finds a date, you must apply a date cell format to cell G14 for the result of the formula to display properly.

In this exercise, you'll create a *VLOOKUP* function to return the destination postal code of deliveries that have ShipmentIDs entered in a specific cell.

 SET UP You need the ShipmentLog workbook located in the Chapter06 practice file folder to complete this exercise. Open the workbook, and then follow the steps.

1   In cell **C3**, enter the formula =**VLOOKUP(B3, Shipments, 5, FALSE)**. Cell **B3**, which the formula uses to look up values in the **Shipments** table, is blank, so the **#N/A** error code appears in cell **C3**.

2   In cell **B3**, enter **SI3049224**, and press **Enter**. The value **51102** appears in cell **C3**.

3   In cell **C3**, edit the formula so that it reads =VLOOKUP(B3, Shipments, 2, FALSE). The formula now finds its target value in table column 2 (the **CustomerID** column), so the value **CI512191** appears in cell **C3**.

4   In cell **C3**, edit the formula so that it reads =VLOOKUP(B3, Shipments, 4, TRUE). Changing the last argument to *TRUE* enables the *VLOOKUP* formula to find an approximate match for the **ShipmentID** in cell **B3**, whereas changing the column to **4** means the formula gets its result from the **OriginationPostalCode** column. The value **14020** appears in cell **C3**.

C3		⋮	✕ ✓	fx	=VLOOKUP(B3,Shipments,4,TRUE)	
◢	A	B	C	D	E	F
1						
2		**ShipmentID**	**Postal Code**			
3		SI3049224	14020			
4						
5						
6		**ShipmentID** ▾	**CustomerID** ▾	**Date** ▾	**OriginationPostalCode** ▾	**DestinationPostalCode** ▾
7		SI3049210	CI384471	5/20/2007	59686	77408
8		SI3049211	CI495231	5/20/2007	24348	91936
9		SI3049212	CI429120	5/20/2007	70216	83501
10		SI3049213	CI418125	5/20/2007	84196	21660
11		SI3049214	CI782990	5/20/2007	13193	92518
12		SI3049215	CI102300	5/20/2007	27910	76842
13		SI3049216	CI560742	5/20/2007	73820	21393
14		SI3049217	CI483289	5/20/2007	34245	33975
15		SI3049218	CI762179	5/20/2007	87569	11471
16		SI3049219	CI278943	5/20/2007	28371	72853
17		SI3049220	CI213987	5/20/2007	18024	31069
18		SI3049221	CI907745	5/20/2007	70812	53604
19		SI3049222	CI299868	5/20/2007	33242	23892
20		SI3049223	CI503324	5/20/2007	58997	37121
21		SI3049224	CI512191	5/20/2007	14020	51102
22		SI3049225	CI932656	5/20/2007	56345	28404
23		SI3049226	CI514577	5/20/2007	34262	99198
24		SI3049227	CI803799	5/20/2007	92043	65330

5   In cell **B3**, enter SI3049209. The value in cell **B3** is smaller than the smallest value in the **Shipments** table's first column, so the *VLOOKUP* formula displays the #N/A error code in cell **C3**.

6   In cell **B3**, enter SI3049245. The **ShipmentID** entered into cell **B3** is greater than the last value in the table's first column, so the *VLOOKUP* formula displays the last value in the target column (in this case, the fourth column). Therefore, the incorrect value **44493** appears in cell **C3**. The error occurs because the *range_lookup* argument is set to *TRUE*.

✖ CLEAN UP Close the ShipmentLog workbook, saving your changes if you want to.

Key points

- You can rearrange the data in a worksheet quickly by clicking either the Sort Ascending or Sort Descending button in the Sort & Filter group on the Data tab.

- Don't forget that you can sort the rows in a worksheet by using orders other than alphabetical or numerical. For example, you can sort a series of days based on their order in the week or by cell color.

- If none of the existing sort orders (days, weekdays, and so on) meets your needs, you can create your own custom sort order.

- You can divide the data in your worksheet into levels and find a subtotal for each level.

- By creating subtotals, you can show or hide groups of data in your worksheets.

- You can use the *VLOOKUP* function to look up a value in one column of data and return a value from another column in the same row.

6

Chapter at a glance

Templates

Use workbooks as templates for other workbooks, page 196

Link

Link to data in other worksheets and workbooks, page 204

	E	F	G	H	I
1					
2	**Facilities**			**Transportation**	
3					
4	Power	$ 1,800,000.00		Truck Fuel	$ 24,808,206
5	Water	$ 900,000.00		Truck Maintenance	
6	Rent	$ 2,350,000.00		Airplane Fuel	
7	Mortgage	$ 4,590,210.00		Airplane Maintenance	

Consolidate

Consolidate multiple sets of data into a single workbook, page 209

	A	B	C	D	E	F	G	H
1								
2								
3			**Hour**					
4		**Call Center**	9:00 AM	10:00 AM	11:00 AM	12:00 PM	1:00 PM	2:00 PM
5		Northeast	15931	15958	13140	25367	19558	20624
6		Atlantic	28432	22326	15436	20884	30000	19770
7		Southeast	13132	12568	19732	14762	18885	20882
8		North Central	17588	26324	24121	24453	20048	21994
9		Midwest	24875	19965	19386	11374	26007	29378
10		Southwest	15353	27755	19718	17889	22116	28816
11		Mountain West	21516	28321	9754	26384	15926	23572
12		Northwest	19806	24154	12389	10151	24078	11642
13		Central	21018	24884	18655	31525	13407	19683
14								

Combining data from multiple sources

7

IN THIS CHAPTER, YOU WILL LEARN HOW TO

- Use workbooks as templates for other workbooks.

- Link to data in other worksheets and workbooks.

- Consolidate multiple sets of data into a single workbook.

Microsoft Excel 2013 gives you a wide range of tools with which to format, summarize, and present your data. After you have created a workbook to hold data about a particular subject, you can create as many worksheets as you need to make that data easier to find within your workbook. For example, you can create a workbook to store sales data for a year, with each worksheet representing a month in that year. To ensure that every year's workbook has a similar appearance, you can create a workbook with the characteristics you want (such as more than the standard number of worksheets, custom worksheet formatting, or a particular color for the workbook's sheet tabs) and save it as a pattern, or *template*, for similar workbooks you will create in the future. The benefit of ensuring that all your sales data worksheets have the same layout is that you and your colleagues immediately know where to look for specific totals. You can use that knowledge to summarize, or consolidate, that data into a single worksheet.

A consequence of organizing your data into different workbooks and worksheets is that you need ways to manage, combine, and summarize data from more than one Excel file. You can always copy data from one worksheet to another, but if the original value were to change, that change would not be reflected in the cell range to which you copied the data. Rather than remembering which cells you need to update when a value changes, you can create a link to the original cell. That way, Excel will update the value for you whenever you open the workbook. If multiple worksheets hold related values, you can use links to summarize those values in a single worksheet.

In this chapter, you'll use a workbook as a template for other workbooks, work with more than one set of data, link to data in other workbooks, and summarize multiple sets of data.

PRACTICE FILES To complete the exercises in this chapter, you need the practice files contained in the Chapter07 practice file folder. For more information, see "Download the practice files" in this book's Introduction.

Using workbooks as templates for other workbooks

After you decide on the type of data you want to store in a workbook and what that workbook should look like, you probably want to be able to create similar workbooks without adding all of the formatting and formulas again. For example, you might have established a design for your monthly sales-tracking workbook.

When you have settled on a design for your workbooks, you can save one of the workbooks as a template for similar workbooks you will create in the future. You can leave the workbook's labels to aid data entry, but you should remove any existing data from a workbook that you save as a template, both to avoid data entry errors and to remove any confusion as to whether the workbook is a template. You can also remove any worksheets you and your colleagues won't need by right-clicking the tab of an unneeded worksheet and, on the shortcut menu that appears, clicking Delete.

If you want your template workbook to have more than the standard number of worksheets (such as 12 worksheets to track shipments for a year, by month), you can add worksheets by clicking the Insert Worksheet button that appears to the right of the existing worksheet tabs.

Before you create your first template, you should identify the path to the default template folder on your computer. The path for users whose Windows local settings are English (US) is typically Program Files (x86)\Microsoft Office\Templates\1033. The language identifier for English (US) is 1033, which is why the path includes that identifier. You can enter that path as your default template path on the Save page of the Excel Options dialog box. To open the Excel Options dialog box, click the File tab and then click Options. In the dialog box, click Save and then, in the Default Personal Templates Location box, enter the template folder's path.

TIP You can discover your template folder's path by opening File Explorer and navigating to the template folder, starting with the Program Files or Program Files (x86) folder, depending on your installation. To copy the path of the folder, click the folder icon at the left end of the File Explorer address box at the top of the File Explorer window and then press Ctrl+C.

To create a template from an existing workbook, save the model workbook as an Excel template file (a file with an .xltx extension), which is a file format you can choose from the Save As Type dialog box. If you ever want to change the template, you can open it like a standard workbook and make your changes. When you have completed your work, save the file by clicking the Save button on the Quick Access Toolbar—it will still be a template.

TIP You can also save your Excel 2013 workbook either as an Excel 97–2003 template (.xlt) or as a macro-enabled Excel 2013 workbook template (.xltm). For information about using macros in Excel 2013 workbooks, see Chapter 12, "Working with macros and forms."

After you save a workbook as a template, you can use it as a model for new workbooks. To create a workbook from a template in Excel, click the File tab to display the Backstage view, and then click New.

7

The New page of the Backstage view displays the blank workbook template, sample templates, a search box you can use to locate helpful templates on Office.com, and a set of sample search terms.

From the list of available templates, you can click the template you want to use as the model for your workbook. Excel creates a new workbook (an .xlsx workbook file, not an .xltx template file) with the template's formatting and contents in place.

In addition to creating a workbook template, you can add a worksheet based on a template to your workbook by right-clicking a sheet tab and then clicking Insert to open the Insert dialog box.

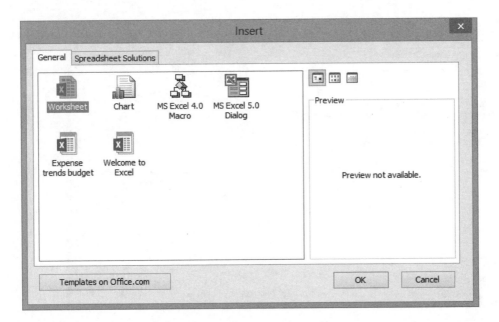

The Insert dialog box splits its contents into two pages. The General page contains icons you can click to insert a blank worksheet, a chart sheet, and any worksheet templates available to you.

TIP The MS Excel 4.0 Macro and MS Excel 5.0 Dialog icons on the General page are there to help users integrate older Excel spreadsheet solutions into Excel 2013.

The Spreadsheet Solutions page contains a set of useful templates for a variety of financial and personal tasks.

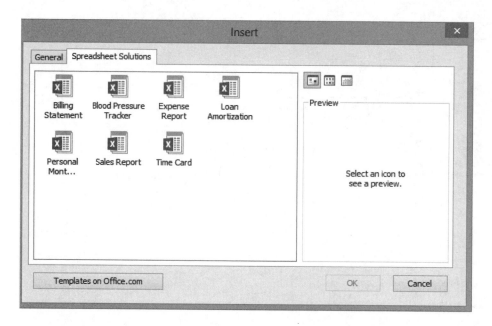

To add a spreadsheet from the Insert dialog box to your workbook, click the template you want, and then click OK. When you click a template, a preview of that template's contents appears in the preview pane, so you can verify you've selected the template you want.

In this exercise, you'll create a workbook from an existing template, save a template to track hourly call volumes to each regional center, and insert a worksheet based on a worksheet template into a new workbook.

 SET UP You need the DailyCallSummary workbook located in the Chapter07 practice file folder to complete this exercise. Open the workbook, and then follow the steps.

1   Click the **File** tab, and then in the **Backstage** view, click **Save As**.

2   On the **Save As** page, click **Computer**.

3   Click **Browse** to open the **Save As** dialog box.

4   In the **Save as type** list, click **Excel Template**.

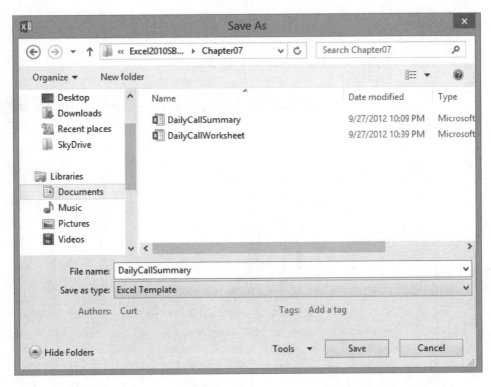

5   Click **Save** to save the workbook as a template and close the **Save As** dialog box.

TIP You must remember where you saved your template file to use it later. If you
updated the Default Personal Templates Location setting in the Excel Options dialog
box and saved the file in that folder, the template you just created will appear on the
New page of the Backstage view.

6   In the **Backstage** view, click **Close** to close the **DailyCallSummary** workbook.

7   Display the **Backstage** view again, and then click **New**.

8   In the templates gallery, click **Expense Trends Budget** to display information about
the template.

9   Click **Create** to create a workbook based on the selected template.

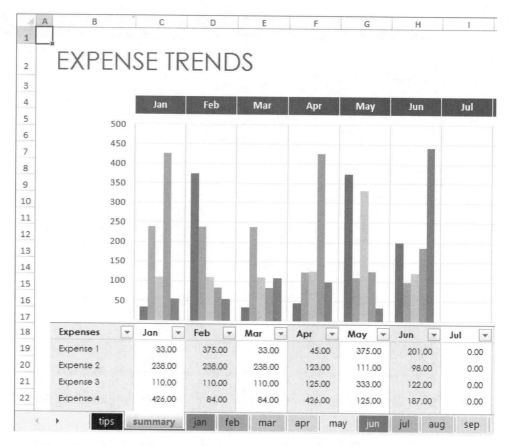

10   On the **Quick Access Toolbar**, click the **Save** button to display the **Backstage** view.

11   On the **Save As** page of the **Backstage** view, click **Computer** and then click **Browse** to open the **Save As** dialog box.

12   In the **File name** box, enter **ExpenseReport**. Use the dialog box controls to browse to the **Chapter07** folder, and then click **Save** to save your workbook.

13   In the **Backstage** view, click **Open** to display that page, and then click **Recent Workbooks**. In the **Recent Workbooks** list, click the **DailyCallSummary** workbook file (not the template) to display the **DailyCallSummary** workbook.

⊿	A	B	C	D	E	F	G
1							
2							
3			**Hour**				
4		**Call Center**	9:00 AM	10:00 AM	11:00 AM	12:00 PM	1:00 PM
5		Northeast					
6		Atlantic					
7		Southeast					
8		North Central					
9		Midwest					
10		Southwest					
11		Mountain West					
12		Northwest					
13		Central					
14							

14   Right-click the **Daily** sheet tab, and then click **Insert** to open the **Insert** dialog box.

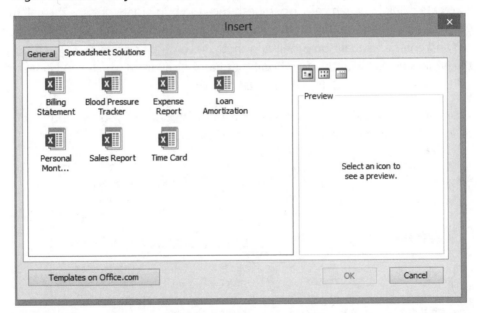

15   On the **Spreadsheet Solutions** page, click **TimeCard**, and then click **OK** to create a new worksheet based on the template.

❌ CLEAN UP Close the DailyCallSummary and ExpenseReport workbooks, saving your changes if you want to.

Linking to data in other worksheets and workbooks

Copying and pasting data from one workbook to another is a quick and easy way to gather related data in one place, but there is a substantial limitation: if the data from the original cell changes, the change is not reflected in the cell to which the data was copied. In other words, copying and pasting a cell's contents doesn't create a relationship between the original cell and the target cell.

You can ensure that the data in the target cell reflects any changes in the original cell by creating a link between the two cells. Instead of entering a value into the target cell by typing or pasting, you create a formula that identifies the source from which Excel will derive the target cell's value and updates the value when it changes in the source cell.

To create a link between cells, open both the workbook that contains the cell from which you want to pull the value and the workbook that has the target cell. Then click the target cell and enter an equal sign, signifying that you want to create a formula. After you enter the equal sign, activate the workbook that has the cell from which you want to derive the value, click that cell, and then press the Enter key.

When you switch back to the workbook with the target cell, you will find that Excel has filled in the formula with a reference to the cell you clicked.

I4		f_x	='[FleetOperatingCosts.xlsx]Truck Fuel'!$C$15	

	E	F	G	H	I
1					
2	**Facilities**			**Transportation**	
3					
4	Power	$ 1,800,000.00		Truck Fuel	$ 24,808,206
5	Water	$ 900,000.00		Truck Maintenance	
6	Rent	$ 2,350,000.00		Airplane Fuel	
7	Mortgage	$ 4,590,210.00		Airplane Maintenance	

For example, the reference =*'[FleetOperatingCosts.xlsx]Truck Fuel'!$C$15* gives three pieces of information: the workbook, the worksheet, and the cell you clicked in the worksheet. The first element of the reference (the name of the workbook) is enclosed in square brackets; the end of the second element (the worksheet) is marked with an exclamation point; and the third element (the cell reference) has a dollar sign before both the row and the column identifier. The single quotes around the workbook name and worksheet name are there to account for the space in the Truck Fuel worksheet's name. This type of reference is known as a *3-D* reference, reflecting the three dimensions (workbook, worksheet, and cell range) that you need in order to point to a group of cells in another workbook.

TIP For references to cells in the same workbook, the workbook information is omitted. Likewise, references to cells in the same worksheet don't use a worksheet identifier.

You can also link to cells in an Excel table. Such links include the workbook name, worksheet name, name of the Excel table, and row and column references of the cell to which you've linked. Creating a link to the Cost column's cell in a table's Totals row, for example, results in a reference such as =*'FleetOperatingCosts.xlsx'!Truck Maintenance[[#Totals],[Cost]]*.

IMPORTANT Hiding or displaying a table's Totals row affects any links to a cell in that row. Hiding the Totals row causes references to that row to display a *#REF!* error message.

Whenever you open a workbook that contains a link to another document, Excel tries to update the information in linked cells. If the program can't find the source, as would happen if a workbook or worksheet is deleted or renamed, an alert box appears, telling you that there is a broken link. At that point, you can click the Update button and then the Edit Links button to open the Edit Links dialog box and find which link is broken. After you identify the broken link, you can close the Edit Links dialog box, click the cell containing the broken link, and create a new link to the data you want.

If you enter a link and you make an error, a *#REF!* error message appears in the cell that contains the link. To fix the link, click the cell, delete its contents, and then either reenter the link or create it by using the method described earlier in this section.

TIP Excel tracks workbook changes, such as when you change a workbook's name, very well. Unless you delete a worksheet or workbook, or move a workbook to a new folder, odds are good that Excel can update your link references automatically to reflect the change.

In this exercise, you'll create a link to another workbook, make the link's reference invalid, use the Edit Links dialog box to break the link, and then re-create the link correctly.

SET UP You need the OperatingExpenseDashboard and FleetOperatingCosts workbooks located in the Chapter07 practice file folder to complete this exercise. Open the workbooks, and then follow the steps.

1   In the **OperatingExpenseDashboard** workbook, in cell **I6**, enter **=**, but do not press Enter.

2   On the **View** tab, in the **Window** group, click **Switch Windows** and then, in the list, click **FleetOperatingCosts** to display the **FleetOperatingCosts** workbook.

3   If necessary, click the **Plane Repair** sheet tab to display the **Plane Repair** worksheet, and then click cell **C15**. Excel updates the formula to **='[FleetOperatingCosts.xlsx] Plane Repair'!$C$15**.

4   Press **Enter**. Excel displays the **OperatingExpenseDashboard** workbook; the value **$2,410,871** appears in cell **I6**.

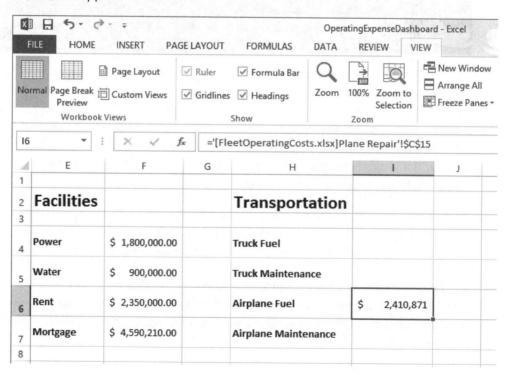

TIP Yes, cell C15 on the Plane Repair worksheet contains the wrong total for the Airplane Fuel category; that's why you replace it later in this exercise.

5   In the **Switch Windows** list, click **FleetOperatingCosts** to display the **FleetOperatingCosts** workbook.

6   Right-click the **Plane Repair** sheet tab, and then click **Delete**. In the message box that appears, click **Delete** to confirm that you want to delete the worksheet.

7   In the **Switch Windows** list, click **OperatingExpenseDashboard** to display the **OperatingExpenseDashboard** workbook. Note that cell **I6** shows a **#REF!** error because the worksheet containing the linked cell has been deleted.

	E	F	G	H	I
1					
2	**Facilities**			**Transportation**	
3					
4	Power	$ 1,800,000.00		Truck Fuel	
5	Water	$ 900,000.00		Truck Maintenance	
6	Rent	$ 2,350,000.00		Airplane Fuel	#REF!
7	Mortgage	$ 4,590,210.00		Airplane Maintenance	
8					

8   On the **Data** tab, in the **Connections** group, click **Edit Links** to open the **Edit Links** dialog box.

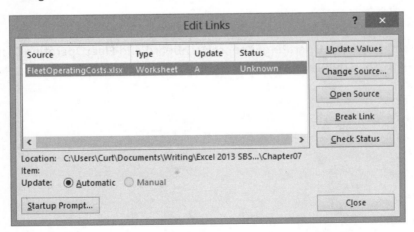

Edit Links dialog box:

Source	Type	Update	Status
FleetOperatingCosts.xlsx	Worksheet	A	Unknown

Update Values
Change Source...
Open Source
Break Link
Check Status

Location: C:\Users\Curt\Documents\Writing\Excel 2013 SBS...\Chapter07
Item:
Update: ● Automatic   ○ Manual

Startup Prompt...   Close

9   Click **Break Link**. Excel displays a warning box asking if you're sure you want to break the link.

10   Click **Break Links** to close the warning box and remove the link from the workbook.

11   Click **Close** to close the **Edit Links** dialog box.

12   In cell **I6**, enter =, but do not press Enter.

13   In the **Switch Windows** list, click **FleetOperatingCosts** to display the **FleetOperatingCosts** workbook.

14   Click the **Plane Fuel** sheet tab to display the **Plane Fuel** worksheet.

15   Click cell **C15**, and then press **Enter** to complete the formula. Excel displays the **OperatingExpenseDashboard** workbook with the value **$52,466,303** in cell **I6**.

I6	▼	:	×	✓	fx	='[FleetOperatingCosts.xlsx]Plane Fuel'!$C$15

	E	F	G	H	I
1					
2	**Facilities**			**Transportation**	
3					
4	Power	$ 1,800,000.00		Truck Fuel	
5	Water	$ 900,000.00		Truck Maintenance	
6	Rent	$ 2,350,000.00		Airplane Fuel	$ 52,466,303
7	Mortgage	$ 4,590,210.00		Airplane Maintenance	
8					

✖ CLEAN UP Close the OperatingExpenseDashboard and FleetOperatingCosts workbooks, saving your changes if you want to.

Consolidating multiple sets of data into a single workbook

When you create a series of worksheets that contain similar data, perhaps by using a template, you build a consistent set of workbooks in which data is stored in a predictable place. For example, consider a workbook template that uses cell C5 to record the number of calls received from 9:00 A.M. to 10:00 A.M. by the Northeast distribution center.

	A	B	C	D	E	F	G
1							
2							
3			**Hour**				
4		**Call Center**	*9:00 AM*	*10:00 AM*	*11:00 AM*	*12:00 PM*	*1:00 PM*
5		*Northeast*					
6		*Atlantic*					
7		*Southeast*					
8		*North Central*					
9		*Midwest*					
10		*Southwest*					
11		*Mountain West*					
12		*Northwest*					
13		*Central*					
14							

Using links to bring data from one worksheet to another gives you a great deal of power to combine data from several sources into a single resource. For example, you can create a worksheet that lists the total revenue just for certain months of a year, use links to draw the values from the worksheets in which the sales were recorded, and then create a formula to perform calculations on the data. However, for large worksheets with hundreds of cells filled with data, creating links from every cell is a time-consuming process. Also, to calculate a sum or an average for the data, you would need to include links to cells in every workbook.

Fortunately, there is an easier way to combine data from multiple worksheets into a single worksheet. By using this process, called *data consolidation*, you can define ranges of cells from multiple worksheets and have Excel summarize the data. You define these ranges in the Consolidate dialog box.

7

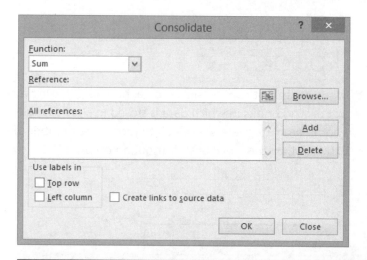

After you open the dialog box, you move to the worksheet that contains the first cell range you want to include in your summary. When you select the cells, the 3-D reference for the range appears in the Consolidate dialog box. Clicking Add stores the reference. You can then choose the other cell ranges that contain data you want to include in the summary, or you can remove a range from the calculation by clicking the range and then clicking Delete.

Cells that are in the same relative position in the ranges have their contents summarized together. When you consolidate the ranges, the cell in the upper-left corner of one range is added to the cell in the upper-left corner of every other range, even if those ranges are in different areas of the worksheet. After you choose the ranges to be used in your summary, you can choose the calculation to perform on the data (sum, average, and so on). When you're done selecting ranges to use in the calculation, click OK to have Excel summarize the data on your target worksheet.

In this exercise, you'll define a data consolidation range consisting of ranges from two other workbooks. You'll then add the contents of the ranges and show the results in a worksheet.

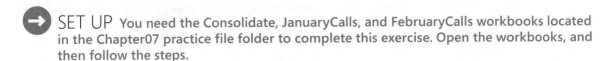 SET UP You need the Consolidate, JanuaryCalls, and FebruaryCalls workbooks located in the Chapter07 practice file folder to complete this exercise. Open the workbooks, and then follow the steps.

1   In the **Consolidate** workbook, on the **Data** tab, in the **Data Tools** group, click **Consolidate** to open the **Consolidate** dialog box.

2   Click the **Collapse Dialog** button at the right edge of the **Reference** field to contract the **Consolidate** dialog box.

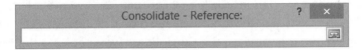

3   On the **View** tab, in the **Window** group, click **Switch Windows** and then, in the list, click **JanuaryCalls** to display the **JanuaryCalls** workbook.

4   Select the cell range **C5:O13**, and then click the **Expand Dialog** button to restore the **Consolidate** dialog box to its full size.

5   Click **Add** to add the selected range to the **All references** box.

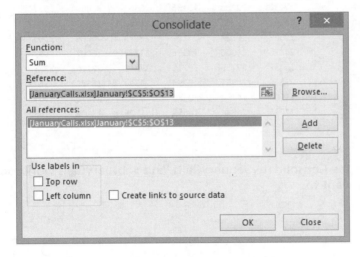

6   Click the **Collapse Dialog** button again to contract the **Consolidate** dialog box.

7   In the **Switch Windows** list, click **FebruaryCalls** to display the **FebruaryCalls** workbook.

8   Select the cell range **C5:O13**, and then click the **Expand Dialog** button to restore the **Consolidate** dialog box to its full size.

9   Click **Add** to add the range '**[FebruaryCalls.xlsx]February**'!$C$5:$O$13 to the **All references** box.

10   Click **OK** to consolidate the **JanuaryCalls** and **FebruaryCalls** workbook data into the range **C5:O13** in the **Consolidate** workbook. You didn't change the **SUM** operation in the **Function** box, so the values in the **Consolidate** workbook are the sum of the other workbooks' values.

⊿	A	B	C	D	E	F	G	H
1								
2								
3			**Hour**					
4		**Call Center**	9:00 AM	10:00 AM	11:00 AM	12:00 PM	1:00 PM	2:00 PM
5		Northeast	15931	15958	13140	25367	19558	20624
6		Atlantic	28432	22326	15436	20884	30000	19770
7		Southeast	13132	12568	19732	14762	18885	20882
8		North Central	17588	26324	24121	24453	20048	21994
9		Midwest	24875	19965	19386	11374	26007	29378
10		Southwest	15353	27755	19718	17889	22116	28816
11		Mountain West	21516	28321	9754	26384	15926	23572
12		Northwest	19806	24154	12389	10151	24078	11642
13		Central	21018	24884	18655	31525	13407	19683
14								

❌ CLEAN UP Close the Consolidate, JanuaryCalls, and FebruaryCalls workbooks, saving your changes if you want to.

Key points

- If you create a lot of workbooks that have the same layout and design, saving a workbook with the common elements (and no data) will save you time when you create similar workbooks in the future.

- You can use data in other worksheets or workbooks in your formulas. You create a link by clicking the cell, which creates a 3-D reference to that cell.

- When you create a link to a cell in a table's Totals row, hiding the Totals row causes Excel to display a #REF! error in the cell in which you created the link.

7

Chapter at a glance

Examine

Examine data by using the Quick Analysis
Lens, page 216

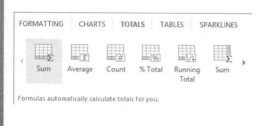

Define

Define an alternative data set,
page 219

Optimize

Find optimal solutions by using Solver,
page 233

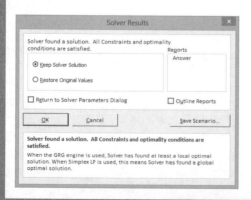

Analyze

Analyze data by using descriptive statistics,
page 240

	A	B	C
1	Column1		
2			
3	Mean	120.7333	
4	Standard Error	7.036955	
5	Median	109	
6	Mode	102	
7	Standard Deviation	27.25401	
8	Sample Variance	742.781	
9	Kurtosis	-1.17215	
10	Skewness	0.642027	
11	Range	74	
12	Minimum	91	

Analyzing data and alternative data sets

8

IN THIS CHAPTER, YOU WILL LEARN HOW TO

- Examine data by using the Quick Analysis Lens.

- Define an alternative data set.

- Define multiple alternative data sets.

- Analyze data by using data tables.

- Vary your data to get a specific result by using Goal Seek.

- Find optimal solutions by using Solver.

- Analyze data by using descriptive statistics.

When you store data in a Microsoft Excel 2013 workbook, you can use that data, either by itself or as part of a calculation, to discover important information about your organization. You can summarize your data quickly by creating charts, calculating totals, or applying conditional formatting. When you track total sales on a time basis, you can find your best and worst sales periods and correlate them with outside events. For businesses such as Consolidated Messenger, package volume increases dramatically during the holidays as customers ship gifts to friends and family members.

The data in your worksheets is great for answering the question, "What happened?" The data is less useful for answering "what-if" questions, such as, "How much money would we save if we reduced our labor to 20 percent of our total costs?" You can always save an alternative version of a workbook and create formulas that calculate the effects of your changes, but you can do the same thing in your existing workbooks by defining one or more alternative data sets and switching between the original data and the new sets you create. Within a single workbook, you can create a data table that calculates the effects of changing one or two variables in a formula.

Excel also provides the tools to determine the input values that would be required for a formula to produce a specified result. For example, the chief operating officer of Consolidated Messenger, Lori Penor, could find out to what level the revenues from three-day shipping would need to rise for that category to account for 25 percent of total revenue.

In this chapter, you'll examine data by using the Quick Analysis Lens, define alternative data sets, and use different methods to determine the necessary inputs to make a calculation produce a specific result.

PRACTICE FILES To complete the exercises in this chapter, you need the practice files contained in the Chapter08 practice file folder. For more information, see "Download the practice files" in this book's Introduction.

Examining data by using the Quick Analysis Lens

One of the refinements in Excel 2013 is the addition of the Quick Analysis Lens, which brings the most commonly used formatting, charting, and summary tools into one convenient location. To examine data by using the Quick Analysis Lens tools, select the data you want to summarize. When you select a range, Excel displays the Quick Analysis button in the lower-right corner of the range. Clicking the Quick Analysis button displays the tools you can use to analyze your data.

KEYBOARD SHORTCUT Press Ctrl+Q to display the Quick Analysis Lens tools. For a complete list of keyboard shortcuts, see "Keyboard shortcuts" at the end of this book.

	A	B	C
1	Region	Packages	
2	Northeast	440,971	
3	Atlantic	304,246	
4	Southeast	444,006	
5	North Central	466,687	
6	Midwest	400,713	
7	Southwest	402,456	
8	Mountain Wes	370,176	
9	Northwest	209,013	
10	Central	234,993	
11			
12			

The Quick Analysis Lens provides a wide range of tools that you can use, including the ability to create an Excel table or PivotTable, insert a chart, or add conditional formatting. You can also add total columns and rows to your data range. For example, you can click the Totals tab of the Quick Analysis Lens, and then click Running Total for columns, identified by the icon labeled Running Total and the blue row at the bottom of the button, to add a row that calculates the running total for each column.

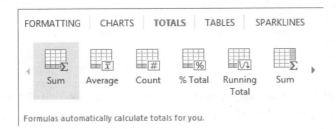

You can add one summary column and one summary row to each data range. If you select a new summary column or row when one exists, Excel displays a confirmation dialog box to verify that you want to replace the existing summary. When you click Yes, Excel makes the change.

In this exercise, you'll use the Quick Analysis Lens to analyze data.

➔ SET UP **You need the PackageAnalysis workbook located in the Chapter08 practice file folder to complete this exercise. Open the workbook, and then follow the steps.**

1   Click any cell in the data range.

2   Press **Ctrl+*** to select the entire data range.

3   Click the **Quick Analysis** button to display the tools available in the **Quick Analysis** gallery.

4   Click the **Totals** tab to display the tools on that tab, point to (but don't click) the **Sum** button that has the blue row at the bottom to display a live preview of the effect of clicking the button, and then click the **Sum** button to add a sum total to the bottom of the data range.

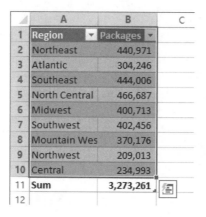

TIP When your data range is an Excel table, as it is in this exercise, you can show or hide the summary by displaying or hiding the table's Total row.

5 In the **Quick Analysis** gallery, click the **Totals** tab again. Then click the arrow on the far right of the gallery to scroll to the right.

6 Click the **% Total** button that has the yellow column at the right edge to add that summary column to the worksheet.

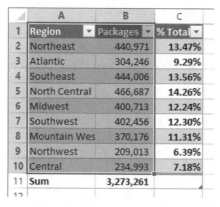

❌ CLEAN UP Close the PackageAnalysis workbook, saving your changes if you want to.

Defining an alternative data set

When you save data in an Excel worksheet, you create a record that reflects the characteristics of an event or object. That data could represent the number of deliveries in an hour on a particular day, the price of a new delivery option, or the percentage of total revenue accounted for by a delivery option. After the data is in place, you can create formulas to generate totals, find averages, and sort the rows in a worksheet based on the contents of one or more columns. However, if you want to perform a what-if analysis or explore the impact that changes in your data would have on any of the calculations in your workbooks, you need to change your data.

The problem with manipulating data that reflects an event or item is that when you change any data to affect a calculation, you run the risk of destroying the original data if you accidentally save your changes. You can avoid ruining your original data by creating a duplicate workbook and making your changes to it, but you can also create alternative data sets, or *scenarios*, within an existing workbook.

When you create a scenario, you give Excel alternative values for a list of cells in a worksheet. You can use the Scenario Manager to add, delete, and edit scenarios.

Clicking the Add button displays the Add Scenario dialog box.

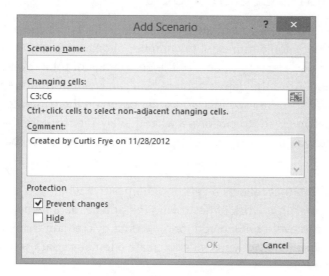

From within this dialog box, you can name the scenario and identify the cells for which you want to define alternative values. After you click OK, the Scenario Values dialog box opens with fields for you to enter the new values.

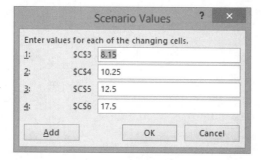

Clicking OK returns you to the Scenario Manager dialog box. From there, clicking the Show button replaces the values in the original worksheet with the alternative values you just defined in the scenario. Any formulas referencing cells that have changed values will recalculate their results. You can then remove the scenario by clicking the Undo button on the Quick Access Toolbar.

> **IMPORTANT** If you save and close a workbook while a scenario is in effect, those values become the default values for the cells changed by the scenario! You should seriously consider creating a scenario that contains the original values of the cells you change or creating a scenario summary worksheet (described in the next section, "Defining multiple alternative data sets").

In this exercise, you'll create a scenario to measure the projected impact on total revenue of a rate increase on two-day shipping.

→ SET UP You need the 2DayScenario workbook located in the Chapter08 practice file folder to complete this exercise. Open the workbook, and then follow the steps.

1   On the **Data** tab, in the **Data Tools** group, click **What-If Analysis** and then, in the list, click **Scenario Manager** to open the **Scenario Manager** dialog box.

2   Click **Add** to open the **Add Scenario** dialog box.

3   In the **Scenario name** field, enter **2DayIncrease**.

4   At the right edge of the **Changing cells** field, click the **Collapse Dialog** button so the worksheet contents are visible.

5   In the worksheet, click cell **C5** and then, in the **Add Scenario** dialog box, click the **Expand Dialog** button. **$C$5** appears in the **Changing Cells** field, and the dialog box title changes to **Edit Scenario**.

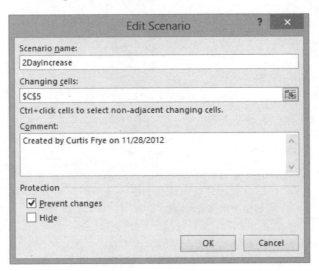

6   Click **OK** to open the **Scenario Values** dialog box.

7   In the value field, enter **13.2**, and then click **OK**. The **Scenario Values** dialog box closes, and the **Scenario Manager** dialog box opens again.

8   If necessary, drag the **Scenario Manager** dialog box to another location on the screen so that you can view the entire table.

9   In the **Scenario Manager** dialog box, click **Show**. Excel applies the scenario, changing the value in cell **C5** to $13.20, which in turn increases the value in cell **E8** to $747,450,000.00.

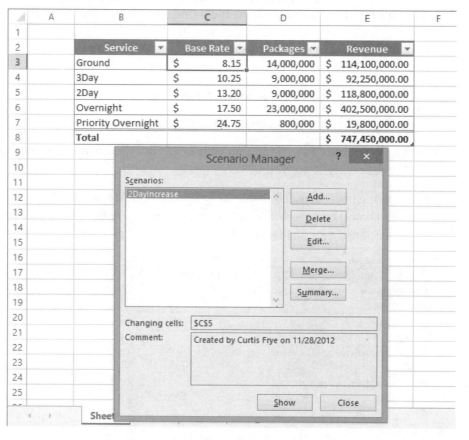

10   In the **Scenario Manager** dialog box, click **Close**.

11   On the **Quick Access Toolbar**, click the **Undo** button to remove the effect of the scenario and prevent Excel from overwriting the original values with the scenario's values if you decide to save the workbook.

❌ CLEAN UP **Close the 2DayScenario workbook, saving your changes if you want to.**

Defining multiple alternative data sets

One great feature of Excel scenarios is that you're not limited to creating one alternative data set—you can create as many scenarios as you like and apply them by using the Scenario Manager. To apply more than one scenario by using the Scenario Manager, click the name of the first scenario you want to display, click the Show button, and then do the same for any subsequent scenarios. The values you defined as part of those scenarios will appear in your worksheet, and Excel will update any calculations involving the changed cells.

TIP If you apply a scenario to a worksheet and then apply another scenario to the same worksheet, both sets of changes appear. If multiple scenarios change the same cell, the cell will contain the value in the most recently applied scenario.

Applying multiple scenarios alters the values in your worksheets. You can understand how those changes affect your formulas, but Excel also gives you a way to view the results of all your scenarios in a single, separate worksheet. To create a worksheet in your current workbook that summarizes the changes caused by your scenarios, open the Scenario Manager, and then click the Summary button. When you do, the Scenario Summary dialog box opens.

8

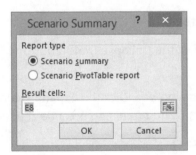

From within the dialog box, you can choose the type of summary worksheet you want to create and the cells you want to display in the summary worksheet. To choose the cells to display in the summary, click the Collapse Dialog button at the right of the Result Cells field, select the cells you want to display, and then expand the dialog box. After you verify that the range in the box represents the cells you want to have included on the summary sheet, click OK to create the new worksheet.

It's a good idea to create an "undo" scenario named *Normal* that holds the original values of the cells you're going to change before they're changed in other scenarios. For example, if you create a scenario named *High Fuel Costs* that changes the sales figures in three cells, your Normal scenario restores those cells to their original values. That way, even if you accidentally modify your worksheet, you can apply the Normal scenario and not have to reconstruct the worksheet from scratch.

TIP Each scenario can change a maximum of 32 cells, so you might need to create more than one scenario to ensure that you can restore a worksheet.

In this exercise, you'll create scenarios to represent projected revenue increases from two rate changes, view the scenarios, and then summarize the scenario results in a new worksheet.

 SET UP You need the MultipleScenarios workbook located in the Chapter08 practice file folder to complete this exercise. Open the workbook, and then follow the steps.

1   On the **Data** tab, in the **Data Tools** group, click **What-If Analysis** and then, in the list, click **Scenario Manager** to open the **Scenario Manager** dialog box.

2   Click **Add** to open the **Add Scenario** dialog box.

3   In the **Scenario name** field, enter **3DayIncrease**.

4   At the right edge of the **Changing cells** field, click the **Collapse Dialog** button to collapse the **Add Scenario** dialog box.

5   In the worksheet, click cell **C4** and then, in the dialog box, click the **Expand Dialog** button. **$C$4** appears in the **Changing Cells** field, and the dialog box title changes to **Edit Scenario**.

6   Click **OK** to open the **Scenario Values** dialog box.

7   In the value field, enter **11.50**.

8   Click **OK** to close the **Scenario Values** dialog box and open the **Scenario Manager**.

9   Click **Add** to open the **Add Scenario** dialog box.

10   In the **Scenario name** field, enter **Ground and Overnight Increase**.

11   At the right edge of the **Changing cells** field, click the **Collapse Dialog** button to collapse the **Add Scenario** dialog box.

12   Click cell **C3**, hold down the **Ctrl** key, and click cell **C6**. Then click the **Expand Dialog** button. **$C$3,$C$6** appears in the **Changing Cells** field, and the dialog box title changes to **Edit Scenario**.

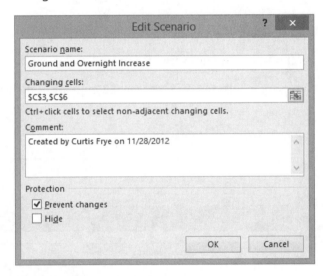

13   Click **OK** to open the **Scenario Values** dialog box.

14   In the **$C$3** field, enter **10.15**.

15   In the **$C$6** field, enter **18.5**.

16   Click **OK** to close the **Scenario Values** dialog box and open the **Scenario Manager** dialog box.

17   Click **Summary** to open the **Scenario Summary** dialog box.

18   Verify that **Scenario summary** is selected and that cell **E8** appears in the **Result cells** field.

19   Click **OK** to create a **Scenario Summary** worksheet.

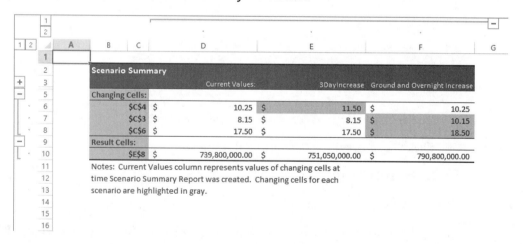

× CLEAN UP Close the MultipleScenarios workbook, saving your changes if you want to.

Analyzing data by using data tables

When you examine business data in Excel, you will often want to discover the result of formulas if you provide different inputs. For example, the executive team of Consolidated Messenger might want to calculate the change in revenue from raising shipping rates, increasing package volume, or both. In Excel 2013, you can calculate the results of those changes by using a data table.

To create a data table that has one variable, you create a worksheet that contains the data required to calculate the variations in the table.

◢	A	B	C	D
1	**Revenue Increases**			**Revenue**
2	Year	2012		$ 2,102,600.70
3	Increase	0%	2%	
4	Package Count	237,582	5%	
5	Rate	$ 8.85	8%	
6				

IMPORTANT The data and formulas must be laid out in a rectangle so the data table you create will appear in the lower-right corner of the cell range you select.

The formula used to summarize the base data appears in cell D2, the cells with the changing values are the range C3:C5, and the cells to contain the calculations based on those values are D3:D5. To create the single-variable data table, select the cell range C2:D5, which encompasses the changing rates, summary formula, and target cells. Then, on the Data tab, click What-If Analysis, and then click Data Table to display the Data Table dialog box.

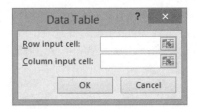

Now you need to identify the cell that contains the summary formula's value that will change in the data table's cells. In this case, that cell is B3. Because the target cells D3:D5 are laid out as a column, you enter the cell address B3 in the Column Input Cell box and click OK.

TIP If your target cells were laid out as a row, you would enter the address of the cell that contains the value to be changed in the Row Input Cell box.

When you click OK, Excel fills in the results of the data table, using the replacement values in cells C3:C5 to provide the values for cells D3:D5.

	A	B	C	D
1	**Revenue Increases**			Revenue
2	Year	2012		$ 2,102,600.70
3	Increase	0%	2%	$ 2,107,352.34
4	Package Count	237,582	5%	$ 2,114,479.80
5	Rate	$ 8.85	8%	$ 2,121,607.26
6				

To create a two-variable data table, you lay your data out with one set of replacement values as row headers and the other set as column headers. For example, you could build a worksheet to calculate total revenue as a function of both rate increases and package count increases.

	A	B	C	D	E
1	**Revenue Increases**		Revenue		
2	Year	2012	$ 2,102,600.70	260,000	300,000
3	Increase	0%	2%		
4	Package Count	237,582	5%		
5	Rate	$ 8.85	8%		
6					

In this case, you select the cell range C2:E5 and then, on the Data tab, click What-If Analysis and then click Data Table to display the Data Table dialog box. Because you're creating a two-variable data table, you need to enter cell addresses for both the Column Input Cell and Row Input Cell. In this case, the column input cell is B3, which represents the rate increase, and the row input cell is B4, which contains the package count. When you click OK, Excel creates your data table.

	A	B	C	D	E
1	**Revenue Increases**		Revenue		
2	Year	2012	$ 2,102,600.70	260,000	300,000
3	Increase	0%	2%	$ 2,306,200.00	$ 2,661,000.00
4	Package Count	237,582	5%	$ 2,314,000.00	$ 2,670,000.00
5	Rate	$ 8.85	8%	$ 2,321,800.00	$ 2,679,000.00
6					

TIP You can't edit the formulas Excel creates when you define a data table. You can only change them successfully by creating another data table that includes the same cells.

In this exercise, you'll create one-variable and two-variable data tables.

➔ SET UP **You need the RateProjections workbook located in the Chapter08 practice file folder to complete this exercise. Open the workbook, and then follow the steps.**

1   If necessary, click the **RateIncreases** sheet tab to display that worksheet.

2   Select cells **C2:D5**.

3   On the **Data** tab, in the **Data Tools** group, click the **What-If Analysis** button and then, in the list, click **Data Table**.

4   In the **Column input cell** box, enter **B3**.

5   Click **OK** to close the **Data Table** dialog box and fill the what-if values into cells **D3:D5**.

6   Click the **RateAndVolume** sheet tab to display that worksheet.

7   Select cells **C2:E5**.

8   On the **Data** tab, in the **Data Tools** group, click the **What-If Analysis** button and then, in the list, click **Data Table**.

9   In the **Row input cell** box, enter **B4**.

10   In the **Column input cell** box, enter **B3**.

11   Click **OK** to close the **Data Table** dialog box and update your worksheet.

▲	A	B	C	D	E
1	**Revenue Increases**		Revenue		
2	Year	2012	$ 2,102,600.70	260,000	300,000
3	Increase	0%	2.00%	$ 2,306,200.00	$ 2,661,000.00
4	Package Count	237,582	4.75%	$ 2,313,350.00	$ 2,669,250.00
5	Rate	$ 8.85	9.25%	$ 2,325,050.00	$ 2,682,750.00
6					

✖ CLEAN UP **Close the RateProjections workbook, saving your changes if you want to.**

Varying your data to get a specific result by using Goal Seek

When you run an organization, you must track how every element performs, both in absolute terms and in relation to other parts of the organization. Just as you might want to reward your employees for maintaining a perfect safety record and keeping down your insurance rates, you might also want to stop carrying products you cannot sell.

When you plan how you want to grow your business, you should have specific goals in mind for each department or product category. For example, Lori Penor of Consolidated Messenger might have the goal of reducing the firm's labor costs by 20 percent as compared to the previous year. Finding the labor amount that represents a 20-percent decrease is simple, but expressing goals in other ways can make finding the solution more challenging. Instead of decreasing labor costs 20 percent over the previous year, Lori might want to decrease labor costs so they represent no more than 20 percent of the company's total outlay.

As an example, consider a worksheet that holds cost figures for Consolidated Messenger's operations and uses those figures to calculate both total costs and the share each category has of that total.

◢	A	B	C	D	E	F	G	H
1								
2			Labor	Transportation	Taxes	Facilities	Total	
3		Cost	$ 18,000,382.00	$35,000,000.00	$ 7,000,000.00	$ 19,000,000.00	$ 79,000,382.00	
4		Share	22.79%	44.30%	8.86%	24.05%		
5								

IMPORTANT In the worksheet, the values in the Share row are displayed as percentages, but the underlying values are decimals. For example, Excel represents *0.3064* as *30.64%*.

Although it would certainly be possible to figure the target number that would make labor costs represent 20 percent of the total, there is an easier way to do it in Excel: by using Goal Seek. To use Goal Seek, you display the Data tab and then, in the Data Tools group, click What-If Analysis. On the menu that is displayed, click Goal Seek to open the Goal Seek dialog box.

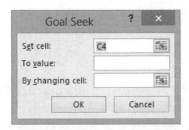

In the dialog box, you identify the cell that has the target value; in this example, it is cell C4, which has the percentage of costs accounted for by the Labor category. The To Value field has the target value (.2, which is equivalent to 20 percent), and the By Changing Cell field identifies the cell that has the value Excel should change to generate the target value of 20 percent in cell C4. In this example, the cell to be changed is C3.

Clicking OK tells Excel to find a solution for the goal you set. When Excel finishes its work, the new values appear in the designated cells, and the Goal Seek Status dialog box opens.

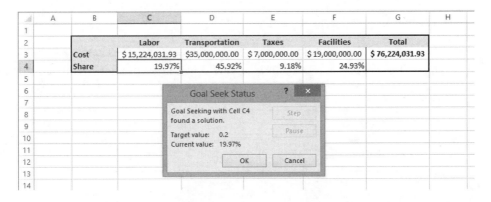

TIP Goal Seek finds the closest solution it can without exceeding the target value. In this case, the closest percentage it could find was 19.97 percent.

In this exercise, you'll use Goal Seek to determine how much you need to decrease transportation costs so that those costs make up no more than 40 percent of Consolidated Messenger's operating costs.

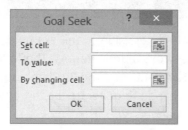 **SET UP** You need the TargetValues workbook located in the Chapter08 practice file folder to complete this exercise. Open the workbook, and then follow the steps.

1   On the **Data** tab, in the **Data Tools** group, click the **What-If Analysis** button, and then, in the list, click **Goal Seek** to open the **Goal Seek** dialog box.

2   In the **Set cell** field, enter **D4**.

3   In the **To value** field, enter **40%**.

4   In the **By changing cell** field, enter **D3**.

5   Click **OK** to display the solution in both the worksheet and the **Goal Seek Status** dialog box. The target value of 0.4 is equivalent to the 40 percent value you entered earlier.

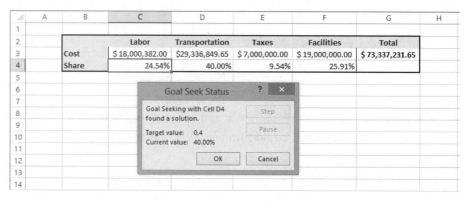

6   Click **Cancel** to close the **Goal Seek Status** dialog box without saving the new worksheet values.

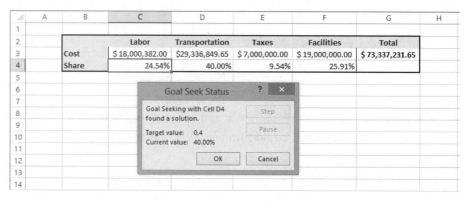 **CLEAN UP** Close the TargetValues workbook, saving your changes if you want to.

Finding optimal solutions by using Solver

Goal Seek is a great tool for finding out how much you need to change a single input value to generate a desired result from a formula, but it's of no help if you want to find the best mix of several input values. For example, marketing vice president Craig Dewar might want to advertise in four national magazines to drive customers to Consolidated Messenger's website, but he might not know the best mix of ads to reach the greatest number of readers. He asked the publishers for ad pricing and readership numbers, which he recorded in a spreadsheet, along with the minimum number of ads per publication (three) and the minimum number of times he wants the ad to be seen (10,000,000). Because one of the magazines has a high percentage of corporate executive readers, Craig does want to take out at least four ads in that publication, despite its relatively low readership. The goal of the ad campaign is for the ads to be seen as many times as possible without costing the company more than the $3,000,000 budget.

	Magazine	Cost per Ad	Readers	Number of Ads	Total Cost	Audience
4	Magazine	Cost per Ad	Readers	Number of Ads	Total Cost	Audience
5	Mag1	$ 30,000.00	100,000	8	$ 240,000.00	800,000
6	Mag2	$ 40,000.00	400,000	8	$ 320,000.00	3,200,000
7	Mag3	$ 27,000.00	350,000	8	$ 216,000.00	2,800,000
8	Mag4	$ 80,000.00	200,000	10	$ 800,000.00	2,000,000
9	Totals				$ 1,576,000.00	8,800,000
10						
11		Constraints			Total Budget	$ 3,000,000.00
12					Minimum Audience	10,000,000
13				Minimum Ads for Magazines 1 through 3		8
14				Minimum Ads for Magazine 4		10
15				Maximum Ads in Any Magazine		20
16						

TIP It helps to spell out every aspect of your problem so that you can identify the cells you want Solver to use in its calculations.

If you performed a complete installation when you installed Excel on your computer, the Solver button is available on the Data tab in the Analysis group. If not, you need to install the Solver Add-In. To do so, click the File tab, and then click Options. In the Excel Options dialog box, click Add-Ins to display the Add-Ins page. At the bottom of the dialog box, in the Manage list, click Excel Add-Ins, and then click Go to display the Add-Ins dialog box. Select the Solver Add-In check box and click OK to install Solver.

TIP You might be prompted for the Microsoft Office system installation CD. If so, put the CD in your CD drive, and click OK.

After the installation is complete, Solver appears on the Data tab, in the Analysis group. Clicking Solver displays the Solver Parameters dialog box.

The first step of setting up your Solver problem is to identify the cell that contains the summary formula you want to establish as your objective. To identify that cell, click in the Set Objective box, click the target cell in the worksheet, and then select the option that represents whether you want to minimize the cell's value, maximize the cell's value, or make the cell take on a specific value. Next, you click in the By Changing Variable Cells box and select the cells Solver should vary to change the value in the objective cell.

If you want to require Solver to find solutions that use only integer values (that is, values that are whole numbers and have no decimal component), you can do so by clicking the Options button in the Solver Parameters dialog box to open the Options dialog box.

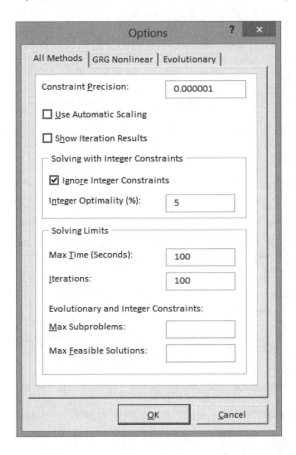

If necessary, clear the Ignore Integer Constraints check box and click OK to save your setting and return to the Solver Parameters dialog box.

Finally, you can create constraints that will set the limits for the values Solver can use. To do so, click Add to open the Add Constraint dialog box. You add constraints to the Solver problem by selecting the cells to which you want to apply the constraint, selecting the comparison operation (such as less than or equal to, greater than or equal to, or must be an integer), and clicking in the Constraint box to select the cell with the value of the constraint. You could also enter a value in the Constraint box, but referring to a cell makes it possible for you to change the constraint later without opening Solver.

TIP After you run Solver, you can use the commands in the Solver Results dialog box to save the results as changes to your worksheet or create a scenario based on the changed data.

In this exercise, you'll use Solver to determine the best mix of ads given the following constraints:

- You want to maximize the number of people who view the ads.

- You must buy at least 8 ads in three magazines and at least 10 in the fourth.

- You can't buy part of an ad (that is, all numbers must be integers).

- You can buy no more than 20 ads in any one magazine.

- You must reach at least 10,000,000 people.

- Your ad budget is $3,000,000.

➡ SET UP You need the AdBuy workbook located in the Chapter08 practice file folder to complete this exercise. Open the workbook, and then follow the steps.

1 If the **Solver** button doesn't appear in the **Analysis** group on the **Data** tab, follow the instructions described earlier to install it.

2 In the **Analysis** group on the **Data** tab, click **Solver** to open the **Solver Parameters** dialog box.

3 In the **Solver Parameters** dialog box, click **Options** to open the **Options** dialog box.

4 On the **All Methods** page of the dialog box, clear the **Ignore Integer Constraints** check box, and then click **OK**.

5 Click in the **Set Objective** box, and then click cell **G9**. $G$9 appears in the **Set Objective** field.

6 Click **Max**.

7   Click in the **By Changing Variable Cells** field, and select cells **E5:E8**. **$E$5:$E$8** appears in the **By Changing Variable Cells** field.

8   Click **Add** to open the **Add Constraint** dialog box.

9   Select cells **E5:E8**. **$E$5:$E$8** appears in the **Cell Reference** field.

10   In the operator list, click **int**. Then click **Add**. Excel adds the constraint to the Solver problem, and the **Add Constraint** dialog box clears to accept the next constraint.

11   Click cell **F9**. **$F$9** appears in the **Cell Reference** field. Verify that the operator **<=** appears in the operator field.

12   Click in the **Constraint** field, and then click cell **G11**. **=$G$11** appears in the **Constraint** field.

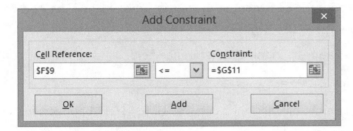

13   Click **Add**. Excel adds the constraint to the Solver problem, and the **Add Constraint** dialog box clears to accept the next constraint.

14   Click cell **G9**. **$G$9** appears in the **Cell Reference** field.

15   In the operator list, click **>=**.

16   Click in the **Constraint** field, and then click cell **G12**. **=$G$12** appears in the **Constraint** field.

17   Click **Add**. Excel adds the constraint to the Solver problem, and the **Add Constraint** dialog box clears to accept the next constraint.

18   Select cells **E5:E7**. **$E$5:$E$7** appears in the **Cell Reference** field.

19   In the operator list, click >=.

20   Click in the **Constraint** field, and then click cell **G13**. =$G$13 appears in the **Constraint** field.

21   Click **Add**. Excel adds the constraint to the Solver problem, and the **Add Constraint** dialog box clears to accept the next constraint.

22   Click cell **E8**. **$E$8** appears in the **Cell Reference** field.

23   In the operator list, click >=.

24   Click in the **Constraint** field, and then click cell **G14**. =$G$14 appears in the **Constraint** field.

25   Click **Add**. Excel adds the constraint to the Solver problem, and the **Add Constraint** dialog box clears to accept the next constraint.

26   Select cells **E5:E8**. **$E$5:$E$8** appears in the **Cell Reference** field.

27   Verify that the <= operator appears in the operator field, click in the **Constraint** field, and then click cell **G15**. =$G$15 appears in the **Constraint** field.

28   Click **OK**. Excel adds the constraint to the Solver problem and closes the **Add Constraint** dialog box, and the **Solver Parameters** dialog box opens again.

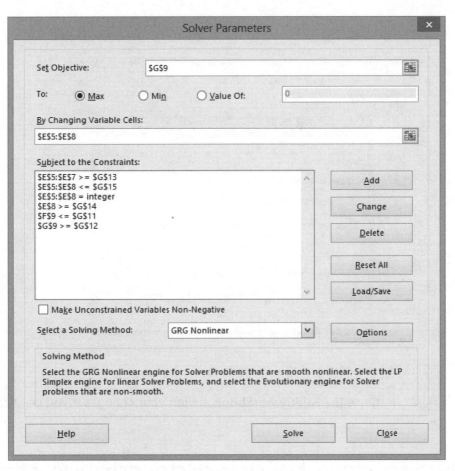

29 Click **Solve**. The **Solver Results** dialog box opens, indicating that Solver found a solution. The result is displayed in the body of the worksheet.

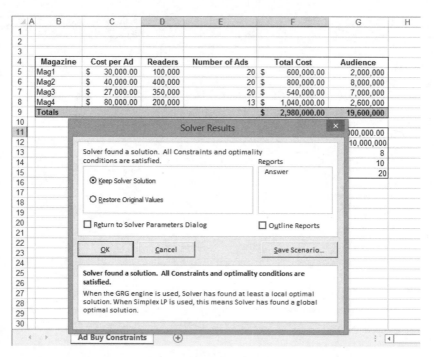

30 Click **OK** to close the **Solver Results** dialog box.

❌ CLEAN UP **Close the AdBuy workbook, saving your changes if you want to.**

Analyzing data by using descriptive statistics

Experienced business people can tell a lot about numbers just by looking at them, such as whether the numbers "feel right." That is, the sales figures are about where they're supposed to be for a particular hour, day, or month; the average seems about right; and sales have increased from year to year. When you need more than an informal assessment, however, you can use the tools in the Analysis ToolPak.

If the Data Analysis item isn't visible in the Analysis group on the Data tab, you can install it. To do so, click the File tab, and then click Options. In the Excel Options dialog box, click Add-Ins to display the Add-Ins page. At the bottom of the dialog box, in the Manage list, click Excel Add-Ins, and then click Go to display the Add-Ins dialog box. Select the Analysis ToolPak check box and click OK.

TIP You might be prompted for the Microsoft Office system installation CD. If so, put the CD in your CD drive, and click OK.

After the installation is complete, the Data Analysis option appears in the Analysis group on the Data tab.

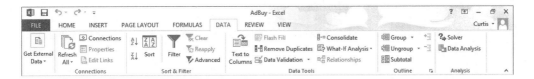

In the list that appears when you click the Data Analysis button, click the item representing the type of data analysis you want to perform, click OK, and use the commands in the resulting dialog box to analyze your data.

In this exercise, you'll use the Analysis ToolPak to generate descriptive statistics of driver sorting time data.

 SET UP **You need the DriverSortTimes workbook located in the Chapter08 practice file folder to complete this exercise. Open the workbook, and then follow the steps.**

1   On the **Data** tab, in the **Analysis** group, click **Data Analysis** to open the **Data Analysis** dialog box.

2   Click **Descriptive Statistics**, and then click **OK** to open the **Descriptive Statistics** dialog box.

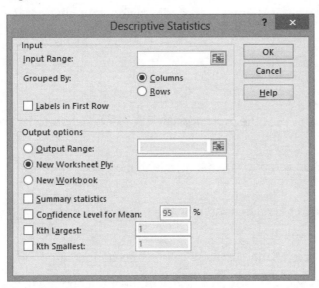

3   Click in the **Input Range** field, and then select cells **C3:C17**. **$C$3:$C$17** appears in the **Input Range** field.

4   Select the **Summary statistics** check box.

5   Click **OK**. A new worksheet that contains summary statistics about the selected data appears.

	A	B	C
1	*Column1*		
2			
3	Mean	120.7333	
4	Standard Error	7.036955	
5	Median	109	
6	Mode	102	
7	Standard Deviation	27.25401	
8	Sample Variance	742.781	
9	Kurtosis	-1.17215	
10	Skewness	0.642027	
11	Range	74	
12	Minimum	91	
13	Maximum	165	
14	Sum	1811	
15	Count	15	
16			

✖ CLEAN UP Close the DriverSortTimes workbook, saving your changes if you want to.

Key points

- The Quick Analysis Lens puts the most popular summary analysis tools at your fingertips.

- By using scenarios, you can describe many potential business cases within a single workbook.

- It's usually a good idea to create a "normal" scenario that you can use to reset your worksheet.

- Remember that you can change up to 32 cells in a scenario, but no more.

- You can summarize your scenarios on a new worksheet to compare how each scenario approaches the data.

- You can use data tables to create useful what-if scenarios by changing one or two variables that provide input to a summary formula.

- You can use Goal Seek to determine what value you need in a single cell to generate the result you want from a formula.

- If you want to vary the values in more than one cell to find the optimal mix of inputs for a calculation, use the Solver Add-In.

- Advanced statistical tools are available in the Analysis ToolPak. You can use them to examine your data thoroughly.

8

Chapter at a glance

Charts

Customize the appearance of charts,
page 254

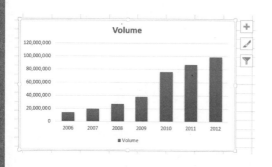

Trendlines

Find trends in your data,
page 262

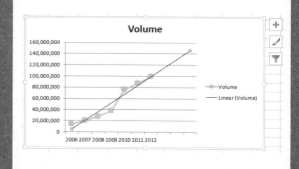

Diagrams

Create diagrams by using SmartArt,
page 273

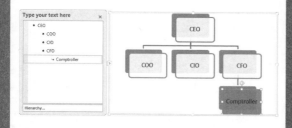

Shapes

Create shapes and mathematical equations,
page 278

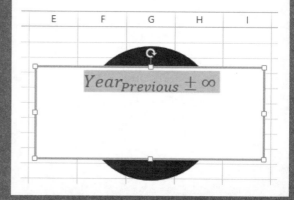

Creating charts and graphics

9

IN THIS CHAPTER, YOU WILL LEARN HOW TO

- Create charts.

- Customize the appearance of charts.

- Find trends in your data.

- Create dual-axis charts.

- Summarize your data by using sparklines.

- Create diagrams by using SmartArt.

- Create shapes and mathematical equations.

When you enter data into a Microsoft Excel 2013 worksheet, you create a record of important events, whether they are individual sales, sales for an hour of a day, or the price of a product. However, a list of values in cells can't communicate easily the overall trends in the data. The best way to communicate trends in a large collection of data is by creating a chart, which summarizes data visually. In addition to the standard charts, with Excel 2013, you can create compact charts called sparklines, which summarize a data series by using a graph contained within a single cell.

You have a great deal of control over your charts' appearance—you can change the color of any chart element, choose a different chart type to better summarize the underlying data, and change the display properties of text and numbers in a chart. If the data in the worksheet used to create a chart represents a progression through time, such as sales over several months, you can have Excel extrapolate future sales and add a trendline to the graph that represents that prediction.

In this chapter, you'll create a chart and customize its elements, find trends in your data, create a dual-axis chart, summarize data by using sparklines, create diagrams by using SmartArt, and create shapes that contain mathematical equations.

Creating charts

With Excel 2013, you can create charts quickly by using the Quick Analysis Lens, which displays recommended charts to summarize your data. To display recommended charts, select the entire data range you want to chart, click the Quick Analysis button, and then click Charts to display the types of charts that Excel recommends.

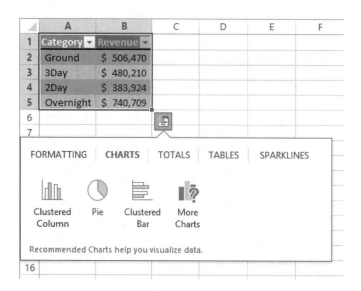

You can display a live preview of each recommended chart by pointing to the icon that represents that chart. Clicking the icon adds the chart to your worksheet.

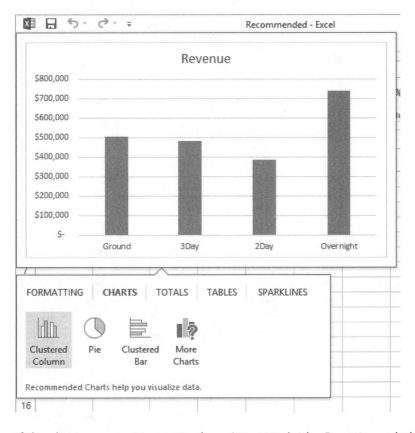

If the chart you want to create doesn't appear in the Recommended Charts gallery, select the data that you want to summarize visually and then, on the Insert tab, in the Charts group, click the type of chart that you want to create to have Excel display the available chart subtypes. When you point to a subtype, Excel displays a live preview of what the chart will look like if you click that subtype.

9

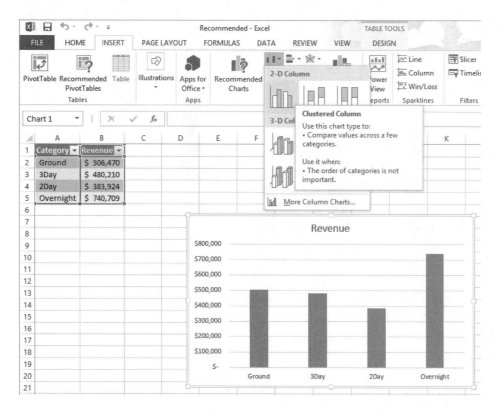

When you click a chart subtype, Excel creates the chart by using the default layout and color scheme defined in your workbook's theme.

KEYBOARD SHORTCUT Press Alt+F11 to create a chart of the default type on the current worksheet or press F11 to create a new chart sheet. Unless you or another user changed the default, Excel creates a column chart. For a complete list of keyboard shortcuts, see "Keyboard shortcuts" at the end of this book.

If Excel doesn't plot your data the way that you want it to appear, you can change the axis on which Excel plots a data column. The most common reason for incorrect data plotting is that the column to be plotted on the horizontal axis contains numerical data instead of textual data. For example, if your data includes a Year column and a Maintenance column, instead of plotting maintenance data for each consecutive year along the horizontal axis, Excel plots both of those columns in the body of the chart and creates a sequential series to provide values for the horizontal axis.

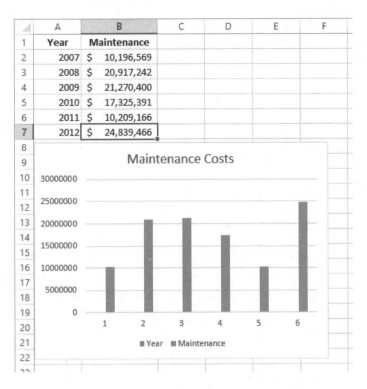

You can change which data Excel applies to the vertical axis (also known as the *y-axis*) and the horizontal axis (also known as the *x-axis*). To make that change, select the chart and then, on the Design tab, in the Data group, click Select Data to open the Select Data Source dialog box.

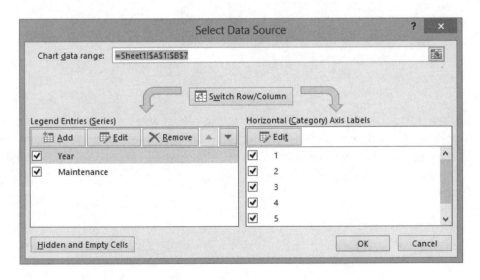

As shown in the preceding graphic, the Year column doesn't belong in the Legend Entries (Series) pane, which corresponds to a column chart's vertical axis. To remove a column from an axis, select the column's name, and then click Remove. To add the column to the Horizontal (Category) Axis Labels pane, click that pane's Edit button to display the Axis Labels dialog box, which you can use to select a range of cells on a worksheet to provide values for an axis.

In the Axis Labels dialog box, click the Collapse Dialog button at the right edge of the Axis Label Range field, select the cells to provide the values for the horizontal axis (not including the column header, if any), click the Expand Dialog button, and then click OK. Click OK again to close the Select Data Source dialog box and revise your chart.

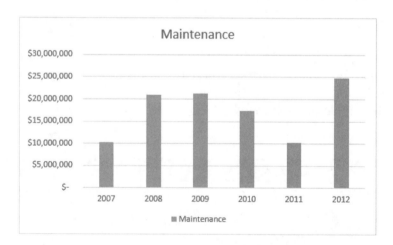

After you create your chart, you can change its size to reflect whether the chart should dominate its worksheet or take on a role as another informative element on the worksheet. For example, Gary Schare, the chief executive officer of Consolidated Messenger, could create a workbook that summarizes the performance of each of his company's business units. In that case, he would display the chart and data for each business unit on the same worksheet, so he would want to make his charts small.

To resize a chart, select the chart, and then drag one of the handles on the chart's edges. By using the handles in the middle of the edges, you can resize the chart in one direction. When you drag a handle on the left or right edge, the chart gets narrower or wider, whereas when you drag the handles on the chart's top and bottom edges, the chart gets shorter or taller. You can drag a corner handle to change the chart's height and width at the same time; and you can hold down the Shift key as you drag the corner handle to change the chart's size without changing its proportions.

Just as you can control a chart's size, you can also control its location. To move a chart within a worksheet, drag the chart to the desired location. If you want to move the chart to a new worksheet, click the chart and then, on the Design tool tab, in the Location group, click Move Chart to open the Move Chart dialog box.

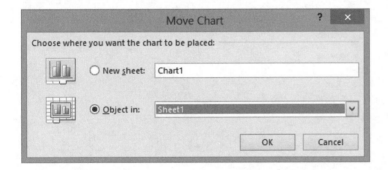

To move the chart to a new chart sheet, click New Sheet and enter the new sheet's name in the accompanying field. Clicking New Sheet creates a chart sheet that contains only your chart. You can still resize the chart on that sheet, but when Excel creates the new chart sheet, the chart takes up the full sheet.

To move the chart to an existing worksheet, click Object In and then, in the Object In list, click the worksheet to which you want to move the chart.

9

In this exercise, you'll create a chart, change how the chart plots your data, move your chart within a worksheet, and move your chart to its own chart sheet.

 SET UP **You need the YearlyPackageVolume workbook located in the Chapter09 practice file folder to complete this exercise. Open the workbook, and then follow the steps.**

1   On the **Data** worksheet, click any cell in the Excel table, and then press **Ctrl+*** to select the entire table.

2   In the lower-right corner of the Excel table, click the **Quick Analysis** button to display tools available in the **Quick Analysis** gallery.

3   Click the **Charts** tab to display the available chart types.

4   Click **Line** to create the recommended line chart.

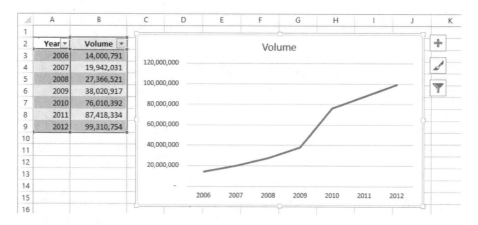

5   Press **Ctrl+Z** to undo the last action and remove the chart from your worksheet.

6   On the **Insert** tab, in the **Charts** group, click **Bar** and then, in the **2D Bar** group, click the first chart subtype, **Clustered Bar**. Excel creates the chart, with both the **Year** and **Volume** data series plotted in the body of the chart.

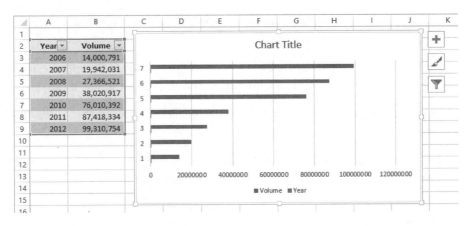

7 On the **Design** tab, in the **Data** group, click **Select Data** to open the **Select Data Source** dialog box.

8 In the **Legend Entries (Series)** area, click **Year**.

9 Click **Remove** to delete the **Year** series.

10 In the **Horizontal (Category) Axis Labels** area, click **Edit** to open the **Axis Labels** dialog box.

11 Select cells **A3:A9**, and then click **OK**. The **Axis Labels** dialog box closes, and the **Select Data Source** dialog box reappears with the years in the **Horizontal (Category) Axis Labels** area.

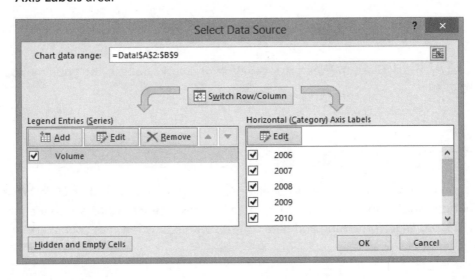

12   Click **OK**. Excel redraws your chart, using the years as the values for the horizontal axis.

13   Point to (don't click) the body of the chart, and when the pointer changes to a four-headed arrow drag the chart up and to the left so that it covers the Excel table.

14   On the **Design** tab, in the **Location** group, click **Move Chart** to open the **Move Chart** dialog box.

15   Click **New sheet**, enter Volume Chart in the sheet name box, and then click **OK**. Your chart appears on a chart sheet named *Volume Chart*.

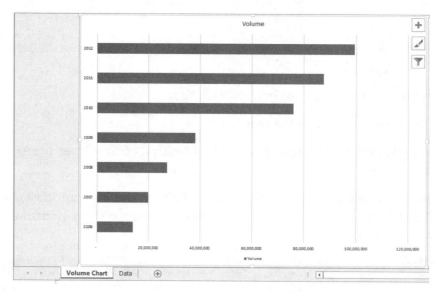

❌ CLEAN UP Close the YearlyPackageVolume workbook, saving your changes if you want to.

Customizing the appearance of charts

If you want to change a chart's appearance, select the chart and then click the Chart Styles button, which appears in a group of three buttons. These buttons, which are new in Excel 2013, put chart formatting and data controls within easy reach of your chart.

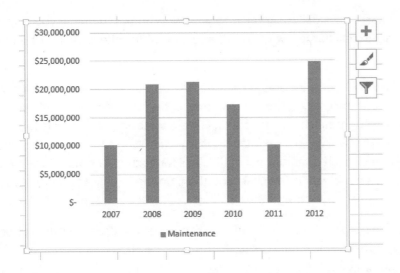

The Chart Styles gallery has two tabs: Style and Color. You can select a new look for you chart by choosing from the many styles on the Style.

TIP If you prefer to work with the ribbon, these same styles appear in the Chart Styles gallery on the Design tab.

Clicking the Color tab in the Chart Styles gallery displays a series of color schemes that you can select to change your chart's appearance.

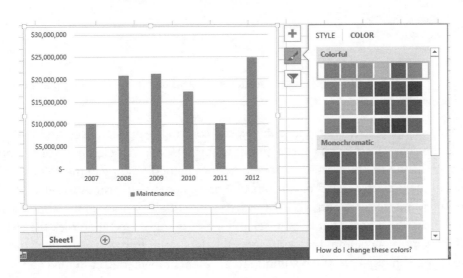

TIP The styles in the Chart Styles gallery are tied to your workbook's theme. If you change your workbook's theme, Excel changes your chart's appearance to reflect the new theme's colors.

When you create a chart by using the tools in the Charts group on the Insert tab, Excel creates an attractive chart that focuses on the data. In most cases, the chart has a title, legend (list of data series displayed in the chart), horizontal lines in the body of the chart to make it easier to discern individual values, and axis labels. If you want to create a chart that has more or different elements, such as additional data labels for each data point plotted on your chart, you can do so by selecting the chart and then, on the Design tab, in the Chart Layouts group, clicking Quick Layouts and then clicking the layout you want.

If you don't find the exact chart layout you want, you can select the chart and then click the Chart Elements action button, which appears to the right of the chart, to control each element's appearance and options.

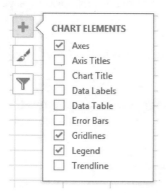

By selecting the Gridlines check box, you can determine whether the chart displays horizontal and vertical gridlines.

In addition to changing your chart's layout, you can control the appearance of each element within the chart. To select a chart element to format, click that element. For example, if you want to change the formatting of the data series named Volume in the column chart you created in the previous exercise, you can click any column in the series to select the entire series. Any formatting changes you make then apply to every point in the entire series. If you want to change a single data point, select the entire series, and then click the chart element (for example, a column) that represents the data point that you want to change. For example, you can highlight the column that represents the year 2011 in the chart you created in the previous exercise.

You can display a list of the selectable chart elements by selecting the chart and then, on the Format tab, in the Current Selection group, clicking the Chart Elements arrow. Then click the desired chart element to select it.

After you select the chart element, you can drag one of the element's handles to resize the element or drag the element to another location within the chart. To change the chart element's format, use the tools and dialog box launchers in the Shape Styles, Word Art Styles, Arrange, and Size groups on the Format tab to change the element's appearance. You can also select the chart element and then, on the Format tab, in the Current Selection group, click Format Selection to display a Format pane that you can use to change the chart element's appearance.

9

You can also display a similar set of formatting controls for a chart element by clicking the Chart Elements action button, pointing to the name of the element you want to change, clicking the right-pointing triangle that appears, and then clicking More Options. Doing so displays the pane related to that element.

With the third action button, Chart Filters, you can focus on specific data in your chart. Clicking the Chart Filters action button displays a filter interface that is very similar to that used to limit the data displayed in an Excel table.

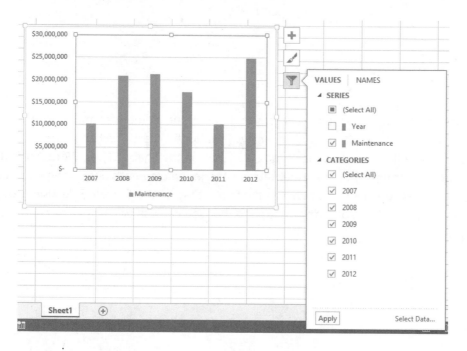

Selecting or clearing a check box displays or hides data related to a specific value within a series, which you can select as well.

If you think you want to apply the same set of changes to charts you'll create in the future, you can save your chart as a chart template. When you select the data that you want to summarize visually and apply the chart template, you'll create consistently formatted charts in a minimum of steps. To save a chart as a chart template, right-click the chart and then click Save As Template. Use the controls in the dialog box that opens to name and save your template. Then, to create a chart based on that template, select the data that you want to summarize and on the Insert tab, in the Charts group, click the dialog box launcher in the lower-right corner of the group to open the Insert Chart dialog box. On the All Charts tab, click Templates, click the template you want to use, and then click OK.

TIP You can apply a template to an existing chart by selecting the chart and then, on the Design tab, in the Type group, clicking Change Chart Type to open the Change Chart Type dialog box. Click Templates, click the template you want to use, and then click OK.

In this exercise, you'll change a chart's layout, apply a new Chart Style, change the number format of the values on the vertical axis, save the chart as a chart template, and apply the template to another chart.

➡ SET UP You need the VolumeByCenter workbook located in the Chapter09 practice file folder to complete this exercise. Open the workbook, and then follow the steps.

1   On the **Presentation** worksheet, select the chart.

2   On the **Design** tab, in the **Chart Layouts** group, click **Quick Layouts**, and then click the first chart layout **Layout 1**.

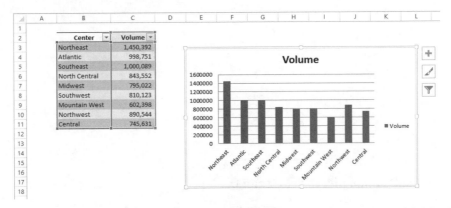

3   To the right of the chart, click the **Chart Styles** action button to display the **Chart Styles** gallery.

4   Click **Style 7** to change the chart's style.

5   Click the **Chart Styles** action button to hide the **Chart Styles** gallery.

6   Click the **Chart Elements** action button, point to the **Axes** entry, click the right-pointing triangle that appears, and then click **More Options** to display the **Format Axis** pane.

7   In the pane, click **Axis Options**, and then click **Vertical (Value) Axis**.

8   Click **Number** to display the **Number** options in the **Format Axis** pane.

9   In the **Category** list, click **Number** to display the **Number** category's style options.

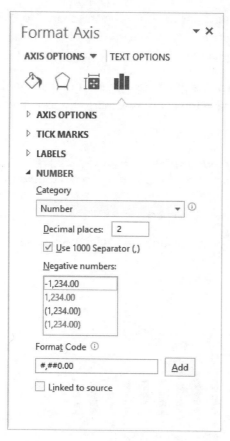

10   In the **Decimal places** field, enter **0**.

11   If necessary, select the **Use 1000 Separator (,)** check box.

12   Click the pane's **Close button**. Excel closes the pane and updates the chart's appearance.

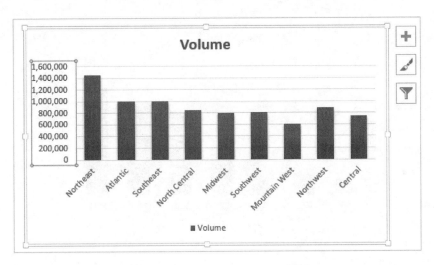

13   Right-click the chart and then click **Save As Template** to open the **Save Chart Template** dialog box.

14   In the **File name** field, enter **Cool Blue**.

15   Click **Save** to save your template.

16   On the tab bar, click the **Yearly Summary** sheet tab to display the **Yearly Summary** worksheet.

17   Select the chart and then, on the **Design** tab, in the **Type** group, click **Change Chart Type** to open the **Change Chart Type** dialog box.

18   Click **Templates** to display the **My Templates** list.

19   Click the **Cool Blue** custom template, and then click **OK** to apply the template to your chart.

9

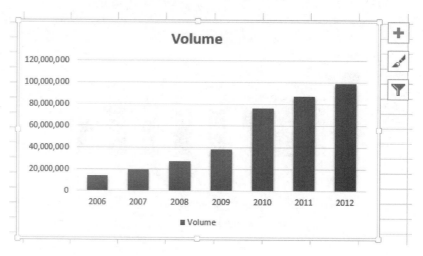

CLEAN UP Close the VolumeByCenter workbook, saving your changes if you want to.

Finding trends in your data

You can use the data in Excel workbooks to discover how your business has performed in the past, but you can also have Excel make its best guess—for example, as to future shipping revenues if the current trend continues. Consider a graph that shows the fleet maintenance costs for the years 2006 through 2012 for Consolidated Messenger.

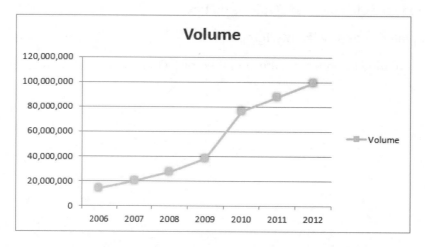

The total has increased from 2006 to 2012, but the growth hasn't been uniform, so guessing how much maintenance costs would increase if the overall trend continued would require difficult mathematical computations. Fortunately, Excel can perform that math. To have Excel project future values in the maintenance costs data series, click the chart, click the Chart Elements action button, point to Trendline, click the right-pointing triangle that appears, and then click More Options to display the Format Trendline pane.

On the Trendline Options page of the Format Trendline pane, you can choose the data distribution that Excel should expect when it makes its projection.

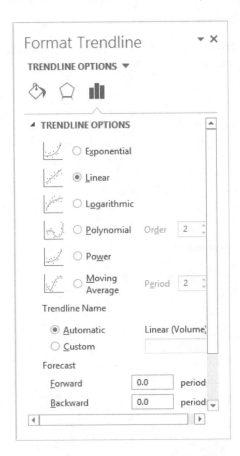

TIP If you don't know which distribution to choose, use Linear, which applies to most business data. The other distributions are used for scientific and engineering applications and you will most likely know, or be told by a colleague, when to use them.

After you choose the distribution type, you can tell Excel how far ahead to project the data trend. The horizontal axis of the chart used in this example shows revenues by year from 2006 to 2012. To tell Excel how far in the future to look, enter a number in the Forecast area's Forward box. In this case, to look ahead one year, enter *1* in the Forward box, and then click OK to add the trendline to the chart.

TIP When you click the Trendline button in the Analysis group, one of the options Excel displays is Linear Forecast Trendline, which adds a trendline with a two-period forecast.

As with other chart elements, you can double-click the trendline to open a formatting dialog box and change the line's appearance.

In this exercise, you'll add a trendline to a chart.

SET UP You need the FutureVolumes workbook located in the Chapter09 practice file folder to complete this exercise. Open the workbook, and then follow the steps.

1   Select the chart.

2   Click the **Chart Elements** action button, point to **Trendline**, click the right-pointing triangle that appears, and then click **More Options**. The **Format Trendline** pane appears.

3   If necessary, in the **Trend/Regression Type** area, click **Linear**.

4   In the **Forecast** area, in the **Forward** field, enter 3.

5   Click the pane's **Close button** to add the trendline to the chart.

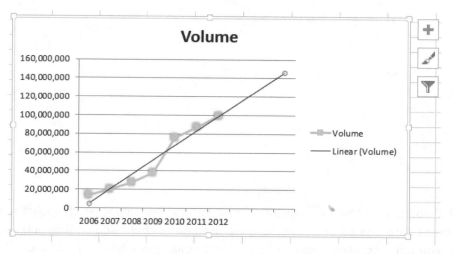

CLEAN UP Close the FutureVolumes workbook, saving your changes if you want to.

Creating dual-axis charts

The Excel 2013 charting engine provides you with the flexibility to plot more than one data series, even if the series use two different scales. For example, Consolidated Messenger might track seasonal package volumes for each regional distribution center by category and, as part of the same data collection, track the number of improperly routed packages.

	A	B	C
1	Month	Volume	Exceptions
2	January	191,442	45
3	February	155,371	31
4	March	207,614	41
5	April	111,977	31
6	May	283,284	29
7	June	109,175	39
8	July	298,858	37
9	August	170,936	47
10	Septembe	195,520	39
11	October	134,432	34
12	Novembe	150,993	23
13	Decembe	195,378	21
14			

When you have two differing but related data series in a table, you can summarize the data by using a dual-axis chart. To create a dual-axis chart, click any cell in the data you want to chart and then, on the Insert tab, click the type of chart you want to create. When you do, Excel plots both data series by using that chart type.

9

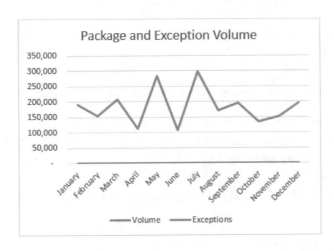

You can plot these two data series using separate axes by creating a combo chart. To do that, click the chart and then, on the Design tool tab, click Change Chart Type to display the dialog box of the same name. In the Change Chart Type dialog box, click the All Charts tab, and then click Combo to display the Combo charts page.

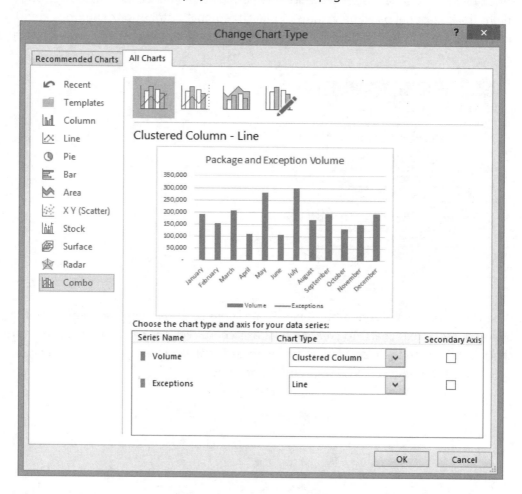

You can now use the controls in the Choose The Chart Type And Axis For Your Data Series area of the dialog box to select how to plot each series. To choose how to format a series, click the Chart Type arrow for that series and select its chart type. If you want the series to be plotted in relation to the values on the left vertical axis, leave the Secondary Axis check box cleared. To have the series plotted in relation to the values on the right vertical axis, select the Secondary Axis check box.

When you click OK, Excel creates your chart.

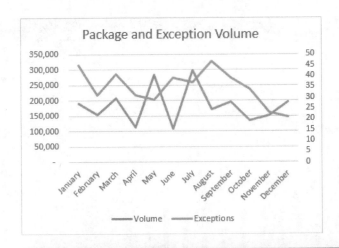

> **IMPORTANT** Dual-axis charts that plot series with widely separated values can be visually deceiving. Be sure to read them carefully.

In this exercise, you'll create a dual-axis chart.

 SET UP **You need the DualAnalysis workbook located in the Chapter09 practice file folder to complete this exercise. Open the workbook, and then follow the steps.**

1 Click any cell in the Excel table.

2 Click the **Insert** tab and then, in the **Charts** group, click the **Insert Column Chart** button and click the first **2D Column** chart subtype, **Clustered Column**. When you do, Excel creates a chart with the two data series.

3 Right-click the **Chart Title** text box and click **Edit Text**. Enter **Comparison** for the chart title.

4 On the **Design** tool tab, click the **Change Chart Type** button to open the **Change Chart Type** dialog box.

5 If necessary, click the **All Charts** tab to display that page of the dialog box. Then, in the list of chart types, click **Combo** to display the **Combo Chart** interface.

6 Verify that the **Volume** series will be plotted by using a **Clustered Column** chart and that the **Exceptions** series will be plotted by using a **Line** chart.

7 Select the **Secondary Axis** check box next to the **Exceptions** series. Doing so adds a second vertical axis to the right edge of the chart. The values on this axis reflect the values in the **Exceptions** series.

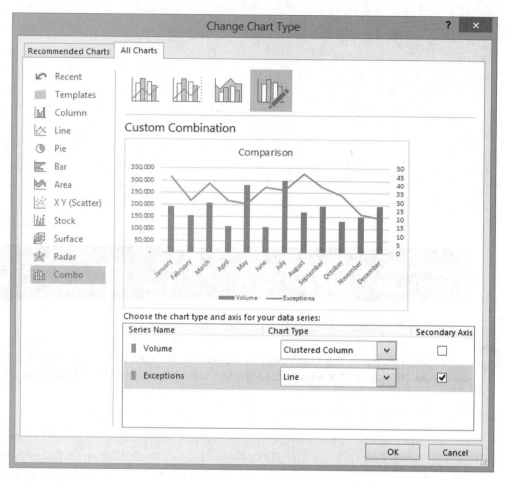

8   Click **OK** to create the chart.

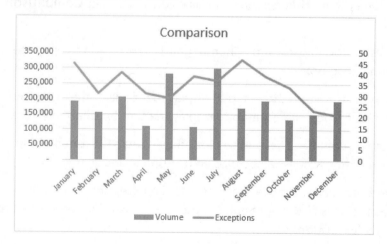

Summarizing your data by using sparklines

You can create charts in Excel workbooks to summarize your data visually by using legends, labels, and colors to highlight aspects of your data. It is possible to create very small charts to summarize your data in an overview worksheet, but you can also use *sparklines* to create compact, informative charts that provide valuable context for your data.

Edward Tufte introduced sparklines in his book *Beautiful Evidence* (Graphics Press, 2006), with the goal of creating charts that imparted their information in approximately the same space as a word of printed text. In Excel, a sparkline occupies a single cell, which makes it ideal for use in summary worksheets. As an example, suppose Lori Penor wanted to summarize the monthly revenue data for one of Consolidated Messenger's local branches.

	A	B	C	D	E	F
1						
2		Month	Revenue	Target	Difference	
3		January	$1,538,468	$1,600,000	$ (61,532)	
4		February	$1,474,289	$1,600,000	$ (125,711)	
5		March	$1,416,242	$1,600,000	$ (183,758)	
6		April	$1,685,377	$1,600,000	$ 85,377	
7		May	$1,573,046	$1,600,000	$ (26,954)	
8		June	$1,979,077	$1,600,000	$ 379,077	
9		July	$1,600,000	$1,600,000	$ -	
10		August	$2,417,226	$1,600,000	$ 817,226	
11		September	$1,872,026	$1,600,000	$ 272,026	
12		October	$2,097,478	$1,600,000	$ 497,478	
13		November	$2,876,025	$2,750,000	$ 126,025	
14		December	$3,825,430	$4,000,000	$ (174,570)	
15						

9

Lori can create three types of sparklines: line, column, and win/loss. The line and column sparklines are compact versions of the standard line and column charts. The win/loss sparkline indicates whether a cell value is positive (a win), negative (a loss), or zero (a tie). To create a line sparkline, you select the data you want to summarize and then, on the Insert tab, in the Sparklines group, click the Line button. When you do, Excel displays the Create Sparklines dialog box.

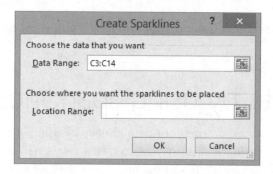

The data range you selected appears in the Data Range box. If the data range is not correct, you can click the Collapse Dialog button to the right of the Data Range box, select the correct cells, and then click the Expand Dialog button. Then, in the Location Range box, enter the address of the cell into which you want to place your sparkline. When you click OK, Excel creates a line sparkline in the cell you specified.

	B	C	D	E	F	G	H
	Month	Revenue	Target	Difference		Trend	By Month
	January	$1,538,468	$1,600,000	$ (61,532)			
	February	$1,474,289	$1,600,000	$ (125,711)			
	March	$1,416,242	$1,600,000	$ (183,758)			
	April	$1,685,377	$1,600,000	$ 85,377			
	May	$1,573,046	$1,600,000	$ (26,954)			
	June	$1,979,077	$1,600,000	$ 379,077			
	July	$1,600,000	$1,600,000	$ -			
	August	$2,417,226	$1,600,000	$ 817,226			
	September	$1,872,026	$1,600,000	$ 272,026			
	October	$2,097,478	$1,600,000	$ 497,478			
	November	$2,876,025	$2,750,000	$ 126,025			
	December	$3,825,430	$4,000,000	$ (174,570)			

You follow the same basic procedure to create a column sparkline, except that instead of clicking the Line button in the Sparklines group on the Insert tab, you click the Column button. To create a win/loss sparkline, you need to ensure that your data contains, or could contain, both positive and negative values. If you measured monthly revenue for

Consolidated Messenger, every value would be positive and the win/loss sparkline would impart no meaningful information. Comparing revenue to revenue targets, however, could result in positive, negative, or tie values, which can be meaningfully summarized by using a win/loss sparkline.

To create a win/loss sparkline, follow the same data selection process and click the Win/Loss button.

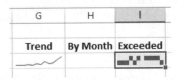

Months in which Consolidated Messenger's branch exceeded its revenue target appear in the top half of the cell in blue, months in which the branch fell short of its target appear in the bottom half of the cell in red, and the month in which the revenue was exactly the same as the target is blank.

After you create a sparkline, you can change its appearance. Because a sparkline takes up the entire interior of a single cell, resizing that cell's row or column resizes the sparkline. You can also change a sparkline's formatting. When you click a sparkline, Excel displays the Design tool tab.

You can use the tools on the Design tool tab to select a new style; show or hide value markers; change the color of your sparkline or the markers; edit the data used to create the sparkline; modify the labels on the sparkline's axes; or group, ungroup, or clear sparklines. You can't delete a sparkline by clicking its cell and then pressing the Delete or Backspace key—you must click the cell and then, on the Design tool tab, click the Clear button.

TIP Remember that sparklines work best when displayed in compact form. If you find yourself adding markers and labels to a sparkline, you might consider using a regular chart to take advantage of its wider range of formatting and customization options.

In this exercise, you'll create a line, column, and win/loss sparkline, change the sparkline's formatting, and clear a sparkline from a cell.

 SET UP You need the RevenueSummary workbook located in the Chapter09 practice file folder to complete this exercise. Open the workbook, and then follow the steps.

1   Select the cell range **C3:C14**.

2   On the **Insert** tab, in the **Sparklines** group, click **Line** to open the **Create Sparklines** dialog box.

3   Verify that **C3:C14** appears in the **Data Range** box. Then, in the **Location Range** box, enter **G3** and click **OK**. Excel creates a line sparkline in cell **G3**.

4   Select the cell range **C3:C14**.

5   On the **Insert** tab, in the **Sparklines** group, click **Column**. The **Create Sparklines** dialog box opens again.

6   Verify that **C3:C14** appears in the **Data Range** box. Then, in the **Location Range** box, enter **H3** and click **OK**. Excel creates a column sparkline in cell **H3**.

7   Drag the right edge of the column **H** header to the right until the cell's width is approximately doubled. Excel displays more details in the sparkline.

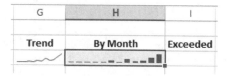

8   Select the cell range **E3:E14**.

9   On the **Insert** tab, in the **Sparklines** group, click **Win/Loss**. The **Create Sparklines** dialog box opens again.

10   Verify that **E3:E14** appears in the **Data Range** box. Then, in the **Location Range** box, enter **I3** and click **OK**. Excel creates a win/loss sparkline in cell **I3**.

11   With cell **I3** still selected, on the **Design** tool tab, in the **Style** gallery, click the rightmost sparkline style. Excel changes the win/loss sparkline's appearance.

12   Click cell **G3** and then, on the **Design** tool tab, in the **Group** group, click the **Clear** button and then click **Clear Selected Sparkline**. The sparkline disappears.

❌ CLEAN UP **Close the RevenueSummary workbook, saving your changes if you want to.**

Creating diagrams by using SmartArt

As an international delivery company, Consolidated Messenger's business processes are quite complex. Many times, chief operating officer Lori Penor summarizes the company's processes for the board of directors by creating diagrams. Excel has just the tool she needs to create those diagrams: SmartArt. To create a SmartArt graphic, on the Insert tab, in the Illustrations group, click SmartArt to display the Choose A SmartArt Graphic dialog box.

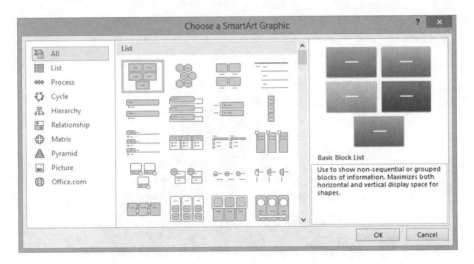

When you click one of the thumbnails in the center pane of the Choose A SmartArt Graphic dialog box, Excel displays a description of the diagram type you selected in the rightmost pane of the dialog box. Clicking All displays every available SmartArt graphic type. The following table lists the types of diagrams you can create by using the Choose A SmartArt Graphic dialog box.

TIP The Office.com category contains SmartArt diagrams available online through Office.com.

Diagram	Description
List	Shows a series of items that typically require a large amount of text to explain
Process	Shows a progression of sequential steps through a task, process, or workflow
Cycle	Shows a process with a continuous cycle or relationships of core elements
Hierarchy	Shows hierarchical relationships, such as those within a company
Relationship	Shows the relationships between two or more items
Matrix	Shows the relationship of components to a whole by using quadrants
Pyramid	Shows proportional, foundation-based, or hierarchical relationships such as a series of skills
Picture	Shows one or more images with captions

TIP Some of the diagram types can be used to illustrate several types of relationships. Be sure to examine all your options before you decide on the type of diagram to use to illustrate your point.

After you click the button that represents the type of diagram you want to create, click OK to add the diagram to your worksheet.

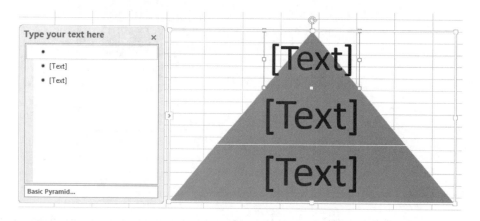

While the diagram is selected, Excel displays the Design and Format tool tabs. You can use the tools on the Design tool tab to change the graphic's layout, style, or color scheme. The Design tool tab also contains the Create Graphic group, which is home to tools you can use to add a shape to the SmartArt graphic, add text to the graphic, and promote or demote shapes within the graphic.

As an example, consider a process diagram that describes how Consolidated Messenger handles a package within one of the company's regional distribution centers.

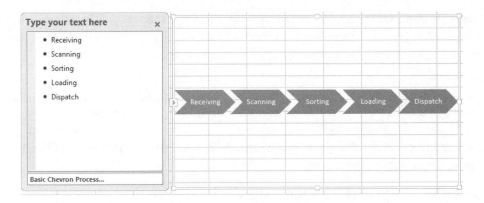

In the text pane, located to the left of the SmartArt graphic, you can add text to a shape without having to click and type within the shape. If you enter the process steps in the wrong order, you can move a shape by right-clicking the shape you want to move and then clicking Cut on the shortcut menu that appears. To paste the shape back into the graphic, right-click the shape to the left of where you want the pasted shape to appear, and then click Paste. For example, if you have a five-step process and accidentally switch the second and third steps, you can move the third step to the second position by right-clicking the third step, clicking Cut, right-clicking the first shape, and then clicking Paste.

If you want to add a shape to a SmartArt graphic, to add a step to a process, for instance, click a shape next to the position you want the new shape to occupy and then, on the Design tool tab, in the Create Graphic group, click Add Shape, and then click the option that represents where you want the new shape to appear in relation to the selected shape.

TIP The options that appear when you click Add Shape depend on the type of SmartArt graphic you created and which graphic element is selected. For instance, the options for an organizational chart are Add Shape After, Add Shape Before, Add Shape Above, Add Shape Below, and Add Assistant.

You can edit the graphic's elements by using the buttons on the Format tool tab or by right-clicking the shape and then clicking Format Shape to display the Format Shape pane. If you have selected the text in a shape, you can use the tools in the Font group on the Home tab to change the text's appearance.

TIP You can use the controls in the Format Shape dialog box to change the shape's fill color, borders, shadow, three-dimensional appearance, and text box properties.

9

In this exercise, you'll create an organization chart, fill in the shapes, delete a shape, add a shape, change the layout of the diagram without changing the information it embodies, and change the formatting of one of the diagram elements.

SET UP You need the OrgChart workbook located in the Chapter09 practice file folder to complete this exercise. Open the workbook, and then follow the steps.

1   On the **Insert** tab, in the **Illustrations** group, click **SmartArt** to open the **Choose a SmartArt Graphic** dialog box.

2   Click **Hierarchy** to display the **Hierarchy** graphic subtypes.

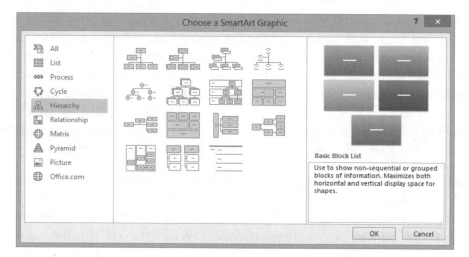

3   Click the first subtype (**Organization Chart**), and then click **OK**. Excel creates the organization chart graphic.

4   In the **Type your text here** pane, in the first text box, enter CEO, and then press the **Down Arrow** key. The value CEO appears in the shape at the top level of the organization chart.

5   In the SmartArt diagram, right-click the assistant box, located below and to the left of the **CEO** shape, and then click **Cut**. Excel removes the shape and moves the shapes on the third level of the organization chart to the second level.

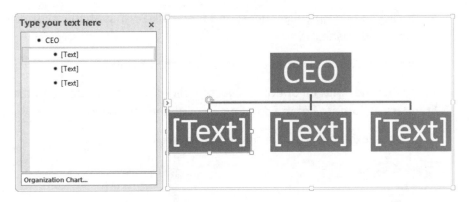

6   Click the leftmost shape on the second level of the organization chart, and then enter COO.

7   Click the middle shape on the second level of the organization chart, and then enter CIO.

8   Click the rightmost shape on the second level of the organization chart, and then enter CFO.

9   Click the **CFO** shape. On the **Design** tool tab, in the **Create Graphic** group, in the **Add Shape** list, click **Add Shape Below**. A new shape appears below the **CFO** shape.

10   In the new shape, type Comptroller.

11   On the **Design** tool tab, in the **Layouts** group, click the second layout from the left on the second line of layouts. Excel applies the new layout to your organization chart.

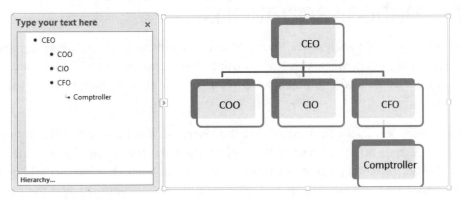

12 Right-click the **Comptroller** shape, and then click **Format Shape** to display the **Format Shape** pane.

13 If necessary, click the **Fill** category to display the fill options.

14 Verify that the **Solid fill** option is selected, click the **Color** button and then, in the **Standard Colors** area of the color picker, click the red swatch.

15 Click **Close**. Excel changes the shape's fill to red.

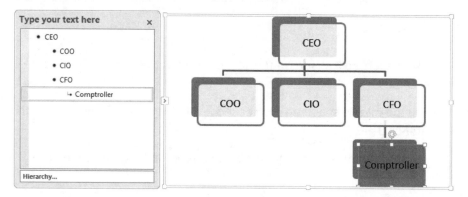

✖ CLEAN UP **Close the OrgChart workbook, saving your changes if you want to.**

Creating shapes and mathematical equations

With Excel, you can analyze your worksheet data in many ways, including summarizing your data and business processes visually by using charts and SmartArt. You can also augment your worksheets by adding objects such as geometric shapes, lines, flowchart symbols, and banners.

To add a shape to your worksheet, click the Insert tab and then, in the Illustrations group, click the Shapes button to display the shapes available. When you click a shape in the gallery, the pointer changes from a white arrow to a thin black crosshair. To draw your shape, click anywhere in the worksheet and drag the pointer until your shape is the size you want. When you release the mouse button, your shape appears and Excel displays the Format tool tab on the ribbon.

TIP Holding down the Shift key while you draw a shape keeps the shape's proportions constant. For example, clicking the Rectangle tool and then holding down the Shift key while you draw the shape causes you to draw a square.

You can resize a shape by clicking the shape and then dragging one of the resizing handles around the edge of the shape. You can drag a handle on a side of the shape to drag that side to a new position; when you drag a handle on the corner of the shape, you affect height and width simultaneously. If you hold down the Shift key while you drag a shape's corner, Excel keeps the shape's height and width in proportion. To rotate a shape, select the shape and then drag the white rotation handle at the top of the selection outline in a circle until the shape is in the orientation you want.

TIP You can assign your shape a specific height and width by clicking the shape and then, on the Format tool tab, in the Size group, entering the values you want in the height and width boxes.

After you create a shape, you can use the controls on the Format tool tab to change its formatting. To apply a predefined style, click the More button in the lower-right corner of the Shape Styles group's gallery and then click the style you want to apply. If none of the predefined styles are exactly what you want, you can use the Shape Fill, Shape Outline, and Shape Effects options to change those aspects of the shape's appearance.

TIP When you point to a formatting option, such as a style or option displayed in the Shape Fill, Shape Outline, or Shape Effects lists, Excel displays a live preview of how your shape would appear if you applied that formatting option. You can preview as many options as you like before committing to a change. If a live preview doesn't appear, click the File tab to display the Backstage view and then click Options to open the Excel Options dialog box. On the General page, select the Enable Live Preview check box and click OK.

If you want to use a shape as a label or header in a worksheet, you can add text to the shape's interior. To do so, select the shape and begin typing; when you're done adding text, click outside the shape to deselect it. You can edit a shape's text by moving the pointer over the text. When the pointer is in position for you to edit the text, it will change from a white pointer with a four-pointed arrow to a black I-bar. You can then click the text to start editing it. If you want to change the text's appearance, you can use the commands on the Home tab or on the Mini Toolbar that appears when you select the text.

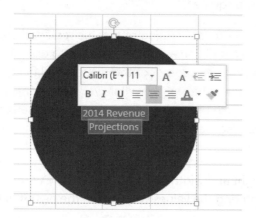

You can move a shape within your worksheet by dragging it to a new position. If your worksheet contains multiple shapes, you can align and distribute them within the worksheet. Horizontal shape alignment means that the shapes are lined up by their top edge, bottom edge, or center. Vertical shape alignment means that they have the same right edge, left edge, or center. To align a series of shapes, hold down the Ctrl key and click the shapes you want to align. Then, on the Format tool tab, in the Arrange group, click Align, and then click the alignment option you want.

Distributing shapes moves the shapes so they have a consistent horizontal or vertical distance between them. To do so, select three or more shapes on a worksheet, click the Format tool tab and then, in the Arrange group, click Align and then click either Distribute Horizontally or Distribute Vertically.

If you have multiple shapes on a worksheet, you will find that Excel arranges them from front to back, placing newer shapes in front of older shapes.

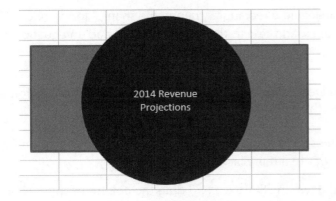

To change the order of the shapes, select the shape in the back, click the Format tool tab, and then, in the Arrange group, click Bring Forward. When you do, Excel moves the back shape in front of the front shape. Clicking Send Backward has the opposite effect, moving the selected shape one layer back in the order. If you click the Bring Forward arrow, you can choose to bring a shape all the way to the front of the order; similarly, when you click the Send Backward arrow, you can choose to send a shape to the back of the order.

One other way to work with shapes in Excel is to add mathematical equations to their interior. As an example, a business analyst might evaluate Consolidated Messenger's financial performance by using a ratio that can be expressed with an equation. To add an equation to a shape, click the shape and then, on the Insert tab, in the Symbols group, click Equation, and then click the Design tool tab to display the interface for editing equations.

TIP Clicking the Equation arrow displays a list of common equations, such as the Pythagorean Theorem, that you can add with a single click.

Click any of the controls in the Structures group to begin creating an equation of that type. You can fill in the details of a structure by adding text normally or by adding symbols from the gallery in the Symbols group.

In this exercise, you'll create a circle and a rectangle, change the shapes' formatting, reorder the shapes, align the shapes, add text to the circle, and then add an equation to the rectangle.

 SET UP You need the Shapes workbook located in the Chapter09 practice file folder to complete this exercise. Open the workbook, and then follow the steps.

1   On the **Insert** tab, in the **Illustrations** group, click the **Shapes** button, and then click the oval. The pointer changes to a thin black crosshair.

2   Starting near cell **C3**, hold down the **Shift** key and drag the pointer to approximately cell **E9**. Excel draws a circle.

3   On the **Format** tool tab, in the **Shapes Styles** group's gallery, click the second style. Excel formats the shape with white text and a black background.

4   On the **Insert** tab, in the **Illustrations** group, click the **Shapes** button, and then click the rectangle shape. The pointer changes to a thin black crosshair.

5   Starting near cell **G3**, drag the pointer to cell **K9**. Excel draws a rectangle.

6   On the **Format** tool tab, in the **Shapes Styles** group's gallery, click the first style. Excel formats the shape with black text, an orange border, and a white background.

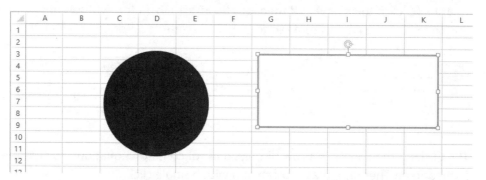

7   Click the circle and enter **2014 Revenue Projections**. Then, on the **Home** tab, in the **Alignment** group, click the **Middle Align** button. Excel centers the text vertically within the circle.

8   On the **Home** tab, in the **Alignment** group, click the **Center** button. Excel centers the text horizontally within the circle.

9   Hold down **Ctrl** and click the circle and the rectangle. Then, on the **Format** tool tab, in the **Arrange** group, click the **Align Objects** button, and then click **Align Center**. Excel centers the shapes horizontally.

10 Without releasing the selection, on the **Format** tool tab, in the **Arrange** group, click the **Align Objects** button, and then click **Align Middle**. Excel centers the shapes vertically.

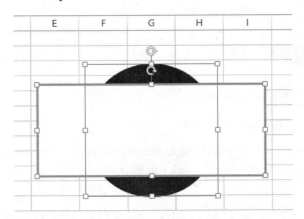

11 Click any spot on the worksheet outside of the circle and rectangle to release the selection, and then click the rectangle.

12 On the **Format** tool tab, in the **Arrange** group, click **Send Backward**. Excel moves the rectangle behind the circle.

13 Press **Ctrl+Z** to undo the last action. Excel moves the rectangle in front of the circle.

14 Click anywhere on the worksheet except on the circle or the rectangle. Click the rectangle and then, on the **Insert** tab, in the **Symbols** group, click **Equation**. The text **Type Equation Here** appears in the rectangle.

15 On the **Design** tool tab, in the **Structures** group, click the **Script** button, and then click the **Subscript** structure (the second from the left in the top row). The **Subscript** structure's outline appears in the rectangle.

9

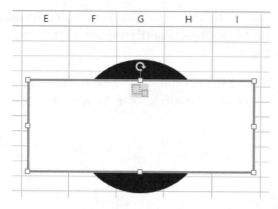

16   Click the left box of the structure and enter Year.

17   Click the right box of the structure and enter Previous.

18   Press the **Right Arrow** key once to move the cursor to the right of the word **Previous** and then, in the **Symbols** group's gallery, click the **Plus Minus** symbol (the first symbol in the top row).

19   In the **Symbols** group's gallery, click the **Infinity** symbol (the second symbol in the top row).

20   Select all of the text in the rectangle and then, on the **Home** tab, in the **Font** group, click the **Increase Font Size** button four times. Excel increases the equation text's font size.

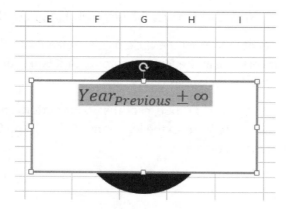

✖ CLEAN UP Close the Shapes workbook, saving your changes if you want to.

Key points

- You can use charts to summarize large sets of data in an easy-to-follow visual format.

- You're not stuck with the chart you create; if you want to change it, you can.

- If you format many of your charts the same way, creating a chart template can save you a lot of work in the future.

- Adding chart labels and a legend makes your chart much easier to follow.

- When you format your data properly, you can create dual-axis charts, which are compact and easy to read.

- If your chart data represents a series of events over time (such as monthly or yearly sales), you can use trendline analysis to extrapolate future events based on the past data.

- With sparklines, you can summarize your data in a compact space, providing valuable context for values in your worksheets.

- With Excel, you can quickly create and modify common business and organizational diagrams, such as organization charts and process diagrams.

- You can create and modify shapes to enhance your workbook's visual impact.

- The improved equation editing capabilities help Excel 2013 users communicate their thinking to their colleagues.

9

Chapter at a glance

Analyze

Analyze data dynamically by using
PivotTables, page 288

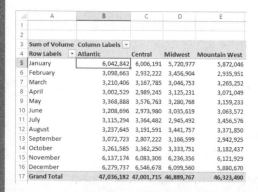

Filter

Filter, show, and hide PivotTable data,
page 298

Format

Format PivotTables,
page 313

Create

Create dynamic charts by using PivotCharts,
page 326

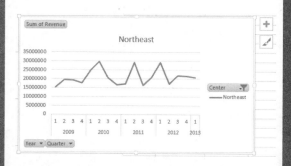

Using PivotTables and PivotCharts

IN THIS CHAPTER, YOU WILL LEARN HOW TO

- Analyze data dynamically by using PivotTables.

- Filter, show, and hide PivotTable data.

- Edit PivotTables.

- Format PivotTables.

- Create PivotTables from external data.

- Create dynamic charts by using PivotCharts.

When you create Microsoft Excel 2013 worksheets, you should consider how you want the data to appear when you show it to your colleagues. You can change the formatting of your data to emphasize the contents of specific cells, sort and filter your worksheets based on the contents of specific columns, or hide rows containing data that isn't relevant to the point you're trying to make.

One limitation of the standard Excel worksheet is that you can't easily change how the data is organized on the page. For example, in a worksheet in which each column represents an hour in the day, each row represents a day in a month, and the body of the worksheet contains the total sales for every hourly period of the month, you can't change the worksheet quickly so that it displays only sales on Tuesdays during the afternoon.

However, Excel has a tool that you can use to create worksheets that can be sorted, filtered, and rearranged dynamically to emphasize different aspects of your data. That tool is the PivotTable.

In this chapter, you'll create and edit PivotTables from an existing worksheet, focus your PivotTable data by using filters, format PivotTables, create a PivotTable that has data imported from a text file, and summarize your data visually by using a PivotChart.

Analyzing data dynamically by using PivotTables

With Excel worksheets, you can gather and present important data, but the standard worksheet can't be changed from its original configuration easily. As an example, consider a worksheet that records monthly package volumes for each of nine distribution centers in the United States.

	A	B	C	D	E
1					
2		**January**	**February**	**March**	**April**
3	**Atlantic**	6,042,842	3,098,663	3,210,406	3,002,529
4	**Central**	6,006,191	2,932,222	3,167,785	2,989,245
5	**Midwest**	5,720,977	3,456,904	3,046,753	3,125,231
6	**Mountain West**	5,872,046	2,935,951	3,265,252	3,071,049
7	**North Central**	6,236,863	3,785,068	2,929,397	2,677,853
8	**Northeast**	6,370,982	3,281,469	3,725,669	3,148,289
9	**Northwest**	6,108,382	4,216,668	3,640,750	2,997,048
10	**Southeast**	6,396,724	4,877,758	4,387,252	3,583,479
11	**Southwest**	5,949,454	4,413,610	3,226,583	3,006,170
12		**54,704,461**	**32,998,313**	**30,599,847**	**27,600,893**

The data in the worksheet is organized so that each row represents a distribution center and each column represents a month of the year. When presented in this arrangement, the monthly totals for all centers and the yearly total for each distribution center are given equal billing: neither set of totals stands out.

Such a neutral presentation of your data is versatile, but it has limitations. First, although you can use sorting and filtering to restrict the rows or columns shown, it's difficult to change the worksheet's organization. For example, in this worksheet, you can't easily reorganize the contents of your worksheet so that the months are assigned to the rows and the distribution centers are assigned to the columns.

To reorganize and redisplay your data dynamically, you can use the PivotTable tool. In Excel 2013, you can create Recommended PivotTables. To open the Recommended PivotTables dialog box for a data set, click any cell in the data range that you want to summarize and then, on the Insert tab of the ribbon, click Recommended PivotTables. When you do, Excel displays a set of PivotTables that you can create quickly.

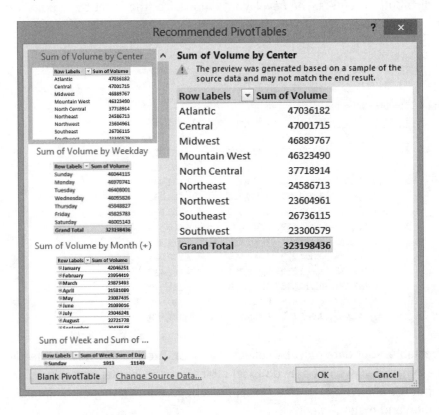

Pointing to a recommended PivotTable shows a preview image of what that PivotTable would look like. To create it, just click the image of the arrangement you want to create and click OK.

TIP If Excel 2013 has no Recommended PivotTables for your data, it displays the option to create a blank PivotTable.

If none of the Recommended PivotTables meet your needs, you can create a PivotTable by adding individual fields. For instance, you can create a PivotTable with the same layout as the worksheet described previously, which emphasizes totals by month, and then change the PivotTable layout to have the rows represent the months of the year and the columns represent the distribution centers. The new layout emphasizes the totals by regional distribution center.

	A	B	C	D	E
1					
2					
3	Sum of Volume	Column Labels			
4	Row Labels	Atlantic	Central	Midwest	Mountain West
5	January	6,042,842	6,006,191	5,720,977	5,872,046
6	February	3,098,663	2,932,222	3,456,904	2,935,951
7	March	3,210,406	3,167,785	3,046,753	3,265,252
8	April	3,002,529	2,989,245	3,125,231	3,071,049
9	May	3,368,888	3,576,763	3,280,768	3,159,233
10	June	3,208,696	2,973,980	3,035,619	3,063,572
11	July	3,115,294	3,364,482	2,945,492	3,456,576
12	August	3,237,645	3,191,591	3,441,757	3,371,850
13	September	3,072,723	2,807,222	3,166,599	2,942,925
14	October	3,261,585	3,362,250	3,333,751	3,182,437
15	November	6,137,174	6,083,306	6,236,356	6,121,929
16	December	6,279,737	6,546,678	6,099,560	5,880,670
17	Grand Total	47,036,182	47,001,715	46,889,767	46,323,490

To create a PivotTable, your data must be collected in a list. Excel tables mesh perfectly with PivotTable dynamic views; not only do Excel tables have a well-defined column and row structure, but the ability to refer to an Excel table by its name also greatly simplifies PivotTable creation and management.

In the Excel table used to create the distribution PivotTable, each row of the table contains a value that represents the distribution center, date, month, week, weekday, day, and volume for every day of the years 2012 and 2013.

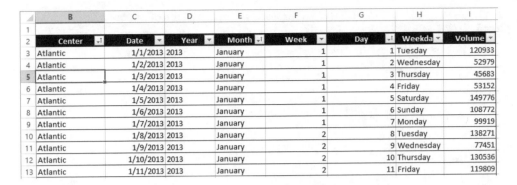

	B	C	D	E	F	G	H	I
1								
2	Center	Date	Year	Month	Week	Day	Weekday	Volume
3	Atlantic	1/1/2013	2013	January	1	1	Tuesday	120933
4	Atlantic	1/2/2013	2013	January	1	2	Wednesday	52979
5	Atlantic	1/3/2013	2013	January	1	3	Thursday	45683
6	Atlantic	1/4/2013	2013	January	1	4	Friday	53152
7	Atlantic	1/5/2013	2013	January	1	5	Saturday	149776
8	Atlantic	1/6/2013	2013	January	1	6	Sunday	108772
9	Atlantic	1/7/2013	2013	January	1	7	Monday	99919
10	Atlantic	1/8/2013	2013	January	2	8	Tuesday	138271
11	Atlantic	1/9/2013	2013	January	2	9	Wednesday	77451
12	Atlantic	1/10/2013	2013	January	2	10	Thursday	130536
13	Atlantic	1/11/2013	2013	January	2	11	Friday	119809

Excel needs that data when it creates the PivotTable so that it can maintain relationships among the data. If you want to filter your PivotTable so that it shows all package volumes on Thursdays in January, for example, Excel must be able to identify January 10, 2013 as a Thursday.

After you create an Excel table, you can click any cell in the table, display the Insert tab and then, in the Tables group, click PivotTable to open the Create PivotTable dialog box.

In this dialog box, you verify the data source for your PivotTable and whether you want to create a PivotTable on a new worksheet or an existing worksheet. After you click OK, Excel displays a new or existing worksheet and displays the PivotTable Fields pane.

TIP You should always place your PivotTable on its own worksheet to avoid cluttering the display.

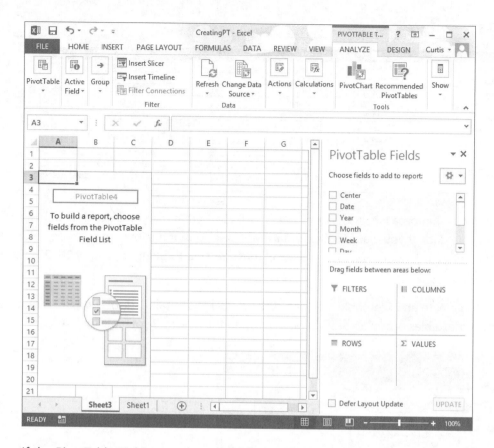

If the PivotTable Fields pane isn't visible, you can display it by clicking any cell in the PivotTable, which displays the PivotTable Tools tabs. On the Options tool tab, in the Show/Hide group, click Field List.

To assign a field, or column of data, to an area of the PivotTable, drag the field header from the Choose Fields To Add To Report area at the top of the PivotTable Fields pane to the Drag Fields Between Areas Below area at the bottom of the pane. For example, if you drag the Volume field header to the Values area, the PivotTable displays the total of all entries in the Volume column.

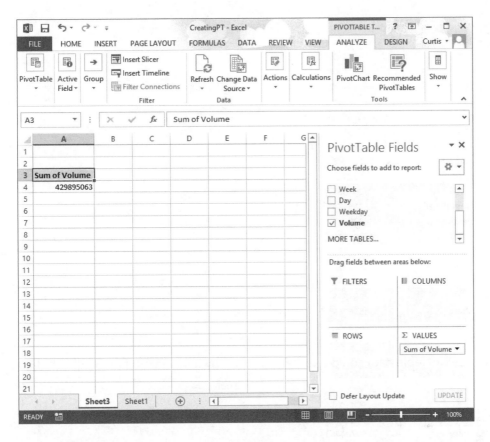

It's important to note that the order in which you enter the fields in the Rows and Columns areas affects how Excel organizes the data in your PivotTable. As an example, consider a PivotTable that groups the PivotTable rows by distribution center and then by month.

3	Row Labels	Sum of Volume
4	⊟ Atlantic	47036182
5	January	6042842
6	February	3098663
7	March	3210406
8	April	3002529
9	May	3368888
10	June	3208696
11	July	3115294
12	August	3237645
13	September	3072723
14	October	3261585
15	November	6137174
16	December	6279737
17	⊟ Central	47001715
18	January	6006191
19	February	2932222
20	March	3167785
21	April	2989245
22	May	3576763
23	June	2973980

The same PivotTable data could also be organized by month and then by distribution center.

3	Row Labels	Sum of Volume
4	⊟ January	54704461
5	Atlantic	6042842
6	Central	6006191
7	Midwest	5720977
8	Mountain West	5872046
9	North Central	6236863
10	Northeast	6370982
11	Northwest	6108382
12	Southeast	6396724
13	Southwest	5949454
14	⊟ February	32998313
15	Atlantic	3098663
16	Central	2932222
17	Midwest	3456904
18	Mountain West	2935951
19	North Central	3785068
20	Northeast	3281469
21	Northwest	4216668
22	Southeast	4877758
23	Southwest	4413610

In the preceding examples, all the field headers are in the Rows area. If you drag the Center header from the Rows area to the Columns area, the PivotTable reorganizes (pivots) its data to form a different configuration.

Sum of Volume	Column Labels			
Row Labels	Atlantic	Central	Midwest	Mountain West
January	6042842	6006191	5720977	5872046
February	3098663	2932222	3456904	2935951
March	3210406	3167785	3046753	3265252
April	3002529	2989245	3125231	3071049
May	3368888	3576763	3280768	3159233
June	3208696	2973980	3035619	3063572
July	3115294	3364482	2945492	3456576
August	3237645	3191591	3441757	3371850
September	3072723	2807222	3166599	2942925
October	3261585	3362250	3333751	3182437
November	6137174	6083306	6236356	6121929
December	6279737	6546678	6099560	5880670
Grand Total	47036182	47001715	46889767	46323490

To pivot a PivotTable, you drag a field header to a new position in the PivotTable Fields pane. As you drag a field within the pane, Excel displays a blue line in the interior of the target area so you know where the field will appear when you release the mouse button. If your data set is large or if you based your PivotTable on a data collection on another computer, it might take some time for Excel to reorganize the PivotTable after a pivot. You can have Excel delay redrawing the PivotTable by selecting the Defer Layout Update check box in the lower-left corner of the PivotTable Fields pane. When you're ready for Excel to display the reorganized PivotTable, click Update.

If you expect your PivotTable source data to change, such as when you link to an external database that records shipments or labor hours, you should ensure that your PivotTable summarizes all the available data. To do that, you can refresh the PivotTable connection to its data source. If Excel detects new data in the source table, it updates the PivotTable contents accordingly. To refresh your PivotTable, click any cell in the PivotTable and then, on the Options tool tab, in the Data group, click Refresh.

10

In this exercise, you'll create a PivotTable by using data from a table, add fields to the PivotTable, and then pivot the PivotTable.

➔ SET UP You need the Creating workbook located in the Chapter10 practice file folder to complete this exercise. Open the workbook, and then follow the steps.

1   Click any cell in the Excel table.

2   On the **Insert** tab, in the **Tables** group, click **Recommended PivotTables** to open the **Recommended PivotTables** dialog box.

3   Click the second icon, labeled **Sum of Volume by Weekday**.

4   Click **OK** to create the PivotTable.

	A	B
1		
2		
3	Row Labels ▼	Sum of Volume
4	Sunday	61253579
5	Monday	62042322
6	Tuesday	62278691
7	Wednesday	60664392
8	Thursday	61694953
9	Friday	61441352
10	Saturday	60519774
11	Grand Total	429895063
12		

5   Click the **Sheet1** worksheet's sheet tab to display that worksheet.

6   If necessary, click any cell in the Excel table.

7   On the **Insert** tab, in the **Tables** group, click the **PivotTable** button to open the **PivotTable** dialog box.

8   Verify that the **DailyVolumes** table name appears in the **Table/Range** field and that the **New Worksheet** option is selected.

9   Click **OK** to create a PivotTable on a new worksheet.

10 In the **PivotTable Fields** pane, drag the **Center** field header to the **Rows** area. Excel adds the **Center** field values to the PivotTable row area.

	A	B
1		
2		
3	Row Labels ▾	
4	Atlantic	
5	Central	
6	Midwest	
7	Mountain West	
8	North Central	
9	Northeast	
10	Northwest	
11	Southeast	
12	Southwest	
13	**Grand Total**	
14		

11 In the **PivotTable Fields** pane, drag the **Year** field header to the **Columns** area. Excel adds the **Year** field values to the PivotTable column area.

12 In the **PivotTable Fields** pane, drag the **Volume** field header to the **Values** area. Excel fills in the body of the PivotTable with the **Volume** field values.

13 In the **PivotTable Fields** pane, in the **Columns** area, drag the **Year** field header to the **Rows** area, and drop it beneath the **Center** field header. Excel changes the PivotTable to reflect the new organization.

10

⊿	A	B
1		
2		
3	**Row Labels** ▾	**Sum of Volume**
4	⊟ **Atlantic**	**47036182**
5	2012	23276049
6	2013	23760133
7	⊟ **Central**	**47001715**
8	2012	23727556
9	2013	23274159
10	⊟ **Midwest**	**46889767**
11	2012	23643436
12	2013	23246331
13	⊟ **Mountain West**	**46323490**
14	2012	23075908
15	2013	23247582
16	⊟ **North Central**	**46680590**
17	2012	24118888
18	2013	22561702
19	⊟ **Northeast**	**48690205**
20	2012	24103492
21	2013	24586713
22	⊟ **Northwest**	**48633350**
23	2012	25028389
24	2013	23604961

✖ CLEAN UP Close the Creating workbook, saving your changes if you want to.

Filtering, showing, and hiding PivotTable data

PivotTables often summarize huge data sets in a relatively small worksheet. The more details you can capture and write to a table, the more flexibility you have in analyzing the data. As an example, consider all the details captured in a table in which each row contains a value that represents the distribution center, date, month, week, weekday, day, and volume for every day of the year.

	B	C	D	E	F	G	H	I
2	Center	Date	Year	Month	Week	Day	Weekday	Volume
3	Atlantic	1/2/2012	2012	January	1	1	Monday	46144
4	Atlantic	1/3/2012	2012	January	1	2	Tuesday	105578
5	Atlantic	1/4/2012	2012	January	1	3	Wednesday	83669
6	Atlantic	1/5/2012	2012	January	1	4	Thursday	100240
7	Atlantic	1/6/2012	2012	January	1	5	Friday	130597
8	Atlantic	1/7/2012	2012	January	1	6	Saturday	123563
9	Atlantic	1/8/2012	2012	January	1	7	Sunday	50054
10	Atlantic	1/9/2012	2012	January	2	8	Monday	78540

Each column, in turn, contains numerous values: there are nine distribution centers, data from two years, 12 months in a year, seven weekdays, and as many as five weeks and 31 days in a month. Just as you can filter the data that appears in an Excel table or other data collection, you can filter the data displayed in a PivotTable by selecting which values you want the PivotTable to include.

SEE ALSO For more information on filtering an Excel table, see "Limiting data that appears on your screen" in Chapter 5, "Focusing on specific data by using filters."

To filter a PivotTable based on a field's contents, click the field's header in the Choose Fields To Add To Report area of the PivotTable Fields pane. When you do, Excel displays a menu of sorting and filtering options.

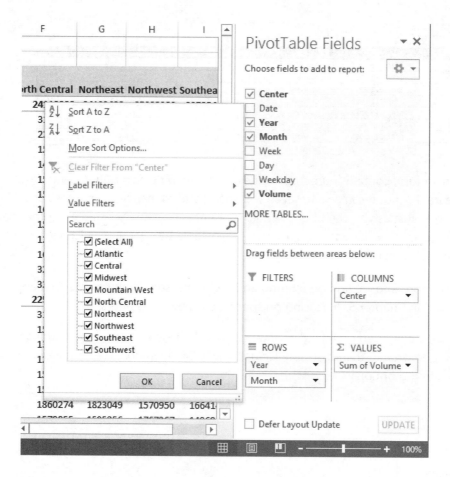

TIP You can also create selection filters for PivotTables by using slicers, which are introduced in Chapter 5, "Focusing on specific data by using filters." To display the Insert Slicers dialog box for a PivotTable, click any cell in the PivotTable, click the Analyze tool tab, and then click Insert Slicer.

The PivotTable displays several sorting options, commands for different categories of filters, and a list of items that appear in the field you want to filter. Every list item has a check box next to it. Items with a check mark in the box are currently displayed in the PivotTable, and items without a check mark are hidden.

The first entry at the top of the item list is the Select All check box. This check box can have one of three states: displaying a check mark, displaying a black square, or empty. If the Select All check box contains a check mark, then the PivotTable displays every item in the list. If the Select All check box is empty, then no filter items are selected. Finally, if the Select

All check box contains a black square, it means that some, but not all, of the items in the list are displayed. Selecting only the Northwest check box, for example, leads to a PivotTable configuration in which only the data for the Northwest center is displayed.

	Sum of Volume	Column Labels	
	Row Labels	Northwest	Grand Total
2012		25028389	25028389
	January	3085352	3085352
	February	2554130	2554130
	March	1932304	1932304
	April	1348145	1348145
	May	1628489	1628489
	June	1475038	1475038
	July	1832445	1832445
	August	1633582	1633582
	September	1638024	1638024
	October	2045639	2045639
	November	3020217	3020217
	December	2835024	2835024
2013		23604961	23604961
	January	3023030	3023030
	February	1662538	1662538
	March	1708446	1708446
	April	1648903	1648903
	May	1607655	1607655

If you'd rather display as much PivotTable data as possible, you can hide the PivotTable Fields pane and filter the PivotTable by using the filter arrows on the Rows and Columns headers within the body of the PivotTable. When you click either of those headers, you can select a field by which you can filter; you can then define the filter by using the same controls that are available when you click a field header in the PivotTable Fields pane.

Excel indicates that a PivotTable has filters applied by placing a filter indicator next to the Columns or Rows header, as appropriate, and the filtered field name in the PivotTable Fields pane.

So far in this example, all the fields by which the PivotTable has been filtered has changed the organization of the data in the PivotTable. Adding some fields to a PivotTable, however, might create unwanted complexity. For example, you might want to filter a PivotTable by weekday, but adding the Weekday field to the body of the PivotTable expands the table unnecessarily.

▲	A	B	C	D	E	F
1						
2						
3	**Sum of Volume**	**Column Labels** ▼				
4		⊟2012				
5	**Row Labels** ▼	Sunday	Monday	Tuesday	Wednesday	Thursday
6	Atlantic	3453319	3349646	3366196	2917606	3567714
7	Central	3320819	3366199	3527584	3365866	3263079
8	Midwest	3667386	3475968	3091127	3463291	3245714
9	Mountain West	3357763	3268404	3068409	3200078	3298019
10	North Central	3457202	3741370	3215869	3428683	3686605
11	Northeast	3496199	3601318	3470147	3593310	3511717
12	Northwest	3791023	3767825	3374432	3812518	3519655
13	Southeast	3268002	3473394	3348605	3575267	3257557
14	Southwest	3178975	3570147	3396272	3632371	3872515
15	**Grand Total**	30990688	31614271	29858641	30988990	31222575

Instead of adding the Weekday field to the Rows or Columns area, you can drag the field to the Filters area near the bottom of the PivotTable Fields pane. Doing so leaves the body of the PivotTable unchanged, but adds a new area above the PivotTable in its worksheet.

▲	A	B	C	D
1	Weekday	(All) ▼		
2				
3	**Sum of Volume**	**Column Labels** ▼		
4	**Row Labels** ▼	2012	2013	**Grand Total**
5	Atlantic	23276049	23760133	47036182
6	Central	23727556	23274159	47001715
7	Midwest	23643436	23246331	46889767
8	Mountain West	23075908	23247582	46323490
9	North Central	24118888	22561702	46680590
10	Northeast	24103492	24586713	48690205
11	Northwest	25028389	23604961	48633350
12	Southeast	23785488	26736115	50521603
13	Southwest	24817582	23300579	48118161
14	**Grand Total**	215576788	214318275	429895063

TIP In Excel 2003 and earlier versions, this area was called the Page Field area.

When you click the filter arrow of a field in the Filters area, Excel displays a list of the values in the field. When you click the filter arrow, you can choose to filter by one value at a time. If you'd like to filter your PivotTable by more than one value, you can do so by selecting the Select Multiple Items check box.

If your PivotTable has more than one field in the Rows area, you can filter values in a PivotTable by hiding and collapsing levels of detail within the report. To do that, you click the Hide Detail control (which looks like a box with a minus sign in it) or the Show Detail control (which looks like a box with a plus sign in it) next to a header.

For example, you might have your data divided by year; clicking the Show Detail control next to the 2012 year header would display that year's details. Conversely, clicking the 2013 year header's Hide Detail control would hide the individual months' values and display only the year's total.

	A	B
1		
2		
3	**Row Labels** ▼	**Sum of Volume**
4	⊟ 2012	215576788
5	Atlantic	23276049
6	Central	23727556
7	Midwest	23643436
8	Mountain West	23075908
9	North Central	24118888
10	Northeast	24103492
11	Northwest	25028389
12	Southeast	23785488
13	Southwest	24817582
14	⊞ 2013	214318275
15	**Grand Total**	429895063

10

Excel 2013 also lets you filter PivotTables using search filters. With a search filter, you can enter in a series of characters for Excel to filter that field's values. To create a search filter, click a field's filter arrow and enter the character string that you want to search for in the filter menu's Search box.

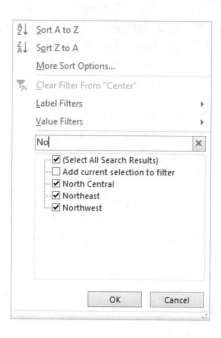

For example, if the PivotTable's Center field contains the values Atlantic, Central, Midwest, Mountain West, North Central, Northeast, Northwest, Southeast, and Southwest, entering the character string *No* limits the values to *North Central*, *Northeast*, and *Northwest*.

TIP Search filters look for the character string you specify anywhere within a field's value, not just at the start of the value. In the previous example, the search filter string *cen* would return both *Central* and *North Central*.

In this exercise, you'll focus the data displayed in a PivotTable by creating a filter, by filtering a PivotTable based on the contents of a field in the Filters area, by showing and hiding levels of detail within the body of the PivotTable, and by using the Search box.

 SET UP **You need the Focusing workbook located in the Chapter10 practice file folder to complete this exercise. Open the workbook, and then follow the steps.**

1 On the **Sheet2** worksheet, click any cell in the PivotTable.

2 In the **Choose fields to add to report** area of the **PivotTable Fields** pane, click the **Center** field header, click the **Center** field filter arrow, and then clear the **(Select All)** check box. Excel clears all the check boxes in the filter menu.

3   Select the **Northwest** check box, and then click **OK**. Excel filters the PivotTable.

⊿	A	B	C
1			
2			
3	Sum of Volume	Column Labels 🔽	
4	Row Labels 🔽	Northwest	Grand Total
5	⊟2012	25028389	25028389
6	January	3085352	3085352
7	February	2554130	2554130
8	March	1932304	1932304
9	April	1348145	1348145
10	May	1628489	1628489
11	June	1475038	1475038
12	July	1832445	1832445
13	August	1633582	1633582
14	September	1638024	1638024
15	October	2045639	2045639
16	November	3020217	3020217
17	December	2835024	2835024
18	⊟2013	23604961	23604961
19	January	3023030	3023030
20	February	1662538	1662538
21	March	1708446	1708446

4   On the **Quick Access Toolbar**, click the **Undo** button to remove the filter.

5   In the **PivotTable Fields** pane, drag the **Weekday** field header from the **Choose fields to add to report area** to the **Filters** area in the **Drag fields between areas below** area.

6   In the **PivotTable Fields** pane, click the **Close** button to close it.

7   In the body of the worksheet, click the **Weekday** filter arrow, and then, if necessary, select the **Select Multiple Items** check box. Excel adds check boxes beside the items in the **Weekday** field filter list.

8   Clear the **All** check box to clear every check box in the list.

9   Select the **Tuesday** and **Thursday** check boxes, and then click **OK**. Excel filters the PivotTable, summarizing only those values from Tuesdays and Thursdays.

10

10   In cell **A5**, click the **Hide Detail** button. Excel collapses rows that contain data from the year 2012, leaving only the subtotal row that summarizes that year's data.

	A	B	C	D
1	Weekday	(Multiple Items) .T		
2				
3	Sum of Volume	Column Labels ▼		
4	Row Labels ▼	Atlantic	Central	Midwest
5	⊞ 2012	6933910	6790663	6336841
6	⊟ 2013	6783726	6541290	6650799
7	January	1017628	1087262	992605
8	February	453202	418419	515009
9	March	467334	359716	367785
10	April	458566	437695	452702
11	May	481096	516957	460397
12	June	302371	416959	450633
13	July	433346	452848	339017
14	August	564377	450209	452780
15	September	353976	278120	381304
16	October	458948	449253	570835
17	November	808929	819627	861745
18	December	983953	854225	805987
19	Grand Total	13717636	13331953	12987640

11   In cell **A5**, click the **Show Detail** button to redisplay the collapsed rows.

12   If the **PivotTable Fields** pane isn't displayed, click the **Analyze** tool tab, click **Show**, and then click **Field List**.

13   In the **PivotTable Fields** pane, click the **Month** field header arrow to open the filter menu.

14   In the **Search** box, enter **Ju**. Excel displays the months **June** and **July** in the filter list.

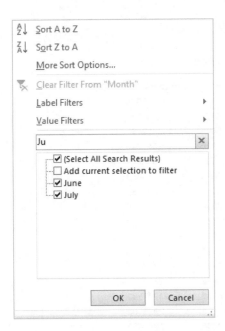

15   Click **OK** to apply the filter.

16   On the **Analyze** tool tab, click the **Actions** button, click **Clear**, and then click **Clear Filters** to remove all filters from the PivotTable.

❌ CLEAN UP   Close the Focusing workbook, saving your changes if you want to.

Editing PivotTables

After you create a PivotTable, you can rename it, edit it to control how it summarizes your data, and use PivotTable cell data in a formula. As an example, consider a PivotTable named *PivotTable2* that summarizes package volumes for every Consolidated Messengers regional distribution hub.

10

	A	B	C	D	E
1					
2					
3	Sum of Volume	Column Labels ▼			
4	Row Labels ▼	Atlantic	Central	Midwest	Mountain West
5	⊟ 2012	23276049	23727556	23643436	23075908
6	January	2966264	3143004	2774877	2942544
7	February	1541726	1407340	2046448	1552098
8	March	1688027	1594434	1600920	1641026
9	April	1445436	1548205	1395802	1653829
10	May	1530319	1813746	1529086	1516453
11	June	1725770	1431518	1458009	1551719
12	July	1581340	1706190	1472534	1672400
13	August	1519538	1577651	1797139	1745152
14	September	1494735	1420065	1672046	1483296
15	October	1743541	1711810	1599927	1655866
16	November	3049369	2921522	3153696	2847752
17	December	2989984	3452071	3142952	2813773
18	⊟ 2013	23760133	23274159	23246331	23247582
19	January	3076578	2863187	2946100	2929502
20	February	1556937	1524882	1410456	1383853

Excel displays the PivotTable name when you click the PivotTable button on the Analyze tool tab. The name *PivotTable2* doesn't help you or your colleagues understand the data the PivotTable contains, particularly if you use the PivotTable data in a formula on another worksheet. To give your PivotTable a more descriptive name, click any cell in the PivotTable and then, on the Options tool tab, in the PivotTable Options group, enter the new name in the PivotTable Name field.

When you create a PivotTable with at least one field in the Rows area and one field in the Columns area of the PivotTable Fields pane, Excel adds a grand total row and column to summarize your data. You can control how and where these summary rows and columns appear by clicking any PivotTable cell and then, on the Design tool tab, in the Layout group, clicking either the Subtotals or Grand Totals button and selecting the desired layout.

After you create a PivotTable, Excel determines the best way to summarize the data in the column you assign to the Values area. For numeric data, for example, Excel uses the *SUM* function. If you want to change a PivotTable summary function, right-click any data cell in the PivotTable values area, point to Summarize Values By, and then click the desired operation. If you want to use a function other than those listed, click More Options to display the Value Field Settings dialog box. On the Summarize Values By page of the dialog box, you can choose the summary operation you want to use.

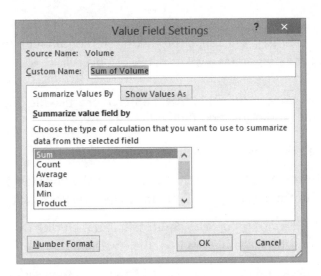

You can also change how the PivotTable displays the data in the Values area. On the Show Values As page of the Value Field Settings dialog box, you can select whether to display each cell's percentage contribution to its column's total, its row's total, or its contribution to the total of all values displayed in the PivotTable.

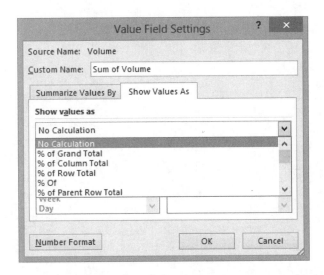

If you want, you can create a formula that incorporates a value from a PivotTable cell. To do so, you click the cell in which you want to create the formula, enter an equal sign, and then click the cell in the PivotTable that contains the data you want to appear in the other cell. A *GETPIVOTDATA* formula appears in the formula box of the worksheet that contains the PivotTable. When you press Enter, Excel creates the *GETPIVOTDATA* formula and displays the contents of the PivotTable cell in the target cell.

10

In this exercise, you'll rename a PivotTable, specify whether subtotal and grand total rows will appear, change the PivotTable summary function, display each cell's contribution to its row's total, and create a formula that incorporates a value in a PivotTable cell.

→ SET UP You need the Editing workbook located in the Chapter10 practice file folder to complete this exercise. Open the workbook, and then follow the steps.

1   On the **PivotTable** worksheet, click any cell in the PivotTable.

2   On the **Analyze** tool tab, click the **PivotTable** button and then, in the **PivotTable Name** field, enter VolumeSummary and press **Enter** to rename the PivotTable.

3   On the **Design** tool tab, in the **Layout** group, click **Subtotals**, and then click **Do Not Show Subtotals**. Excel removes the subtotal rows from the PivotTable.

4   On the **Design** tool tab, in the **Layout** group, click **Grand Totals**, and then click **On for columns only**. Excel removes the cells that calculate each row's grand total.

H	I	J	K	L	
Northwest	**Southeast**	**Southwest**			
3085352	3470295	3029490			
2554130	1988929	2692383			
1932304	1441894	1646946			
1348145	1631240	1525005			
1628489	1749378	1452226			
1475038	1422265	1428581			
1832445	1511712	1503100			
1633582	1671246	1414763			
1638024	1510884	1407402			
2045639	1427066	2888565			
3020217	2848642	2728934			
2835024	3111937	3100187			

5   On the **Quick Access Toolbar**, click the **Undo** button to reverse the last change.

6   Right-click any data cell in the PivotTable, point to **Summarize Values By**, and then click **Average** to change the **Value** field summary operation.

▲	A	B	C	D	E
1					
2					
3	**Average of Volume**	**Column Labels** ▾			
4	**Row Labels** ▾	**Atlantic**	**Central**	**Midwest**	**Mountain West**
5	⊟**2012**				
6	January	95685.93548	101387.2258	89512.16129	94920.77419
7	February	55061.64286	50262.14286	73087.42857	55432.07143
8	March	54452.48387	51433.35484	51642.58065	52936.32258
9	April	48181.2	51606.83333	46526.73333	55127.63333
10	May	49365.12903	58507.93548	49325.35484	48917.83871
11	June	57525.66667	47717.26667	48600.3	51723.96667
12	July	51010.96774	55038.3871	47501.09677	53948.3871
13	August	49017.35484	50891.96774	57972.22581	56295.22581
14	September	49824.5	47335.5	55734.86667	49443.2
15	October	56243.25806	55219.67742	51610.54839	53415.03226
16	November	101645.6333	97384.06667	105123.2	94925.06667
17	December	96451.09677	111357.129	101385.5484	90766.87097
18	⊟**2013**				
19	January	99244.45161	92360.87097	95035.48387	94500.06452
20	February	55604.89286	54460.07143	50373.42857	49423.32143

7   On the **Quick Access Toolbar**, click the **Undo** button to reverse the last change.

8   Right-click any data cell in the PivotTable, and then click **Value Field Settings** to open the **Value Field Settings** dialog box.

9   Click the **Show Values As** tab to display the **Show Values As** page.

10 In the **Show Values As** list, click **% of Row Total**.

11 Click **OK** to change how Excel calculates the values in the PivotTable.

10

▲	A	B	C	D	E
1					
2					
3	Sum of Volume	Column Labels ▼			
4	Row Labels ▼	Atlantic	Central	Midwest	Mountain West
5	⊟ 2012				
6	January	10.75%	11.39%	10.06%	10.66%
7	February	8.63%	7.88%	11.46%	8.69%
8	March	11.40%	10.77%	10.81%	11.08%
9	April	10.68%	11.43%	10.31%	12.22%
10	May	10.76%	12.75%	10.75%	10.66%
11	June	12.70%	10.54%	10.73%	11.42%
12	July	10.94%	11.81%	10.19%	11.58%
13	August	10.43%	10.83%	12.34%	11.98%
14	September	10.95%	10.40%	12.25%	10.87%
15	October	10.57%	10.37%	9.70%	10.03%
16	November	11.38%	10.90%	11.77%	10.63%
17	December	10.68%	12.33%	11.22%	10.05%
18	⊟ 2013				
19	January	11.35%	10.56%	10.87%	10.81%
20	February	10.28%	10.07%	9.31%	9.14%
21	March	9.64%	9.96%	9.15%	10.28%

12　On the **Quick Access Toolbar**, click the **Undo** button to reverse the last change.

13　On the **Design** tab, in the **Layout** group, click **Subtotals**, and then click **Show All Subtotals at Bottom of Group** to display subtotals in the workbook.

14　Click the **Package Summary** sheet tab to display the **Package Summary** worksheet.

15　In cell **C4**, enter =, but do not press Enter.

16　Click the **PivotTable** sheet tab to display that worksheet.

17　Click cell **K32**, and then press **Enter**. When you do, Excel creates the formula **=GETPIVOTDATA("Volume",Sheet2!$A$3,"Year",2013)** in cell **C4**.

CLEAN UP Close the Focusing workbook, saving your changes if you want to.

Formatting PivotTables

PivotTables are the ideal tools for summarizing and examining large data collections, even those containing more than 10,000 or even 100,000 rows. Even though PivotTables often end up as compact summaries, you should do everything you can to make your data more comprehensible. One way to improve your data's readability is to apply a number format to the PivotTable Values field. To apply a number format to a field, right-click any cell in the field, and then click Number Format to open the Format Cells dialog box. Select or define the format you want to apply, and then click OK to enact the change.

SEE ALSO For more information on selecting and defining cell formats by using the Format Cells dialog box, see "Formatting cells" in Chapter 4, "Changing workbook appearance."

Analysts often use PivotTables to summarize and examine organizational data with an eye to making important decisions about the company. For example, chief operating officer Lori Penor might examine monthly package volumes handled by Consolidated Messenger and notice that there's a surge in package volume during the winter months in the United States.

10

	H	I	J	K	L
	Northwest	Southeast	Southwest	Grand Total	
	25,028,389	23,785,488	24,817,582	215,576,788	
	3,085,352	3,470,295	3,029,490	27,595,133	
	2,554,130	1,988,929	2,692,383	17,854,654	
	1,932,304	1,441,894	1,646,946	14,804,110	
	1,348,145	1,631,240	1,525,005	13,539,264	
	1,628,489	1,749,378	1,452,226	14,225,789	
	1,475,038	1,422,265	1,428,581	13,587,254	
	1,832,445	1,511,712	1,503,100	14,448,166	
	1,633,582	1,671,246	1,414,763	14,568,966	
	1,638,024	1,510,884	1,407,402	13,650,679	
	2,045,639	1,427,066	2,888,565	16,501,082	
	3,020,217	2,848,642	2,728,934	26,798,138	
	2,835,024	3,111,937	3,100,187	28,003,553	

Excel extends the capabilities of your PivotTables by enabling you to apply a conditional format to the PivotTable cells. What's more, you can select whether to apply the conditional format to every cell in the Values area, to every cell at the same level as the selected cell (that is, a regular data cell, a subtotal cell, or a grand total cell) or to every cell that contains or draws its values from the selected cell's field (such as the Volume field in the previous example).

To apply a conditional format to a PivotTable field, click a cell in the Values area. On the Home tab, in the Styles group, click Conditional Formatting, and then create the desired conditional format. After you do, Excel displays a Formatting Options action button, which offers three options for applying the conditional format:

- **Selected Cells** Applies the conditional format to the selected cells only

- **All Cells Showing Sum of field_name Values** Applies the conditional format to every cell in the data area, regardless of whether the cell is in the data area, a subtotal row or column, or a grand total row or column

- **All Cells Showing Sum of field_name Values for Fields** Applies the conditional format to every cell at the same level (for example, data cell, subtotal, or grand total) as the selected cells

SEE ALSO For more information on creating conditional formats, see "Changing the appearance of data based on its value" in Chapter 4, "Changing workbook appearance."

In Excel, you can take full advantage of the Microsoft Office system enhanced formatting capabilities to apply existing formats to your PivotTables. Just as you can create Excel table formats, you can also create your own PivotTable formats to match your organization's desired color scheme.

To apply a PivotTable style, click any cell in the PivotTable and then, on the Design tool tab, in the PivotTable Styles group, click the style that you want to apply. If you want to create your own PivotTable style, click the More button to display a menu containing a gallery, and then click New PivotTable Style below the gallery to open the New PivotTable Style dialog box.

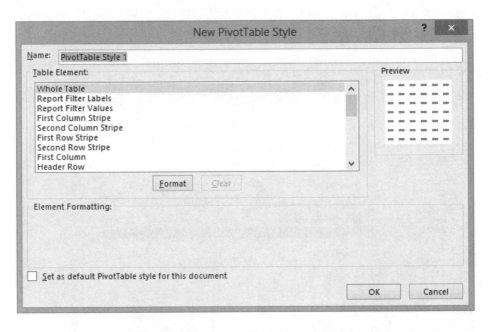

Enter a name for the style in the Name field, click the first table element you want to customize, and then click Format. Use the controls in the Format Cells dialog box to change the element's appearance. After you click OK to close the Format Cells dialog box, the New PivotTable Quick Style dialog box Preview pane displays the style's appearance. If you want Excel to use the style by default, select the Set As Default PivotTable Style For This Document check box. After you finish creating your formats, click OK to close the New PivotTable Quick Style dialog box and save your style.

The Design tool tab contains many other tools that you can use to format your PivotTable, but one of the most useful is the Banded Columns check box, which you can find in the PivotTable Style Options group. If you select a PivotTable style that offers banded rows as an option, selecting the Banded Rows check box turns banding on. If you prefer not to have Excel band the rows in your PivotTable, clearing the check box turns banding off.

In this exercise, you'll apply a number format to a PivotTable values field, apply a PivotTable style, create your own PivotTable style, apply banded rows to your PivotTable, and apply a conditional format to a PivotTable.

→ SET UP You need the Formatting workbook located in the Chapter10 practice file folder to complete this exercise. Open the workbook, and then follow the steps.

1   On the **Sheet2** worksheet, right-click any data cell, and then click **Number Format** to open the **Format Cells** dialog box.

2   In the **Category** list, click **Number** to display the **Number** page of the dialog box.

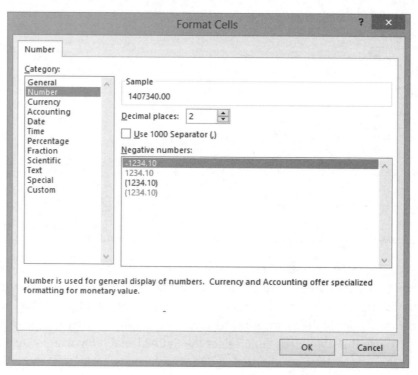

3   In the **Decimal places** field, enter **0**.

4   Select the **Use 1000 Separator (,)** check box.

5   Click **OK** to reformat your PivotTable data.

⁄	A	B	C	D
1				
2				
3	**Sum of Volume**	**Column Labels** ▾		
4	**Row Labels** ▾	**Atlantic**	**Central**	**Midwest**
5	⊟**2012**	**23,276,049**	**23,727,556**	**23,643,436**
6	January	2,966,264	3,143,004	2,774,877
7	February	1,541,726	1,407,340	2,046,448
8	March	1,688,027	1,594,434	1,600,920
9	April	1,445,436	1,548,205	1,395,802
10	May	1,530,319	1,813,746	1,529,086
11	June	1,725,770	1,431,518	1,458,009
12	July	1,581,340	1,706,190	1,472,534
13	August	1,519,538	1,577,651	1,797,139
14	September	1,494,735	1,420,065	1,672,046
15	October	1,743,541	1,711,810	1,599,927
16	November	3,049,369	2,921,522	3,153,696
17	December	2,989,984	3,452,071	3,142,952
18	⊟**2013**	**23,760,133**	**23,274,159**	**23,246,331**
19	January	3,076,578	2,863,187	2,946,100
20	February	1,556,937	1,524,882	1,410,456
21	March	1,522,379	1,573,351	1,445,833

6   If necessary, on the **Design** tool tab, in the **PivotTable Style Options** group, select the **Banded Rows** check box.

7   On the **Design** tool tab, in the **PivotTable Styles** group, click the **More** button. Then, in the top row of the gallery, click the third style from the left (**Pivot Style Light 2.**). Clicking the style causes Excel to apply it to your PivotTable.

10

	A	B	C	D
1				
2				
3	Sum of Volume	Column Labels ▼		
4	Row Labels ▼	Atlantic	Central	Midwest
5	⊟2012	23,276,049	23,727,556	23,643,436
6	January	2,966,264	3,143,004	2,774,877
7	February	1,541,726	1,407,340	2,046,448
8	March	1,688,027	1,594,434	1,600,920
9	April	1,445,436	1,548,205	1,395,802
10	May	1,530,319	1,813,746	1,529,086
11	June	1,725,770	1,431,518	1,458,009
12	July	1,581,340	1,706,190	1,472,534
13	August	1,519,538	1,577,651	1,797,139
14	September	1,494,735	1,420,065	1,672,046
15	October	1,743,541	1,711,810	1,599,927
16	November	3,049,369	2,921,522	3,153,696
17	December	2,989,984	3,452,071	3,142,952
18	⊟2013	23,760,133	23,274,159	23,246,331
19	January	3,076,578	2,863,187	2,946,100
20	February	1,556,937	1,524,882	1,410,456

8   In the lower-right corner of the **PivotTable Styles** menu, click the **More** button to display the gallery.

9   Click **New PivotTable Style** to open the **New PivotTable Style** dialog box.

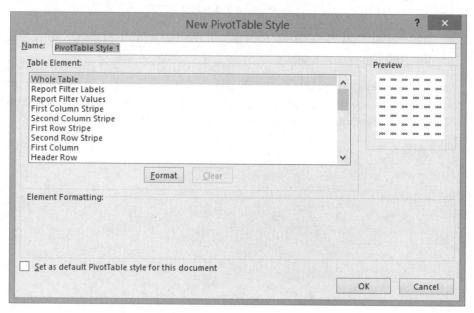

10   In the **Name** field, enter Custom Style 1.

11   In the **Table Element** list, click **Header Row**, and then click **Format** to open the **Format Cells** dialog box.

12   On the **Font** page, in the **Color** list, click the white swatch.

13   On the **Border** page, in the **Presets** area, click **Outline**.

14   On the **Fill** page, in the **Background Color** area, click the purple swatch in the lower-right corner of the color palette.

15   Click **OK** to close the **Format Cells** dialog box. The style change appears in the **Preview** pane of the **New PivotTable Quick Style** dialog box.

16   In the **Table Element** list, click **Second Row Stripe**, and then click **Format** to open the **Format Cells** dialog box.

17   On the **Fill** page, in the middle part of the **Background Color** area, click the eighth swatch in the second row (it's a light, dusty purple).

18   Click **OK** twice to close the **Format Cells** dialog box. Your format appears in the **PivotTable Styles** group.

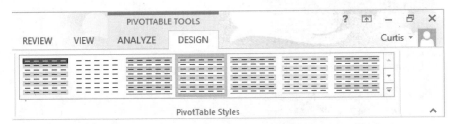

19   Click the **More** button in the lower-right corner of the **PivotTable Styles** group, and then click your new style to reformat the PivotTable.

20   On the **Design** tool tab, in the **PivotTable Style Options** group, clear the **Banded Rows** check box. Excel removes the banding from your PivotTable and from the preview of the custom style.

10

⊿	A	B	C	D	E
1					
2					
3	Sum of Volume	Column Labels ▼			
4	Row Labels ▼	Atlantic	Central	Midwest	Mountain West
5	⊟2012	23,276,049	23,727,556	23,643,436	23,075,908
6	January	2,966,264	3,143,004	2,774,877	2,942,544
7	February	1,541,726	1,407,340	2,046,448	1,552,098
8	March	1,688,027	1,594,434	1,600,920	1,641,026
9	April	1,445,436	1,548,205	1,395,802	1,653,829
10	May	1,530,319	1,813,746	1,529,086	1,516,453
11	June	1,725,770	1,431,518	1,458,009	1,551,719

21 Select the cell ranges **K6:K17** and **K19:K30**.

22 On the **Home** tab, in the **Styles** group, click **Conditional Formatting**, point to **Color Scales**, and in the top row, click the second three-color scale from the left to apply the conditional format to the selected cells.

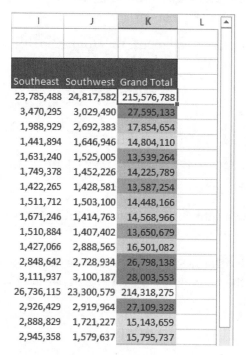

I	J	K	L
Southeast	Southwest	Grand Total	
23,785,488	24,817,582	215,576,788	
3,470,295	3,029,490	27,595,133	
1,988,929	2,692,383	17,854,654	
1,441,894	1,646,946	14,804,110	
1,631,240	1,525,005	13,539,264	
1,749,378	1,452,226	14,225,789	
1,422,265	1,428,581	13,587,254	
1,511,712	1,503,100	14,448,166	
1,671,246	1,414,763	14,568,966	
1,510,884	1,407,402	13,650,679	
1,427,066	2,888,565	16,501,082	
2,848,642	2,728,934	26,798,138	
3,111,937	3,100,187	28,003,553	
26,736,115	23,300,579	214,318,275	
2,926,429	2,919,964	27,109,328	
2,888,829	1,721,227	15,143,659	
2,945,358	1,579,637	15,795,737	

✖ CLEAN UP Close the Formatting workbook, saving your changes if you want to.

Creating PivotTables from external data

Although most of the time you will create PivotTables from data stored in Excel worksheets, you can also bring data from outside sources into Excel. For example, you might need to work with data created in another spreadsheet program by using a file format that Excel can't read directly. Fortunately, you can export the data from the original program into a text file, which Excel then translates into a worksheet.

TIP The data import technique shown here isn't exclusive to PivotTables. You can use this procedure to bring data into your worksheets for any purpose.

Spreadsheet programs store data in cells, so the goal of representing spreadsheet data in a text file is to indicate where the contents of one cell end and those of the next cell begin. The character that marks the end of a cell is a *delimiter*, in that it marks the end (or "limit") of a cell. The most common cell delimiter is the comma, so the delimited sequence *15, 18, 24, 28* represents data in four cells. The problem with using commas to delimit financial data is that larger values—such as *52,802*—can be written by using commas as thousands markers. To avoid confusion when importing a text file, the most commonly used delimiter for financial data is the Tab character.

To import data from a text file, on the Data tab, click Get External Data group, and then click From Text to display the Import Text File dialog box.

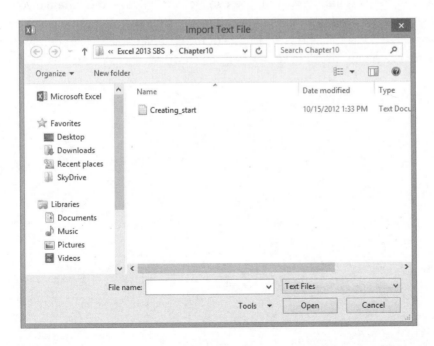

From within the Import Text File dialog box, browse to the directory that contains the text file you want to import. When you double-click the file, Excel launches the Text Import wizard.

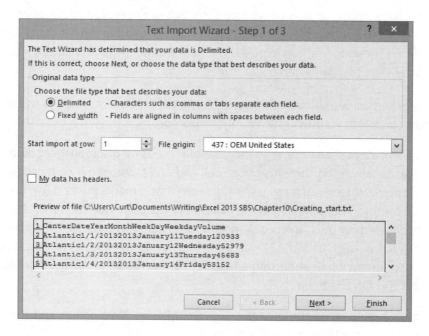

On the first page of the Text Import wizard, you can indicate whether the data file you are importing is Delimited or Fixed Width; Fixed Width means that each cell value will fall within a specific position in the file. Clicking Next to accept the default choice, Delimited (which Excel assigns after examining the data source you selected), advances you to the next wizard page.

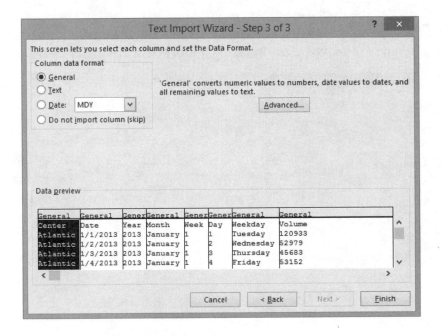

On this page, you can choose the delimiter for the file (in this case, Excel detected tabs in the file and selected the Tab check box for you) and you can preview what the text file will look like when imported. Clicking Next advances you to the final wizard page.

On this page, you can change the data type and formatting of the columns in your data. Because you'll assign number styles and PivotTable Quick Styles after you create the PivotTable, you can click Finish to import the data into your worksheet. After the data is in Excel, you can work with it normally.

In this exercise, you'll import data into Excel from a text file and then create a PivotTable based on that data.

SET UP You need the Creating text file located in the Chapter10 practice file folder to complete this exercise. Don't open the file yet; just follow the steps.

1   Create a new Excel workbook. On the **Data** tab, click the **Get External Data** button, and then click **From Text** to open the **Import Text File** dialog box.

2   Navigate to the **Chapter10** practice file folder, and then double-click the **Creating** text file to start the **Text Import** wizard.

3   Verify that the **Delimited** option is selected, and then click **Next** to display the next page of the wizard.

4   In the **Delimiters** area, verify that the **Tab** check box is selected and also verify that the data displayed in the **Data preview** area reflects the structure you expect.

5   Click **Finish** to skip the third page of the wizard, which has commands you can use to assign specific data types to each column. Excel assigns data types for you, so you don't need to do so. After you click **Finish**, the **Import Data** dialog box opens.

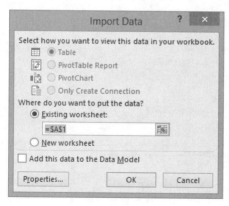

6   Verify that **Existing worksheet** is selected, and then click **OK** to import the data into your workbook.

7   On the **Home** tab, in the **Styles** group, click **Format as Table**, and then click the first table style to display the **Format As Table** dialog box.

8   Verify that the **My table has headers** check box is selected and that the range =$A$1:$H$6571 appears in the **Where is the data for your table?** box, and then click **OK**.

9   In the confirmation dialog box, click **Yes** to confirm that you want to create the Excel table and break its link to the external data source. Excel creates an Excel table from your imported data.

10   On the **Insert** tab, click **PivotTable** to open the **Create PivotTable** dialog box.

11   Verify that **Select a table or range** is selected, that **Table1** appears in the **Table/Range** field, and that the **New Worksheet** option is selected.

12   Click **OK** to create the PivotTable on a new worksheet.

13   In the **PivotTable Fields** pane, drag the **Volume** field header to the **Values** area.

14   Drag the **Weekday** field header to the **Columns** area.

15   Drag the **Center** field header to the **Rows** data area.

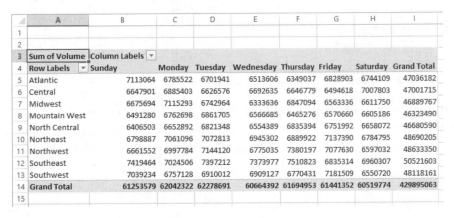

Row Labels	Sunday	Monday	Tuesday	Wednesday	Thursday	Friday	Saturday	Grand Total
Atlantic	7113064	6785522	6701941	6513606	6349037	6828903	6744109	47036182
Central	6647901	6885403	6626576	6692635	6646779	6494618	7007803	47001715
Midwest	6675694	7115293	6742964	6333636	6847094	6563336	6611750	46889767
Mountain West	6491280	6762698	6861705	6566685	6465276	6570660	6605186	46323490
North Central	6406503	6652892	6821348	6554389	6835394	6751992	6658072	46680590
Northeast	6798887	7061096	7072813	6945302	6889922	7137390	6784795	48690205
Northwest	6661552	6997784	7144120	6775035	7380197	7077630	6597032	48633350
Southeast	7419464	7024506	7397212	7373977	7510823	6835314	6960307	50521603
Southwest	7039234	6757128	6910012	6909127	6770431	7181509	6550720	48118161
Grand Total	61253579	62042322	62278691	60664392	61694953	61441352	60519774	429895063

10

❌ CLEAN UP Close the Imported Data workbook, saving your changes if you want to.

Creating dynamic charts by using PivotCharts

Just as you can create PivotTables that you can reorganize on the fly to emphasize different aspects of the data in a list, you can also create dynamic charts, or PivotCharts, to reflect the contents and organization of a PivotTable.

Creating a PivotChart is fairly straightforward. Just click any cell in a list or Excel table that you would use to create a PivotTable, and then click the Insert tab. In the Charts group, click the PivotChart button to create the chart. When you do, Excel 2013 opens the Create PivotChart dialog box.

To create a PivotChart from an existing PivotTable, click a cell in the PivotTable, display the Insert tab and then, in the Charts group, click the type of chart you want to create. After you complete either of these procedures, Excel displays a new PivotChart in your workbook.

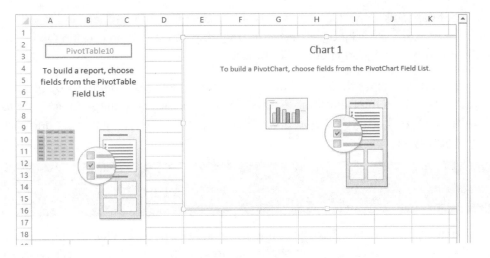

Any changes to the PivotTable on which the PivotChart is based are reflected in the PivotChart. For example, if the data in an underlying data set changes, clicking the Refresh button in the Data group on the Analyze tool tab will change the PivotChart to reflect the new data. Also, if you filter the contents of a PivotTable, the filter will be reflected in the PivotChart. For instance, if you click 2009 in the Year list of a revenue analysis PivotTable and then click OK, both the PivotTable and the PivotChart will show only revenues from 2009.

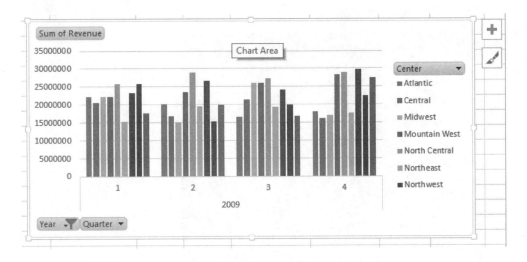

SEE ALSO For more information on manipulating PivotTables, see "Filtering, showing, and hiding PivotTable data" earlier in this chapter.

A PivotChart has tools with which you can filter the data in the PivotChart and PivotTable. Clicking the Year arrow, clicking (All) in the list that appears, and then clicking OK will restore the PivotChart to its original configuration.

If you ever want to change the chart type of an existing chart, you can do so by selecting the chart and then, on the Design tab, in the Type group, clicking Change Chart Type to display the Change Chart Type dialog box. When you select the type you want and click OK, Excel re-creates your chart.

> **IMPORTANT** If your data is the wrong type to be represented by the chart type you select, Excel displays an error message.

In this exercise, you'll create a PivotTable and associated PivotChart, change the underlying data and update the PivotChart to reflect that change, change the PivotChart's type, and then filter a PivotTable and PivotChart.

→ SET UP You need the RevenueAnalysis workbook located in the Chapter10 practice file folder to complete this exercise. Open the workbook, and then follow the steps.

1   On the **Through 2012** worksheet, click any cell in the Excel table.

2   On the **Insert** tab, in the **Charts** group, click the **PivotChart** button to open the **Create PivotChart** dialog box.

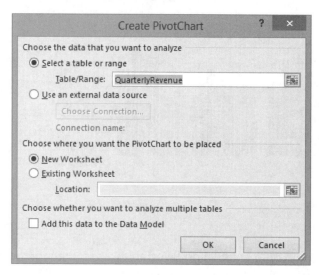

3   Verify that the **QuarterlyRevenue** table appears in the **Table/Range** field and that **New Worksheet** is selected.

4   Click **OK** to create the PivotChart and associated PivotTable.

5   In the **PivotChart Fields** pane, drag the **Center** field header from the **Choose fields to add to report** area to the **Legend (Series)** area.

6   Drag the **Year** field header from the **Choose fields to add to report** area to the **Axis (Category)** area.

7   Drag the **Quarter** field header from the **Choose fields to add to report** area to the **Axis (Category)** area, positioning it below the **Year** field header.

8   Drag the **Revenue** field header from the **Choose fields to add to report** area to the **Values** area. Excel updates the PivotChart to reflect the field placements.

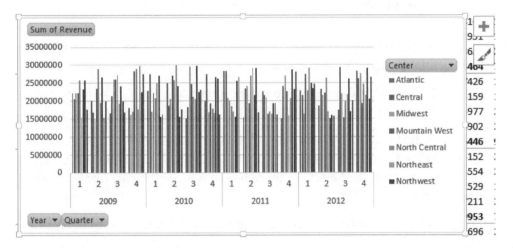

9   Click the **2013** sheet tab to display that worksheet.

10   Select the data in cells **B2:E10**, and then press **Ctrl+C**. Excel copies the data to the Microsoft Office Clipboard.

11   On the tab bar, click the **Through 2012** sheet tab to display that worksheet.

12   Select cell **B147**, and then press **Ctrl+V** to paste the data into the worksheet and include it in the Excel table.

13   Click the tab of the worksheet that contains the PivotTable and the PivotChart. The PivotChart appears.

14   Select the PivotChart and then, on the **Analyze** tool tab, in the **Data** group, click **Refresh** to add the data to your PivotChart.

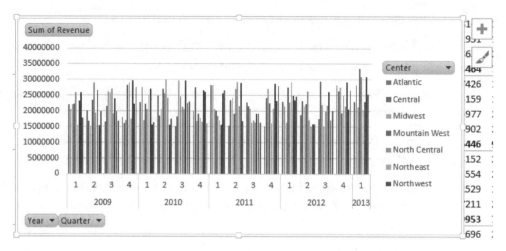

15   On the **Design** tool tab, in the **Type** group, click **Change Chart Type** to open the **Change Chart Type** dialog box.

16   Click **Line**, click the first **Line** chart subtype, and then click **OK** to change your PivotChart to a line chart.

17   In the **PivotTable Fields** pane, in the **Choose fields to add to report** area, point to the **Center** field header. Click the filter arrow that appears and then, in the filter menu, clear the **Select All** check box to remove the check boxes from the filter list items.

18   Select the **Northeast** check box, and then click **OK** to filter the PivotChart.

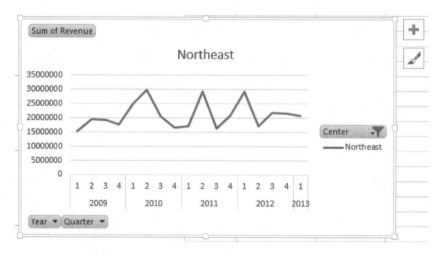

❌ CLEAN UP Close the RevenueAnalysis workbook, saving your changes if you want to.

Key points

- A PivotTable is a versatile tool that you can use to rearrange your data dynamically, enabling you to emphasize different aspects of your data without creating new worksheets.

- PivotTable data must be formatted as a list. By using a data table as the PivotTable data source, you can streamline the creation process by referring to the table name instead of being required to select the entire range that contains the data you want to summarize.

- You can choose from a variety of styles when you create PivotTables.

- With the PivotTable Fields pane, you can create your PivotTable by using a straightforward, compact tool.

- Just as you can limit the data shown in a static worksheet, you can use filters to limit the data shown in a PivotTable.

- If you have data in a compatible format, such as a text file, you can import that data into Excel and create a PivotTable from it.

- You can summarize your data visually by using a PivotChart, which you can pivot just like a PivotTable.

10

Chapter at a glance

Headers

Add headers and footers to printed pages,
page 334

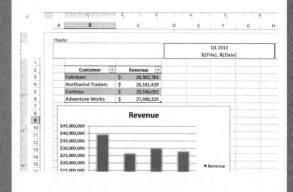

Prepare

Prepare worksheets for printing,
page 340

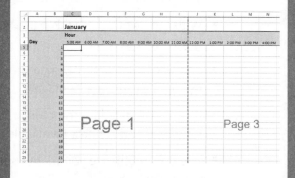

Print

Print parts of worksheets,
page 352

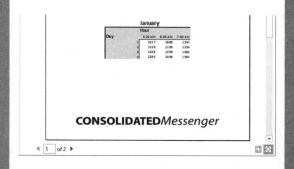

Charts

Print charts,
page 357

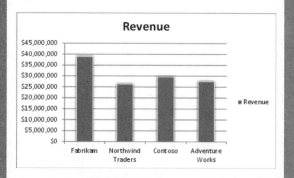

Printing worksheets and charts

IN THIS CHAPTER, YOU WILL LEARN HOW TO

- Add headers and footers to printed pages.

- Prepare worksheets for printing.

- Print worksheets.

- Print parts of worksheets.

- Print charts.

Microsoft Excel 2013 provides you with a wide range of tools that you can use to create and manipulate your data. By using filters, by sorting, and by creating PivotTables and charts, you can change your worksheets so that they convey the greatest possible amount of information. After you configure your worksheet so that it shows your data to best advantage, you can print your Excel documents to use in a presentation or include in a report. You can choose to print all or part of any of your worksheets, change how your data and charts appear on the printed page, and even suppress any error messages that might appear in your worksheets.

In this chapter, you'll add headers and footers to your worksheets, prepare your worksheets for printing, print all of and part of a worksheet, and print a chart.

PRACTICE FILES To complete the exercises in this chapter, you need the practice files contained in the Chapter11 practice file folder. For more information, see "Download the practice files" in this book's Introduction.

Adding headers and footers
to printed pages

If you want to ensure that the same information appears at the top or bottom of every printed page, you can do so by adding headers or footers. A *header* is a section that appears at the top of every printed page; a *footer* is a section that appears at the bottom of every printed page. To create a header or footer in Excel, you display the Insert tab and then, in the Text group, click Header & Footer to display the Design tool tab.

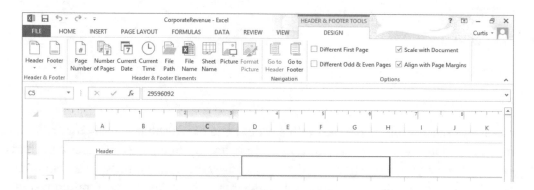

When you display your workbook's headers and footers, Excel displays the workbook in Page Layout view. Page Layout view shows you exactly how your workbook will look when printed, while still enabling you to edit your file, a capability not provided by Print Preview. You can also switch to Page Layout view by displaying the View tab and then, in the Workbook Views group, clicking Page Layout.

SEE ALSO For information about editing your workbook in Print Preview mode, see "Previewing worksheets before printing" later in this chapter.

Excel divides its headers and footers into left, middle, and right sections. When you point to an editable header or footer section, Excel highlights the section to indicate that clicking the mouse button will open that header or footer section for editing.

When you click a header or footer section, Excel displays the Design tool tab on the ribbon. The Design tool tab contains several standard headers and footers, such as page numbers by themselves or followed by the name of the workbook. To add an Auto Header to your workbook, display the Design tool tab and then, in the Header & Footer group, click Header. Then click the header you want to apply. The list of headers that appears will vary depending on the properties and contents of your worksheet and workbook.

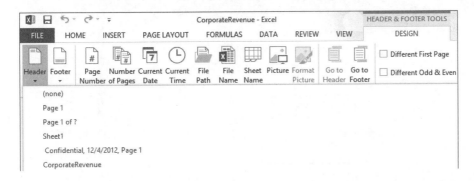

You can also create custom headers by entering your own text or by using the commands in the Header & Footer Elements group to insert a date, time, worksheet name, or page number. You can also add a graphic, such as a company logo, to a header or footer. For example, if you include a worksheet in a printed report that is distributed outside your company, adding your company's logo to the worksheet can identify the worksheet with your company. After you insert a graphic into a header or footer, the Format Picture button in the Header & Footer Elements group will become available. When you click that button, a dialog box opens with tools for editing your graphic.

When you print or display a worksheet, you might want to have different headers for odd and even pages. For example, Consolidated Messenger's document standards might require the current date on odd-numbered pages and the page number on even-numbered pages. To establish different headers and footers for odd-numbered and even-numbered pages,

11

click the View tab and then click the Page Layout button to display your workbook in Page Layout view. Click within a header or footer and then, on the Design tool tab, select the Different Odd & Even Pages check box. Now when you change a header or footer, Excel indicates whether it applies to an odd or even page.

Your worksheet's header and footer will always be the same width as the printed worksheet. If you want to adjust the vertical size of a header or footer, click the Page Layout tab, click the Margins button, and then click the Custom Margins command at the bottom of the menu to display the Margins page of the Page Setup dialog box.

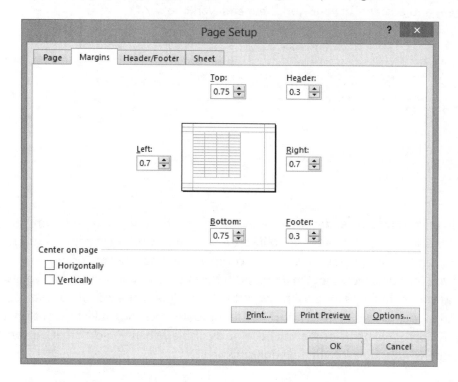

The Margins page of the Page Setup dialog box has boxes for you to enter your desired header and footer sizes. Enter the values you want and then click OK to apply your changes.

In this exercise, you'll create a custom header for a workbook. You'll then add a graphic to the footer and edit the graphic by using the Format Picture dialog box.

→ **SET UP** You need the RevenueByCustomer workbook and the ConsolidatedMessenger image located in your Chapter11 practice file folder to complete this exercise. Open the workbook, and then follow the steps.

1   On the **Insert** tab, click the **Text** button, and then click **Header & Footer** to display your workbook in **Page Layout** view.

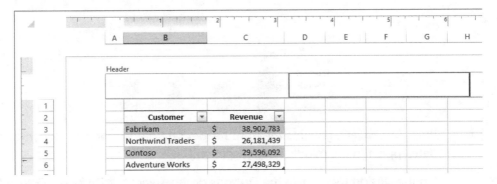

2   In the middle header section, enter **Q1 2013**, and then press **Enter**.

3   On the **Design** tool tab, in the **Header & Footer Elements** group, click **File Name** to add the **&[File]** code to the header.

4   To the right of the **&[File]** code, enter a comma, and then press the **Spacebar**.

5   On the **Design** tool tab, in the **Header & Footer Elements** group, click **Current Date**. Excel changes the contents of the middle header section to **&[File], &[Date]**.

11

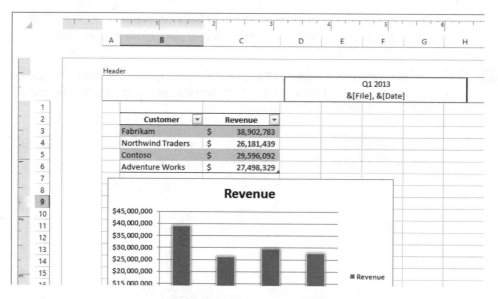

6　Press **Tab**. Excel highlights the right header section. The workbook name and current date appear in the middle header section.

7　On the **Design** tool tab, in the **Options** group, select the **Different Odd & Even Pages** check box to print the header you defined on odd-numbered pages only and to leave the header on even-numbered pages blank. Excel changes the header label from **Header** to **Odd Page Header**.

8　On the **Design** tool tab, in the **Navigation** group, click **Go to Footer** to highlight the right footer section.

9　Click the middle footer section.

10　On the **Design** tool tab, in the **Header & Footer Elements** group, click **Picture** to open the **Insert Pictures** dialog box.

11　Click **From a File** to display the **Insert Picture** dialog box.

12　Navigate to the **Chapter11** folder, and then double-click the **ConsolidatedMessenger** image file. The code **&[Picture]** appears in the middle footer section.

13　Click any worksheet cell above the footer to display the worksheet as it will be printed.

14   Click the image in the footer and then, on the **Design** tool tab, click **Format Picture** to open the **Format Picture** dialog box.

15   Click the **Size** tab if the **Size** page is not already displayed.

16   In the **Scale** area of the dialog box, in the **Height** field, enter 80%, and then press **Enter** to close the **Format Picture** dialog box.

17   Click any worksheet cell above the footer to display the reformatted picture.

18   On the **Page Layout** tab, click **Margins**, and then click the **Custom Margins** command at the bottom of the menu to display the **Margins** page of the **Page Setup** dialog box.

19   In the **Header** box, enter .5.

20   In the **Footer** box, enter .5 and click **OK** to reformat your worksheet.

❌ CLEAN UP Close the RevenueByCustomer workbook, saving your changes if you want to.

11

Preparing worksheets for printing

When you are ready to print your workbook, you can change the workbook's properties to ensure that your worksheets display all your information and that printing is centered on the page. In Excel, all of these printing functions are gathered together in one place: the Backstage view. To preview your workbook in the Backstage view, click the File tab and then click Print.

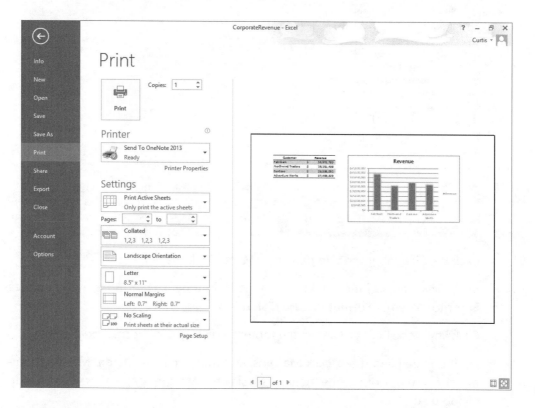

KEYBOARD SHORTCUT Press Ctrl+P to preview your worksheet in the Backstage view. For a complete list of keyboard shortcuts, see "Keyboard shortcuts" at the end of this book.

Excel comes with three margin settings: Normal, Wide, and Narrow. Excel applies the Normal setting by default, but you can select any of the three options by displaying the workbook in the Backstage view and then, in the Settings area, clicking the Margins button and clicking the setting you want. If you want finer control over your margins, click the Margins button and then click Custom Margins to display the Margins page of the Page Setup dialog box.

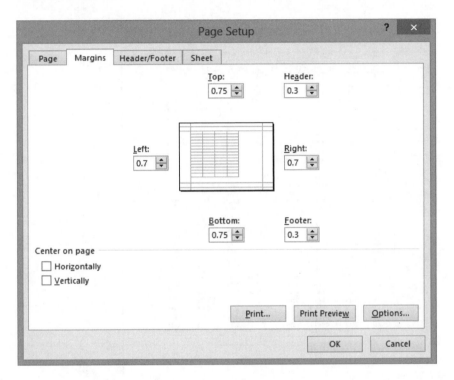

If you want to display a worksheet's margins while you have its workbook open in the Backstage view, click the Show Margins button near the lower-right corner of the Backstage view.

11

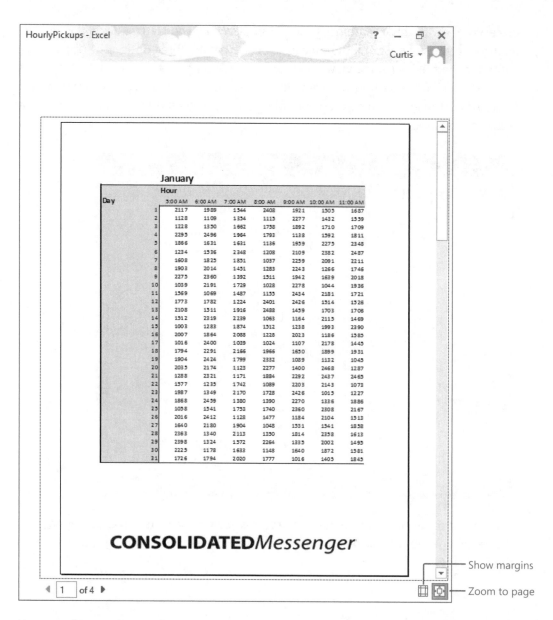

You can drag each margin line to change the corresponding margin's position, increasing or decreasing the amount of space allocated to each worksheet section. Do bear in mind that increasing the size of the header or footer reduces the size of the worksheet body, meaning that fewer rows can be printed on a page.

Another issue with printing worksheets is that the data in worksheets tends to be wider horizontally than a standard sheet of paper. You can use the commands in the Backstage view to change the alignment of the rows and columns on the page. When the columns parallel the long edge of a piece of paper, the page is laid out in portrait mode; when the columns parallel the short edge of a piece of paper, it is in landscape mode.

Changing between portrait and landscape mode can result in a better fit, but you might find that not all of your data will fit on a single printed page. This is where the options available on the Scaling button in the Backstage view come to the rescue. By using the options on the Scaling button, you can perform three tasks: reduce the size of the worksheet's contents until the worksheet can be printed on a single page, reduce the size of the worksheet's contents until all of the worksheet's columns fit on a single page, or reduce the size of the worksheet's contents until all of the worksheet's rows fit on a single page. You can make the same changes (and more) by using the controls in the Page Setup dialog box. To display the Page Setup dialog box, click the Page Layout tab, and then click the Page Setup dialog box launcher.

Previewing worksheets before printing

You can view your worksheet as it will be printed by displaying the Backstage view and then clicking Print in the left pane. When Excel displays your worksheet in the Backstage view, it shows the active worksheet as it will be printed with its current settings. At the bottom of the Backstage view, Excel indicates how many pages the worksheet will require when printed and the number of the page you are viewing.

TIP When you display a workbook in the Backstage view, you can view the next printed page by clicking the preview image and pressing the Page Down key; to move to the previous page, press the Page Up key. You can also use the Previous and Next arrows at the bottom of the Backstage view, enter a page number in the Current Page box, or scroll through the pages by using the vertical scroll bar at the right edge of the Backstage view.

Changing page breaks in a worksheet

Another way to affect how your worksheet will appear on the printed page is to change where Excel assigns its page breaks. A page break is the point at which Excel prints all subsequent data on a new sheet of paper. You can make these changes indirectly by modifying a worksheet's margins, but you can do so directly by displaying your document in Page Break Preview mode. To display your worksheet in this mode, on the View tab, in the Workbook Views group, click Page Break Preview.

11

Day	5:00 AM	6:00 AM	7:00 AM	8:00 AM	9:00 AM	10:00 AM	11:00 AM	12:00 PM	1:00 PM	2:00 PM	3:00 PM	4:00 PM
1	2117	1989	1544	2408	1921	1505	1687	2391	1486	2075	1626	1326
2	1128	1109	1354	1115	2277	1432	1559	2103	2493	1317	1519	1836
3	1228	1350	1662	1758	1892	1710	1709	1889	1495	1405	1513	1493
4	2295	2496	1964	1793	1138	1592	1811	1479	2339	1839	2416	1838
5	1866	1631	1631	1136	1959	2275	2348	1355	1346	1947	2098	1163
6	1234	1536	2348	1208	2109	2382	2487	2464	1755	2086	1261	1989
7	1608	1825	1851	1037	2259	2091	2211	1195	1395	1727	1171	1753
8	1903	2014	1451	1283	2243	1266	1746	2243	1385	1414	1675	2274
9	2275	2360	1392	1511	1942	1639	2018	2468	2247	2493	1827	2261
10	1039	2191	1729	1028	2278	1044	1936	1233	1677	1988	1690	1649
11	1569	1069	1487	1155	2434	2181	1721	2235	1534	1407	1187	1581
12	1773	1782	1224	2401	2426	1514	1526	1086	1478	1943	1028	1988
13	2108	1511	1916	2488	1459	1703	1706	2083	2305	2348	1662	2218
14	1512	2319	2239	1068	1164	2115	1469	1629	2398	1970	1665	1343
15	1003	1288	1874	1512	1238	1993	2390	2040	1366	1422	2344	1144
16	2007	1864	2088	1228	2023	1186	1585	1422	1486	2232	1907	2001
17	1016	2400	1039	1024	1107	2178	1445	1452	1506	1605	1925	2223
18	1794	2291	2166	1966	1650	1899	1931	2124	1166	1630	2178	1185
19	1904	2424	1799	2332	1089	1132	1045	1203	1364	2346	1654	1483

The blue lines in the window represent the page breaks. If you want to set a page break manually, you can do so by displaying your worksheet in Page Break Preview mode, right-clicking the row header of the row below where you want the new page to start, and clicking Insert Page Break. In other words, if you right-click the row header of row 15 and then click Insert Page Break, row 14 will be the last row on the first printed page, and row 15 will be the first row on the second printed page. The same technique applies to columns: if you right-click the column H column header and click Insert Page Break, column G will be the last column on the first printed page, and column H will be the first column on the second printed page.

You can also add page breaks without displaying your workbook in Page Break Preview mode. To add a page break while your workbook is open in Normal view, click a row or column header and then, on the Page Layout tab, in the Page Setup area, click Breaks, and click Insert Page Break. You can use the commands in the Breaks list to delete a page break or to reset all of the page breaks in your worksheets.

> **IMPORTANT** Be sure to click a row header or column header when you want to insert a single page break. If you view a workbook in Page Break Preview mode, right-click a cell within the body of a worksheet, and then click Insert Page Break, Excel creates both a vertical page break to the left of the selected cell and a horizontal page break above the selected cell.

To move a page break, drag the line that represents the break to its new position. Excel will change the worksheet's properties so that the area you defined will be printed on a single page.

Changing the page printing order for worksheets

When you view a document in Page Break Preview mode, Excel indicates the order in which the pages will be printed with light gray words on the worksheet pages. (These indicators appear only in Page Break Preview mode; they don't show up when the document is printed.) You can change the order in which the pages are printed by displaying the Page Layout tab, clicking the Page Setup dialog box launcher, and displaying the Sheet page of the Page Setup dialog box.

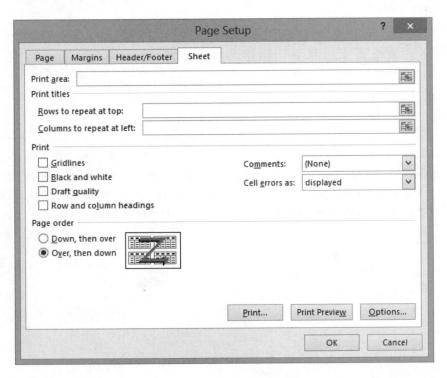

11

In the Page Order area of the dialog box, you can select the Over, Then Down option to change the order in which the worksheets will be printed from the default Down, Then Over. You might want to change the printing order to keep certain information together on consecutive printed pages. For example, suppose you have a worksheet that is designed to hold hourly package pickup information; the columns represent hours of the day, and the rows represent days of the month. If you want to print out consecutive days for each hour, you use Down, Then Over. In a typical configuration, pages 1 and 2 display the 5:00 A.M. to 11:00 A.M. pickups for the months of January and February, pages 3 and 4 display the 12:00 P.M. to 5:00 P.M. pickups for those months, and so on.

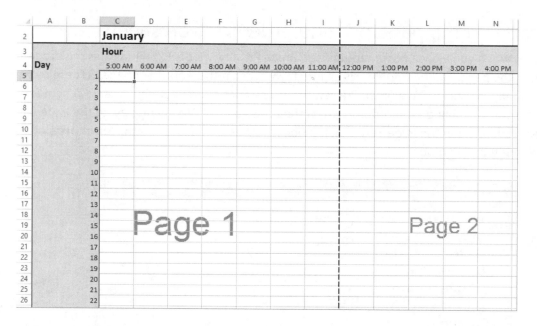

Changing the print order to Over, Then Down for the previous example would print consecutive hours for each day. Pages 1 and 2 would display the 5:00 A.M. to 5:00 P.M. pickups for January, and pages 3 and 4 would display the same pickups for February.

⊿	A	B	C	D	E	F	G	H	I	J	K	L	M	N
1														
2			January											
3			Hour											
4	Day		5:00 AM	6:00 AM	7:00 AM	8:00 AM	9:00 AM	10:00 AM	11:00 AM	12:00 PM	1:00 PM	2:00 PM	3:00 PM	4:00 PM
5		1												
6		2												
7		3												
8		4												
9		5												
10		6												
11		7												
12		8												
13		9												
14		10												
15		11												
16		12												
17		13												
18		14				Page 1							Page 3	
19		15												
20		16												
21		17												
22		18												
23		19												
24		20												
25		21												
26		22												

In this exercise, you'll preview a worksheet before printing it, change the worksheet's margins, change its orientation, reduce its size, add a page break, and change the page printing order.

SET UP You need the PickupsByHour workbook located in the Chapter11 practice file folder to complete this exercise. Open the workbook, and then follow the steps.

1   While displaying the **JanFeb** worksheet, click the **File** tab to display the **Backstage** view, and then click **Print**.

2   On the **Print** page of the **Backstage** view, click the **Orientation** button, and then click **Landscape Orientation** to reorient the worksheet.

3   In left pane of the **Backstage** view, click the **Go Back** button to return to the workbook.

11

4   On the **Page Layout** tab, in the **Scale to Fit** group, enter **80%** in the **Scale** box, and then press **Enter** to resize your worksheet.

5   Click the row header for row **38** to highlight that row.

6   On the **Page Layout** tab, in the **Page Setup** group, click **Breaks**, and then click **Insert Page Break** to set a horizontal page break above row **38**.

▲	A	B	C	D	E
37					
38		**February**			
39					
40				**Hour**	
41		**Day**		5:00 AM	6:00 AM
42			1	2117	1989
43			2	1128	1109
44			3	1228	1350
45			4	2295	2496

7   On the tab bar, click the **MarJun** sheet tab to display the **MarJun** worksheet.

8   On the **Page Layout** tab, in the **Page Setup** group, click **Margins**, and then click **Wide** to apply wide margins to the worksheet.

9   On the **Page Layout** tab, click the **Page Setup** dialog box launcher to open the **Page Setup** dialog box.

10   If necessary, click the **Sheet** tab to display the **Sheet** page of the dialog box.

11   In the **Page order** area, click **Over, then down**.

12   Click **OK**.

13   If you want, display the **Backstage** view, click **Print** to display the **Print** page, and then click the **Print** button to print your worksheet.

✖ CLEAN UP   Close the PickupsByHour workbook, saving your changes if you want to.

Printing worksheets

When you're ready to print a worksheet, all you have to do is display the Backstage view, click Print, and then click the Print button. If you want a little more say in how Excel prints your worksheet, you can use the commands on the Print page of the Backstage view to determine how Excel prints your worksheet. For example, you can choose the printer to which you want to send this print job, print multiple copies of the worksheet, and select whether the copies are collated (all pages of a document are printed together) or not (multiple copies of the same page are printed together).

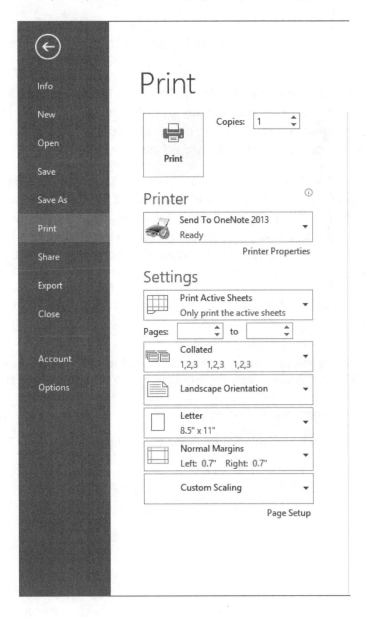

If you want to print more than one worksheet from the active workbook, but not every worksheet in the workbook, you can select the worksheets to print from the tab bar. To select specific worksheets to print, hold down the Ctrl key while you click the sheet tabs of the worksheets you want. Then display the Backstage view, click Print, and click the Print button.

TIP The worksheets you select for printing do not need to be next to one another in the workbook.

One helpful option on the Sheet page of the Page Setup dialog box is the Cell Errors As box, which you can use to select how Excel will print any errors in your worksheet. You can print an error as it normally appears in the worksheet, print a blank cell in place of the error, or choose one of two other indicators that are not standard error messages.

After you prepare your workbook for printing, you can specify which elements to print by displaying the Print page of the Backstage view and then clicking the Print What button, which displays Print Active Sheets by default. To print the entire worksheet, verify that the Print What button displays Print Active Sheets, and then click the Print button. To print every worksheet in the active workbook, click the Print What button, click Print Entire Workbook, and then click the Print button.

In this exercise, you'll print nonadjacent worksheets in your workbook and suppress errors in the printed worksheet.

 SET UP You need the SummaryByCustomer workbook located in the Chapter11 practice file folder to complete this exercise. Open the workbook, and then follow the steps.

1   If necessary, display the **Summary** worksheet.

2   On the **Page Layout** tab, click the **Page Setup** dialog box launcher to open the **Page Setup** dialog box.

3   Click the **Sheet** tab to display the **Sheet** page of the dialog box.

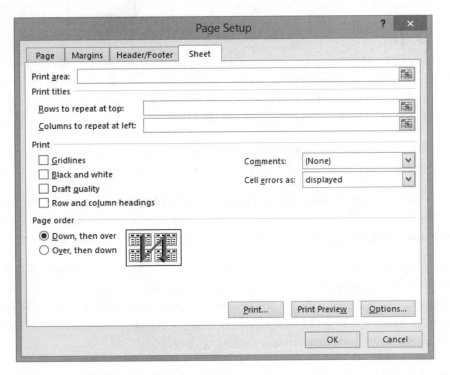

4   In the **Cell errors as** list, click **<blank>**.

5   Click **OK**.

6   Hold down the **Ctrl** key and then, on the tab bar, click the **Northwind** sheet tab to select the **Summary** and **Northwind** worksheets.

7   Display the **Backstage** view, and then click **Print**.

8   In the **Settings** area of the **Print** page, verify that **Print Active Sheets** is selected.

9   Click the **Go Back** button at the top of the left pane to cancel printing, or click the **Print** button if you want to print the worksheets.

11

✖ CLEAN UP Close the SummaryByCustomer workbook, saving your changes if you want to.

Printing parts of worksheets

Excel gives you a great deal of control over what your worksheets look like when you print them, but you also have a lot of control over which parts of your worksheets will be printed. For example, you can use the commands available on the Print page of the Backstage view to choose which pages of a multipage worksheet you want to print.

In the Settings area of the Print page, you can fill in the page numbers you want to print in the Pages From and To boxes.

TIP You can also use the Page Break Preview window to determine which pages to print, and if the pages aren't in an order you like, you can use the commands on the Sheet page of the Page Setup dialog box to change the order in which they will be printed.

Another way you can modify how a worksheet will be printed is to have Excel fit the entire worksheet on a specified number of pages. For example, you can have Excel resize a worksheet so that it will fit on a single printed page. Fitting a worksheet onto a single page is a handy tool when you need to add a sales or other summary to a report and don't want to spread important information across more than one page.

To have Excel fit a worksheet on a set number of pages, display the Page Layout tab and use the controls in the Scale To Fit group. In the Width and Height lists, you can select how many pages wide or tall you want your printout to be.

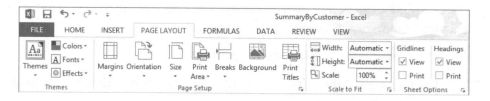

If you want to print a portion of a worksheet instead of the entire worksheet, you can define the area or areas that you want to have printed. To identify the area of the worksheet you want to print, select the cells with the data you want to print and, on the Page Layout tab, in the Page Setup group, click Print Area and then click Set Print Area. Excel marks the area with a dotted line around the border of the selected cells and prints only the cells you selected. To remove the selection, click Print Area, and then click Clear Print Area.

TIP You can include noncontiguous groups of cells in the area to be printed by holding down the Ctrl key as you select the cells. Noncontiguous print areas will be printed on separate pages.

After you define a print area, you can use the options in the Page Setup dialog box to position the print area on the page. Specifically, you can have Excel center the print area on the page by selecting the Horizontally and Vertically check boxes in the Center On Page area of the Margins page.

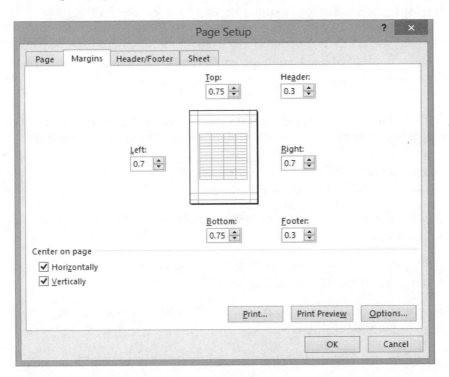

If the contents of a worksheet will take up more than one printed page, you can have Excel repeat one or more rows at the top of the page or columns at the left of the page. For example, if you want to print a lengthy worksheet that contains the mailing addresses of customers signed up to receive your company's monthly newsletter, you could repeat the column headings Name, Address, City, and so forth at the top of the page. To repeat rows at the top of each printed page, on the Page Layout tab, in the Page Setup group, click Print Titles. Excel will display the Sheet page of the Page Setup dialog box.

11

On the Sheet page of the Page Setup dialog box, you can use the commands in the Print Titles area to select the rows or columns to repeat. To choose rows to repeat at the top of the page, click the Collapse Dialog button next to the Rows To Repeat At Top box, select the rows, and then click the Expand Dialog button. The rows you selected appear in the Rows To Repeat At Top box.

Similarly, to have a set of columns appear at the left of every printed page, click the Collapse Dialog button next to the Columns To Repeat At Left box, select the columns, and then click the Expand Dialog button. When you're done, click OK to accept the settings.

In this exercise, you'll select certain pages of a worksheet to print, have Excel fit your printed worksheet on a set number of pages, define a multi-region print area, center the printed material on the page, and repeat columns at the left edge of each printed page.

➡ SET UP **You need the HourlyPickups workbook located in the Chapter11 practice file folder to complete this exercise. Open the workbook, and then follow the steps.**

1   On the **Page Layout** tab, in the **Page Setup** group, click **Print Titles** to open the **Page Setup** dialog box with the **Sheet** page displayed.

2   At the right edge of the **Columns to repeat at left** field, click the **Collapse Dialog** button to collapse the dialog box.

3   Select the column **A** header, and drag to select the column **B** header. The reference **$A:$B** appears in the **Columns To Repeat At Left** field.

4   At the right edge of the **Columns to repeat at left** field, click the **Expand Dialog** button to expand the dialog box.

5   Click **Print Preview** to display your worksheet in the **Backstage** view.

    TIP Even though nothing in the preview indicates that columns A and B will appear on every printed page, scrolling through the preview shows those columns on each page.

		January						
		Hour						
Day		5:00 AM	6:00 AM	7:00 AM	8:00 AM	9:00 AM	10:00 AM	11:00 AM
	1	2117	1989	1344	2408	1921	1505	1687
	2	1128	1109	1354	1115	2277	1432	1559
	3	1228	1350	1662	1758	1892	1710	1709
	4	2295	2496	1964	1793	1138	1592	1811
	5	1866	1631	1631	1136	1959	2273	2348
	6	1234	1536	2348	1208	2109	2382	2487
	7	1608	1825	1851	1037	2259	2091	2211
	8	1903	2014	1451	1283	2243	1266	1746
	9	2275	2360	1392	1511	1942	1639	2018
	10	1039	2191	1729	1028	2278	1044	1936
	11	1569	1069	1487	1135	2434	2181	1721
	12	1773	1782	1224	2401	2426	1514	1526
	13	2108	1511	1916	2488	1459	1703	1706
	14	1512	2319	2239	1063	1164	2115	1469
	15	1003	1283	1874	1512	1238	1993	2390
	16	2007	1864	2088	1228	2023	1186	1585
	17	1016	2400	1039	1024	1107	2178	1445
	18	1794	2291	2166	1966	1650	1899	1931
	19	1904	2424	1799	2332	1089	1132	1045
	20	2035	2174	1123	2277	1400	2468	1287
	21	1288	2321	1171	1884	2292	2437	2465
	22	1577	1235	1742	1089	2203	2143	1073
	23	1987	1349	2170	1728	2426	1013	1227
	24	1868	2459	1380	1390	2270	1336	1886
	25	1058	1541	1753	1740	2360	2308	2167
	26	2016	2412	1128	1477	1184	2104	1513
	27	1640	2180	1904	1048	1531	1541	1838
	28	2363	1340	2113	1350	1814	2358	1613
	29	2398	1324	1572	2264	1335	2002	1495
	30	2223	1178	1633	1148	1640	1872	1581
	31	1726	1794	2020	1777	1016	1403	1845

CONSOLIDATED*Messenger*

◄ 1 of 4 ►

6   Below **Pages** in the **Settings** area, in the **From** field, enter **1**; in the **To** field, enter **2**.

7   Click the **Go Back** button at the top of the left pane and then, on the ribbon, click the **Page Layout** tab; in the **Scale to Fit** group, click the **Width** arrow and then, in the list that appears, click **1 page**.

8   Click the **Height** arrow and then, in the list that appears, click **2 pages**. Excel resizes your worksheet so that it will fit on two printed pages. The new scaling and size values appear in the **Scale to Fit** group on the **Page Layout** tab.

11

9   Select the cell range **A1:E8**, hold down the **Ctrl** key, and then select the cell range **A38:E45**.

10 On the **Page Layout** tab, in the **Page Setup** group, click the **Print Area** button, and then click **Set Print Area**.

11 Click the **Page Setup** dialog box launcher to open the **Page Setup** dialog box.

12 On the **Margins** page of the dialog box, in the **Center on page** area, select the **Horizontally** and **Vertically** check boxes.

13 Click **Print Preview** to display your worksheet in the **Backstage** view.

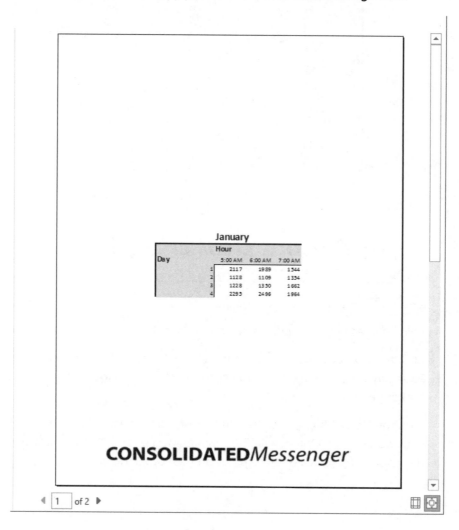

14   Click the **Go Back** button to exit the **Backstage** view and then, on the ribbon, click the **Page Layout** tab to display your worksheet in **Normal** view.

15   In the **Page Setup** group, click **Print Area**, and then click **Clear Print Area** to remove the print areas defined for the **JanFeb** worksheet.

❌ CLEAN UP Close the HourlyPickups workbook, saving your changes if you want to.

Printing charts

With charts, which are graphic representations of your Excel data, you can communicate lots of information by using a single picture. Depending on your data and the type of chart you make, you can show trends across time, indicate the revenue share for various departments in a company for a month, or project future sales by using trendline analysis. After you create a chart, you can print it to include in a report or use in a presentation.

If you embed a chart in a worksheet, however, the chart might obscure some of your data unless you move the chart elsewhere on the worksheet. That's one way to handle printing a chart or the underlying worksheet, but there are other ways that don't involve changing the layout of your worksheets.

To print a chart without printing any other part of the underlying worksheet, click the chart, display the Backstage view, and then click Print. In the Settings area of the Print page, Print Selected Chart will be the only option available. If you click anywhere on the worksheet outside the chart, the Print What area opens with Print Active Sheets selected, meaning that the chart and underlying worksheet are printed as they appear on the screen. When you're ready to print the chart, click the Print button.

TIP Even if the selected chart is smaller than the worksheet on which it resides, it will be scaled to print at the full size of the printer's page.

11

In this exercise, you'll print a chart.

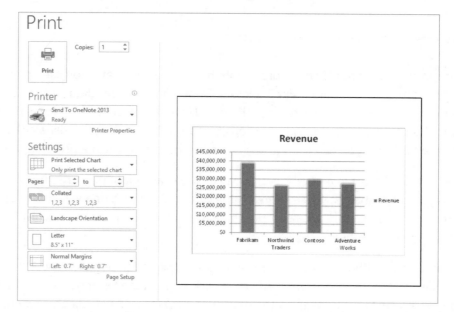

→ SET UP You need the CorporateRevenue workbook located in the Chapter11 practice file folder to complete this exercise. Open the workbook, and then follow the steps.

1   Select the chart.

2   Click the **File** tab to display the **Backstage** view, and then click **Print**.

3   Verify that **Print Selected Chart** is selected, and then click **Print** (or click the **Go Back** button to exit the **Backstage** view if you don't want to print the chart).

✖ CLEAN UP Close the CorporateRevenue workbook.

Key points

- In the Backstage view, you have complete control over how your worksheets appear on the printed page. Don't be afraid to experiment until you find a look you like.

- When you display a worksheet in the Backstage view, you can preview what your worksheet will look like on paper before you print.

- You can preview where the page breaks will fall when you print a worksheet, and you can change them if you want.

- Don't forget that you can have Excel avoid printing error codes!

- You can repeat rows or columns in a printed worksheet.

- If you want to print a chart without printing the rest of the accompanying worksheet, be sure to select the chart before you start the printing procedure.

11

Chapter at a glance

Modify

Create and modify macros,
page 369

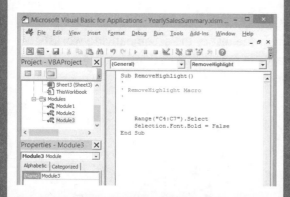

On-click

Run macros when a button is clicked,
page 372

On-open

Run macros when a workbook is opened,
page 376

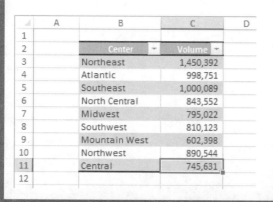

Controls

Insert form controls and set form properties,
page 379

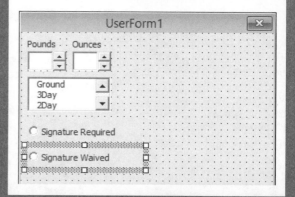

Working with macros and forms

IN THIS CHAPTER, YOU WILL LEARN HOW TO

- Enable and examine macros.

- Create and modify macros.

- Run macros when a button is clicked.

- Run macros when a workbook is opened.

- Insert form controls and set form properties.

Many tasks you perform in Microsoft Excel 2013 are done once (for example, entering sales data for a particular day or adding formulas to a worksheet) or can be repeated quickly by using tools in Excel (for example, changing the format of a cell range). However, you probably have one or two tasks you perform frequently that require a lot of steps to accomplish. For example, you might have several cells in a worksheet that contain important data you use quite often in presentations to your colleagues. Instead of going through a lengthy series of steps to highlight the cells that have the important information, you can create a macro, which is a recorded series of actions, to perform the steps for you. After you have created a macro, you can run, edit, or delete it as needed.

In Excel, you run and edit macros by using the items available in the Macros group on the View tab. You can make your macros easier to access by creating new buttons on the Quick Access Toolbar, to which you can assign your macros. If you run a macro to highlight specific cells in a worksheet every time you show that worksheet to a colleague, you can save time by adding a Quick Access Toolbar button that runs the macro to highlight the cells for you.

Another handy feature of Excel macros is that you can create macros that run when a workbook is opened. For example, you might want to ensure that no cells in a worksheet are highlighted when the worksheet opens. You can create a macro that removes any special formatting from your worksheet cells when its workbook opens, which enables you to emphasize the data you want as you present the information to your colleagues.

You can also use form controls and macros to create custom solutions for your business. By adding controls such as text boxes, spin controls, and list boxes, you can design a user-friendly interface for you and your colleagues to enter data quickly while minimizing errors.

In this chapter, you'll open, run, create, and modify macros; create Quick Access Toolbar buttons and shapes that you can use to run macros with a single mouse click; run a macro when a workbook is opened; and add controls and set form properties for a UserForm.

PRACTICE FILES To complete the exercises in this chapter, you need the practice files contained in the Chapter12 practice file folder. For more information, see "Download the practice files" in this book's Introduction.

Enabling and examining macros

It's possible for unscrupulous programmers to write viruses and other harmful programs by using the Microsoft Visual Basic for Applications (VBA) programming language, so you need to be sure that you don't run macros from unknown sources. In addition to running protective software such as Windows Defender, you can also change your Excel macro security settings to control when macros can be run. After you're sure a macro is safe, you can open it in the Visual Basic Editor to examine its code.

Changing macro security settings

In versions of Excel prior to Excel 2007, you could define macro security levels to determine which macros, if any, your workbooks would be allowed to run, but there was no workbook type in which all macros were disallowed. Excel 2013 has several file types that you can use to control whether a workbook will allow macros to be run. The following table summarizes the macro-related file types.

Extension	Description
.xlsx	Regular Excel workbook; macros are *disabled*
.xlsm	Regular Excel workbook; macros are *enabled*
.xltx	Excel template workbook; macros are *disabled*
.xltm	Excel template workbook; macros are *enabled*

When you open a macro-enabled workbook, the Excel program-level security settings might prevent the workbook from running the macro code. When that happens, Excel displays a security warning on the Message Bar.

To allow a workbook's macros to run, click the Enable Content button on the Message Bar. Always take the time to verify the workbook's source and consider whether you expected the workbook to contain macros before you enable the content. If you decide not to enable the macros in a workbook, click the Close button at the right edge of the Message Bar.

You can change your program-level security settings to make them more or less restrictive; to do so, click the File tab to display the Backstage view, click Options in the left pane, and then, in the Excel Options dialog box that opens, click the Trust Center category. On the page that appears, click the Trust Center Settings button to display the Trust Center dialog box.

12

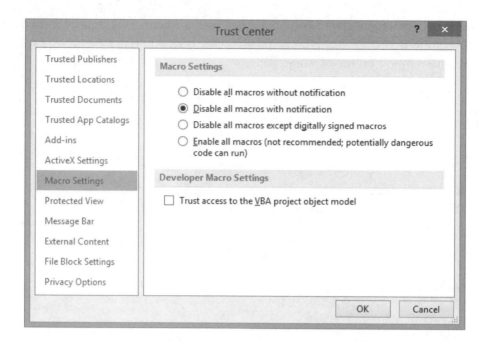

The Excel default macro security level is Disable All Macros With Notification, which means that Excel displays a warning on the Message Bar but allows you to enable the macros manually. Selecting the Disable All Macros Without Notification option does exactly what the label says. If Consolidated Messenger's company policy is to disallow all macros in all Excel workbooks, its employees would select the Disable All Macros Without Notification option.

> **IMPORTANT** Because it is possible to write macros that act as viruses, potentially causing harm to your computer and spreading copies of themselves to other computers, you should never choose the Enable All Macros security setting, even if you have virus-checking software installed on your computer.

Examining macros

The best way to get an idea of how macros work is to examine an existing macro. To do that, display the View tab. In the Macros group, click the Macros button, and then click View Macros.

TIP In the Macro dialog box, you can display the macros available in other workbooks by clicking the Macros In box and selecting a workbook by name or selecting All Open Workbooks to display every macro in any open workbook. If you select either of those choices, the macro names that are displayed include the name of the workbook in which the macro is stored. Clicking This Workbook displays the macros in the active workbook.

The Macro dialog box displays a list of macros in your workbook. To view the code behind a macro, you click the macro's name and then click Edit to open the Visual Basic Editor.

```
Sub HighlightSouthern()
'
' HighlightSouthern Macro
'


    Range("B4:C4").Select
    With Selection.Font
        .Color = -16776961
        .TintAndShade = 0
    End With
    Range("B5:C5").Select
    With Selection.Font
        .Color = -16776961
        .TintAndShade = 0
    End With
    Range("B8:C8").Select
    With Selection.Font
        .Color = -16776961
        .TintAndShade = 0
    End With
End Sub
```

KEYBOARD SHORTCUT Press Alt+F11 to open and close the Visual Basic Editor. For a complete list of keyboard shortcuts, see "Keyboard shortcuts" at the end of this book.

Excel macros are recorded by using VBA. Consider, for example, the code for a macro that selects the cell range B4:C4 and changes the cells' formatting to bold. The first line of the macro identifies the cell range to be selected (in this case, cells C4:C9). After the macro selects the cells, the next line of the macro changes the formatting of the selected cells to bold, which has the same result as when you click a cell and then click the Bold button in the Font group on the Home tab.

To test how the macro works, you can open the Macro dialog box, click the name of the macro you want to examine, and then click Step Into. The Visual Basic Editor opens, with a highlight around the instruction that will be executed next.

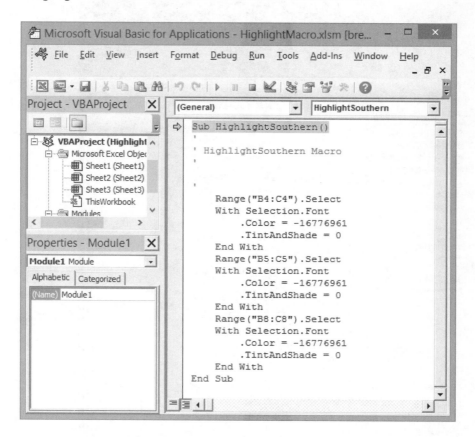

To execute an instruction, press F8. The highlight moves to the next instruction, and your worksheet then changes to reflect the action that resulted from the execution of the preceding instruction.

You can run a macro without stopping after each instruction by opening the Macro dialog box, clicking the macro to run, and then clicking Run. You'll usually run the macro this way; after all, the point of using macros is to save time.

In this exercise, you'll examine a macro in the Visual Basic Editor, move through the first part of the macro one step at a time, and then run the entire macro without stopping.

→ SET UP **You need the VolumeHighlights workbook located in the Chapter12 practice file folder to complete this exercise. Open the workbook, click the Enable Content button on the Message Bar (if necessary), and then follow the steps.**

1   On the **View** tab, in the **Macros** group, click the **Macros** arrow and then, in the list that appears, click **View Macros** to open the **Macro** dialog box.

2   If necessary, click the **HighlightSouthern** macro, and then, to display the macro code, click **Edit**. The Visual Basic Editor opens, with the code for the **HighlightSouthern** macro displayed in the **Module1 (Code)** window.

3   In the Visual Basic Editor window, click the **Close** button to close the window and redisplay the workbook.

4   In the **Macros** list, click **View Macros** to open the **Macro** dialog box.

5   Click the **HighlightSouthern** macro, and then click **Step Into**. The macro appears in the Visual Basic Editor, with the first macro instruction highlighted.

6   Press the **F8** key to highlight the next instruction.

7   Press **F8** again to execute the step that selects the **Atlantic** row in the table.

8   Press **F8** twice to execute the steps that change the **Atlantic** row's text color to red.

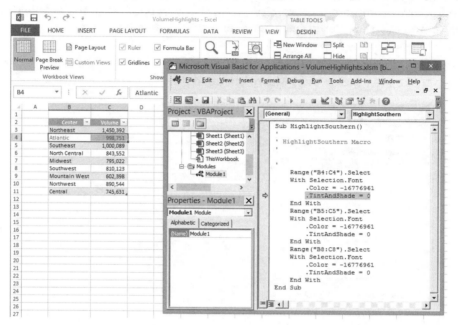

9   Click the **Close** button in the Visual Basic Editor.

10 When a warning dialog box opens, indicating that closing the Visual Basic Editor will stop the debugger, click **OK**.

11 In the **Macros** list, click **View Macros** to open the **Macro** dialog box.

12 Click the **HighlightSouthern** macro.

13 Click **Run** to close the **Macro** dialog box and run the entire macro.

◢	A	B	C	D
1				
2		Center ⌄	Volume ⌄	
3		Northeast	1,450,392	
4		Atlantic	998,751	
5		Southeast	1,000,089	
6		North Central	843,552	
7		Midwest	795,022	
8		Southwest	810,123	
9		Mountain West	602,398	
10		Northwest	890,544	
11		Central	745,631	
12				

❌ CLEAN UP Close the VolumeHighlights workbook, saving your changes if you want to.

Creating and modifying macros

The first step of creating a macro is to plan the process you want to automate. Computers today are quite fast, so adding an extra step that doesn't affect the outcome of a process doesn't slow you down noticeably, but leaving out a step means you will need to re-record your macro. After you plan your process, you can create a macro by clicking the View tab and then, in the Macros group, clicking the Macros arrow. In the list that appears, click Record Macro. When you do, the Record Macro dialog box opens.

After you enter the name of your macro in the Macro Name box, click OK. You can now perform the actions that you want Excel to repeat later; when you're done recording your macro, in the Macros list, click Stop Recording to add your macro to the list of macros available in your workbook.

TIP The Record and Stop Recording icons also appear on the status bar.

To modify an existing macro, you can simply delete the macro and re-record it. Or if you just need to make a quick change, you can open it in the Visual Basic Editor and add to or change the macro's instructions. To delete a macro, open the Macro dialog box, click the macro you want to delete, and then click Delete.

SEE ALSO For more information about using the Visual Basic Editor, press Alt+F11 to display the Visual Basic Editor, and then press F1 to display the Visual Basic Help dialog box.

In this exercise, you'll record, edit, save, and run a macro that removes the bold formatting from selected cells.

SET UP You need the YearlySalesSummary workbook located in the Chapter12 practice file folder to complete this exercise. Open the workbook, click the Enable Content button on the Message Bar (if necessary), and then follow the steps.

1. On the **View** tab, in the **Macros** group, click the **Macros** arrow and then, in the list that appears, click **Record Macro** to open the **Record Macro** dialog box.

2. In the **Macro name** box, replace the existing name with **RemoveHighlight**.

3. Click **OK** to close the **Record Macro** dialog box.

4. Select the cell range **C4:C7**. (The text in these cells is currently bold.)

5. On the **Home** tab, in the **Font** group, click the **Bold** button to remove the bold formatting.

6. On the **View** tab, in the **Macros** list, click **Stop Recording** to stop recording the macro.

7. In the **Macros** list, click **View Macros** to open the **Macro** dialog box.

8. In the **Macro name** area, click **RemoveHighlight**, and then click **Edit** to display the macro in the Visual Basic Editor.

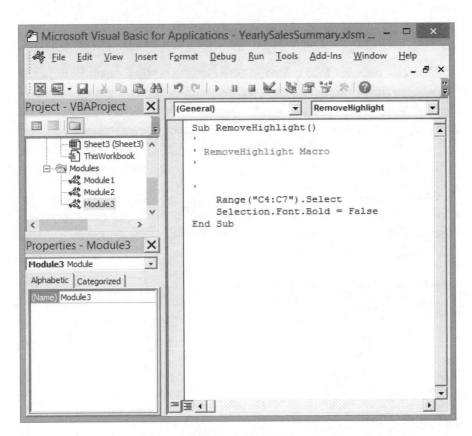

9   Edit the line of code that currently reads **Range("C4:C7").Select** so that it reads
    Range("C3:C9").Select. This macro statement selects the cell range **C3:C9**, not the
    incorrect range **C4:C7**.

10 On the **Standard** toolbar of the Visual Basic Editor, click the **Save** button to save your
    change.

11 On the title bar of the Visual Basic Editor window, click the **Close** button.

12 Select cells **C3:C9** and format them as bold.

13 In the **Macros** list, click **View Macros** to open the **Macro** dialog box.

14 Click **RemoveHighlight**, and then click **Run**. The macro removes the bold formatting
    from cells **C3:C9**.

✖ CLEAN UP Close the YearlySalesSummary workbook, saving your changes if you
want to.

Running macros when a button is clicked

You can quickly discover the commands built into Excel by looking though the commands on the ribbon. However, it can take a few seconds to display the View tab, open the Macro dialog box, select the macro you want to run, and click the Run button. When you're in the middle of a presentation, taking even those few seconds can reduce your momentum and force you to regain your audience's attention. Excel offers several ways for you to make your macros more accessible.

If you want to display the Macro dialog box quickly, you can add the View Macros button to the Quick Access Toolbar. To do so, click the Customize Quick Access Toolbar button at the right edge of the Quick Access Toolbar, and then click More Commands to display the Quick Access Toolbar page of the Excel Options dialog box.

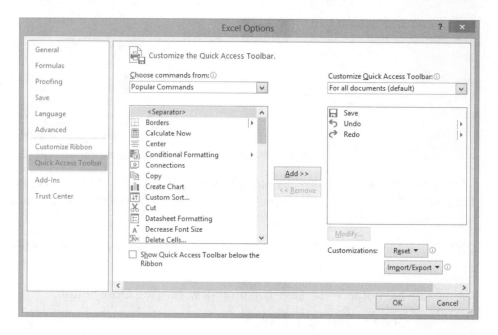

SEE ALSO For more information about customizing the Quick Access Toolbar, see "Customizing the Excel 2013 program window" in Chapter 1, "Setting up a workbook."

In the Popular Commands command group, the last item in the command pane is View Macros. When you click the View Macros command, click the Add button, and then click OK, Excel adds the command to the Quick Access Toolbar and closes the Excel Options dialog box. Clicking the View Macros button on the Quick Access Toolbar opens the Macro dialog box, which saves a significant amount of time compared to when you display the View tab and move the pointer to the far right edge of the ribbon.

If you prefer to run a macro without having to display the Macro dialog box, you can do so by adding a button representing the macro to the Quick Access Toolbar. Clicking that button runs the macro immediately, which is very handy when you create a macro for a task you perform frequently. To add a button that represents a macro to the Quick Access Toolbar, click the Customize Quick Access Toolbar button at the right edge of the Quick Access Toolbar, and then click More Commands to display the Quick Access Toolbar page of the Excel Options dialog box. From there, in the Choose Commands From list, click Macros. Click the macro that you want represented on the Quick Access Toolbar, click Add, and then click OK.

If you add more than one macro button to the Quick Access Toolbar or if you want to change the button that represents your macro on the Quick Access Toolbar, you can select a new button from more than 160 options. To assign a new button to your macro, click the macro command in the Customize Quick Access Toolbar pane and click the Modify button to display your choices. Click the symbol you want, enter a new text value to appear when a user points to the button, and then click OK twice (the first time to close the Modify Button dialog box and the second to close the Excel Options dialog box).

Finally, you can have Excel run a macro when you click a shape in your workbook. By assigning macros to shapes, you can create "buttons" that are graphically richer than those available on the Quick Access Toolbar. If you're so inclined, you can even create custom button layouts that represent other objects, such as a remote control. To run a macro when you

12

click a shape, right-click the shape, and then click Assign Macro on the shortcut menu that opens. In the Assign Macro dialog box, click the macro that you want to run when you click the shape, and then click OK.

> **IMPORTANT** When you assign a macro to run when you click a shape, don't change the name of the macro that appears in the Assign Macro dialog box. The name that appears refers to the object and what the object should do when it is clicked; changing the macro name breaks that connection and prevents Excel from running the macro.

In this exercise, you'll add the View Macros button to the Quick Access Toolbar, add a macro button to the Quick Access Toolbar, assign a macro to a workbook shape, and then run the macros.

➡ SET UP You need the PerformanceDashboard workbook located in the Chapter12 practice file folder to complete this exercise. Open the workbook, click the Enable Content button on the Message Bar (if necessary), and then follow the steps.

1   On the **Quick Access Toolbar**, click the **Customize Quick Access Toolbar** button, and then click **More Commands**. The **Quick Access Toolbar** page of the **Excel Options** dialog box opens, displaying the **Popular Commands** category in the **Choose Commands From** pane.

2   In the list of available commands, click **View Macros**.

3   Click **Add** to add the **View Macros** command to the **Customize Quick Access Toolbar** pane.

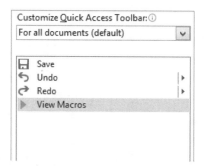

4   In the **Choose commands from** list, click **Macros** to display the available macros in the pane below the list.

5   In the **Choose commands from** pane, click **SavingsHighlight**.

If macros in the workbook are not enabled, the SavingsHighlight macro will not appear in the list.

6   Click **Add** to add the **SavingsHighlight** macro to the **Customize Quick Access Toolbar** pane.

7   In the **Customize Quick Access Toolbar** pane, click the **SavingsHighlight** command.

8   Click **Modify** to open the **Modify Button** dialog box.

9   Click the gray button with the white circle inside it (the fourth button from the left on the top row).

10 Click **OK** twice to close the **Modify Button** dialog box and the **Excel Options** dialog box. The **View Macros** and **SavingsHighlight** buttons appear on the **Quick Access Toolbar**.

11 On the worksheet, right-click the **Show Efficiency** shape, and then click **Assign Macro** to open the **Assign Macro** dialog box.

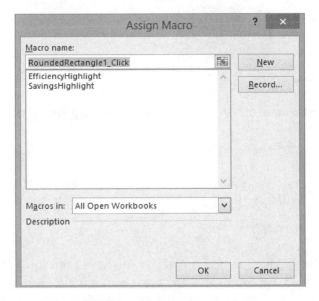

12 Click **EfficiencyHighlight**, and then click **OK** to assign the macro to the button and close the **Assign Macro** dialog box.

13 On the **Quick Access Toolbar**, click the **SavingsHighlight** button. Excel runs the macro, which applies a conditional format to the values in the **Savings** column of the table on the left.

14 Click the **Show Efficiency** shape. Excel runs the macro, which applies a conditional format to the values in the **Efficiency** column of the table on the right.

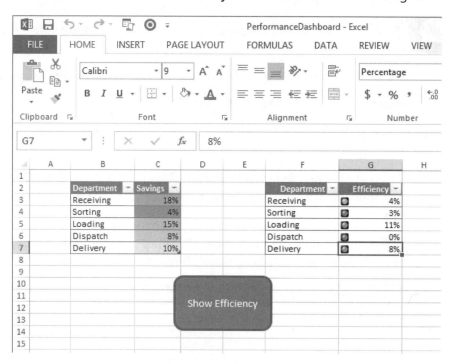

⊗ CLEAN UP Close the PerformanceDashboard workbook, saving your changes if you want to.

Running macros when a workbook is opened

One advantage of writing Excel macros in VBA is that you can have Excel run a macro whenever a workbook is opened. For example, if you use a worksheet for presentations, you can create macros that render the contents of selected cells in bold type, italic, or different typefaces to set the data apart from data in neighboring cells. If you close a workbook without removing that formatting, however, the contents of your workbook will still have that formatting applied when you open it. Although this is not a catastrophe, returning the workbook to its original formatting might take a few seconds to accomplish.

Instead of running a macro manually, or even from a toolbar button or a menu, you can have Excel run a macro whenever a workbook is opened. The trick of making that happen is in the name you give the macro. Whenever Excel finds a macro with the name Auto_Open, it runs the macro when the workbook to which it is attached is opened.

TIP If you have your macro security set to the Disable With Notification level, clicking the Options button that appears on the Message Bar, selecting the Enable This Content option, and then clicking OK allows the Auto_Open macro to run.

In this exercise, you'll create and test a macro that runs whenever someone opens the workbook to which it is attached.

 SET UP **You need the RunOnOpen workbook located in the Chapter12 practice file folder to complete this exercise. Open the workbook, click the Enable Content button on the Message Bar (if necessary), and then follow the steps.**

1   On the **View** tab, in the **Macros** group, click the **Macros** arrow and then, in the list that appears, click **Record Macro** to open the **Record Macro** dialog box.

2   In the **Macro name** box, delete the existing name, and then enter Auto_Open.

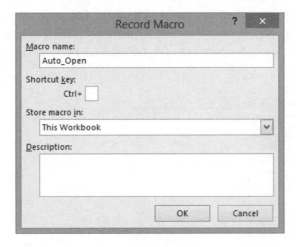

3   Click **OK** to close the **Record Macro** dialog box.

4   Select the cell range **B3:C11**.

5   On the **Home** tab, in the **Font** group, click the **Bold** button twice. The first click of the **Bold** button formats all the selected cells in bold; the second click removes the bold formatting from all the selected cells.

6   Click cell **C11** and then, in the **Macros** list, click **Stop Recording** to stop recording your macro.

7   In the **Macros** list, click **View Macros** to open the **Macro** dialog box.

8   Click **Highlight**, and then click **Run**. The macro formats the contents of cells **C4**, **C6**, and **C10** in bold type.

	A	B	C	D
1				
2		Center	Volume	
3		Northeast	1,450,392	
4		Atlantic	**998,751**	
5		Southeast	1,000,089	
6		North Central	**843,552**	
7		Midwest	795,022	
8		Southwest	810,123	
9		Mountain West	602,398	
10		Northwest	**890,544**	
11		Central	745,631	
12				

9   On the **Quick Access Toolbar**, click the **Save** button.

10 Click the **Close** button to close the **RunOnOpen** workbook.

11 Display the **Backstage** view, click **Recent Workbooks**, and then click **RunOnOpen. xlsm**. If a warning appears, click **Enable Content**, and then click **OK** to enable macros. **RunOnOpen** opens, and the contents of cells **C4**, **C6**, and **C10** change immediately to regular type.

	A	B	C	D
1				
2		Center	Volume	
3		Northeast	1,450,392	
4		Atlantic	998,751	
5		Southeast	1,000,089	
6		North Central	843,552	
7		Midwest	795,022	
8		Southwest	810,123	
9		Mountain West	602,398	
10		Northwest	890,544	
11		Central	745,631	
12				

❌ CLEAN UP Close the RunOnOpen workbook, saving your changes if you want to.

Inserting form controls and setting form properties

UserForms are Excel objects that you create to provide a user-friendly interface for data entry. You can allow open-ended text entry by adding a text box, define specific items in a list box, or combine the two approaches in a combo box.

To create a UserForm, press Alt+F11 to open the Visual Basic Editor, and then on the Insert menu, click UserForm. You can then change the form's name by clicking in the Properties pane and entering a new value in the Name field.

You can change the size of a UserForm by dragging any of the handles on its sides or corners. By dragging a handle in the middle of a side, you can change the UserForm's height or width; dragging a handle at a UserForm's corner changes both height and width.

TIP The Name property is the internal representation of the UserForm (that is, how you will refer to it in your code), so you should consider putting the letters *frm* at the start of the name to indicate that it represents a form.

The Caption property contains the word or words that appear on a UserForm's title bar. To change the UserForm's caption, click the UserForm and then, in the Properties panel, click the box next to the Caption property and edit its value.

Adding text boxes to UserForms

You can create a text box in a UserForm so that users can enter textual information. If the Toolbox isn't displayed in the Visual Basic Editor, on the Insert menu, click Toolbox. Then click the TextBox button in the Toolbox and drag in the body of the UserForm to define the text box. When you do, the text box's properties appear in the Properties panel.

As with the UserForm object, you can change the name of a text box. To do that, click the text box control and then, in the Properties pane, enter a new value in the *Name* property's box.

12

You can also add a label to identify the control and indicate the data to be entered. To add a label, display the Toolbox, click the Label button, and drag to define the label in the body of the form. Position the label so that it's in line with the text box and then change the label's *Caption* property so that it contains the text required to identify its related control.

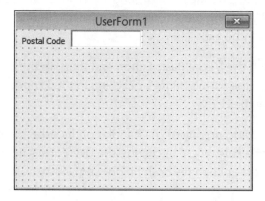

TROUBLESHOOTING A control's name may not be a reserved word, such as *Number* or *Date*.

Adding list boxes to UserForms

In a text box, users can enter any text they want into the control. If you prefer to have users select from a list of values, you can create a list box. List boxes increase data entry accuracy at the expense of user flexibility.

To create a list box, display a UserForm in the Visual Basic Editor and then, in the Toolbox, click the ListBox button, and drag on the UserForm to create the list box. When you do, the list box appears on the UserForm and its properties appear in the Properties panel on the left side of the Visual Basic Editor window.

A list box control draws its values from a range of worksheet cells. To assign a cell range to a list box, you enter the range's definition into the list box's *RowSource* property. In Excel 2013, the easiest way to define the row source for a list box is to create a one-column Excel table.

SEE ALSO For more information about creating an Excel table, see Chapter 2, "Working with data and Excel tables."

With your data source defined, enter an equal sign (=) followed by the name of the table in the *RowSource* property for your list box. When you run the UserForm, you can use the list box's arrows to scroll through the list of available values. When you find the value you want, click it to highlight it.

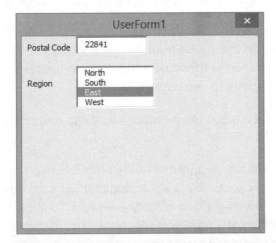

IMPORTANT When you enter data in a UserForm's list box, you must click the item in the list box so that it is highlighted. The item displayed isn't necessarily the selected item.

Adding combo boxes to UserForms

In a list box, users can select a value from a predetermined list of values; in a text box, they can enter any text value they want. A combo box provides either mode of entry, which is more flexible than a list box but introduces the possibility that misspellings might lead to inconsistent data entry.

To add a combo box to a UserForm, display the UserForm in the Visual Basic Editor and then, in the Toolbox, click the Combobox button. Draw the outline of the combo box on the body of the UserForm to create it.

As with the list box, you can provide its values by assigning an Excel table to the *RowSource* property, using a statement such as *=ServiceLevels*.

Adding option buttons to UserForms

With option buttons, users can indicate whether an option, such as whether a delivery requires signature confirmation, is turned on or turned off. You can also create groups of option buttons that lets users select at most one option from the group at a time.

To add an option button to a UserForm, display the UserForm and then, in the Toolbox, click the Option Button control. Draw the option button on the UserForm. Its properties will be displayed in the Properties panel. The most common properties you'll change are the button's *Name* and *Caption* properties.

The *Name* property controls how you refer to the option button in your VBA code. To change the control's label text, you need to change the value of the *Caption* property. For example, you could change the caption property to read *Signature*.

TIP If you want an option button to be selected by default, change its Value property from False to True.

You can also create groups of option buttons where only one of the buttons can be selected at a time. For example, you might want a user to select a shipping method from among the options of ground, two day, three day, overnight, and priority overnight. To allow only one option button of those five to be selected at a time, you assign the same *GroupName* property value to each button. You could create the Methods group to allow one selection from the alternatives.

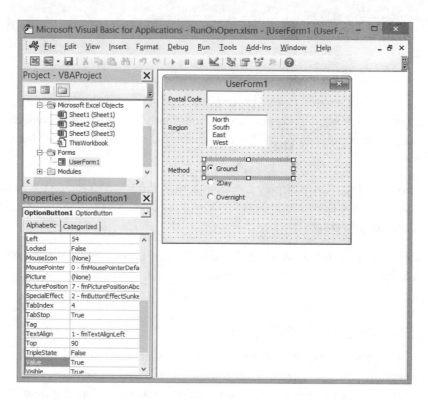

Adding graphics to UserForms

One way to add some visual interest or useful information to a VBA UserForm is by adding graphics. To add an image to a UserForm, display the UserForm in the Visual Basic Editor and then, in the Toolbox, click the Image button. Drag on the UserForm to define the frame within which the image should appear.

To select the graphic you want to display on the UserForm, click the image control on the UserForm and then, in the Properties panel, click in the box next to the Picture property name. Click the Browse button that appears, navigate to the folder that contains the image you want to add to the UserForm, click the image, and then click Open to display it.

Unless the image you selected fits exactly in the frame, just a portion of it is displayed on the UserForm. You can control the way the image fits within the frame by assigning the value you want to the *PictureSizeMode* property. That property has three possible values:

- **0 – fmPictureSizeModeClip** Displays as much of the image as possible within the frame

- **1 – fmPictureSizeModeStretch** Displays the entire image within the frame but stretches the image so that it fills the entire frame

- **3 – fmPictureSizeModeZoom** Displays the entire image within the frame but keeps the vertical and horizontal dimensions in their original ratio

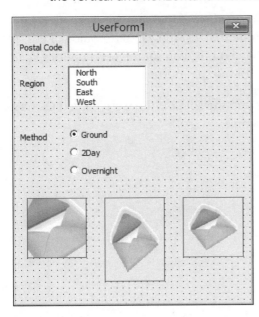

12

Adding spin buttons to UserForms

With Excel VBA UserForms, you and your colleagues can enter data quickly. Text boxes are flexible, but you can take more control over the numbers a user enters by linking a spin button to a text box. Clicking the spin button's up or down arrow changes the value in the attached control by an amount that you define.

To create a spin button, click the UserForm and then, in the Toolbox, click the SpinButton control and draw the spin button on the UserForm. Next, click the spin button and then, in the Properties panel, change the values of these properties:

- **Max** The largest value allowed in the spin button
- **Min** The smallest value allowed in the spin button
- **SmallChange** The amount that each click changes the spin button's value

Suppose you create a spin button with a *Min* value of *1*, *Max* value of *10*, and *SmallChange* value of *1*. Each click of the up button would increase the value by 1 (to a maximum of 10) and each click of the down button would decrease the value by 1 (to a minimum of 1).

After you create the spin button, create a text box to display the value assigned to the spin control. Write down the name of the text box, which you can discover by clicking the text box and observing the value of the *Name* property in the Properties panel.

Right-click the spin button and, from the shortcut menu that appears, click View Code. Doing so displays the outline of the event code that will run when the value of the spin button changes. To link the spin button with the text box, you set the text control's *Value* property so that it is equal to the same property of the spin button.

If the text box were named *PackageOunces* and the spin button were named *OuncesSpin*, your code would look like the following example.

```
Private Sub OuncesSpin_Change()
PackageOunces.Value = OuncesSpin.Value
End Sub
```

Writing UserForm data to a worksheet

After you've created your UserForm, you need to write VBA code to record the controls' values to a worksheet. You do that by adding a command button to your form and assigning code to the button's *On_Click* event that reads the controls' values and writes them to a worksheet.

The process to read and write these values identifies the first empty row in the target worksheet and then uses the *Value* property of the *Cells* object to write the data into the target cells. As an example, suppose you have a UserForm that collects four pieces of data for a shipment: the customer's name, origination postal code, destination postal code, and shipping method.

Next, create a command button to which you can attach code that writes the values to the worksheet. To create the command button, display a UserForm and then, in the Toolbox, click the CommandButton button. Draw the button on the UserForm and, if you want, change the button's Caption property so that the button's text describes its function.

Right-click the button and, from the shortcut menu that appears, click View Code to display the button's *On_Click* event handling code. You could use the following routine to find the first empty cell in column A of your worksheet, read the values in the four controls, and write values into the worksheet.

```
Private Sub CommandButton1_Click()
Dim lngFirstRow As Long

Worksheets("Sheet1").Activate
lngFirstRow = Worksheets("Sheet1").Range("A1048576").End(xlUp).Row + 1

Cells(lngFirstRow, 1) = txtCompName.Value
Cells(lngFirstRow, 2) = txtOrigPostCode.Value
Cells(lngFirstRow, 3) = txtDestPostCode.Value
Cells(lngFirstRow, 4) = lstMethod.Value
Cells(lngFirstRow, 4).Activate
End Sub
```

12

If two records were already in the target worksheet and you entered data from the UserForm, the result would be the following list.

	A	B	C	D
1	Company	Originating Postal Code	Destination Postal Code	Method
2	Contoso	22841	97220	Ground
3	Tailspin Toys	11210	54382	3Day
4	Northwind Traders	98013	33010	Overnight
5				

TIP On the Developer tab of the ribbon, you will also find buttons that you can use to add worksheet Form controls and ActiveX controls. You can use the skills learned in this section to create those controls and assign VBA code to them.

Displaying, loading, and hiding UserForms

After you create a UserForm, you must display it so that the user can interact with it. As an example, suppose you have a form named *frmShipmentEntry*. All you need to do to display the form is enter the name of the form followed by a period and the Show method. For example, the code to display *frmShipmentEntry* would be as follows.

```
frmShipmentEntry.Show
```

You can test a UserForm from within the Visual Basic Editor by displaying the UserForm and pressing the F5 key. You can also enter a UserForm into Excel's memory without displaying it by using the *Load* method. The command to load the same form into the Excel program's memory is as follows.

```
frmCustomerEntry.Load
```

When you want to display the UserForm in Excel, you can call the *Show* method as noted earlier.

Hiding a UserForm relies on the *Hide* method. The syntax follows the pattern used for the *Show* and *Load* methods.

```
frmCustomerEntry.Hide
```

The most common way to invoke the *Hide* method is to create a command button with the label Cancel and add the code including the *Hide* method in the command button's *On_ Click* event handler. You can also hide a UserForm by clicking the Close box in the upper-right corner of the UserForm.

In this exercise, you'll create a UserForm, add a text box, add a list box, and then add a series of option buttons within a single group. You'll also add spin button controls to two text boxes, and use existing code to display the form and write its data to a worksheet.

SET UP You need the PackageWeight workbook located in the Chapter12 practice file folder to complete this exercise. Open the workbook, click the Enable Content button on the Message Bar (if necessary), and then follow the steps.

1 Press **Alt+F11** to open the Visual Basic Editor.

2 On the menu bar, click **Insert**, and then click **UserForm** to create a blank UserForm.

3 In the **Toolbox**, click the **Label** button and draw a label in the upper-left corner of the UserForm. Then, with the label still selected, in the **Caption** property box of the **Properties** panel, enter Pounds.

4 Click on the body of the UserForm and then, in the **Toolbox**, click the **Label** button and draw a label to the right of the **Pounds** label. Then, with the label still selected, in the **Caption** property box of the **Properties** panel, enter Ounces. Resize the label control so that the **Ounces** text fits within it.

5 Click on the body of the UserForm and then, in the **Toolbox**, click the **TextBox** button. Draw a text box below the **Pounds** label on the UserForm. Click the **TextBox** button again and, leaving some space for another control, draw a second text box below the **Ounces** label.

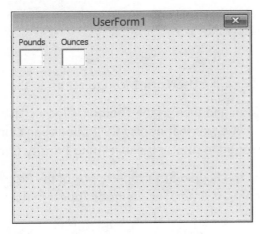

6 In the **Toolbox**, click the **SpinButton** button and then draw a spin button to the right of the text box beside the **Pounds** label.

7   With the new spin button still selected, in the **Properties** panel, enter **49** in the **Max** field. The spin button will now accept values from 0 to 49.

8   In the **Toolbox**, click the **SpinButton** button, and then draw a new spin button to the right of the text box beside the **Ounces** label.

9   With the new spin button still selected, in the **Properties** panel, enter **15** in the **Max** field. The spin button will now accept values from 0 to 15.

10   Click the spin button to the right of the text box below the **Pounds** label and make a note of its name (which is probably SpinButton1).

11   Right-click the spin button below the **Pounds** label and then click **View Code**. In the code window that appears, edit the code so it reads as follows.

```
Private Sub SpinButton1_Change()
TextBox1.Value = SpinButton1.Value
End Sub
```

TROUBLESHOOTING The preceding code assumes the text box is named TextBox1 and the spin button is named SpinButton1. If they aren't, edit the code to reflect the controls' actual names.

12   Right-click the spin button below the **Ounces** label, and then click **View Code**. In the code window that appears, edit the code so it reads as follows.

```
Private Sub SpinButton2_Change()
TextBox2.Value = SpinButton2.Value
End Sub
```

13   In the **Project** window, double-click the **UserForm1** icon to return to the UserForm.

14   Click on the body of the UserForm and then, in the **Toolbox**, click the **ListBox** button. Draw a list box below the text boxes that display the **Pounds** and **Ounces** values. Your list box should be wide enough to display the text string **Priority Overnight**.

15   With the list box still selected, in the **RowSource** property box of the **Properties** panel, enter **=ShipMethods** and then press **Enter**. The methods appear in the list box.

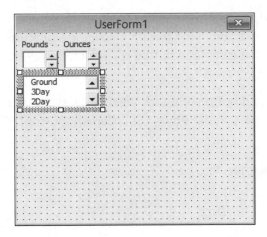

16   Click on the body of the UserForm and then, in the **Toolbox**, click the **OptionButton** button. Click in the body of the UserForm below the list box you just created. When you do, an option button appears.

17   With the option button still selected, in the **Caption** box of the **Properties** panel, enter Signature Required and press **Enter**. Then, in the **GroupName** box, enter Sig and press **Enter**.

18   Repeat step 16 to create an option button below the first option button you created. With the new option button still selected, in the **Caption** box, enter Signature Waived and press **Enter**. Then, in the **GroupName** box, enter Sig and press **Enter**.

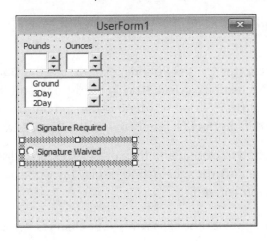

12

19   Click on the body of the UserForm and then, in the **Toolbox**, click the
     CommandButton button. Draw a command button below the **Signature Waived**
     option button and then, with the command button still selected, in the **Caption** box,
     enter Submit and press **Enter**.

20   Right-click the **Submit** command button and click **View Code** to display the button's
     On_Click event handling routine. Edit the **Private Sub CommandButton1_Click()** sub-
     routine so it reads as follows.

```
Private Sub CommandButton1_Click()
Dim lngFirstRow As Long

Worksheets("Records").Activate
lngFirstRow = Worksheets("Records").Range("A1048576").End(xlUp).Row + 1

Cells(lngFirstRow, 1) = TextBox1.Value
Cells(lngFirstRow, 2) = TextBox2.Value
Cells(lngFirstRow, 3) = ListBox1.Value
Cells(lngFirstRow, 4) = OptionButton1.Value
Cells(lngFirstRow, 5) = OptionButton2.Value
Cells(lngFirstRow, 5).Activate

End Sub
```

21   In the **Project** pane, click **UserForm1** to display it and then press **F5** to run the
     UserForm.

22   Use the **Pounds** spin button to enter **4** in the **Pounds** text box; use the **Ounces** spin
     button to enter **8** in the **Ounces** text box; select **3Day** in the list box; and then select
     the **Signature Waived** option button. Click the **Submit** command button. When you
     do, the UserForm writes your data to the first empty row in the **Records** worksheet.

23   Click the UserForm's **Close** button to close it and then press **Alt+F11** to display the
     workbook. If necessary, click the **Records** sheet tab to display the worksheet of the
     same name to view the data you entered.

❌ CLEAN UP Close the PackageWeight workbook, saving your changes if you want to.

Key points

- Macros are handy tools that you can use to perform repetitive tasks quickly, such as inserting blocks of text.

- You don't have to be a programmer to use macros; you can record your actions and have Excel save them as a macro.

- Excel uses macro-enabled workbook types, which have the file extensions .xlsm (a macro-enabled workbook) and .xltm (a macro-enabled template workbook).

- If you're curious about what a macro looks like, you can display it in the Visual Basic Editor. If you know a little VBA, or if you just want to experiment, feel free to modify the macro code to find out what happens.

- You can create Quick Access Toolbar buttons and shapes that, when clicked, run a macro.

- If you want a macro to run whenever you open a workbook, create a macro named Auto_Open.

- UserForms provide a customizable interface for data entry.

12

Chapter at a glance

Link

Link to Office documents from workbooks,
page 394

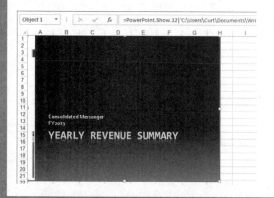

Embed

Embed workbooks into other Office
documents, page 398

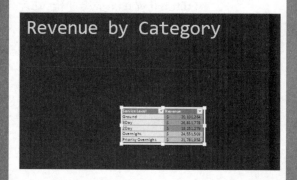

Create

Create hyperlinks,
page 401

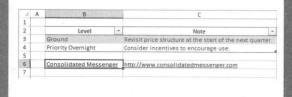

Paste

Paste charts into other Office documents,
page 407

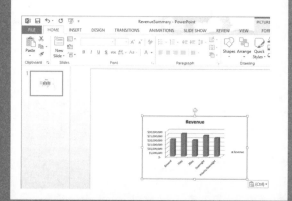

Working with other Office programs

13

IN THIS CHAPTER, YOU WILL LEARN HOW TO

- Link to Office documents from workbooks.

- Embed workbooks into other Office documents.

- Create hyperlinks.

- Paste charts into other Office documents.

By itself, Microsoft Excel 2013 provides a broad range of tools that you can use to store, present, and summarize your financial data. When you use other Microsoft Office 2013 programs, you can extend your capabilities even further, by creating databases, presentations, written reports, and custom webpages through which you can organize and communicate your data in print and over networks.

All the Office programs interact with each other in many useful ways. For example, you can include a file created with another Office program in an Excel workbook. If you use Microsoft Word 2013 to write a quick note about why a customer's shipping expenditures decreased significantly in January, you can include the report in your workbook. Similarly, you can include your Excel workbooks in documents created with other Office programs. If you want to copy only part of a workbook, such as a chart, into another Office document, you can do that as well.

Excel integrates well with the web. If you know of a web-based resource that would be useful to someone who is viewing a document, you can create a hyperlink to connect from a document to a place in the same file or to another file anywhere on a network or the Internet that the user's computer can reach.

In this chapter, you'll link to an Office document from a worksheet, embed an Excel workbook into another Office document, create hyperlinks, and paste an Excel chart into another document.

Linking to Office documents from workbooks

One benefit of working with Excel 2013 is that, because it is part of Office 2013, it is possible to combine data from Excel and other Office programs to create informative documents and presentations. Just as you can combine data from one Excel workbook into another, you can combine information from another Office document with an Excel workbook, either by pasting the other document into the Excel workbook or by creating a link between the two.

There are two advantages to creating a link between your Excel workbook and the other file. The first benefit is that linking to the other file, as opposed to copying the entire file into your workbook, keeps the file size of your Excel workbook small. If the workbook is copied to another drive or computer, you can maintain the link by copying the linked file along with the Excel workbook or by re-creating the link if the linked file is on the same network as the Excel workbook. The second benefit of linking to another file is that any changes in the file to which you link are reflected in your Excel workbook. If the linked file has been moved or isn't available over a network, then any changes to the linked file won't be reflected in your workbook.

You create a link between an Excel workbook and another Office document by clicking the cell in which you want the document to appear, clicking the Insert tab and then, in the Text group, clicking Object to display the Object dialog box. In the Object dialog box, click the Create From File tab.

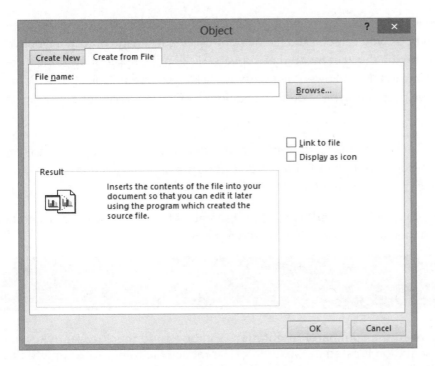

When you click the Browse button on the Create From File page, the Browse dialog box opens. In this dialog box, you can browse to the folder that contains the file you want to link to. After you locate the file, double-clicking it closes the Browse dialog box and adds the file's name and path to the File Name box of the Object dialog box. To create a link to the file, select the Link To File check box, and click OK. When you do, a preview of the file appears in your workbook near the active cell.

If you want to link a file to your workbook but don't want the file image to take up much space on the screen, you can also select the Display As Icon check box. After you select the file and click OK, the file will be represented by the same program icon used to represent it in Windows. Double-clicking the icon opens the file.

13

After you have linked a file—for example, a Microsoft PowerPoint 2013 presentation—to your Excel workbook, you can edit the file by right-clicking its image or icon in your workbook and then, on the shortcut menu that appears, clicking the appropriate Object command and clicking Edit. For a PowerPoint file, you click Presentation Object. The file will open in its native program. When you finish editing the file, your changes appear in your workbook.

TIP The specific menu command you click changes to reflect the program used to create the file to which you want to link. For a Word 2013 document, for example, the menu command you click is Document Object.

In this exercise, you'll link a PowerPoint 2013 presentation to an Excel workbook and then edit the presentation after it opens in PowerPoint from within Excel.

IMPORTANT You must have PowerPoint 2013 installed on your computer to complete this exercise.

 SET UP You need the **SummaryPresentation** workbook and the **2013YearlyRevenue-Summary** presentation located in the Chapter13 practice file folder to complete this exercise. Open the workbook, and then follow the steps.

1   In the **SummaryPresentation** workbook, on the **Insert** tab, in the **Text** group, click **Object** to open the **Object** dialog box.

2   Click the **Create from File** tab to display the **Create From File** page.

3   Click **Browse** to open the **Browse** dialog box.

4   Browse to the **2013YearlyRevenueSummary.pptx** presentation, and then click **Insert**. The **Browse** dialog box closes, and the full file path of the **2013YearlyRevenueSummary** presentation appears in the **File name** box.

5   Select the **Link to file** check box, and then click **OK** to create a link from your work-
    book to the presentation.

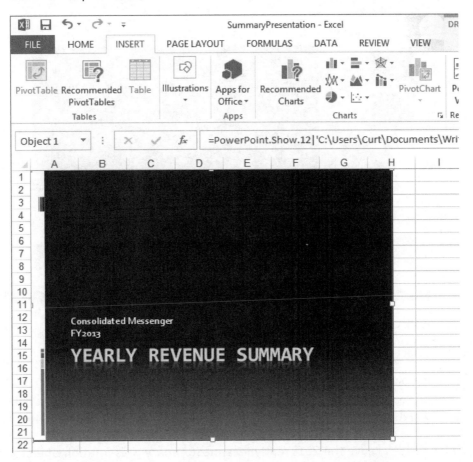

6   Right-click the presentation image in the workbook, click **Presentation Object**, and
    then click **Edit** to open the presentation in a PowerPoint 2013 window.

13

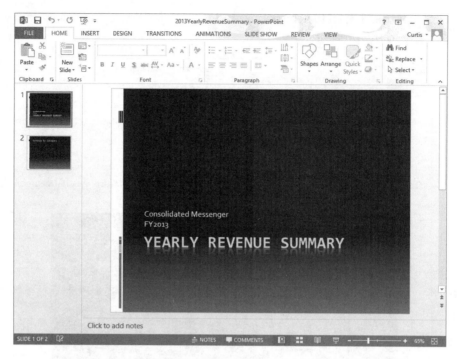

7 Click **Consolidated Messenger FY2013** to activate its text box.

8 Select the **FY2013** text, and then enter Calendar Year 2013.

9 In PowerPoint, on the **Quick Access Toolbar**, click the **Save** button. (You'll use this presentation again in the next exercise.) Because the presentation is linked to the workbook, Excel updates the linked object's appearance to reflect the new text.

❌ CLEAN UP Leave the 2013YearlyRevenueSummary presentation open for the next exercise. Close the SummaryPresentation workbook, saving your changes if you want to.

Embedding workbooks into other Office documents

In the preceding section, you linked to another file from within your Excel workbook. The advantages of linking to a second file are that the file size of your workbook is kept small and any changes in the second document will be reflected in your workbook. The disadvantage is that the second document must be copied with the workbook—or at least be on a network-accessible computer. If Excel can't find or access the second file where the link says it is located, Excel can't display it. You can still open your workbook, but the linked file's contents won't be displayed.

If file size isn't an issue and you want to ensure that the second document is always available, you can embed the file in your workbook. Embedding another file in an Excel workbook means that the entirety of the other file is saved as part of your workbook. Wherever your workbook goes, the embedded file goes along with it. Of course, the embedded version of the file is no longer connected to the original file, so changes in one aren't reflected in the other.

IMPORTANT To view a linked or embedded file, you must have the program used to create it installed on the computer on which you open the workbook.

You can embed a file in an Excel workbook by following the procedure described in the preceding section but leaving the Link To File check box cleared.

It is also possible to embed your Excel workbooks in other Office documents. In PowerPoint, for example, you can embed an Excel file in a presentation by displaying the Insert tab in PowerPoint and then, in the Text group, clicking Object to display the Insert Object dialog box. Then in the Insert Object dialog box, select Create From File.

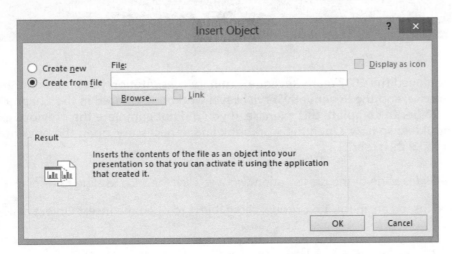

13

To identify the file that you want to embed, click the Browse button and then, in the Browse dialog box that opens, navigate to the folder in which the file is stored and double-click the file. The Browse dialog box closes, and the file path appears in the File box. Click OK to embed your workbook in the presentation.

If you want to embed a workbook in a file created with any other Office program but don't want the worksheet to take up much space on the screen, select the Display As Icon check box. After you select the file to embed and click OK, the file is represented by the same icon used to represent it in Windows. Double-clicking the icon opens the embedded document in its original application.

TROUBLESHOOTING If your Excel workbook's cells don't have a background fill color (that is, you have the No Fill option selected), PowerPoint treats the cells' backgrounds as if they were transparent. If you were to place cells with black text and no background fill over a dark background, the text would not be visible. To make your text visible, fill the cells with a very light gray color so that the presentation's background doesn't show through.

To open an embedded Excel workbook for editing, right-click the workbook (or the icon representing it) and then, on the shortcut menu that appears, click Worksheet Object and click Edit. After you finish making your changes, you can click anywhere outside the workbook to return to the presentation.

IMPORTANT You must have PowerPoint 2013 installed on your computer to complete this exercise.

 SET UP You need the 2013YearlyRevenueSummary presentation you created in the previous exercise, and the RevenueByServiceLevel workbook located in the Chapter13 practice file folder to complete this exercise. If you did not complete the previous exercise, you should do so now. Open the workbook and, if necessary, open the presentation. Then follow the steps.

1   In the **Slides** pane of the presentation window, click the second slide to display it.

2   On the **Insert** tab, in the **Text** group, click **Object** to open the **Insert Object** dialog box.

3   Select **Create from file**. The **Insert Object** dialog box changes to allow you to enter a file name.

4   Click **Browse** to open the **Browse** dialog box.

5   Browse to the **RevenueByServiceLevel** workbook and double-click it. The **Browse** dialog box closes, and the file's full path appears in the **File** box of the **Insert Object** dialog box for PowerPoint.

6   Click **OK** to add the workbook to your presentation.

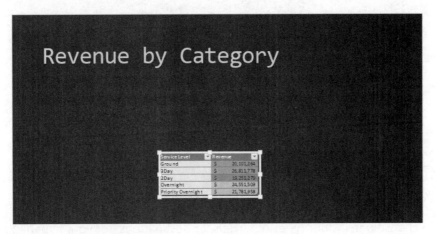

❌ CLEAN UP Close the RevenueByServiceLevel workbook and the 2013YearlyRevenue-Summary presentation, saving your changes if you want to.

Creating hyperlinks

One of the characteristics of the web is that documents published on webpages can have references, or *hyperlinks*, to locations in the same document or to other web documents. A hyperlink functions much like a link between two cells or between two files, but hyperlinks can reach any computer on the web, not just those on a corporate network. Hyperlinks that haven't been clicked usually appear as underlined blue text, and hyperlinks that have been followed appear as underlined purple text, but those settings can be changed.

⊿	A	B	C	D
1				
2		Level ▾	Note ▾	
3		Ground	Revisit price structure at the start of the next quarter.	
4		Priority Overnight	Consider incentives to encourage use.	
5				
6		Consolidated Messenger	http://www.consolidatedmessenger.com	
7				

13

To create a hyperlink, click the cell in which you want to insert the hyperlink and then, on the Insert tab, click Hyperlink. The Insert Hyperlink dialog box opens.

KEYBOARD SHORTCUT Press Ctrl+K to open the Insert Hyperlink dialog box. For a complete list of keyboard shortcuts, see "Keyboard shortcuts" at the end of this book.

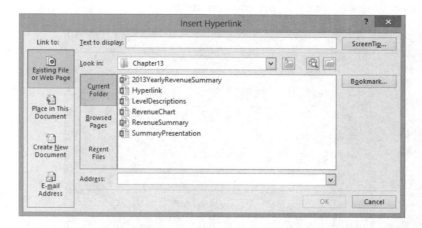

You can choose one of four types of targets, or destinations, for your hyperlink: an existing file or webpage, a place in the current document, a new document you create on the spot, or an email address. By default, the Insert Hyperlink dialog box displays the tools to connect to an existing file or webpage.

To create a hyperlink to another file or webpage, you can use the Look In navigation tool to locate the file. If you recently opened the file or webpage to which you want to link, you can click either the Browsed Pages or the Recent Files button to display the webpages or files in your History list.

If you want to create a hyperlink to another place in the current Excel workbook, you can click the Place In This Document button to display a list of available targets in the current workbook.

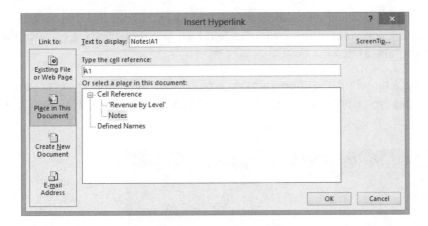

To select the worksheet to which you want to refer, you click the worksheet name in the Or Select A Place In This Document box. When you do, a reference with the name of the worksheet and cell A1 on that worksheet appears in the Text To Display box.

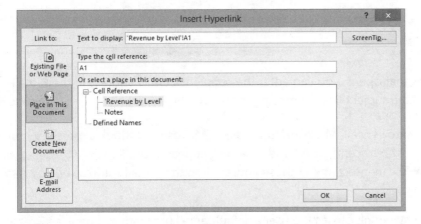

If you want to refer to a cell other than A1 on the selected worksheet, click the worksheet name in the Or Select A Place In This Document box, and then change the cell reference in the Type The Cell Reference box.

13

To have explanatory text appear when the user points to a hyperlink, click the ScreenTip button, enter the text you want in the ScreenTip Text box, and then click OK to close the Set Hyperlink ScreenTip dialog box.

You can also create a hyperlink that generates an email message to an address of your choice. To create this type of hyperlink, which is called a *mailto* hyperlink, click the E-mail Address button.

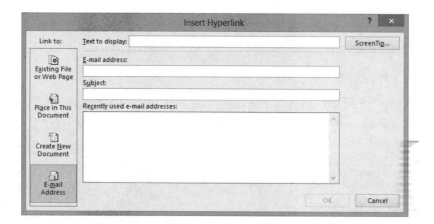

In the dialog box that opens, you can enter the recipient's email address in the E-mail Address box and the subject line for messages sent via this hyperlink in the Subject box.

TIP If you use Windows Mail, Microsoft Outlook, or Microsoft Outlook Express as your email program, a list of recently used addresses will appear in the Recently Used E-mail Addresses box. You can insert any of those addresses in the E-mail Address box by clicking the address.

Clicking a mailto hyperlink causes the user's default email program to open and create a new email message. The email message is addressed to the address you entered in the E-mail Address box, and the subject is set to the text you entered in the Subject box.

Regardless of the type of hyperlink you create, you can specify the text you want to represent the hyperlink in your worksheet. You enter that text in the Text To Display box. When you click OK, the text you enter there appears in your worksheet, formatted as a hyperlink.

TIP If you leave the Text To Display box empty, the actual link will appear in your worksheet.

To edit an existing hyperlink, right-click the cell that contains the hyperlink and then, on the shortcut menu that appears, click Edit Hyperlink. You can also click Open Hyperlink to go to the target document or create a new email message, or click Remove Hyperlink to delete the hyperlink.

TIP If you delete a hyperlink from a cell, the text from the Text To Display box remains in the cell, but it no longer functions as a hyperlink.

In this exercise, you'll create a hyperlink to another document and then a second hyperlink to a different location in the current workbook.

➡ SET UP **You need the Hyperlink and LevelDescriptions workbooks located in the Chapter13 practice file folder to complete this exercise. Open the Hyperlink workbook, and then follow the steps.**

1   In the **Hyperlink** workbook, on the **Revenue by Level** worksheet, click cell **B9**.

2   On the **Insert** tab, in the **Links** group, click the **Hyperlink** button to open the **Insert Hyperlink** dialog box.

3   If necessary, click the **Existing File or Web Page** button.

4   If necessary, use the controls to the right of the **Look in** box to navigate to the **Chapter13** practice file folder and display the files in the **Insert Hyperlink** dialog box.

5   In the file list, click the **LevelDescriptions** workbook. The workbook's name appears in the **Text To Display** box and the **Address** box.

6   In the **Text to display** box, edit the value so that it reads **LevelDescriptions**.

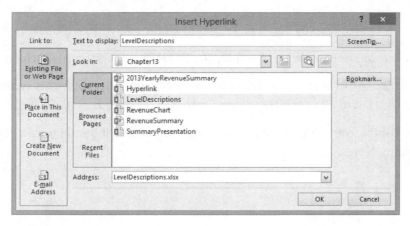

7   Click **OK**.

8   Click the hyperlink in cell **B9** to open the **LevelDescriptions** workbook.

9   In the **LevelDescriptions** workbook, display the **Backstage** view, and then click **Close** to close the workbook.

10   Right-click cell **B11**, and then click **Hyperlink** to open the **Insert Hyperlink** dialog box.

11   In the **Link to** pane, click **Place in This Document**. The document elements to which you can link appear in the dialog box.

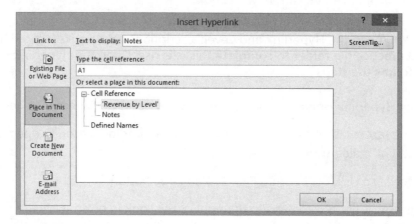

12   In the **Or select a place in this document** pane, click **Notes**.

13   Click **OK** to close the **Insert Hyperlink** dialog box and create a hyperlink in cell **B11**.

14   Right-click cell **B11**, and then click **Edit Hyperlink** to open the **Edit Hyperlink** dialog box.

15   Edit the **Text to display** box's value so that it reads Revenue Notes.

16   Click the **ScreenTip** button to display the **Set Hyperlink ScreenTip** dialog box.

17   In the **ScreenTip text** box, enter Link to Notes worksheet in this workbook and then click **OK** to close the **Hyperlink ScreenTip** dialog box.

18   Click **OK** to close the **Edit Hyperlink** dialog box and change the text in cell **B11** to **Revenue Notes**.

⊿	A	B	C	D	E
1					
2		Service Level ⌄	Revenue ⌄		
3		Ground	$ 20,101,264		
4		3Day	$ 26,811,778		
5		2Day	$ 19,251,279		
6		Overnight	$ 24,551,509		
7		Priority Overnight	$ 21,781,958		
8					
9		LevelDescriptions			
10					
11		Revenue Notes			
12					
13					

✖ CLEAN UP Close the Hyperlink and LevelDescriptions workbooks, saving your changes if you want to.

Pasting charts into other Office documents

One more way to include objects from one workbook in another Office document is to copy the object you want to share and then paste it into its new location. For example, you can copy Excel charts to Word documents and PowerPoint presentations to reuse your data without inserting a worksheet into the file and re-creating your chart in that new location.

Pasting a copied chart into another Office document by using Ctrl+V creates a link between the workbook and the other Office document. Whenever the original data changes, both copies of the chart will change as long as the files can connect on a computer or over a network. You can also select the Use Destination Theme & Link Data option or the Keep Source Formatting & Link Data option from the Paste Options list to create this link and control how the pasted chart should appear.

When you want to copy the current appearance of the chart to another document without creating a link back to the chart, you can right-click the chart and click Copy on the shortcut menu to copy the chart to the Microsoft Office Clipboard. Then, in the document into which you want to paste the chart's image, on the Home tab, in the Clipboard group, click the Paste button's arrow to display the menu of paste options that are available. The last option on the right, Picture, pastes an image of the chart in its current state.

13

In this exercise, you'll copy a chart to the Clipboard and paste an image of the chart into a PowerPoint presentation.

> **IMPORTANT** You must have PowerPoint 2013 installed on your computer to complete this exercise.

SET UP You need the RevenueChart workbook and the RevenueSummary presentation located in the Chapter13 practice file folder to complete this exercise. Open the workbook and the presentation. Then follow the steps.

1. In the **RevenueChart** workbook, right-click the chart, and then click **Copy** to copy the chart to the Clipboard.

2. Display the **RevenueSummary** presentation, which contains a single, blank slide.

3. Right-click a blank spot in the visible slide, and then, in the **Paste Options** area of the shortcut menu, click the **Picture** icon to paste the chart as a static image.

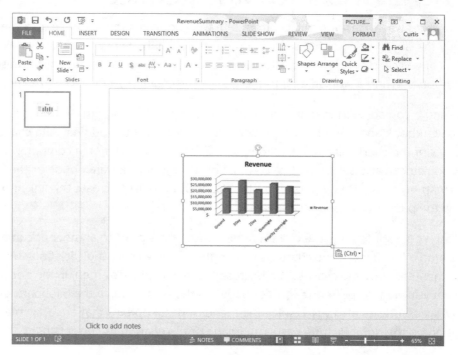

CLEAN UP Close the RevenueChart workbook and the RevenueSummary presentation, saving your changes if you want to..

Key points

- Excel is a versatile program. You can exchange data between Excel and other Office programs in just a few steps.

- Because Excel is part of Office 2013, you can embed Excel worksheets into other Office documents and embed other Office documents into Excel workbooks.

- Excel works smoothly with the web You can add hyperlinks that go to webpages, other documents, or specific locations in the current workbook by using the options in the Insert Hyperlink dialog box.

- After you create a hyperlink, you can edit it to add a ScreenTip, change the text that appears in the link, or change the link's target.

- You can easily create charts in Excel. After you create a chart, you can paste it directly into another Office document.

13

Chapter at a glance

Manage

Manage comments,
page 418

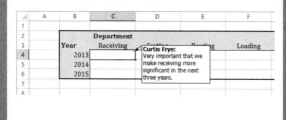

Track

Track and manage colleagues' changes,
page 420

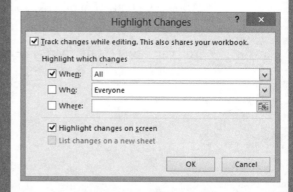

Protect

Protect workbooks and worksheets,
page 424

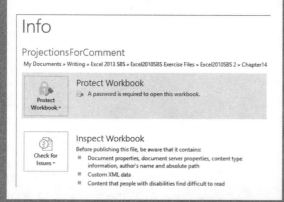

Save

Save workbooks as web content,
page 436

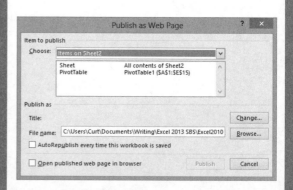

Collaborating with colleagues

14

IN THIS CHAPTER, YOU WILL LEARN HOW TO

- Share workbooks.

- Save workbooks for electronic distribution and as web content.

- Manage comments, and track and manage colleagues' changes.

- Protect workbooks and worksheets.

- Authenticate workbooks.

- Import and export XML data.

- Work with SkyDrive and Excel Web App.

Even though one individual might be responsible for managing an organization's financial data and related information, many people provide input about revenue projections. You and your colleagues can enhance the Microsoft Excel 2013 workbook data you share by adding comments that offer insight into the information the data represents, such as why revenue was so strong during a particular month or whether a service level might be discontinued. If the workbook in which those projections and comments will be stored is available on a network or an intranet site, you can allow more than one user to access the workbook at a time by turning on workbook sharing. When a workbook has been shared with your colleagues, you can have the workbook mark and record any changes made to it. You can then decide which changes to keep and which to reject.

If you prefer to limit the number of colleagues who can view and edit your workbooks, you can add password protection to a workbook, worksheet, cell range, or even an individual cell. By adding password protection, you can prevent changes to critical elements of your workbooks. You can also hide formulas used to calculate values.

If you work in an environment in which you and your colleagues, both inside and outside your organization, exchange files frequently, you can use a digital signature to help verify that your workbooks and any macros they contain are from a trusted source.

Finally, if you want to display information on a website, you can do so by saving a workbook as a webpage. Your colleagues won't be able to edit the workbook, but they will be able to view it and comment by email or phone.

In this chapter, you'll share a workbook, save a workbook for electronic distribution, manage comments in workbook cells, track and manage changes made by colleagues, protect workbooks and worksheets, digitally sign your workbooks, and save your workbooks as web content. You'll also experiment with Microsoft SkyDrive and Microsoft Excel Web App.

PRACTICE FILES To complete the exercises in this chapter, you need the practice files contained in the Chapter14 practice file folder. For more information, see "Download the practice files" in this book's Introduction.

Sharing workbooks

For several users to edit a workbook simultaneously, you must turn on workbook sharing. Workbook sharing is perfect for an enterprise such as Consolidated Messenger, whose employees need to look up customer information, shipment numbers, and details on mistaken deliveries.

To turn on workbook sharing, on the Review tab, in the Changes group, click Share Workbook. On the Editing page of the Share Workbook dialog box, turn on workbook sharing by selecting the Allow Changes By More Than One User At The Same Time check box. You can then set the sharing options for the active workbook by clicking the Advanced tab.

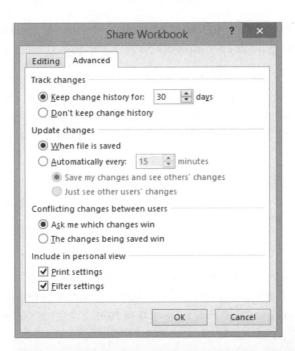

IMPORTANT You can't share a workbook that contains an Excel table. To share the workbook, convert the Excel table to a regular cell range by clicking the Excel table, clicking the Design tab and then, in the Tools group, clicking Convert To Range. Click Yes in the dialog box that opens to confirm the change.

On the Advanced page of the Share Workbook dialog box, two settings are of particular interest. The first determines whether Excel should maintain a history of changes made to the workbook and, if so, for how many days it should keep the history. The default setting is for the program to retain a record of all changes made in the past 30 days, but you can enter any number of days you want. If you revisit your workbook on a regular basis, maintaining a list of all changes for the past 180 days might not be unreasonable. For a workbook that changes less frequently, a history reaching back 365 days (one year) could meet your tracking and auditing needs. Excel deletes the record of any changes made earlier than the time you set.

14

TIP You should find out whether your organization has an information retention policy that would affect the amount of time you should keep your workbooks' change histories.

The other important setting on this page deals with how Excel decides which of two conflicting changes in a cell should be applied. For example, a service level's price might change, and two of your colleagues might enter in what they think the new price should be. When Ask Me Which Changes Win is selected, you can decide whether to keep the original price or the changed price.

You can share a workbook with your colleagues in two main ways:

- You can make it available over your organization's network.
- You can send a copy of the file to your colleagues via email.

Every organization's network is different, so you should check with your network administrators to determine the best way to share a file. Similarly, although the specific command to attach a file to an email message is different in every email program, the most common method of attaching a file is to create a new email message and then click the Attach button, as you do in Microsoft Outlook 2013.

In this exercise, you'll turn on workbook sharing and then attach the file to an Outlook 2013 email message.

> **IMPORTANT** You must have Outlook 2013 installed on your computer to follow this procedure exactly.

 SET UP **You need the CostProjections workbook located in the Chapter14 practice file folder to complete this exercise. Open the workbook, and start Outlook. Then follow the steps.**

1 In Excel, on the **Review** tab, in the **Changes** group, click **Share Workbook** to open the **Share Workbook** dialog box.

2 Select the **Allow changes by more than one user at the same time** check box.

> **TIP** Workbook merging is the process of bringing changes from several copies of a shared workbook into the source workbook. For more information about the topic, press F1 to display the Excel Help dialog box, search for *workbook merging*, and then click the Merge Copies Of A Shared Workbook link.

3 Click **OK**. When you do, a message box appears, indicating that you must save the workbook for the action to take effect.

4 Click **OK** to save and share the workbook.

5 Click the **File** tab, click **Share**, click **Email**, and then click **Send as Attachment** to create a new email message with the **CostProjections** workbook attached.

14

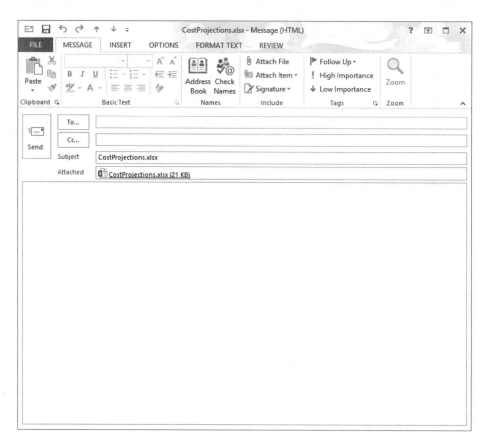

6   Enter an address in the **To** box.

7   Click **Send** to send the message. If Excel had to open your email program to send the message, the program would close at this point.

CLEAN UP **Exit Oulook and close the CostProjections workbook.**

Saving workbooks for electronic distribution

You can create a more secure, read-only copy of a workbook for electronic distribution by saving it as a Portable Document Format (PDF) or XML Paper Specification (XPS) file. The controls you use to do so are available on the Export page of the Backstage view.

The image shows the Excel Backstage view Export page with navigation options (Info, New, Open, Save, Save As, Print, Share, Export, Close) on the left. The Export page shows "Create PDF/XPS Document" and "Change File Type" options, with a "Create a PDF/XPS Document" panel describing: Preserves layout, formatting, fonts, and images; Content can't be easily changed; Free viewers are available on the web. A "Create PDF/XPS" button is shown. Book1 - Excel appears at top.

Click the Create PDF/XPS button to open the Publish As PDF Or XPS dialog box. Enter a name for the destination file in the File Name box, select the file type you want from the Save As Type list, and then click Publish.

TIP You can also save a workbook as a PDF or XPS document by clicking Save As in the Backstage view. Then, in the Save As dialog box, in the Save As Type list, select either PDF or XPS to create the type of file you want.

In this exercise, you will save a workbook as a PDF file.

SET UP You need the ProjectionsDistro workbook located in the Chapter14 practice file folder to complete this exercise. Open the workbook, and then follow the steps.

1   Click the **File** tab to display the **Backstage** view, and then click **Export** to display the Export page.

2   Click **Create PDF/XPS Document**, and then click the **Create PDF/XPS** button.

3   In the **Publish As PDF Or XPS** dialog box, select the file format you want.

4   If you plan to distribute the file online but not print it, click **Minimum Size**.

5   If you want to specify what portion of the workbook or types of content to publish, click the **Options** button, make your selections, and then click **OK**.

6   Click **Publish**.

CLEAN UP Close the ProjectionsDistro workbook.

14

Managing comments

Excel makes it easy for you and your colleagues to insert comments in workbook cells. Those comments can add insights that go beyond the cell data; for example, if a regional processing center's package volume is exceptionally high on a particular day, the center's manager can add a comment to the cell in which shipments are recorded for that day, and note that two very large bulk shipments accounted for the disparity.

When you add a comment to a cell, a flag appears in the upper-right corner of the cell. When you point to a cell that contains a comment, the comment appears in a box next to the cell, along with the user name of the person who was logged on to the computer on which the comment was created.

IMPORTANT Note that the name attributed to a comment might not be the same as the name of the person who actually created it. Access controls, such as those that require users to enter account names and passwords when they access a computer, can help track the person who made a comment or change.

You can add a comment to a cell by clicking the cell, clicking the Review tab, and then clicking New Comment. When you do, the comment flag appears in the cell, and a comment box appears next to the cell. You can enter the comment in the box and, when you're done, click another cell to close the box.

If you want a comment to be shown the entire time the workbook is open, click the cell that contains the comment, click the Review tab and then, in the Comments group, click Show/Hide Comment. You can hide the comment by clicking the same button when the comment appears in the workbook, and delete the comment by clicking the Review tab and then, in the Comments group, clicking Delete. Or you can open the comment for editing by clicking Edit Comment in the Comments group.

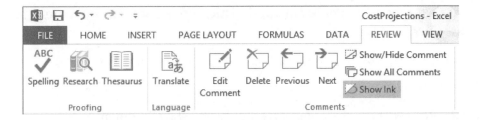

TIP You can also manage comments by right-clicking a cell that contains a comment and then using the commands on the shortcut menu.

IMPORTANT When someone other than the original user edits a comment, that person's input is marked with the new user's name and is added to the original comment.

You can control whether a cell displays just the comment indicator or the indicator and the comment itself by clicking a cell that contains a comment and then, on the Review tab, clicking the Show/Hide Comment button. Clicking the Show/Hide Comment button again reverses your action. If you've just begun to review a worksheet and want to display all of the comments on the sheet, display the Review tab and click the Show All Comments button. To move through the worksheet's comments one at a time, click the Previous or Next button.

In this exercise, you'll add comments to two cells. You will then highlight the cells that contain comments, review a comment, and delete that comment.

➡️ SET UP You need the ProjectionsForComment workbook located in the Chapter14 practice file folder to complete this exercise. Open the workbook, and then follow the steps.

1   Click cell **E6**.

2   On the **Review** tab, in the **Comments** group, click **New Comment**. When you do, a red comment flag appears in cell **E6** and a comment box appears next to the cell.

	A	B	C	D	E	F	G	H
1								
2					**Efficiency Improvement Projections**			
3								
4			Department					
5		Year	Receiving	Sorting	Routing	Curtis Frye:		
6		2014	9%	8%	20%			19%
7		2015	9%	6%	7%			5%
8		2016	17%	11%	5%			14%
9								

14

3   In the comment box, enter **Seems optimistic; move some improvement to the next year?**

4   Click any cell outside the comment box to hide the comment box.

5   Click cell **G7**.

6   On the **Review** tab, in the **Comments** group, click **New Comment**.

7   In the comment box, enter **Should have more increases as we integrate new processes.**

8   Click any cell outside the comment box to hide the comment box.

9   Click cell **G7**.

10   On the **Review** tab, in the **Comments** group, click **Delete** to remove the comment.

✖ CLEAN UP **Close the ProjectionsForComment workbook, saving your changes if you want to.**

Tracking and managing colleagues' changes

Whenever you collaborate with your colleagues to produce or edit a document, you should consider tracking the changes each user makes. When you turn on change tracking, any changes made to the workbook are highlighted in a color assigned to the user who made the changes. One benefit of tracking changes is that if you have a question about a change, you can quickly identify who made the change and verify whether the change is correct. In Excel, you can turn on change tracking in a workbook by clicking the Review tab and then, in the Changes group, clicking Track Changes, and clicking Highlight Changes.

In the Highlight Changes dialog box that opens, select the Track Changes While Editing check box. Selecting this check box saves your workbook, turns on change tracking, and also shares your workbook, which enables more than one user to access the workbook simultaneously.

You can use the commands in the Highlight Changes dialog box to choose which changes to track. When the When, Who, and Where check boxes are selected, Excel will track all changes. By selecting a check box and using the commands to specify a time frame, users, or areas of the workbook, you can limit which changes are highlighted. Each user's changes are displayed in a unique color. When you point to a cell that contains a change, the date and time when the change was made and the name of the user who made it appear as a ScreenTip.

TIP Selecting the When check box and choosing the All option has the same effect as clearing the check box.

After you and your colleagues finish modifying a workbook, anyone with permission to open the workbook can decide which changes to accept and which changes to reject. To start the process, click the Review tab. In the Changes group, click Track Changes, and then click Accept Or Reject Changes. After you clear the message box that indicates Excel will save your workbook, the Select Changes To Accept Or Reject dialog box opens. From the When list, you can choose which changes to review. The default choice is Not Yet Reviewed, but you can also click Since Date to open a dialog box in which you can enter the starting date of changes you want to review. To review all changes in your workbook, clear the When, Who, and Where check boxes.

TIP After you and your colleagues have finished making changes, you should turn off workbook sharing to help ensure that you are the only person able to review the changes and decide which to accept.

14

When you are ready to accept or reject changes, click OK. The Accept Or Reject Changes dialog box opens and displays the first change, which is described in the body of the dialog box. Clicking the Accept button finalizes the change; clicking the Reject button removes the change, restores the cell to its previous value, and erases any record of the change. Clicking Accept All or Reject All finalizes all changes or restores all cells to their original values, but you should choose one of those options only if you are absolutely certain you are doing the right thing.

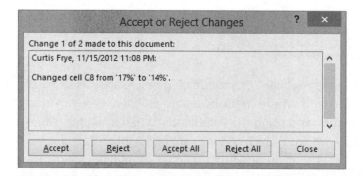

IMPORTANT Clicking the Undo button on the Quick Access Toolbar or pressing Ctrl+Z will not undo the operation.

You can create an itemized record of all changes made since the last time you saved the workbook by adding a History worksheet to your workbook. To add a History worksheet, click Track Changes in the Changes group, and then click Highlight Changes to open the Highlight Changes dialog box. Select the List Changes On A New Sheet check box. When you click OK, a new worksheet named History opens in your workbook. Excel will delete the History worksheet the next time you save your workbook.

In this exercise, you'll turn on change tracking in a workbook, make changes to the workbook, accept the changes, and create a History worksheet.

→ SET UP You need the ProjectionChangeTracking workbook located in the Chapter14 practice file folder to complete this exercise. Open the workbook, and then follow the steps.

1   On the **Review** tab, in the **Changes** group, click **Track Changes**, and then click **Highlight Changes** to open the **Highlight Changes** dialog box.

2   Select the **Track changes while editing** check box to activate the **Highlight which changes** area, and then clear the **When** check box.

3   Click **OK**. When you do, a message box appears, indicating that Excel will save the workbook.

4   Click **OK** to close the message box. Excel saves the workbook and begins tracking changes.

5   In cell **E6**, enter **16%**, and then press **Enter**. A blue flag appears in the upper-left corner of cell **E6**, indicating that the cell was changed.

6   In cell **E7**, enter **14%**, and then press **Enter**.

◢	A	B	C	D	E	F	G	H
1								
2				**Efficiency Improvement Projections**				
3								
4			Department					
5		Year	Receiving	Sorting	Routing	Loading	Delivery	
6		2014	9%	8%	16%	13%	19%	
7		2015	9%	6%	14%	5%	5%	
8		2016	17%	11%	5%	5%	14%	
9								

7   On the **Quick Access Toolbar**, click the **Save** button to save your work.

8   On the **Review** tab, in the **Changes** group, click **Track Changes**, and then click **Highlight Changes** to open the **Highlight Changes** dialog box.

9   Select the **List changes on a new sheet** check box, clear the **When** check box, and then click **OK**. Excel creates and displays a worksheet named **History**, which contains a list of all changes made since the last time a user accepted or rejected changes.

◢	A	B	C	D	E	F	G	H	I	J	K	L
1	Action Number ▾	Date ▾	Time ▾	Who ▾	Change ▾	Sheet ▾	Range ▾	New Value ▾	Old Value ▾	Action Type ▾	Losing Action ▾	
2	1	11/15/2012	11:09 PM	Curtis Frye	Cell Change	Sheet1	E6	16%	20%			
3	2	11/15/2012	11:09 PM	Curtis Frye	Cell Change	Sheet1	E7	14%	17%			
4												
5	The history ends with the changes saved on 11/15/2012 at 11:09 PM.										
6												

10   Click the **Sheet1** sheet tab to display the **Sheet1** worksheet.

11   On the **Review** tab, in the **Changes** group, click **Track Changes**, and then click **Accept/Reject Changes**. The **Select Changes to Accept or Reject** dialog box opens.

12   Click **OK** to display the first change in the **Accept or Reject Changes** dialog box.

14

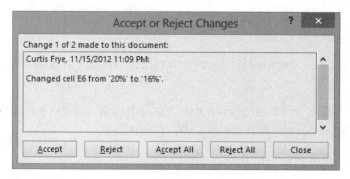

13   Click **Accept** to keep the change and display the next change.

14   Click **Accept** to keep the change and delete the **History** worksheet. The **Accept or Reject Changes** dialog box closes.

✖ CLEAN UP Close the ProjectionChangeTracking workbook, saving your changes if you want to.

Protecting workbooks and worksheets

Excel gives you the ability to share your workbooks over the web, over a corporate intranet, or by creating copies of files for other users to take on business trips. An important part of sharing files, however, is ensuring that only those users who you want to have access to the files can open or modify them. For example, Consolidated Messenger might have a series of computers available in a processing center so that supervisors can look up package volumes and handling efficiency information. Although those computers are vital tools for managing the business process, it doesn't help the company to have unauthorized personnel, even those with good intentions, accessing critical workbooks.

You can limit access to your workbooks or elements within workbooks by setting passwords. When you set a password for an Excel workbook, any users who want to access the protected workbook must enter the workbook's password in a dialog box that opens when they try to open the file. If users don't know the password, they cannot open the workbook.

To set a password for a workbook, open the workbook to be protected, and display the workbook in the Backstage view. On the Info page of the Backstage view, click the Protect Workbook button, and then click Encrypt With Password. The Encrypt Document dialog box opens, with a Password box in which you can enter your password. After you click OK, the Confirm Password dialog box opens, in which you can verify the password required to open the workbook. After you have confirmed the password, click OK. Now the Info page indicates that users must enter a password to open the file.

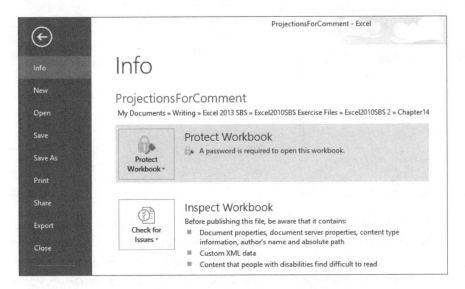

To remove the password from a workbook, repeat these steps, but delete the password from the Encrypt Document dialog box and save the file.

TIP The best passwords are long strings of random characters, but random characters are hard to remember. One good method of creating hard-to-guess passwords is to string two or more words and a number together. For example, the password *genuinestarcalibration302* is 24 characters long, combines letters and numbers, and is easy to remember. If you must create a shorter password to meet a system's constraints, avoid dictionary words and include uppercase letters, lowercase letters, numbers, and any special symbols such as ! or # if they are allowed.

14

If you want to allow anyone to open a workbook but want to prevent unauthorized users from editing a worksheet, you can protect a worksheet by displaying that worksheet, clicking the Review tab and then, in the Changes group, clicking Protect Sheet to open the Protect Sheet dialog box.

In the Protect Sheet dialog box, you can select the Protect Worksheet And Contents Of Locked Cells check box to protect the sheet. You can also set a password that a user must enter before protection can be turned off again, and choose which elements of the worksheet a user can change while protection is turned on. To allow a user to change a worksheet element without entering the password, select the check box next to that element's name.

The check box at the top of the worksheet mentions locked cells. A locked cell is a cell that can't be changed when worksheet protection is turned on. You can lock or unlock a cell by right-clicking the cell and then clicking Format Cells. In the Format Cells dialog box, you click the Protection tab and select the Locked check box.

When worksheet protection is turned on, selecting the Locked check box prevents unauthorized users from changing the contents or formatting of the locked cell, whereas selecting the Hidden check box hides the formulas in the cell. You might want to hide the formula in a cell if you draw sensitive data, such as customer contact information, from another workbook and don't want the name of the workbook in a formula to be viewed by casual users.

Finally, you can password-protect a cell range. For example, you might want to let users enter values in most worksheet cells but also want to protect the cells by using formulas that perform calculations based on those values. To password-protect a range of cells, select the cells to protect, click the Review tab and then, in the Changes group, click Allow Users To Edit Ranges. The Allow Users To Edit Ranges dialog box opens.

To create a protected range, click the New button to display the New Range dialog box. Enter a name for the range in the Title box, and then enter a password in the Range Password box. When you click OK, Excel asks you to confirm the password; after you do, click OK in the Confirm Password dialog box and again in the Allow Users To Edit Ranges dialog box to protect the range. Now, whenever users try to edit a cell in the protected range, they are prompted for a password.

TIP Remember that a range of cells can mean just one cell.

In this exercise, you'll password-protect a workbook, a worksheet, and a range of cells. You will also hide the formula in a cell.

→ SET UP You need the SecureInfo workbook located in the Chapter14 practice file folder to complete this exercise. Open the workbook, and then follow the steps.

1   Display the **Backstage** view, and then, if necessary, click **Info** to display the **Info** page.

2   Click the **Protect Workbook** button, and then click **Encrypt with Password** to open the **Encrypt Document** dialog box.

3   Enter work14pro in the **Password** box.

4   Click **OK**. When you do, the **Confirm Password** dialog box opens.

5   In the **Reenter password** box, enter work14pro.

6   Click **OK** to close the **Confirm Password** dialog box.

7   Click the **Go Back** button in the upper-left corner of the **Backstage** view.

8   Click the **Review** tab and, if necessary, click the **Performance** sheet tab to display the **Performance** worksheet.

9   Right-click cell **B8**, and then click **Format Cells** to open the **Format Cells** dialog box.

10 Click the **Protection** tab to display the **Protection** page of the dialog box.

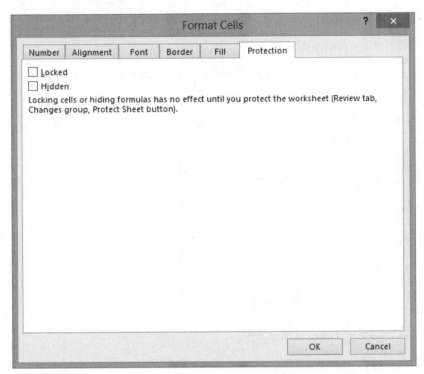

11 Select the **Hidden** and **Locked** check boxes, and then click **OK**. Excel formats cell **B8** so that it won't display its formula after you protect the worksheet.

12 On the **Review** tab, in the **Changes** group, click **Protect Sheet** to open the **Protect Sheet** dialog box.

13 In the **Password to unprotect sheet** box, enter prot300pswd.

14 Clear the **Select locked cells** and **Select unlocked cells** check boxes, and then click **OK**. When you do, the **Confirm Password** dialog box opens.

14

15   In the **Reenter password to proceed** box, enter prot300pswd, and then click **OK**.

16   Click the **Weights** sheet tab to display the **Weights** worksheet.

17   Select the cell range **B2:C7**.

18   On the **Review** tab, in the **Changes** group, click **Allow Users to Edit Ranges** to open the **Allow Users to Edit Ranges** dialog box.

19   Click **New**. When you do, the **New Range** dialog box opens, with the range **B2:C7** displayed in the **Refers to cells** box.

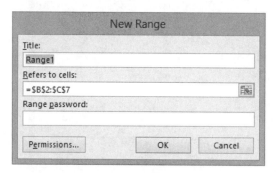

20   In the **Title** box, enter AllWeights.

21   In the **Range password** box, enter work14pro, and then click **OK**.

22   In the **Confirm Password** dialog box, reenter the password work14pro. The range appears in the **Allow Users to Edit Ranges** box.

23   Click **Protect Sheet** to open the **Protect Sheet** dialog box.

24   In the **Password to unprotect sheet** box, enter work14pro, and then click **OK**.

25   In the **Confirm Password** dialog box, reenter the password work14pro, and then click **OK**.

❌ CLEAN UP Close the SecureInfo workbook, saving your changes if you want to.

Finalizing workbooks

Distributing a workbook to other users carries many risks, not the least of which is the possibility that the workbook might contain private information you don't want to share with users outside your organization. With Excel, you can inspect a workbook for information you might not want to distribute to other people, and create a read-only final version that prevents other people from making changes to the workbook content.

Using the Document Inspector, you can quickly locate comments and annotations, document properties and personal information, custom XML data, headers and footers, hidden rows and columns, hidden worksheets, and invisible content. You can then easily remove any hidden or personal information that the Document Inspector finds.

To start the Document Inspector, save the file, and then display the Info page of the Backstage view. Click the Check For Issues button, and then click Inspect Document to open the Document Inspector dialog box.

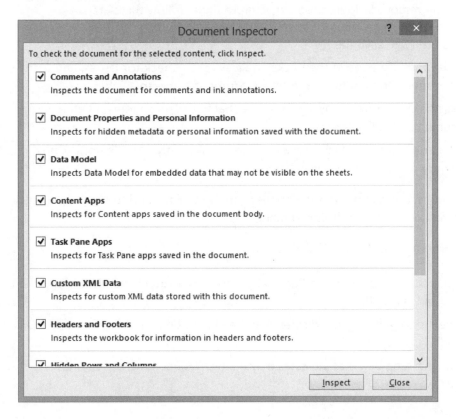

14

The Document Inspector checks your document for every category of information that is selected in the list. Clear the check box of any type of information you want to remain in the workbook, and then click Inspect. In the inspection results dialog box that appears, click the Remove All button to the right of any data you want to remove.

When you're done making changes to a workbook, you can mark it as final. Marking a workbook as final sets the status property to Final and turns off data entry and editing commands. To mark a workbook as final, display the Info page of the Backstage view, click Protect Workbook, click Mark As Final, and then click OK to verify that you want to finalize the workbook.

To restore functionality to a workbook that has been marked as final, display the Info page of the Backstage view, click Protect Workbook, and then click Mark As Final to change its status.

To inspect and remove hidden or personal information, follow these steps:

1 Press **Ctrl+S** to save the file.
2 Display the **Info** page of the **Backstage** view, click **Check for Issues**, and then click **Inspect Document** to open the **Document Inspector** dialog box.
3 Clear the check box of any content type that you want to remain in the document, and click **Inspect**.
4 In the inspection results list, click the **Remove All** button to the right of any category of data that you want to remove.

Marking a workbook as final sets the status property to Final and turns off data entry, editing commands, and proofreading marks.

To mark a workbook as final, follow these steps:

1 Display the **Info** page of the **Backstage** view, click **Protect Workbook**, and then click **Mark as Final**.
2 In the message box that indicates that the file will be marked as final and then saved, click **OK**.
3 In the message box that indicates that the file has been marked as final, click **OK**.

Authenticating workbooks

The unfortunate reality of exchanging files over networks, especially over the Internet, is that you need to be sure you know the origin of the files you're working with. One way an organization can guard against files with viruses or substitute data is to authenticate every workbook by using a digital signature. A digital signature is a character string created by combining a user's unique secret digital signature file mathematically with the contents of the workbook, which programs such as Excel can recognize and use to verify the identity of the user who signed the file. A good analogy for a digital signature is a wax seal, which was used for thousands of years to verify the integrity and origin of a document.

TIP The technical details of and procedure for managing digital certificates are beyond the scope of this book, but your network administrator should be able to create a digital certificate for you. You can also directly purchase a digital signature from a third party, which can usually be renewed annually for a small fee. For the purposes of this book, you can use the selfcert.exe Microsoft Office accessory program to generate a certificate with which to perform the exercise in this topic. This type of certificate is useful for certifying a document as part of a demonstration, but other users will not accept it as a valid certificate.

To create a digital certificate that you can use as a demonstration, navigate to the folder that contains your Office 2013 program files. Whether you have the selfcert.exe file and the specific folder it's in if you do have it depends on your computer's configuration, the drive onto which you installed Office 2013, and whether you installed all available files when you installed Office 2013. One typical folder is C:\Program Files (x86)\Microsoft Office\Office15. In that folder, which contains a large number of files, you will find the selfcert.exe program. Double-click the program to run it.

In the Create Digital Certificate dialog box, enter a name for your certificate and click OK to have the program create your trial certificate. Then, in Excel, display the Info page of the Backstage view, click Protect Workbook, and click Add A Digital Signature. In the Sign dialog box, enter your purpose for signing the document, select the certificate you want to use, and then click Sign to sign your workbook.

IMPORTANT After you click Add A Digital Signature, Excel checks your computer for usable digital certificates. If it can't find one, Excel displays a dialog box that indicates that you can buy digital signatures from third-party providers. To get information about those services, click the Signature Services From The Office Marketplace button. You won't be able to add a digital signature to a file until you acquire a digital certificate, either by generating a test certificate using the included selfcert.exe program or by purchasing one through a third-party vendor.

14

If you have several certificates from which to choose, and the desired certificate doesn't appear in the Sign dialog box, you can click Change to display the Select Certificate dialog box. In the Select Certificate dialog box, click the certificate with which you want to sign the workbook, and then click OK. The Select Certificate dialog box closes, and the certificate with which you signed the workbook appears in the Sign dialog box. As before, click Sign to sign your document by using the digital certificate.

In this exercise, you'll create a digital certificate and digitally sign a workbook by using the certificate.

IMPORTANT You must have a digital certificate, such as one generated by selfcert.exe or purchased through a third-party vendor, to complete this exercise. If you don't have a third-party digital certificate and don't have selfcert.exe installed on your computer, read through the steps of the procedure to become familiar with the process.

➡ SET UP You need the ProjectionsSigned workbook located in the Chapter14 practice file folder to complete this exercise. Open the workbook, and then follow the steps.

1   On the drive where you installed Office 2013, navigate to the folder (such as *C:\Program Files (x86)\Microsoft Office\Office15*) that contains the Office 2013 program files, and then double-click **selfcert.exe**. The **Create Digital Certificate** dialog box opens.

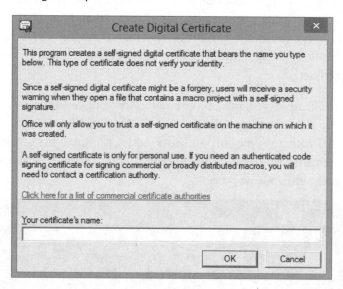

2 In the **Your certificate's name** box, enter Excel2013SBS, and then click **OK**. When you do, a message box indicates that the program created your certificate successfully.

3 Click **OK** to close the message box.

4 Display the **Backstage** view, and then, if necessary, click **Info**. Click **Protect Workbook**, and then click **Add a Digital Signature** to open the **Sign** dialog box.

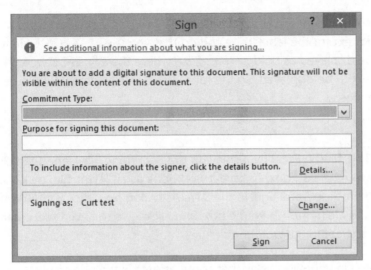

5 In the **Purpose for signing this document** box, enter Testing.

6 Verify that the name of your certificate appears in the **Signing as** area of the dialog box, and then click **Sign**. When you do, a dialog box opens, indicating that using a selfcert.exe certificate prevents users from validating the signature.

7 Click **OK** to acknowledge the message and display the **Signature Confirmation** dialog box.

8 Click **OK**. The **Signatures** pane opens and the workbook is marked as final. If you edit the workbook, it will invalidate the digital signature, which is based on the workbook's contents at the time you signed it.

❌ CLEAN UP Close the ProjectionsSigned workbook, saving your changes if you want to.

14

Saving workbooks as web content

With Excel, you can save your workbooks as web documents, so you and your colleagues can view workbooks over the Internet or an organization's intranet. For a document to be viewable on the web, it must be saved as an HTML file. These files, which end with either an *.htm* or an *.html* extension, include tags that tell a web browser such as Windows Internet Explorer how to display the contents of the file.

For example, you might want to set the data labels in a workbook apart from the rest of the data by using bold text for the labels. The coding that you use in an HTML file to indicate that text should be displayed as bold is *...*, where the ellipsis between the tags is replaced by the text to be displayed. So the following HTML fragment would be displayed as **Excel** in a webpage.

```
<b>Excel</b>
```

You can create HTML files in Excel by displaying the Backstage view, and then clicking Save As to open the Save As dialog box. To save a workbook as an HTML file, click the Save As Type arrow, and then click Web Page. In the Save As dialog box, click Entire Workbook, enter a name for the file in the File Name box, and click Save to have Excel create an HTML document for each sheet in the workbook.

TIP If the only sheet in your workbook that contains data is the one displayed when you save the workbook as a webpage, Excel saves only that worksheet as a webpage.

After you save an Excel workbook as a set of HTML documents, you can open it in your web browser. To open the Excel file, start Internet Explorer, and then click Open in the Backstage view to open the Open dialog box. In the Open dialog box, click the Browse button to open the Windows Internet Explorer dialog box. You can use the commands in that dialog box to identify the file you want to open.

When you double-click the file you want to open, the Windows Internet Explorer dialog box closes and the file's name and path appear in the Open box. To display the Excel workbook, click OK, and the workbook appears in Internet Explorer. You can move among the workbook's worksheets by clicking the sheet tabs in the lower-left corner of the page.

When you save a workbook to an organization's intranet site, you can share data with your colleagues. For example, Consolidated Messenger's chief operating officer, Lori Penor, could save a daily report on package misdeliveries to her team's intranet site so that everyone could examine what happened, where the problem occurred, and how to fix the problem. It's also possible to save a workbook as a web file that retains a link to the original workbook. Whenever someone updates the workbook, Excel updates the web file to reflect the new content.

To publish a workbook to the web, display the Backstage view, click Save As and then, in the Save As Type list, click Web Page. When you do, Excel displays the Publish button; when you click the Publish button, the Publish As Web Page dialog box opens.

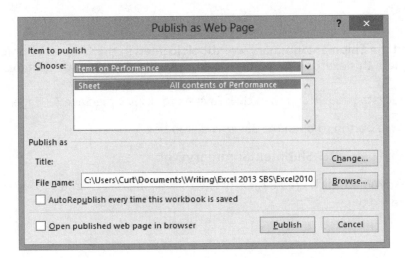

14

You can use the options in the Publish As Web Page dialog box to select which elements of your workbook you want to publish to the web. Clicking the Choose arrow displays a list of publishable items, including the option to publish the entire workbook, items on specific sheets, or a range of cells. To have Excel update the webpage whenever someone updates the source workbook, select the AutoRepublish Every Time This Workbook Is Saved check box. You can also specify what text appears on the web page's title bar. To do so, click the Change button, enter the page title in the Set Title dialog box, and click OK. When you save a workbook that has AutoRepublish turned on, Excel displays a dialog box that indicates that the changes will update the associated web file.

> **IMPORTANT** When you save a PivotTable to the web, the PivotTable doesn't retain its interactivity. Instead, Excel publishes a static image of the PivotTable's current configuration. For information about publishing a workbook with an interactive PivotTable to the web, see "Working with SkyDrive and Excel Web App" later in this chapter.

In this exercise, you'll save a workbook as a webpage and then publish a worksheet's PivotTable to the web.

 SET UP **You need the ShipmentSummary workbook located in the Chapter14 practice file folder to complete this exercise. Open the workbook, and then follow the steps.**

1   Display the **Backstage** view, and then click **Save As** to display the **Save As** page.

2   Click the **Browse** button to open the **Save As** dialog box.

3   In the **File name** box, enter **ShipmentSummaryWeb**.

4   In the **Save as type** list, click **Web Page**. The **Save As** dialog box changes to reflect the **Web Page** file type.

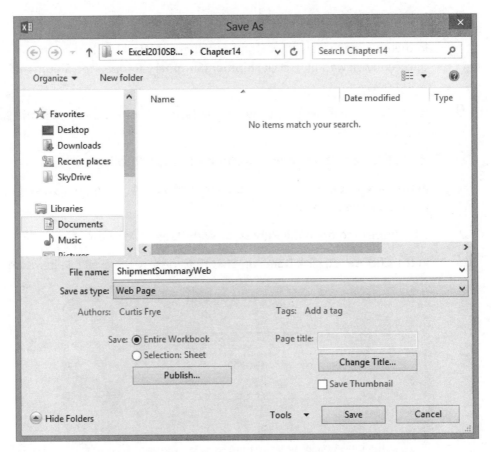

5   Click **Save**. When you do, a warning message box appears, indicating that the workbook might contain elements that can't be saved in a webpage.

6   Click **Yes** to save the workbook as a web file. The message box closes, and Excel saves the workbook as a webpage.

14

7   Display the **Backstage** view, and then click **Close**.

8   In the **Backstage** view, click **Open**, click **Recent Workbooks**, and then, in the list of recently viewed files, click **ShipmentSummary** to open the **ShipmentSummary** workbook.

9   In the **Backstage** view, click **Save As**, and then click **Browse** to open the **Save As** dialog box.

10 In the **File name** box, enter **ShipmentSummaryPublish**.

11 In the **Save as type** list, click **Web Page**. The **Save As** dialog box changes to reflect the **Web Page** file type.

12 Click **Publish** to open the **Publish as Web Page** dialog box.

13 In the **Choose** list, click **Items on Sheet2** to display the available items on **Sheet2**.

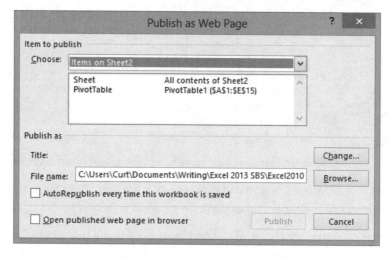

14 In the **Item to publish** list, click **PivotTable**.

15 Select the **AutoRepublish every time this workbook is saved** check box.

16 Click **Publish** to publish the PivotTable to a webpage. Excel will update the contents of the webpage whenever a user saves the **ShipmentSummary** workbook.

✖ CLEAN UP Close the ShipmentSummary workbook, saving your changes if you want to.

Importing and exporting XML data

By using HTML, you can determine how a document will be displayed in a web browser, such as by telling Internet Explorer to display certain text in bold type or to start a new paragraph. However, HTML doesn't tell you anything about the meaning of data in a document. Internet Explorer might "know" it should display a set of data in a table, but it wouldn't "know" that the data represented an Excel spreadsheet.

You can add metadata, or data about data, to web documents by using XML. Although a full discussion of XML is beyond the scope of this book, the following bit of XML code shows how you might identify two sets of three values (Month, Category, and Exceptions) by using XML.

```
<?xml version="1.0" encoding="UTF-8" standalone="yes"?>
<ns2:exceptions xmlns:ns2="http://www.w3schools.com">
<exception>
    <Month>January</Month>
    <Category>2Day</Category>
    <Exceptions>14</Exceptions>
</exception>
<exception>
    <Month>January</Month>
    <Category>3Day</Category>
    <Exceptions>3</Exceptions>
</exception>
</ns2:exceptions>
```

XML is meant to be a universal language, allowing data to move freely from one program to another. Excel might display those two sets of Exceptions data as rows of data in an Excel worksheet.

	A	B	C
1	Month	Category	Exceptions
2	January	2Day	14
3	January	3Day	3
4			

14

Other programs could display or process the XML file's contents in other ways, but you wouldn't have to change the underlying XML file. All of the work is done by the other programs' programmers.

To work with XML data in Excel, you must use the controls on the Developer tab. If the Developer tab doesn't appear on the ribbon in your copy of Excel 2013, display the Backstage view, and then click Options to open the Excel Options dialog box. Click Customize Ribbon to display that page of the dialog box and then, in the Main Tabs list in the panel on the right, select the Developer tab's check box.

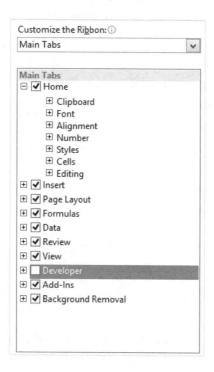

When you click OK, the Developer tab appears on the ribbon.

To import XML data into an Excel worksheet, click the cell in which you want the first value to appear. Next, click the Developer tab and then, in the XML group, click the Import button to open the Import XML dialog box. Click the XML file you want to import and then click Open. When you do, Excel will display a dialog box that indicates that the XML source file doesn't refer to a schema, so the program will create one for you. Click OK, verify that the cell you selected appears in the XML Table In Existing Worksheet box of the next dialog box that opens, and click OK to import the data.

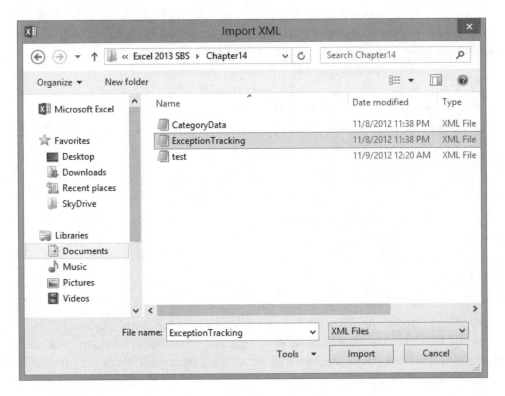

TIP If you think the XML data file has changed, click the Refresh Data button in the Developer tab's XML group to update your worksheet.

14

To export XML data, click any cell in an XML table and then, on the Developer tab, click the Export button to display the Export XML dialog box. Navigate to the folder in which you want to export your data, enter a name for the file, ensure that the Save As Type field's value is XML Files, and click Export.

For programs to process XML data properly, developers must create a formal model of the data's structure. That model is called a schema. The schema for the Exceptions data collection is as follows.

```xml
<?xml version="1.0"?>
<xs:schema xmlns:xs="http://www.w3.org/2001/XMLSchema"
           targetNamespace="http://www.w3schools.com"
           xmlns="http://www.w3schools.com"
           elementFormDefault="qualified">
 <xs:element name="exception">
  <xs:complexType>
    <xs:sequence>
      <xs:element name="Month"      type="xs:string"/>
      <xs:element name="Category"   type="xs:string"/>
      <xs:element name="Exceptions" type="xs:integer"/>
    </xs:sequence>
  </xs:complexType>
 </xs:element>
</xs:schema>
```

Toward the bottom of the schema's text are the elements for Month, Category, and Exceptions, plus their data types. Creating a schema is a technical challenge that's beyond the scope of this book, but Excel can create a schema from your XML data for all but the most complicated data sets.

In this exercise, you'll display the Developer tab of the ribbon, import XML data into a workbook, create a schema based on the structure of the data, and then export the data to another XML file.

SET UP You need the CategoryXML workbook and the ExceptionTracking.xml file located in your Chapter14 practice file folder to complete this exercise. Open the workbook, and then follow the steps.

1 If the **Developer** tab doesn't appear on the ribbon, display the **Backstage** view, and then click **Options** to open the **Excel Options** dialog box.

2 In the **Excel Options** dialog box, click **Customize the Ribbon** to display that page of the dialog box.

3 In the **Customize the Ribbon** list at the right side of the dialog box, select the **Developer** check box to indicate that you want Excel to display that tab on the ribbon.

4 Click **OK** to apply your changes.

5 Click the **Developer** tab, and then, in the **XML** group, click **Import** to open the **Import XML** dialog box.

6 Navigate to the **Chapter14** practice file folder, click **ExceptionTracking**, and then click **Open** to start the import process.

7 In the alert box that appears, click **OK** to have Excel create a schema for the imported data and display the **Import Data** dialog box.

8 Verify that cell **A1** appears in the **XML table in existing worksheet** box, and then click **OK** to import the data.

	A	B	C	D
1	Month	Category	Exceptions	
2	January	2Day	14	
3	January	3Day	3	
4	January	Ground	7	
5	January	Overnight	1	
6	January	PriorityOvernight	0	
7	February	2Day	9	
8	February	3Day	2	
9	February	Ground	20	
10	February	Overnight	10	
11	February	PriorityOvernight	0	
12				

9 With the active cell still in the imported data range, click the **Developer** tab and then, in the **XML** group, click **Export**. The **Export XML** dialog box opens.

14

10   In the **File name** field, enter **ExceptionsExport**, and then click the **Export** button to create your new XML file.

✖ CLEAN UP **Close the CategoryXML workbook, saving your changes if you want to.**

Working with SkyDrive and Excel Web App

As information workers become increasingly mobile, they need to access their data from anywhere and to have a single version of a file to which they can turn. Excel 2013 is integrated with SkyDrive, a Microsoft cloud service that stores your files remotely and lets you access them over the Internet.

To use SkyDrive, go to *www.skydrive.com*. You will need a Microsoft account to use SkyDrive.

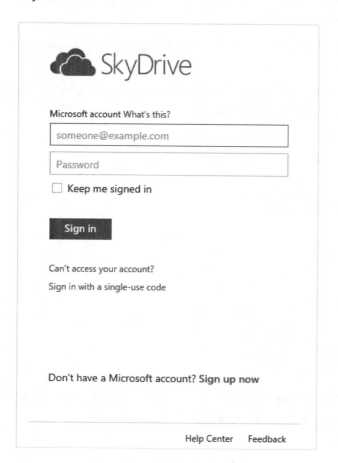

If you don't have a Microsoft account, click the Sign Up Now link to create one. After you create your account, sign in by using those credentials. When you do, the Files page of your SkyDrive account is displayed.

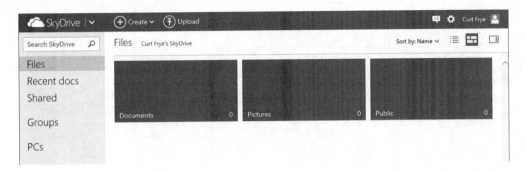

You can upload files to your SkyDrive account by clicking the Upload button on the menu bar at the top of the page and then clicking Select Them From Your Computer to display the Open dialog box. Select the files you want to upload, and click Open to add them to your account.

To open a folder, such as Documents, Pictures, or Public, click that folder in the Files pane. You can create a new folder anywhere in the SkyDrive site structure by clicking the Create button and then clicking Folder.

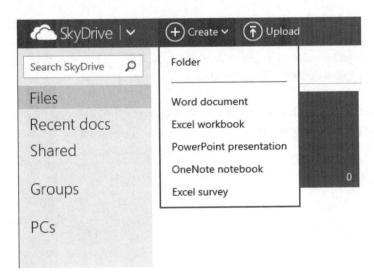

14

When you click Create, SkyDrive also displays options to create a Word document, an Excel workbook, a PowerPoint presentation, a OneNote notebook, or an Excel survey. If you click Create and then click Excel Workbook, SkyDrive displays the New Microsoft Excel Workbook dialog box. Enter a name for the new file, and then click Create to create it by using Excel Web App.

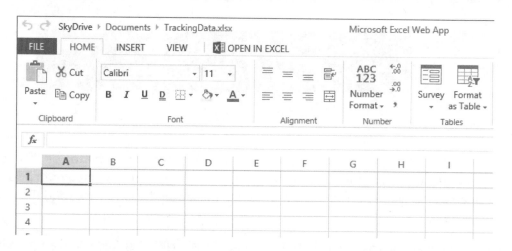

TIP Excel Web App saves your workbook every time you edit a cell, so there's no Save button on the Quick Access Toolbar.

Excel Web App provides a rich set of capabilities that you can use to create new workbooks and edit workbooks you created in the desktop version of the program. If you find you need some features that aren't available in Excel Web App, click Open In Excel on the ribbon to open the file in the Excel 2013 desktop program.

TROUBLESHOOTING You might encounter a series of dialog boxes that ask you to sign back in to your Microsoft account and to provide other information. These queries are normal and expected.

In this exercise, you'll upload an Excel workbook to your SkyDrive account, open the workbook in Excel Web App, and open the file in the Excel desktop program.

> **IMPORTANT** You need an active SkyDrive account and a working Internet connection to successfully complete the following exercise.

➡ SET UP You need the SkyDriveFile workbook located in the Chapter14 practice file folder to complete this exercise. Don't open the workbook yet; just follow the steps.

1 Start Internet Explorer, go to **http://www.skydrive.com**, and sign in to your SkyDrive account.

2 On the menu bar at the top of the SkyDrive **Files** page, click **Upload** to open the **Choose File to Upload** dialog box.

3 Navigate to the **Chapter14** practice file folder, click **SkyDriveFile**, and then click **Open** to upload your file.

4 When SkyDrive displays a dialog box that indicates that the file was uploaded successfully, click the **Close** button in the dialog box to dismiss it.

5 In SkyDrive, click the **SkyDriveFile** workbook's tile to open it in Excel Web App.

6 Click cell **A14**, enter April into the cell, and press **Tab**; enter Ground into cell **B14** and press **Tab**; then enter 102 in cell **C14** and press **Enter**.

14

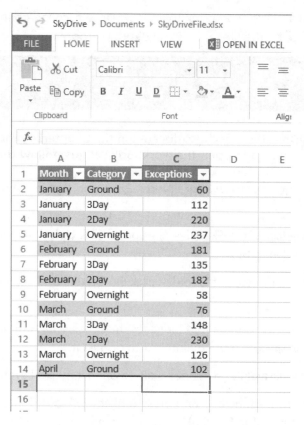

7   On the Excel Web App ribbon, click **Open in Excel** to start the process of opening the file in the Excel desktop program.

8   Click **Yes** or **OK** as appropriate to clear the message boxes that appear. When you're done, the **SkyDriveFile** workbook opens in Excel.

9   Close Excel. Then, in Internet Explorer, click **Close the Excel Web App** to indicate that you opened the file successfully in the desktop program.

❌ CLEAN UP   **Exit Internet Explorer and, if necessary, Excel.**

Key points

- When you share a workbook, more than one user can view and edit the data at one time, which is useful in group projects in which each member has a distinct area of responsibility.

- You can send files by email to efficiently collaborate with colleagues.

- You can add comments to cells to quickly let your colleagues know what you're thinking without taking up valuable space in a cell.

- Tracking changes is vital when you share responsibility for a workbook with several other people.

- When your workbook's data is too important to leave lying around in the open, use passwords to protect all or part of the file!

- Authenticating workbooks with digital signatures helps to identify the source of your files, so you won't have to guess about the origins of that next attachment in your email Inbox.

- Saving a workbook as a web-accessible HTML document is as easy as saving it as a regular Excel file, and opening a workbook saved for the web is just as easy as opening any other webpage.

- Use the AutoRepublish feature to update Excel files on the web. Whenever anyone changes the original workbook, Excel writes the edits to the HTML version of the file.

- You can import and export XML data in Excel 2013. When you import XML data, Excel creates the schema required to manage the data within the program.

- With SkyDrive and Excel Web App, you can work with data in the native Excel 2013 workbook format wherever you have web access. If you have Excel 2013 installed on your computer, you can open a file stored on SkyDrive and edit it by using the full power of the desktop program.

14

Glossary

3-D reference A pattern for referring to the workbook, worksheet, and cell from which a value should be read.

absolute reference A cell reference, such as $B$3, that doesn't change when you copy a formula that contains the reference to another cell. See also *relative reference*.

active cell The cell that is currently selected and open for editing.

add-in A supplemental program that can be used to extend functions in Excel.

alignment The manner in which a cell's contents are arranged within that cell (for example, centered).

arguments The specific data that a function requires to calculate a value.

aspect ratio The relationship between a graphic's height and its width.

auditing The process of examining a worksheet for errors.

AutoComplete The Excel functionality that completes data entry for a cell based on similar values in other cells in the same column.

AutoFill The Excel functionality that extends a series of values based on the contents of a single cell. See also *FillSeries, Flash Fill*.

AutoFilter An Excel tool that you can use to create filters.

AutoRepublish An Excel technology that maintains a link between a web document and the worksheet on which the web document is based, and updates the web document whenever the original worksheet is saved.

Backstage view A view introduced in Excel 2010, accessed by clicking the File tab, that gathers workbook management tasks into a single location.

browser A program with which users view web documents.

cell The box at the intersection of a row and a column.

cell range A group of cells.

cell reference The letter and number combination, such as C16, that identifies the row and column intersection of a cell.

chart A visual summary of worksheet data; also called a *graph*.

column Cells that are on the same vertical line in a worksheet.

conditional format A format that is applied only when cell contents meet specific criteria.

conditional formula A formula that calculates a value by using one of two different expressions, depending on whether a third expression is true or false.

data bar A horizontal line within a cell that indicates the relative magnitude of the cell's value.

data consolidation Summarizing data from a set of similar cell ranges.

dependent A cell with a formula that uses the value from a particular cell.

Document Inspector A utility with which you can inspect an Excel workbook for personal information, tracked changes, and other sensitive data.

embed To save a file as part of another file, as opposed to linking one file to another. See also *link*.

error code A brief message that appears in a worksheet cell, describing a problem with a formula or a function.

Excel table An Excel object with which you can store and refer to data based on the name of the table and the names of its columns and rows.

Excel Web App A browser-enabled version of the Excel desktop program.

field A column of data used to create a PivotTable.

fill handle The square at the lower-right corner of a cell that can be dragged to indicate other cells that should hold values in the series defined by the active cell.

FillSeries The ability to extend a series of values based on the contents of two cells, where the first cell has the starting value for the series and the second cell shows the increment. See also *AutoFill*, *Flash Fill*.

filter A rule that Excel uses to determine which worksheet rows to display.

Flash Fill A capability that senses patterns of data combination and separation and offers to continue the pattern for the remainder of the rows in a data list. See also *AutoFill*, *FillSeries*.

format A predefined set of characteristics that can be applied to cell contents.

formula An expression used to calculate a value.

Formula AutoComplete The Excel functionality with which you can enter a formula quickly by selecting functions, named ranges, and table references that appear when you begin to enter the formula into a cell.

formula bar The area just above the worksheet grid that displays the active cell's formula and within which you can edit the formula.

function A predefined formula.

Goal Seek An analysis tool that finds the value for a selected cell that would produce a given result from a calculation.

graph A visual summary of worksheet data; also called a *chart*.

header An area of the worksheet that appears above the contents of the worksheet grid when you print the worksheet or view it in Layout view.

HTML A document-formatting system that tells a web browser such as Windows Internet Explorer how to display the contents of a file.

hyperlink A connection from a hyperlink anchor such as text or a graphic that you can follow to display a link target such as a file, a location in a file, or a website. Text hyperlinks are usually formatted as colored or underlined text, but sometimes the only indication is that when you point to them, the pointer changes to a hand..

icon set A conditional format that uses distinct visual indicators to designate how a value compares to a set of criteria.

landscape mode A display and printing mode whereby columns run parallel to the short edge of a sheet of paper.

link A formula that has a cell show the value from another cell. See also *embed*.

Live Preview A feature of Excel that displays the result of an operation, such as pasting data or applying a cell style, without implementing the change until you complete the operation.

locked cell A cell that cannot be modified if its worksheet is protected.

macro A series of recorded automated actions that can be replayed.

mailto hyperlink A special type of hyperlink with which a user creates an email message to a particular email address.

map A correspondence between an XML schema and an Excel worksheet.

Merge And Center An operation that combines a contiguous group of cells into a single cell. Selecting a merged cell and clicking the Merge And Center button splits the merged cells into the original group of separate cells.

named range A group of related cells defined by a single name.

Paste Options A button that appears after you paste an item from the Microsoft Office Clipboard into your workbook, and which provides options for how the item appears in the workbook.

Pick From List The Excel functionality that you can use to enter a value into a cell by choosing the value from the set of values already entered into cells in the same column.

pivot To reorganize the contents of a PivotTable.

PivotChart A chart, which can be linked to a PivotTable, that can be reorganized dynamically to emphasize different aspects of the underlying data.

PivotTable A dynamic worksheet that can be reorganized by a user.

portrait mode A display and printing mode whereby columns run parallel to the long edge of a sheet of paper.

precedent A cell that is used in a formula.

primary key A field or group of fields with values that distinguish a row of data from all other rows.

property A file detail, such as an author name or project code, that helps identify the file.

Quick Access Toolbar A customizable toolbar that contains a set of commands that are independent of the ribbon.

Quick Analysis A selection of tools that a user can use to summarize data quickly by using formulas and charts.

range A group of related cells.

Recommended Chart A chart, designed by the Excel program, that summarizes a selected data range.

Recommended PivotTable A PivotTable, designed by the Excel program, that summarizes a selected data range.

refresh To update the contents of one document when the contents of another document are changed.

relative reference A cell reference in a formula, such as =B3, that refers to a cell that is a specific distance away from the cell that contains the formula. For example, if the formula =B3 were in cell C3, copying the formula to cell C4 would cause the formula to change to =B4. See also *absolute reference*.

ribbon The tab-based user interface introduced in Microsoft Office 2007.

row Cells that are on the same horizontal line in a worksheet.

scenario An alternative data set with which you view the impact of specific changes on your worksheet.

schema A defined structure that a program can use to interpret the contents of an XML file.

search filter A filter in which you enter a string of characters and have Excel display every value within an Excel table, data set, or PivotTable that contains that character string.

sharing Making a workbook available for more than one user to open and modify simultaneously.

sheet tab The indicator for selecting a worksheet, located at the bottom of the workbook window.

SkyDrive An online service, accessed through a Microsoft account, that a user can use to store data in the cloud.

slicer An Excel tool with which you can filter an Excel table, data list, or PivotTable while indicating which items are displayed and which are hidden.

Solver An Excel add-in that finds the optimal value for one cell by varying the results of other cells.

sort To reorder the contents of a worksheet based on a criterion.

sparkline A compact chart that summarizes data visually within a single worksheet cell.

subtotal A partial total for related data in a worksheet.

template A workbook used as a pattern for creating other workbooks.

theme A predefined format that can be applied to a worksheet.

tracer arrow An arrow that indicates the formulas to which a cell contributes its value (a dependent arrow) or the cells from which a formula derives its value (a precedent arrow).

trendline A projection of future data (such as sales) based on past performance.

validation rule A test that data must pass to be entered into a cell without generating a warning message.

watch Display of a cell's contents in a separate window even when the cell is not visible in the Excel workbook.

what-if analysis Analysis of the contents of a worksheet to determine the impact that specific changes have on your calculations.

workbook The basic Excel document, consisting of one or more worksheets.

worksheet A page in an Excel workbook.

XML A content-marking system with which you store data about the contents of a document in that document.

Keyboard shortcuts

This list of shortcuts is a comprehensive list derived from Microsoft Excel 2013 Help. Some of the shortcuts might not be available in every edition of Excel 2013.

Ctrl combination shortcut keys

Key	Description
Ctrl+Shift+(	Unhides any hidden rows within the selection.
Ctrl+Shift+&	Applies the outline border to the selected cells.
Ctrl+Shift+_	Removes the outline border from the selected cells.
Ctrl+Shift+~	Applies the General number format.
Ctrl+Shift+$	Applies the Currency format with two decimal places (negative numbers in parentheses).
Ctrl+Shift+%	Applies the Percentage format with no decimal places.
Ctrl+Shift+^	Applies the Scientific number format with two decimal places.
Ctrl+Shift+#	Applies the Date format with the day, month, and year.
Ctrl+Shift+@	Applies the Time format with the hour and minute, and A.M. or P.M.
Ctrl+Shift+!	Applies the Number format with two decimal places, thousands separator, and minus sign (-) for negative values.
Ctrl+Shift+*	Selects the current region around the active cell (the data area enclosed by blank rows and blank columns). In a PivotTable, it selects the entire PivotTable report.
Ctrl+Shift+:	Enters the current time.
Ctrl+Shift+"	Copies the value from the cell above the active cell into the cell or the formula bar.
Ctrl+Shift+Plus (+)	Opens the Insert dialog box to insert blank cells.
Ctrl+Minus (-)	Opens the Delete dialog box to delete the selected cells.
Ctrl+;	Enters the current date.
Ctrl+`	Toggles between displaying cell values and displaying formulas in the worksheet.
Ctrl+'	Copies a formula from the cell above the active cell into the cell or the formula bar.
Ctrl+1	Opens the Format Cells dialog box.

Key	Description
Ctrl+2	Toggles to apply or remove bold formatting.
Ctrl+3	Toggles to apply or remove italic formatting.
Ctrl+4	Toggles to apply or remove underlining.
Ctrl+5	Toggles to apply or remove strikethrough.
Ctrl+6	Toggles between hiding and displaying objects.
Ctrl+8	Toggles to display or hide the outline symbols.
Ctrl+9	Hides the selected rows.
Ctrl+0	Hides the selected columns.
Ctrl+A	Selects the entire worksheet. If the worksheet contains data, pressing Ctrl+A selects the current region. Pressing Ctrl+A a second time selects the entire worksheet. When the cursor is to the right of a function name in a formula, pressing Ctrl+A opens the Function Arguments dialog box.
Ctrl+Shift+A	Inserts the argument names and parentheses when the cursor is to the right of a function name in a formula.
Ctrl+B	Toggles to apply or remove bold formatting.
Ctrl+C	Copies the selected cells.
Ctrl+D	Uses the Fill Down command to copy the contents and format of the topmost cell of a selected range into the cells below.
Ctrl+F	Opens the Find And Replace dialog box, with the Find page active. Shift+F5 also displays this page, whereas Shift+F4 repeats the last Find action.
Ctrl+Shift+F	Opens the Format Cells dialog box, with the Font page active.
Ctrl+G	Opens the Go To dialog box. F5 also opens this dialog box.
Ctrl+H	Opens the Find And Replace dialog box, with the Replace page active.
Ctrl+I	Toggles to apply or remove italic formatting.
Ctrl+K	Opens the Insert Hyperlink dialog box for new hyperlinks or the Edit Hyperlink dialog box for selected existing hyperlinks.
Ctrl+L	Opens the Create Table dialog box.
Ctrl+N	Creates a new, blank workbook.
Ctrl+O	Opens the Open dialog box to open or find a file.
Ctrl+Shift+O	Selects all cells that contain comments.
Ctrl+P	Displays the Print page in the Backstage view.
Ctrl+Shift+P	Opens the Format Cells dialog box, with the Font page active.
Ctrl+R	Uses the Fill Right command to copy the contents and format of the leftmost cell of a selected range into the cells to the right.
Ctrl+S	Saves the active file with its current file name, location, and file format.
Ctrl+T	Opens the Create Table dialog box.

Key	Description
Ctrl+U	Toggles to apply or remove underlining.
Ctrl+Shift+U	Toggles between expanding and collapsing the formula bar.
Ctrl+V	Inserts the contents of the Microsoft Office Clipboard at the cursor and replaces any selection. Available only after you have cut or copied an object, text, or cell contents.
Ctrl+Alt+V	Opens the Paste Special dialog box. Available only after you have cut or copied an object, text, or cell contents on a worksheet or in another program.
Ctrl+W	Closes the selected workbook window.
Ctrl+X	Cuts the selected cells.
Ctrl+Y	Repeats the last command or action, if possible.
Ctrl+Z	Performs the Undo command to reverse the last command or to delete the last entry that you entered.

TIP The Ctrl combinations Ctrl+E, Ctrl+J, Ctrl+M, and Ctrl+Q are currently unassigned to any shortcuts.

Function keys

Key	Description
F1	Displays the Excel Help pane.
Ctrl+F1	Displays or hides the ribbon.
Alt+F1	Creates an embedded chart of the data in the current range.
Alt+Shift+F1	Inserts a new worksheet.
F2	Opens the active cell for editing and positions the cursor at the end of the cell contents. It also moves the cursor into the formula bar when editing in a cell is turned off.
Ctrl+F2	Displays the print preview area on the Print page in the Backstage view.
Shift+F2	Adds a cell comment or opens an existing comment for editing.
F3	Opens the Paste Name dialog box. Available only if names exist in the workbook.
Shift+F3	Opens the Insert Function dialog box.
F4	Repeats the last command or action, if possible.
Ctrl+F4	Closes the selected workbook window.
Alt+F4	Exits Excel.

Key	Description
F5	Opens the Go To dialog box.
Ctrl+F5	Restores the window size of the selected workbook window.
F6	Switches between the worksheet, ribbon, pane, and Zoom controls. In a worksheet that has been split, F6 includes the split panes when switching between panes and the ribbon area.
Ctrl+F6	Switches to the next workbook window when more than one workbook window is open.
Shift+F6	Switches between the worksheet, Zoom controls, pane, and ribbon.
F7	Opens the Spelling dialog box to check spelling in the active worksheet or selected range.
Ctrl+F7	Performs the Move command on the workbook window when it is not maximized. Use the arrow keys to move the window, and when finished press Enter or Esc to cancel.
F8	Turns extend mode on or off. In extend mode, *Extended Selection* appears in the status line, and the arrow keys extend the selection.
Ctrl+F8	Performs the Size command (on the Control menu for the workbook window) when a workbook is not maximized.
Alt+F8	Opens the Macro dialog box to create, run, edit, or delete a macro.
Shift+F8	Enables you to add a nonadjacent cell or range to a selection of cells by using the arrow keys.
F9	Calculates all worksheets in all open workbooks.
Ctrl+F9	Minimizes a workbook window to an icon.
Shift+F9	Calculates the active worksheet.
Ctrl+Alt+F9	Calculates all worksheets in all open workbooks, regardless of whether they have changed since the last calculation.
Ctrl+Alt+Shift+F9	Rechecks dependent formulas, and then calculates all cells in all open workbooks, including cells not marked as needing to be calculated.
F10	Turns key tips on or off. (Pressing Alt does the same thing.)
Ctrl+F10	Maximizes or restores the selected workbook window.
Shift+F10	Displays the shortcut menu for a selected item.
Alt+Shift+F10	Displays the menu or message for an Error Checking button.
F11	Creates a chart of the data in the current range in a separate Chart sheet.
Alt+F11	Opens the Microsoft Visual Basic Editor, in which you can create a macro by using Visual Basic for Applications (VBA).
Shift+F11	Inserts a new worksheet.
F12	Opens the Save As dialog box.

Other useful shortcut keys

Key	Description
Arrow keys	Moves one cell up, down, left, or right in a worksheet.
Ctrl+Arrow key	Moves to the edge of the current data region (range of cells that contains data and that is bounded by empty cells or datasheet borders) in a worksheet.
Shift+Arrow key	Extends the selection of cells by one cell.
Ctrl+Shift+Arrow key	Extends the selection of cells to the last nonblank cell in the same column or row as the active cell, or if the next cell is blank, extends the selection to the next nonblank cell.
Left Arrow or Right Arrow	Selects the tab to the left or right when the ribbon is selected. When a submenu is open or selected, these arrow keys switch between the main menu and the submenu.
Down Arrow or Up Arrow	Selects the next or previous command when a menu or submenu is open. When a ribbon tab is selected, these keys navigate up or down the tab group. In a dialog box, arrow keys move between options in an open drop-down list, or between options in a group of options.
Down Arrow or Alt+Down Arrow	Displays a selected drop-down list.
Backspace	Deletes one character to the left in the formula bar. Also clears the content of the active cell. In cell editing mode, deletes the character to the left of the cursor.
Delete	Removes the cell contents (data and formulas) from selected cells without affecting cell formats or comments. In cell editing mode, deletes the character to the right of the cursor.
End	Turns End mode on. In End mode, you can press an arrow key to move to the next nonblank cell in the same column or row as the active cell. If the cells are blank, pressing End followed by an arrow key moves to the last cell in the row or column. End also selects the last command on the menu when a menu or submenu is visible.
Ctrl+End	Moves to the last cell on a worksheet, to the lowest used row of the rightmost used column. If the cursor is in the formula bar, Ctrl+End moves the cursor to the end of the text.

Key	Description
Ctrl+Shift+End	Extends the selection of cells to the last used cell on the worksheet (lower-right corner). If the cursor is in the formula bar, Ctrl+Shift+End selects all text in the formula bar from the cursor position to the end—this does not affect the height of the formula bar.
Enter	Completes a cell entry from the cell or the formula bar, and selects the cell below (by default). In a data form, moves to the first field in the next record. Displays a selected menu (press F10 to activate the menu bar) or performs the action for a selected command. In a dialog box, performs the action for the default command button in the dialog box (the button with the bold outline, often the OK button).
Alt+Enter	Starts a new line in the same cell.
Ctrl+Enter	Fills the selected cell range with the current entry.
Shift+Enter	Completes a cell entry and selects the cell above it.
Esc	Cancels an entry in the cell or formula bar. Closes an open menu or submenu, dialog box, or message window. Also closes full screen mode when this mode has been applied, and returns to normal screen mode to display the ribbon and status bar again.
Home	Moves to the beginning of a row in a worksheet. Moves to the cell in the upper-left corner of the window when Scroll Lock is turned on. Selects the first command on the menu when a menu or submenu is visible.
Ctrl+Home	Moves to the beginning of a worksheet.
Ctrl+Shift+Home	Extends the selection of cells to the beginning of the worksheet.
Page Down	Moves one screen down in a worksheet.
Alt+Page Down	Moves one screen to the right in a worksheet.
Ctrl+Page Down	Moves to the next sheet in a workbook.
Ctrl+Shift+Page Down	Selects the current and next sheet in a workbook.
Page Up	Moves one screen up in a worksheet.
Alt+Page Up	Moves one screen to the left in a worksheet.
Ctrl+Page Up	Moves to the previous sheet in a workbook.
Ctrl+Shift+Page Up	Selects the current and previous sheet in a workbook.
Spacebar	In a dialog box, performs the action for the selected button, or selects or clears a check box.
Ctrl+Spacebar	Selects an entire column in a worksheet.
Shift+Spacebar	Selects an entire row in a worksheet.

Key	Description
Ctrl+Shift+Spacebar	Selects the entire worksheet. If the worksheet contains data, pressing Ctrl+Shift+Spacebar selects the current region. Pressing Ctrl+Shift+Spacebar a second time selects the current region and its summary rows. Pressing Ctrl+Shift+Spacebar a third time selects the entire worksheet. When an object is selected, pressing Ctrl+Shift+Spacebar selects all objects on a worksheet.
Alt+Spacebar	Displays the Control menu for the Excel window.
Tab	Moves one cell to the right in a worksheet. Moves between unlocked cells in a protected worksheet. Moves to the next option or option group in a dialog box.
Shift+Tab	Moves to the previous cell in a worksheet or the previous option in a dialog box.
Ctrl+Tab	Switches to the next page in a dialog box.
Ctrl+Shift+Tab	Switches to the previous page in a dialog box.

Index

F

X

Y

About the author

Curtis Frye is a writer, speaker, and performer who lives in Portland, Oregon. He is the author or coauthor of more than 20 books, including *Microsoft Excel 2010 Step by Step* and *Microsoft Excel 2010 Plain & Simple*. In addition to his writing, Curt presents keynote addresses on Excel and motivational topics.

How To Download Your eBook

To download your eBook, go to
http://go.microsoft.com/FWLink/?Linkid=224345
and follow the instructions.

Please note: You will be asked to create a free online account and enter the access code below.

Your access code:

TWLQPNM

Microsoft® Excel® 2013 Step by Step

Your PDF eBook allows you to:

- Search the full text
- Print
- Copy and paste

Best yet, you will be notified about free updates to your eBook.

If you ever lose your eBook file, you can download it again just by logging in to your account.

Need help? Please contact:
mspinput@microsoft.com

What do you think of this book?

We want to hear from you!

To participate in a brief online survey, please visit:

microsoft.com/learning/booksurvey

Tell us how well this book meets your needs—what works effectively, and what we can do better. Your feedback will help us continually improve our books and learning resources for you.

Thank you in advance for your input!

Microsoft®
Press